THE **Home School Manual**

THE **Home School Manual**

For parents who teach their own children

Third Edition

General author and editor
Theodore E. Wade, Jr.

Authors of special chapters
☆ Meg Johnson ☆ Sue Welch
☆ Sandy Peterson ☆ Margaret Savage
☆ Ginny Baker ☆ Christopher Klicka
☆ Sandy Gogel ☆ Cindy Short

Other contributors
☆ Monroe Morford ☆ Velma Woodruff
☆ J. Michael Smith ☆ Jessica Hulcy
☆ Gregg Harris ☆ Mary Pride ☆ Kim Solga
☆ Raymond and Dorothy Moore

Gazelle Publications

Acknowledgments for quoted material appear
at the back of the book in Appendix I.

Library of Congress Catalog Card Number: 88-81518.
International Standard Book Number: 0-930192-19-2.

For parents who see education
as more than schooling
and who sense a responsibility
for guiding their children
to wholesome development
in every area of life

Contents

Priority reading is suggested by bold-faced chapter numbers.

AREAS OF LEARNING

THEORY INTO PRACTICE

APPENDIX SECTIONS

0

About this book

I and my colleagues have written about purposes, methods and rewards for parents who teach their own children instead of sending them off to school. A glance at the table of contents reveals the broad scope of topics from planning and finding help, to making it work for your own situation.

What to expect from this book

Don't be frightened by the mass of information presented. If you haven't taught home school before and don't have time to read the whole book at once, you may first want to breeze through it, picking up what you need most to get started. Then as you begin teaching, you can return to review topics you see as especially important. Priority chapters are suggested by bold-faced numbers in the table of contents. If you have preschoolers, add the chapter, "Early learning."

Whether novice or veteran, you'll find here a whole warehouse of ideas to help make your teaching better and more fun. And, after all, your real purpose for teaching centers in your children. We trust that their experience will be richer and more enjoyable.

Although I have arranged the chapters in a logical order, they should also make sense independently.

Since 1980, when my first book on the topic appeared, home schooling has become much more popular and better understood. Legislatures have made laws dealing specifically with home teaching, and a large flock of programs, newsletters and support groups have sprung into life. We have updated, clarified and expanded material from the second edition of *The Home School Manual* adding six chapters and two appendix sections. I have described a number of products marketed to home school families and have organized the appendix information better.

In explaining educational principles, we express our own convictions. The decisions belong to you. Responsible home teaching calls for purpose and effort—for guiding your children to wholesome development in every area of life. In the process, you are building a relationship to enjoy now and for the years to come.

Information such as I have shown about supporting organizations, publishers and laws will change in time, but having access to these resources is worth the trouble of a few invalid entries. "Ideas that work," one of the appendix sections added for this edition, is a gold mine of concepts for good teaching.

The more I learn about learning, the more I see the principles of real life preparation illuminated in God's ancient Book. Of course we have written for *all* parents who love their kids. Here and there we mention a Bible principle, but we have tried to minimize elaboration leaving you to draw your own conclusions. Occasional Scripture references invite further study for those who are interested.

About the other authors

Now let me introduce my co-writers—the people who have given this book its breadth of viewpoint. All of them love children and write from considerable experience.

Meg Johnson lives in New Hampshire. The material for her two chapters was first prepared for her Home Education Resource Center which is now inactive. She gives realistic advice for making school successful in the already complex home environment. Her four children are home taught. Of course she realizes that education is more than schooling. "It is the development of our children as total human beings," she explains, "that concerns most of us who keep our children out of school."

Across the continent in Portland, Oregon, Sue Welch edits *The Teaching Home,* a topnotch home schooling periodical. Like the other contributors to this book, she writes with solid old-fashioned conviction.

Cindy Short is Sue Welch's sister. They are both qualified to write about support groups. Sue has pointed out that a support group is only a part of the Christian's larger support system with God at the center. Cindy, with her husband Bill, have been teaching their children at home since 1980. They live in Bend, Oregon.

Sandy Gogel provides some basic ideas about selecting learning materials. She and her husband, Bill, home teach and operate the Sycamore Tree, a busy supplies and guidance center. Her contribution "practicalizes" my chapter, "Teaching in the home school."

Jessica Hulcy's article on teaching writing (from *The Teaching Home*) caught my attention. I am using part of it in my chapter on the topic. She is co-author of the KONOS curriculum.

I found Sandy Peterson in Colorado teaching her boys, and full of ideas about planning and organizing materials for home school. Since her specialty is art education, she was the ideal choice for a chapter on that topic. Kim Solga has enriched the chapter with more good ideas. Kim's periodical, *KidsArt News,* is described in the bibliography.

I won't tell you much about Margaret Savage because she tells her own story in her two chapters. Your home situation and background probably aren't just like hers, and your home school will be a little different, too. But you'll appreciate her specific ideas on what it takes to do the job.

Ginny Baker wrote an article on multi-grade teaching which appeared in *The Teaching Home.* Thinking that you would appreciate a little of her common-sense approach, I asked if I could include it in this book. She and her husband, Charles, are seasoned home school parents now living in Texas.

I've known Monroe Morford and his wife for a long time. In fact, they were teaching in Uganda when my young family lived in the neighboring country of Rwanda. Our dialogue in the chapter on teaching math occurred before he left California to teach in Egypt. The discussion is about how to help children make sense out of math.

Velma Woodruff's letter appeared in my first home education book, *School at Home*, but it's such a good testimony for home school social development and the success of long-term home schooling that I asked to use it again. Her home is now in Georgia.

J. Wesley Taylor, V (That's right, there were four JWTs before him) is a personal acquaintance. He has provided insights into his doctoral research study on self-confidence, and hence social development, of home schooled children. He was, himself, home educated through high school by correspondence growing up in a missionary family serving in Central and South America. He now teaches at Montemorelos University in Mexico.

J. Michael Smith is an attorney associated with the Home School Legal Defense Association (HSLDA), and also a home school father. He shares some ideas (updated for this edition) about how to face a legal threat.

You will appreciate Chris Klicka's observations on the dynamics of the struggles a few families have had defending their right to teach their own children. Attorney Klicka is executive director of HSLDA. The chapter has been adapted from the March-June, 1987 issue of *The Home School Court Report,* HSLDA's newsletter.

You have likely heard about the Colfaxes, a home schooling family whose third son, Reed, has now followed his two older brothers as a student at Harvard. Always eager for contributions to this book, I phoned them to inquire about getting a few pearls of wisdom on quality in home education. Dr. Colfax told me about the appearance of a new book he and his wife had written. I found the copy he sent to be enlightening. In my chapter, "Educating for superior achievement," I'll share some ideas with you about why I think their plan succeeded. The three boys in the Archer family have similarly become superior scholars. We discuss them, too. (I learned about the Archers from *Home Education Magazine*.) My own horizons have widened from considering these ideas. Maybe yours will, too.

Jon Wartes is what you might call a home schooling convert. He is a high school guidance counselor who sensed the divergence between viewpoints of home educators and school educators and decided to take an honest look. I appreciate his desire to help both camps avoid exaggerated positions. He explains his research results in Chapter 1.

Many others like the Moores, Jon Lindvall, Mary Pride, and Gregg Harris graciously permitted me to share some of their ideas with you.

Then there's one more person that just must be mentioned—my wife, Karen, who helps set the direction for our little publishing company. She is also full-time business manager for Weimar Institute and has her own small public accounting practice.

By the way, Melvin, our youngest, is now married so, for us, parenting means activities like long-distance calls rather than wiping runny noses. I've mentioned our two sons in the book. We also have a daughter, Dorothea, who is married and working in health education. (Now, don't turn the page yet! I'm stopping the family history recitation right here.)

From all of us

Your reactions to this book will be appreciated. Your ideas about what should be added, deleted or changed for a future edition will make it better for other readers.

We have written out our thoughts for you, the individual reader, and we have enjoyed thinking how you would study our words and make some of the ideas work for your own home school. We wish you the best of success with what will probably be one of the most important jobs you will ever do—teaching your own children.

Theodore E. Wade, Jr. (Ted)
Summer, 1988

PRINCIPLES
OF HOME EDUCATION

1

The home school alternative

As parents you are fundamentally responsible for the development of your children. The school is an extension of the home. Education always begins at home, even when parents don't care about their children and have no plan for guiding them. Most parents, however, do care, at least to a degree, how their children develop. And this concern doesn't stop when the children are sent off to school. As a rule teachers, too, want good education for the children sent to them, and they work for it.

Then why do some parents teach their own children at home? The most common reason is no doubt because they feel that public schools have the wrong influence and they have not found a private school they like or can afford. Some others feel that the child should not be taught but allowed to learn without being told just what to study and when. For still others, special beliefs about education or special needs of children, prompt the decision to teach them at home.

Questions to answer

You no doubt already have particular reasons for feeling that the popular system of education is unsuitable for your children. We won't take much paper and ink trying to convince you about what you already believe. But is school at home really your ideal solution or might another alternative be better? Are you qualified to teach? What all is involved in a good home school program?

Can legal problems be avoided? When and how should home education begin?

In this book, I and my co-authors will help you answer these questions for your own family. Then if you choose home education, we provide nuts and bolts for getting started plus advanced ideas to help you lead your children on to excellence.

Even before home schooling became well publicized, people were teaching their own children. Most of these, however, needed an alternative because they were too far from a school or because exceptional needs of a child prevented success in the classroom; while a few braved tradition to teach at home just because they realized they could do it better.

The great majority of home schooling parents now enjoy the full cooperation or the tacit approval of the public school authorities, fulfilling a responsibility they consider to be their own—raising their children. A few have had to stand up for their rights—and yours.

Facing a school problem

To help you as a parent think through the question of whether or not you should teach your own children, we will first assume that you see a problem with the school situation they would otherwise face.

Conflicts or problems are often developed by differences in philosophy. Everyone has a philosophy. You have one, too. Your philosophy is the way you feel you should relate to the world around you. It's what you consider to be truth—how you decide what is right and wrong. As a parent, you train your children based on your philosophy or understanding of truth.

Before you plant your flag pole for a home school, let's consider some other options for solving a school problem:

Reform the school. This is in somewhat the same category as moving mountains but there are ways to go about it if your philosophy is in harmony with that of a significant number of other parents. Just remember to honor the convictions of those who may

think differently when your choice would jeopardize their freedom of conscience.

Help the teacher see your need. This is certainly worth considering if the issue centers around the teacher. You could run into a brick wall here, but more than likely you will be surprised to learn that the teacher will have already noticed the problem and will welcome your suggestions. You may even learn that your child is contributing more to the problem than you would like to admit. In that case, solid cooperation between home and school may be wiser than running away and taking the problem with you. We will discuss this more in Chapter 3.

Talk with the principal if you have not been able to work out a satisfactory understanding with the teacher. Keep your mind open to the possibility that you may have misinterpreted the situation. It may be possible to have your child changed to a different section and teacher for the same grade.

Consider private school enrollment. Ask about the school's philosophy of education. Visit the school. If it's a junior or senior high, it will likely have a school paper. Ask to see copies. Look through some of the textbooks. Study the school catalog. If you find a reasonable match with your own ideals, including what you consider to be a proper balance between moral, intellectual, and physical education, this could be your solution.

Hire a teacher and establish a private school. This could be expensive, but the teacher's salary may not be as much of a hurdle if several families join together. Of course, with more children in more grades you may need teacher aides to help. You may even have high-school level students in your small private school studying all or most of their courses by correspondence. If you are a church member, consult your pastor about setting up a school under the responsibility of the church.

Due to past struggles for religious liberty, private schools are more or less free to teach what they want, usually with uncertified teachers. As a rule, however, private schools that accept students outside the home (and in some places, ones that don't) must still comply with attendance, health, and safety standards. Your state or provincial department of education can send you a copy of the regulations which apply to private schools. (See Appendix Section C or D.) You will find that someone in the education office specializes in dealing with private schools and possibly even home schools. You will be able to discuss your particular situation.

Consider a home school. Probably you already have since that's what this book is all about. Home schools are operated in a variety of ways from being closely tied to a classroom to being entirely independent. I'll list the general categories in that order.

Home school organizational options

Ask a public or private classroom school to enroll your child as an extension student. This may be called independent study. Most any school can enroll your child as a home student. They routinely supervise home study for those who are sick and unable to come to school. However, the school principal, if not in sympathy with home schools, may refuse because even once-a-week visits mean more teacher time and increased expense. This and other options are discussed further in the chapter, "Choosing an Educational Framework."

Arrange for a supervising teacher. In-home guidance by a certified teacher is a legal option in some states. You may be able to arrange for your teacher through a controlling organization. You still do most of the teaching, but you have help a certain number of hours each week.

Establish a home school by correspondence. Several schools offer home study programs. (See Appendix A, Parts 1 and 2.) At the elementary level, the parent or tutor teaches from lesson plans and materials furnished by the school. Secondary level students follow a study guide for each course which coordinates their study from books and other materials; lessons are sent in for grading, and supervised examinations are taken at regular intervals.

Choose a curriculum package. A number of programs are available which provide basic materials for practically a whole learning program for the elementary grades. This option is similar to correspondence school enrollment, except that textbooks and workbooks are replaced by materials created by the organization

and, in many cases, you buy the package without ongoing guidance.

The fact that these programs are designed for home teaching is an advantage, but they have the potential danger of not having the breadth characteristic of traditional textbooks. Granted that the textbooks often have more than you want to have your child spend time with, but they are designed as tools. Skipping parts is often appropriate. Please understand that I am not offering this as a blanket criticism, but as a possibility that you might want to be alert to. You may find the package still the best for your needs. You can add enrichment, as appropriate, following your child's interests.

Enroll your child with a home schooling guidance center. This may also be called a school services organization or an umbrella school. You carry the primary responsibility for your school. The center may provide such services as helping you decide what to teach and selling you some or all of the materials. It may provide standardized tests and keep your records on file. You would be expected to ask for counsel whenever you need it. Your home school may be considered a branch of the supporting organization.

Organize a cooperative or multi-family school. This plan uses the abilities of several families. It could include some study in individual homes. The extra transportation and administrative time needed compared to the one-family school may offset some of the saving in teaching time, but for many homes there could be significant advantages. More on this in Chapters 8 and 9.

Establish an independent home school where you do the planning as well as the teaching. This is a good choice at the preschool level for parents who have chosen to delay their child's entrance into formal learning. Also, it is an obvious choice for parents who feel that learning should have relatively little formal structure. Although the independent home school which follows the typical school curriculum requires more preparation, it is possible for most parents at the elementary level. In secondary school, it might be a little more difficult to do a good job without subject matter and/or teaching expertise.

The topic of establishing various types of home schools is discussed throughout this book.

Advantages of school at home

Teaching your own children at home is a serious commitment, not a decision you can easily change from day to day like subscribing to a newspaper. You can weigh the pros and cons for your own family as you read through the pages of this book. To start your thinking, here are some points to consider. Some may not apply in your situation, and you may want to add others.

In a home school you can educate your children according to your own convictions. For example, if you believe God inspired the Scriptures as a guide for living, you will certainly want the Bible to be a key source in the education of your children.

Your child cannot live around other children who think constantly about sex and drugs, and who lie, cheat, steal, and use obscenities without being influenced. If you are tempted to think that your kids know better, that they will turn out all right in spite of their surroundings, beware! Mistakes here are for keeps. You will never be able to turn back the years to do your job over again.

Nearly all classroom schools are highly competitive. Children compete in sports. They compete for grades, for popularity, and beginning in the junior high years, for friends of the opposite sex. Children who have developed a degree of maturity can handle mild competition without taking it personally, but school is the major occupation for children and youth. It counts big. In a home school, the child can focus attention on achieving goals rather than on trying to be better than the rest or worrying about being a loser.

A home environment enhances social development. Home schools have a more restricted social atmosphere. This most obvious distinction is often considered a disadvantage. The question deserves attention. In our chapter on early education you will see that for the social development of small children, home is far better than school. Older children and youth are naturally more peer-oriented and certainly need to know how to relate. Home

school parents should assure that they, and even the younger children, can be around friends. However, the most important society even for high school youth is the family unit. This association should provide the principal elements for social development: love, security, discipline, interdependence and responsibility. Friends outside the family are important, but they don't have to be present every day for the formation of socially well-developed individuals. In the chapter on social development, I have quoted a letter describing the Woodruff family home school. Their children were obviously not socially impaired even though taught at home through high school.

School at home encourages what we might call "self-propelled" learning. In a classroom it's easy to drift along with the crowd depending on the calendar to get through the year. Studying alone, the learner soon realizes that progress is a direct result of effort.

The self-directed student selects and independently pursues objectives and projects—under supervision, of course. The greater motivation leads to more achievement. Although home school doesn't automatically result in self-directed learning, the one-to-one relationship gives more opportunity to provide for it.

Home schools educate children and youth who live too far away to attend the public school or to attend a private school with a compatible philosophy. Often even when school bus service is available, the ride to and from school takes too much time and provides too much poorly supervised association. For parents who travel extensively and for those in foreign countries, distance is an obvious reason to choose home school; authorities don't generally question it under these circumstances.

School at home is often an advantage for children with problems which threaten their opportunity to achieve. Self-confidence and self-control are easily crushed in a competitive classroom environment. Children can't concentrate on school assignments, and they begin to fail. At the same time, their behavior problems generally increase. They can't get along with other students. Sometimes they withdraw. They view themselves

as abnormal and unable, and everyone else sees them in that same light.

Removed from the damaging atmosphere for a year or so and given patient encouragement, the child can begin to achieve. Success builds self-confidence, and self-confidence restores the normal independent psychological function of the individual.

Some children with serious physical or mental handicaps are often better off in a special environment outside of regular schools. Attendance laws provide for this type of exception, although specially trained teachers may be required.

Relief from tuition expense. Many parents for whom public school is out of the question feel unable to afford school fees. Tuition for one child may be cheaper than lost wages, but when there are several or when the mother's presence at home is valued for the sake of a preschooler, keeping her from a paying job anyway, home school becomes the best choice.

School at home brings parents a sense of satisfaction. It's not easy, but rewarding accomplishments seldom are. You can develop a much fuller relationship with your children if you teach them yourself. And as a bonus, you will sharpen your own knowledge and skills in the subjects they are learning.

Disadvantages

On the other side of the coin, what difficulties might home school parents face?

Conflicts with school authorities. This concern may cause those considering home school the greatest hesitation. Actually, only a small number of home schools are challenged and some of them would not have been if they had taken more care to establish good legal footing. There are ways to deal with the problem. We discuss them in Chapter 4, "Keeping peace with school authorities."

Time. Although you will probably spend less time than a classroom teacher, you cannot just give your child a book and go off to town. Quality home teaching takes time. We discuss this more later.

*A poor home environment.* Not many parents in an unsatisfactory home even consider teaching their own children. When they do, the children at greatest risk are ones whose parents are least apt to admit their weaknesses. The biggest question to ask is, How are my children being influenced by my own attitudes and habits? Let's continue this discussion in the next chapter.

Transfer to a conventional school

Parents are sometimes concerned about whether children from home education programs can easily transfer to classroom schools. This does not qualify as a "disadvantage," but it's appropriate to discuss in this context. Transfer seldom presents any serious difficulty. Tests may be given if the school personnel doubt your judgment about grade placement. Faithfully taught home school students generally show up very well. The fact that your home school was unofficial or that you were uncertified is not likely to cause a problem. Most administrators would take other factors into consideration, too. Accreditation is more a problem in accepting secondary school credits.

Being placed in the wrong grade is unlikely. Deciding the proper grade should depend on more than test results. Most students who slip behind become discouraged and may never catch up if required to repeat a grade. They are bigger than the other kids and considered stupid. If you face this situation, you may want to continue home schooling and push for a little better achievement.

A child ahead of grade level may face more social problems. If your child isn't really ready for the grade you expected, the challenge may be too great and may lead to burnout. On the other hand, if your child missed studying South America and a minor math concept which the others were exposed to, but could handle the extra study to catch up, you would not want him or her in the lower grade. You might ask for a trial period or seek wider counsel.

Whenever students make a transition from one type of school to another, a certain degree of adjustment in learning style is necessary. Home schooled students coming into a classroom situation sometimes have to learn: (1) to get more information from lectures, (2) to move more with the class, performing particular learning tasks at stipulated times, (3) to move ahead in a study task without someone standing by to prompt each step, (4) not to leave their seats at liberty, and (5) that they don't "know it all."

These minor adjustments may be a little more difficult than changes students make in the transition from one school to another, but you can prepare your child by: expecting self-direction, planning opportunities for learning from lectures, and by arranging for group interaction.

Evidence of success

Do children taught at home really learn as well as they would in a traditional classroom school? I've told you they can, but how do you know I'm right? Other authors have described their success with home education, but you have to ask whether or not their cases are typical. Parents whose home schooling experience failed would not likely write a book about it.

Research studies provide reliable indications of the validity of home schooling if care is taken not to overgeneralize the findings. Unfortunately, an unbiased sampling of all home schools is difficult even to approach. Evidence from the success of home schooled students (contrary to how it appears) does not clearly prove the superiority of studying at home. Children of parents who care that much usually do better anyway. Still research helps us understand.

In 1977 I made two studies of elementary students at Home Study International. The first was simply a summary of the results of standardized reading tests parents were asked to give as part of the regular reading evaluation in grades one to six. The average percentile rank was 81. In other words, these children tended to read better than 80% of the students in their grade levels across the nation.

The second study assessed opinions of parents of 118 (out of a sampling of 171) elementary students. Three of the items and the percentage of parents who marked either "agree" or "strongly agree" were:

The home instructor filled adequately the role of helping the home student learn, 97%.

The child probably learned as well as (if not better than) he/she would have in a regular classroom, 95%.

The social development of the child (getting along with others, et cetera) has not been jeopardized by studying at home, 96%.

Results from the 1987 testing of 873 Washington home schooled children provide the most meaningful information available.* {Notes and references for this book are all in Appendix I.} These were all the students in grades K-12 tested by six testing services cooperating with the project. They appear to fairly represent families who follow the legal requirements for home schooling.

Scores on the Stanford Achievement Test averaged at or above the national average for 104 out of 120 test cells (testing categories). The median (middle) category was at the 65th percentile (meaning that 64 out of 100 American students would do worse than the average home schooled child). Scores were highest in science and in the verbal areas of listening, vocabulary and word reading. The lowest scores were in math computation, although math application scores were stronger.

I asked Jon Wartes, Project Leader, for his observations on what research really tells us about the achievement of home educated students. Here is his reply:

> The question is "How well does homeschooling work academically?" In the interest of precision, I would propose breaking the question into three parts: (1) Does homeschooling work? (2) Do homeschoolers do better than conventionally educated students? (3) Is homeschooling a superior educational method compared to conventional schooling?
>
> 1. Does homeschooling work? The answer is "yes". There is a wealth of anecdotal information in the homeschooling literature showing positive examples of homeschooling. Also, virtually all

existing tabulations of test score data from homeschooler groups around the nation have produced mean scores in the average to above average range.

2. Do homeschoolers do better than conventionally educated students? The present evidence is inconclusive. The best studies so far (those having the least sources of potential bias and the largest sample size) have frequently shown above average scores for home schooled children, but not always strongly so. The primary problem with all of these studies is that test scores from a significant proportion of homeschoolers are not available to the researcher. There is a belief that parents of the lower scoring students would be less likely to have the child tested or to report the scores compared to parents of higher scoring children. Because homeschoolers tend to be an independent lot, obtaining a systematic sampling remains a difficult challenge to homeschool researchers.

3. Is homeschooling an academically superior educational method compared to conventional schooling? There is virtually no empirical evidence available on this topic. While homeschoolers commonly do well, the proper research design would need to show that any difference is not due to other factors. For example, it is commonly acknowledged that the homeschoolers have parents who are more dedicated and supportive than usual. Is the academic outcome a result of the homeschooling or of having supportive parents? It is commonly observed that conventionally educated children who have supportive parents also tend to do well.

The state of Alaska offers a correspondence program to many of their youth. Test results make these students look very good compared with classroom students at the same levels. Conclusions about the superiority of home schooling based on this information, however, is on rather shaky ground for several reasons: (1) The program is not like most home school programs: It is structured, administered from the correspondence office and has a traditional curriculum. (2) Results of tests given at home may be influenced by hints or carelessness of parents who want their children to make good grades. And (3), most serious, a large percentage of the tests (one fifth in 1985) are either not taken or not returned to the correspondence office. The averages reported for correspondence students do not take them into consideration. We can get some good clues from these score comparisons, but can't take them seriously. I was pleased to learn of the Washington studies which give us a little more reliable picture.

In the chapter, "Social Development," we look at evidence that home schooling does more for children socially than giving them an equal opportunity.

Some of the best help in deciding whether or not to teach your children at home can come from others who are doing it. Talk to several families including one who has been home teaching for several years. Talk with the kids, too.

As you evaluate the possibility of school at home for your family, many factors must figure into your consideration. Some parents have to reject the idea, but the overall advantages are greater than many people realize.

2

Parents and education

Teaching is as natural for parents as learning is for children. Loving is sharing, and sharing—when it involves ideas—is teaching. You teach as you communicate with your children, as you take care of them, and as you play with them. To a young child the world is new, interesting, and sometimes frightening. You as a parent are the interpreter. Your child's natural curiosities, fears, needs and wants are your cues.

As you love your child you want him or her to be happy, to develop and learn. So you teach. And as your child develops and acquires new needs and interests, your teaching naturally adapts. At a certain stage it is such fun to get love and attention from Mommy and Daddy through the teaching-learning process that the child seems to make up the questions like a perpetual quiz show. You may not know every answer in detail but details are not important at this age anyway.

This process of learning and expanding horizons is moving along at top speed when, according to popular thinking, the parents suddenly become "inadequate." When most children are five or six, professionally trained educators take over a giant part of the teaching.

This pattern is especially alarming when you consider that the most important things you have to teach your child are not facts and skills, but values—your philosophy. Although you have been laying the essential groundwork for habits and obedience, sending your child off to school tends to interrupt the process of teaching values and places it in other hands. At the typical school entrance age, children do what you tell them because they want to please, not because they have an internal sense of right and wrong. Conscience is developed later.

If you love your children and have the skills and knowledge of a normal literate adult, of course you can teach them. You will have to spend time. You will need to find materials. And you should sometimes get counsel. But you can do it.

Parents as teachers—four stages

I'm not suggesting that you will want to try to teach your children everything they ever learn in life. Your ability to teach obviously depends on their level of learning.

As children mature, the relationship of their parents as teachers goes through four general stages: *should, can, might,* and *can't.* At the beginning, parents *should* teach their children. During the earliest years they are by nature the best teachers. Later, they *can* do a perfectly adequate job but so can someone else. As the young scholars mature, parents *might* be able to teach them the total normal school program. At this stage providing an adequate education is difficult. Finally, if the children continue the pursuit of knowledge, their learning needs definitely pass beyond the competence of any one or two people. Their parents *can't* teach what they need to know.

Unfortunately, the common thinking of most people—educators and parents included—allows for only two of these stages. Usually it is a very short *can* followed by *can't.* More fortunate children come from homes where the early teaching attitude is *should* instead of *can,* but even for most of these, *can't* begins around age six.

As you continue reading the pages of this book, think about your own situation. Do you see a *can* extending past the typical school entrance age and a *might* for a few years after that?

Another open question for you to consider is where to draw the lines between these stages. Of course this depends on many factors, and even when all the information is known, opinions vary.

Also, it is not a question to decide precisely ahead of time. Your final decision will depend on the development and changing needs of your child, as well as on your own obligations and resources.

What is teaching?

To get a better idea of whether or not you should establish a home school and if so, when, let's look briefly at what teaching is. Seeing what teachers do and what skills they need will help clarify what it will take for you to teach.

For state certification, teachers are required to study various aspects of education including philosophy, psychology, and methodology; they must practice teaching under supervision; and they must have a solid general background for the subject areas they will be teaching. In addition, they need whatever other courses are required for a college degree. It is understandable, then, to question how a parent without this preparation and often without any college training, could successfully conduct a home school.

A tailor produces a suit from cloth. A baker uses flour to bake bread. A hairdresser makes a change in a person's appearance. By applying their skills to raw materials, these people produce the desired results. But a teacher does not in the same sense cause learning. Learning is very much the job of the individual who learns. Until that person feels the need to learn, receives the information, assimilates it, and is willing to apply it, we can't say that successful learning has occurred.

I am not making a case for the elimination of teachers. Nor do I feel that the teacher's responsibility is unimportant. Although teachers don't create learning, they certainly help it happen.

Most people (and even some teachers) think of teaching primarily as lecturing, although they realize that making assignments, giving tests, and grading papers are also part of the job. This very narrow concept of teaching overlooks the more important ways of presenting information, and it totally ignores the essential task of shaping the student's environment to make the desired learning possible.

In helping students learn, teachers have basically two functions. They assure that conditions are right for the learner to receive the instruction, and they present or make available the information, skills, and attitudes to be learned. Now let's examine these two functions in more detail to give you a general idea of what teaching involves. In later chapters you will find more specific suggestions on how to do it.

Controlling learning conditions

Teaching is like painting a house. Choosing the right color of paint and spreading it evenly is important, but the job involves much more than applying paint. If your experience has been like mine, you have found that most of the work lies in getting the surface ready. So in teaching, making sure that conditions are favorable—that the learner is as nearly ready as possible to receive instruction—is the groundwork of the educator's responsibility. A good learning environment depends on several factors.

The student must, first of all, be physically ready to learn. He or she must have a clear, alert mind. This preparation includes such taken-for-granted health practices as good nutrition, ample rest, physical exercise, and freedom from the use of stimulating or depressing substances of all kinds (including some sold as food).

The environment where the student comes to learn also has an effect on learning efficiency. Proper light, fresh air, and a comfortable temperature as well as the absence of distracting sights and sounds are obviously important.

An individual's emotional condition has a profound effect on learning. In homes where parents are fighting or have recently separated, children are almost sure to have difficulty learning. The stimulation of sports competition upsets the calm interest important for serious study. The isolation and hurt that children feel from being shut out of a social circle or from being a loser on the playfield or in the classroom can block learning entirely. The trauma of boyfriend-girlfriend interaction which is inevitable and necessary as young people look forward to marriage, often creates an obstacle to learning even in the elementary school.

A large part of the teacher's responsibility in controlling the emotional environment at school is in maintaining good discipline. A calm command of the situation along with an interesting learning program and a sincere demonstration of appreciation for good work is what it takes. The goal of good discipline is to develop self-discipline.

One of the most elusive, hard-to-analyze teaching skills is fostering motivation. The amount of learning that occurs depends directly on the individual's desire to learn.

One possible approach to assuring motivation is to teach only what the student indicates an interest in wanting to know. This obviously risks omitting certain fundamental concepts naturally uninteresting to the child, but which the adult needs and would regret having missed. The other extreme would be to present a structured body of knowledge, insensitive to student interest. Good teaching seems to lie somewhere in the middle. To a limited degree, students should be able to choose what they want to study but the framework and most learning activities are usually prearranged.

Good teachers are careful to build interest in a topic as the first step in presenting it for learning. Interest is developed by helping the student see purpose and importance in what he or she is expected to know.

Several things make people want to learn. The ideal motivation is interest in the subject itself. Mature scholars view the end result to which the learning will finally be applied as sufficient reason to persevere, but this is a rather remote objective for children. Grades are important mostly to good students who are also easily motivated by a more direct interest in the subject. Certain other specially arranged rewards for learning sometimes help and may be worth experimenting with.

Appropriate praise is no doubt the most successful motivator. Not praise which nourishes self-centeredness, but sincere appreciation focused on work well done. Even students who are naturally interested in the topic to be studied generally perform their learning tasks to please the teacher and sometimes for their peers. Imagine how most students would feel if, after completing a test or turning in their homework, the teacher announced that this was their lucky day. Everyone would get an A. Then without being read, the whole stack of papers were dropped directly into the trash. All of us like to be appreciated and have someone notice what we do. Students who work hard on a written assignment are disappointed if the teacher doesn't read it. A few words of appropriate encouragement and praise make most of us eager to perform nearly any reasonable task.

Another condition for learning is having the background knowledge necessary to understand what is presented. We acquire any new concept by breaking it down and relating its components to prior learning. Thus before learning to add fractions a person must be able to find lowest common denominators along with a host of other number skills, not to mention vocabulary and writing abilities. In order to learn the reasons for changes in the prime interest rate, a person must first understand how banks operate by borrowing and lending money.

Seeing that the student has the necessary background understanding is not as difficult a task for the perceptive teacher as it might seem. First, a carefully planned curriculum builds the structure in a logical order. Frequent reviews and a variety of approaches not only reinforce learning but provide repeated opportunities for those who might not have caught on at first. Textbook authors generally plan their materials for this repetition of key concepts.

Even with the best materials and well-prepared teachers, students sometimes come to new learning goals with gaps in their backgrounds. Although patience and individual attention are needed, it usually isn't too difficult to analyze where a student got left behind and to help him or her catch up. The teacher breaks down the new concept with the student into the elements necessary to understand it. Then either the student suddenly gets all the pieces together or else the missing foundation block becomes apparent.

Finally, the readiness of young learners depends on their maturity. As children grow into adolescents and then into adults their natural interest and aptitudes go through many complex

changes. Understanding how children develop physically, socially, mentally and morally helps the teacher evaluate their readiness for particular learning tasks. All too often pressures from eager parents, school entrance laws and the typical curriculum push children into school study tasks before they are ready. This problem is discussed in another chapter.

Presentation of ideas to be learned

We have explored the principles of assuring that the student is ready to receive instruction. Now we will discuss delivering it. Even if you delegate most of the planning to a curriculum-providing organization, you will still have a part in presenting the ideas. A quick look at the more general job of teaching will help you understand your part better.

The process is sometimes as simple as handing the individual a book or turning on the television. However, to make learning efficient and to achieve specific desirable results, the instructional process requires considerable thought and usually a good deal of effort.

The first step in making learning available to the receptive student is choosing goals and objectives. Teachers have a limited general influence on the goals or purposes of the educational system. They have a little more to say about the objectives of what is taught in their school. But they are largely responsible for the interpretation of these objectives into specific learning outcomes in their classrooms.

As a parent you have a responsibility to know and to care about what your children are learning and why. Most people don't often question where modern schools are leading their children. They figure if everyone is following along they must be headed for a good destination. But if you view the school as an extension of the home—as a service to help you educate your children—you will care very much what happens there.

For a home school, the process of choosing desired outcomes is much simpler than it sounds. We'll discuss it more in Chapter 8. My point here is that good teaching begins with a sense of direction. When you know where you are headed, it is time to select textbooks and other learning materials to help achieve your goals and objectives.

Textbooks will probably be your most important materials purchase. Schools also use other teaching aids such as filmstrips, sound recordings, laboratory equipment, video equipment, computers and library books.

Next is planning. A teacher who doesn't plan well typically plods along in the textbook having students read and answer questions from it until the school year comes to an end. Using good materials is never a substitute for planning. Even if the plan is to adopt a preplanned plan, the teacher must know the objectives and have a clear, functional idea of how they can be achieved. The general plan for the school year is laid out according to the goals set for the grade or class. Then each day or week during the course of the year more precise plans are prepared. The plans are modified constantly as students' needs become evident.

With students ready to learn, directions set, materials chosen, and plans made, the stage is set for the learner's reception of the desired concepts. Communicating these understandings, skills, and values, or making them available and attractive to the student is what we think of in the narrow sense as "teaching."

When considering how to teach, most people think first of lecturing. But because the brain seems to remember best what it is actively involved in acquiring, talk should be limited. Concepts are learned from books and other materials, from experimentation, from other people including teachers and, in brief, from the total environment.

A good teacher knows best how to communicate ideas by focusing on the learner—by being constantly perceptive to his or her needs and achievements. Teaching is like guiding travelers across an unfamiliar wilderness. The instructor must know not only the destination and how to get to it, but must also watch and direct the travelers. Can you imagine the guide saying, "If you are smart you will follow me," then proceeding to cross the wilderness with great speed and skill, never looking back?

Tests or examinations stimulate learning in several ways. Most importantly, they provide a short-range reason for study. Also, during the time of the examination the mind is usually very alert. Reinforcement occurs, and, when ideas are to be combined in new ways, original learning often occurs.

Evaluation is the final step in the teaching process as well as a continuous part of it. Students, parents and teachers must know how well learning objectives are being met in order to modify teaching and learning strategies and to set new goals. Examinations and written assignments provide only a part of the information for evaluation. Observation and counseling are also important.

Grades are a convenient, condensed expression of evaluation. Unfortunately, when grades are used to compare individuals, they too often build pride for some and create poor self-images for others. Descriptive evaluation reports help learners focus more on the achievement of objectives and less on competition with other students.

The total process

Although I have divided the teaching responsibility into categories to describe it clearly, most of these activities go on simultaneously, and all blend into the teaching process.

I have outlined what teachers need to achieve, but have said little in practical terms about how it might be accomplished. My purpose here has been to analyze what teaching basically is, whether for a classroom in Africa, for the school down the street, or for a tutor working with an individual. Suggestions for operating a home school appear later in this book.

Perfection is impossible. No one can be absolutely sure that every student is completely ready and that instruction is given in a way which will be perfectly understood and assimilated. An attempt to perfect one area would risk not getting around to the others. Good teachers know how to balance their efforts to achieve the best results. The human mind is amazingly adaptable and often learns even with imperfect teaching.

Can parents play the role of school teacher?

Teaching is a natural result of communication. Parents teach even without planning to. But as we have seen, teaching with a purpose is complex. Should parents without formal training in the field of education try it?

Consider first the general area of making sure that conditions are right for learning to occur. This is the real art of teaching—helping students be ready to receive instruction. As a parent you have a distinct advantage here. Much of what we have discussed as controlling learning conditions, good parents do anyway. You probably know well how to assure a good physical and emotional environment. You may not feel as skilled in motivation but, with practice, the art of appropriate encouragement can be steadily improved. Being sure that background learning has occurred may seem like more of a challenge to you, but if you progress carefully through a well-planned program and patiently analyze reasons for lack of success when it occurs, you should have no difficulty. Missing prerequisite understanding is much less of a problem in one-to-one teaching than it is in a classroom because the direct contact with a single student allows for the kind of communication which tends to identify deficiencies immediately and precisely.

Parents who have spent time learning to understand their children—which is usually the case for those who want a home school—tend to achieve most of the right learning conditions naturally. A good home atmosphere is generally also a good learning atmosphere.

Presenting ideas to be learned—the other teaching skills area—is greatly simplified by using the services of a guidance center or enrolling your child in a correspondence school. (See Appendix Section A.) Even parents who set up their own independent home schools find help from most student textbooks and from guidelines provided in teachers' editions. A supervising teacher, who visits the home from time to time, can help the parent keep on target particularly in setting up the curriculum and in evaluation.

Operating a home school requires time and effort, but most parents can do it very well.

Responsibilities and rights

The statewide support group, Georgians for Freedom in Education, have outlined their convictions and goals so well that I asked to quote them. Reading the "beliefs" may help you sort out your own convictions about parents and education. The list of "goals" will help you better understand general support groups. You may want to refer back to it when you read the chapter on that topic.

We believe:

— That our children do not belong to the state; that it is the responsibility of *parents* to properly direct the needs of their children mentally, emotionally, spiritually, socially, and physically.

— That parents have the constitutional right to choose the best method of providing for each of these needs, including the child's formal education.

— That the learning process begins at home from the moment of birth, and parents *are* the prime educators of their children.

— That conscientious parents can provide in the home a very adequate and often superior comprehensive program for their children's education.

— That home schools offer the very best method of teaching: *one-to-one tutoring.*

— That a child's educational needs can be met on a more individual basis in a home environment; that the flexible nature of a home school program allows each child to progress at his own ideal pace in every subject, without stressful competition or pressure.

— That the home school atmosphere encourages an intensive adventure into learning through natural self-discovery; this builds self-confidence and individual thinking rather than peer dependence.

— That home education encourages valuable social interaction with people of *all* ages, in the home and in the community. This helps the child learn to relate well to people outside his own peer group.

— That the *family* is the basic link in the structure of any society, and that America has seen a definite weakening of the family unit in recent years. Home schoolers have found that the relaxed, intimate interaction between parent and child in the home school serves to strengthen family unity as well as providing the best possible alternative for education.

Our goals are:

— To support and encourage parents desiring to educate their children at home.

— To provide helpful information in every way possible to parents who choose home education.

— To promote legislation in support of the parents' primary and constitutionally guaranteed rights in education.

— To promote public awareness of the parents' right to choose the educational environment for their children, and awareness of the alternative to educate them at home.

— To support the highest standards possible for education of children in every school situation—in public and private schools and well as home schools.

— To support minimal governmental control and maximum local and family control of education.

3

When not to try home schooling

In the preceding chapter we examined the teaching-learning process and concluded that parents can generally succeed as teachers for their own children. Applying the principles of good education at home does not require the same level of professional training and competence as does teaching in a classroom. It's easier to monitor the needs of a single individual than it is to intelligently teach a whole classroom of students guided by feedback from a few vocal ones. For the individual, learning difficulties can be cleared quickly, keeping anxiety to a minimum.

Most parents who care enough about their children to want to teach them at home have the necessary qualifications. Still, for various reasons, home school beyond the preschool years is not for every family. Before you decide to be a school teacher for your own children, consider several important requirements.

Teaching is full time work

The amount of time needed will vary from much to very much, depending to a degree on your skill, the needs of your child and the assistance you get from a guidance center or correspondence course. But even if you are a trained teacher and purchase a well-prepared materials package, as long as you need to have a job outside the home, either hire a qualified tutor or forget about the idea of a home school.

First graders take the greatest amount of time because they learn mostly from you and from your direct guidance. You obviously can't send them off to read and follow printed instructions. Also they have short attention spans and need very brief learning tasks. As children mature they become more able to concentrate on serious learning goals and require less of your direct attention. You can expect no sense of self-directed learning from children starting school unless you have delayed beginning their formal study until well past the typical school entrance age of six.

High school students, even on a correspondence program, still require your time. But your major responsibility at this level is encouragement, occasional help, and often gentle pushing. Difficult learning tasks may appear to the young learner as insurmountable obstacles. The help you give is valuable not because you are more skilled at the subject involved but because you lend courage and stability to the struggler.

Teaching requires good discipline

Parents who are seriously concerned about their children's training generally have good home discipline. If your home doesn't—if you seem to have a personality conflict with your children, they will probably be better off in a classroom school where a more significant part of their direction and development can come from people outside the home.

In most homes children are occasionally ill-tempered and exhibit unpleasant behavior. Normal parents slip once in a while, too, and act unwisely. But when a tense parent-child relationship is the rule rather than the exception, home school is not a good idea. Children in these cases need the influence of other adults. People can't learn well in an atmosphere of high anxiety.

I'm not suggesting that sending your children off to school will solve a serious home discipline problem. There are things you can and should do, especially if your children are still quite young. But until the situation is under control, a home school is probably not your best option.

Teaching requires commitment and organization

Most parents find that setting up school and teaching at home is a very interesting idea. But unlike a hobby that can be put aside when it ceases to be fun, your school program requires steady rain-or-shine commitment. If you aren't in the habit of following through on long projects, or if you anticipate frequent periods of time during the school year when "more urgent" tasks are apt to "unexpectedly" take you away from your teaching, you had better send your child away to a conventional school to begin with.

Of course you can build your school schedule around necessary trips and special projects. Vacations are important too. You will be successful in getting through your school program as long as you have a plan that is not apt to be interrupted whenever you hear of a good sale, or when someone asks you to help arrange a wedding, or when you have a hard time finding help to pick your peach orchard, or when the house needs painting or when hundreds of other very worthy tasks demand your attention. I'm not saying never, never stop to pick peaches, but weigh the value to your children. Then if it seems worthy and it doesn't interfere with meeting your objectives, change your plan to allow for it.

Organization is related to commitment. Do you tend to plan your time and follow through on your plan? Do you see the tasks you want to do as having various degrees of importance? And do you sometimes put aside low priority activities for what you consider more important? Do you plan your shopping to avoid frequent trips? Are you master of the TV and the telephone, or do they dictate what else you accomplish and when?

Organization can be improved with effort. But if you seldom accomplish a great deal in a day, your school program could suffer. You could plod along for twelve months and still not complete what should have taken nine. If you have a serious organization problem, don't try home school until you have made some giant steps toward improvement.

Home teaching requires knowledge

As already explained, you should know something about how to guide learning and control the learning environment. Hopefully this book can help. You also need to have some basic knowledge in the areas you are teaching, although not much more than you plan to teach. To some extent you can learn along with your child, but don't try home school without certain minimum understandings and abilities. First of all, you need basic reading skills. Speed reading ability isn't necessary, but being a very poor reader would be a handicap in all your teaching.

In math, you should be able to handle with ease (and without a calculator) the basic operations of addition, subtraction, multiplication, and division. For middle grades and beyond you should have a simple understanding of fractions. Refinements of these math skills and additional concepts such as percents and metric units can be sharpened up as you go.

Finally, you should be able to use standard English. Your child's ability to communicate as an adult depends on the quality of language heard all day every day as well as on the skill with which his or her written and spoken language is corrected. I would not argue that different dialects are bad, and I am not referring to accent, but if an individual can't use standard English when it is expedient to do so, his or her future opportunities are certain to be limited.

Of course, knowing more than these minimum elements is better as long as you are patient and don't lose your feel for the young learner just beginning to grapple with what you take for granted as obvious.

Running away might teach the wrong lesson

Although most parents who withdraw their children from a regular school to teach them at home are giving them a greater future, a few are encouraging negative character traits instead.

Consider your motivation. What led to your idea that home school is better? If your mother-hen instinct got all fluffed up because your little chick wasn't assigned to the advanced reading group; or if, without asking your opinion, your early adolescent boy was counseled about being too familiar with a certain girl; or if your young cherub lost points because the *teacher* thought she was cheating when *you* know she would never do such a thing, beware! You may be teaching your child that anything that crosses the ego should be squashed or escaped. You could be gaining better reading opportunities at the expense of a calm, unselfish character.

Rules needed for keeping the classroom in order seem quite restrictive to the child used to getting his way at home. Rebellion then surfaces naturally. Efforts to help him overcome the problem are sometimes thwarted by his parents' defense of the behavior. They have always given him free reign hardly realizing the strength of his self-will, and they take any suggestion of his wrongdoing as a personal affront. After all, he does it at home and its being "wrong" at school challenges their judgment. If the child is taken out of school at this point to be taught at home, you can see what happens to character development.

The parents' mistaken attitude is sometimes camouflaged when the teacher hasn't handled the situation prudently. He or she may have misjudged, or maybe the rule wasn't really that important. Also, the child's own bias in explaining what happened might have distorted the facts. Even if the teacher is wrong, the child is seldom entirely innocent. A "win" for the parents may settle things well between them and the teacher, but the child loses!

While we are on the topic, we should also point out that parents' opposite overreaction to school discipline by denouncing and harshly punishing the child at home can equally sow seeds of bitterness and rebellion.

I'm not saying that conflicts in opinion should always be ignored, or that an unpleasant situation should never prompt a change in the school environment. Just try to find a solution in a spirit of respect and cooperation. Your own attitude teaches more valuable lessons than can ever come from math or science or reading. Finally, if the problem is serious and it persists, then withdraw calmly.

Handicapped children have special needs

Teaching children with certain handicaps often requires special preparation. You may be able to teach your handicapped child quite well. In fact, your extra degree of love and patience are very valuable. You can help develop in your child a positive self-image which, even for normal children, is far more important than school subjects. If your child does have a special need, you should find out about learning to meet it. Contact the Council for Exceptional Children or The National Information Center for Handicapped Children and Youth.*

In considering a home school remember that because handicapped individuals are different. They tend to be sidetracked by society and miss much of the normal interaction with other people needed for social development. On the other hand, although home school means associating with fewer people, it may be a necessity for your situation. Or it may be highly desirable for part of your child's learning program. In principle, however, life is already abnormal for your handicapped child. You will want to do all you can to help him or her feel like an important part of the big world. That may mean the regular classroom for as much of formal education as possible.

As you may already know, state education funds often pay an extension teacher from the local school system to visit homes of handicapped children who cannot easily fit into the school system. Ask your area schools office.

Home school needs a balanced approach

Parents who are interested in school at home are not usually run-of-the-mill people. They have distinctive opinions, and when decisions are to be made, they don't often look around first to be sure all their friends approve of what they are about to do.

Acting on the basis of principle instead of popularity is commendable. Occasionally, however, independent thinkers specialize in a single idea. They write, talk, plan and dream about it. The risk I see for them is not in teaching the idea to their children. Parents have a responsibility to pass on what they consider valuable information and right principles. The danger is that learning essential to success in life might be neglected. The children's future is at stake.

A course of study could differ from what is normally taught in the public schools and still prepare the student for a successful life, but in my opinion, it could not be satisfactory while ignoring the essentials of the major subjects most schools try to teach.

Before you decide that the curriculum set for schools in your state is totally terrible, find out exactly what it is and what rationale lies behind it. You may be pleased to learn that considerable flexibility is permitted. Appendix Section C lists the state offices of education. Another chapter will discuss how to decide what to teach.

If you are not ready to provide your child the essential array of skills and knowledge in sufficient depth to function efficiently and effectively as an adult, you should let a more traditional school do the job. You can teach your special idea at home after school hours.

But

If you are naturally timid, don't be too quick to conclude from this chapter that you can't teach. I've described important qualities for the home teacher, but I believe that most people who want to teach their own children and who are concerned enough to read this book have what it takes. Look back over the qualifications. If you are really bad in one or more areas, OK, throw in the towel. But if you see some weaknesses that aren't clearly problems, go have a heart-to-heart chat with someone who knows you and is sympathetic to the home school idea (if there exists such a person). Maybe you are underselling yourself. All of us have stronger and weaker areas.

If your final decision is to give it a try, then pick up your courage and really go to work.

4

Keeping peace
with school authorities

We don't need to look back past very many yesterdays to see the time when few children had any significant amount of schooling. Before the Civil War, a typical American child whose parents saw the importance of education might have attended school for a few months out of the year when his or her time couldn't have been more "profitably" spent working.

Although the Massachusetts legislature passed a compulsory school attendance law in 1852, no other state followed the example until after the Civil War. The Massachusetts law required children between eight and fourteen years of age to attend school for at least twelve weeks every school year. Parents unable to afford the tuition were exempted from the fine set for violation. Now, every state requires attendance for certain ages.

As early as 1642 a colonial Massachusetts law required parents to teach their children how to read. But only gradually and many years later when education became tax-supported and compulsory, and when laws restricted child labor, did school become a standard and significant part of American childhood. Even as recently as 1898, for example, the average school year was 143 days compared to our present 170 or 180. But the average days of attendance for those who were enrolled as pupils was only 98.

Now, let's come a little closer to the question of why educators today might question your teaching your own children at home instead of sending them to a classroom school. Several factors influence them.

First of all, many don't understand how parents could really do a good job. Too often children suffer from their parents' selfish interests, and nonconformists are easily assumed to be violating human rights.

Most school leaders like to do their jobs well. They are people who entered the field of education because they like young people and enjoy helping them learn. Anyone who, through years of study and experience, has gained expertise in a particular profession, might naturally take a dim view of novices who claim to have a better way.

In addition to parents wanting to teach their own children, several other factors already threaten school attendance standards: Truancy is increasing. Many of the better students attend private schools. A number of parents are delaying starting their children until after the mandatory entrance age. And some people even argue that attendance laws should be abolished altogether. After all, couldn't nonscholastic individuals prepare for life better outside the typical school environment? and good scholars would attend anyway. Thus some educators fear that to allow greater freedom in the establishment of home schools would only accelerate the erosion of control over school attendance.

While policy makers may be concerned that home-schooled children might be missing something, I am increasingly convinced that the bigger reason for defending erosion of school attendance in most cases has nothing to do with what's good for kids. Instead, many teachers, through their unions, want to protect their job security.

Disclaimer

Before we discuss what you might expect in relating to school laws, please understand: <u>Nothing in this book is intended as legal advice.</u> Laws and regulations, as well as their interpretations, change in time. Advice for one situation in one place may not apply to someone else's problem elsewhere.

The law and home schools

You probably want to know simply whether the law will permit you to teach your children at home. Under the right (and sometimes unreasonable) circumstances, yes. Laws differ from state to state, and in Canada provincial laws vary, too.

Often the superintendent or board of the local school district authorizes or screens home schools. The plan of local authority is reasonable. Sometimes, however the local decision makers are not. Each year, laws and regulations relating to home schools are better defined. But interpretations still often seem prejudiced, and sometimes the school boards succeed in frightening home school parents into submission by get-tough tactics.

Legal requirements in various areas

Statutes differ from state to state, and with increasing interest in home schools, new legislation is constantly in the making. Case law (or the body of precedents of interpretation that are being established by the courts and which are used as the basis of future decisions) is rapidly expanding and changing.

To learn about the laws and regulations governing your state or province: (1) Contact a local or state home school support group. (See Appendix Section C, D or E.) (2) Get precise information from the summary provided by HSLDA or by the Rutherford Institute (Appendix A, Part 4). (3) Ask your state or provincial office of education. School authorities in local districts could also be helpful, but in some cases they attempt to discourage home schools. (4) Your public library might have a section of state statutes. Look under school attendance laws and under regulations pertaining to home schools or private schools.

Some areas are certainly more favorable than others to home schools. Often statutes that permit home schools set the minimum number of days per year for giving instruction. Some laws require attendance records, some indicate that the subjects taught be the same as in public school or that instruction be "equivalent," and some require standardized examinations.

The most difficult problem that faces parents in some areas relates to their own qualifications as teachers. Statutes in a few states specify certification for tutors or home teachers; and in some other states where the requirement is for "qualified" or "competent" teachers, these terms are sometimes interpreted to mean practically the same as "certified." A few states require home teachers to pass competency examinations.

If you investigate the particular situation where you are, you may find it easier to set up a private school than to get an exemption from school attendance unless your state specifically provides for home instruction. Most states restrict private schools less than public schools. Usually, teacher certification is not required.

Religious liberty

Parents' religious convictions that public schools have a bad influence on their children may be the reason for starting most home schools. Private church-operated schools would be a satisfactory solution for some of these families, but often they feel unable to afford it or no suitable school is close enough.

The First Amendment to the United States Constitution states that "Congress shall make no law respecting an establishment of religion, or prohibiting the free exercise thereof. . . ." A number of Supreme Court rulings based on this amendment relate to education. Among them is the decision supporting the right of parents to send their children to nonpublic schools.[1] Furthermore, the term "religion" has been interpreted to mean a sincere belief in God or any "sincere and meaningful belief which occupies a place in the believer's life parallel to that filled by orthodox belief in God."[2]

A number of other religious liberty decisions of interest to home school parents have come from lower courts. A religious school in Ohio was granted the right to follow a curriculum which did not meet the state's established standards.[3] Private school teachers in Kentucky no longer have to be certified or hold college degrees.[4] And a Michigan district court has determined that parents with religious convictions conflicting with teacher certification may teach their own children without it.[5] These are encouraging decisions; and although they do not have the force of law outside the jurisdictions where they were made, and do not necessarily open the door to home schools, the precedents set will help establish parallel rights in other places. Several significant rulings are discussed later in this chapter.

Claiming religious rights

A great deal of anxiety can develop in relating to authorities in situations where you believe statutes or the way they are handled to be unfair. Since objections are often based on religious belief, let me share a concern with you who are my fellow Christians. School attendance requirements commonly conflict with what many of us perceive as religious duty. We are quick to insist that our children belong to God, not to the state. And they certainly do. God has given us the responsibility to educate them (Deuteronomy 11:18-21).

When the local government tried to stop the apostles from teaching about Jesus, Peter had a straight answer. "We ought to obey God rather than men" (Acts 5:29). But Paul, in Romans 13, and Jesus, in Mark 12:17, point out the importance of compliance with civil authority. To me these verses clarify our responsibility to cooperate with government requirements not in conflict with what my Lord asks me to do. Let's remember that Christianity means more than protecting our rights (Matthew 5:38-44).

Applying for approval

Before approaching your school district office about approval, contact home school leaders in your area. Ask them for suggestions or guidelines so you can check the strength of your own situation. Some states (Ohio, New York, Pennsylvania and others) pass the responsibility for approval down to local superintendents or boards of education who determine some of their own policies.

For example, if they expect teaching parents to have college degrees, and you don't have one, learning about this policy in advance gives you time to look for alternatives or to consider your defense before getting accused of truancy.

Fortunately, school authorities in most areas do deal fairly with parents wanting to teach their own children and recognize home schooling as a viable alternative to the more traditional educational systems.

In applying for approval, you may need to provide a considerable amount of information about your goals and curriculum plan, about methods and equipment you expect to use, about your schedule, and about your own qualifications; or you may be asked only to declare that you are teaching certain standard subjects for a minimum number of days per year.

Often parents and educational administrators each view the other group as adversaries. Parents are frightened when they hear about school people whose unreasonable actions are apparently motivated by a desire to protect teachers' jobs, to assure tax dollars from the state, or simply to control the situation. And educators who misunderstand school at home, or confuse parents wanting to educate their own children with those who don't care, often feel an obligation to be tough. Communication reduces misunderstanding, and a demonstration of good faith and cooperation eases restrictions. Many home school parents across North America consider training their own children to be a fundamental right and responsibility.

Reducing the possibility of trouble

Most home school parents don't want a confrontation with the law even if they feel they are doing the right thing and that they could win in court. Here are several suggestions that may help keep you out of trouble:

(1) Know the statutes for your area that apply to school attendance and teaching children at home. Learn what you can about court cases where these statutes have been tested and interpretations established. This helps you know where you stand

and gives you a background for intelligent discussion of your position. Unless you know your local superintendent to be sympathetic, ask your state or provincial office for information. People at this higher level will probably have less vested interest in your child's classroom enrollment and they may know more.

(2) Do your job well. Intelligent, well-adjusted students constitute a powerful argument for your educational program whether you are called into court or whether you need to convince your relatives that you aren't ruining your children.

(3) Keep careful records of your child's progress. A daily log in a teacher's plan book would be excellent evidence of a serious educational plan. Keep samples of school work. Keep good teaching materials, especially any you make. Keep any records you have from a previously attended school.

(4) Beginning school during the summer after your child has had a brief vacation from the previous school term might, under certain circumstances, convince school authorities that you are doing the right thing. No regulations are violated by conducting school at home during the summer. If responsibility or teaching ability is the issue and you faithfully make steady progress, you will have strong evidence of your qualifications.

(5) Cooperate in every way you can. Cooperation disarms prejudice and reduces unnecessary differences. If you should be called into court, your case will be much easier to defend if it involves interpretation of the law rather than rationale for disobedience. For example, private or home schools are often required by law to file certain reports. Should your school status be challenged, having filled out and submitted the reports would show that you were complying with the law as you interpreted it. Of course I'm not suggesting you do something that violates your conscience and casts doubt on your sincerity.

(6) Consider joining a legal insurance group. The directors of the Home School Legal Defense Association in their brochure, state their belief that "God imposes a responsibility on all parents to train their children in a manner pleasing to Him," and that "home schooling, when it is responsibly done, is legally protected by the Constitution . . . ." The National Association for the Legal Support

of Alternative Schools also has an insurance plan. For information, see Appendix Section A.

(7) If your competency to teach might be an issue, and if classroom teachers (and not home teachers) in your area are required to pass a general abilities exam, consider taking it yourself. It will probably cover major school subjects at the eighth-grade level. In case you don't pass, authorities wouldn't need to know, and you could brush up weak areas. An acceptable test score would certainly be evidence of ability. Ask your nearest university teachers' college for information.

When you are told, "Send them to school or else!"

Attorney J. Michael Smith, in addressing a home schooling conference and later in personal letters, has outlined a typical approach that school authorities might take in an effort to get your children enrolled in "school," and he has suggested how you might react.

The ideas here apply most directly where the legal situation is not entirely clear and where you feel you have a right to teach your children. As time passes, laws address the home schooling issue more specifically. Each situation is obviously different and your responses should depend on the particular circumstances.

(1) When the school principal learns that your children have not returned to school after being enrolled the previous year or when a neighbor complains, the superintendent's office gets called, and you are contacted by personal letter, by telephone or by a visit from a truancy officer to let you know that your children must be enrolled within a certain few days.

I'll add a few comments here to expand on Attorney Smith's first point. Some parents who have no intentions of teaching at home just don't bother to enroll their children. They need some kind of push to get their kids in school before Christmas, so the intent of the contact isn't always bad.

If you get your neighbors on your side of the question before they get the wrong ideas, you might never receive a letter from the superintendent's office. After you have gotten acquainted, let them know what you are doing and what a good opportunity it is for your children. Anticipating questions that might come to their minds, show that your children are learning better than they would in school and how their social contacts are helping them develop. Have the kids do some special things for the neighbors.

(2) Many times the mother is the one contacted. If the father lives with the family, she should obtain the school official's name and phone number promising that the father will respond promptly. This gives time to prepare an intelligent response after consulting with others, and it puts the husband in his God-given responsibility as the family protector and covering.

If you are told at the door or on the phone, certain things about what you must do, ask for statements in writing and suggest that the caller check with an attorney due to the possibility of civil rights violation under 42 U.S.C. 1983. If you feel it is appropriate, state that the U.S. Supreme Court decision, *Wisconsin* v. *Yoder* gives parents a prior right to educate their children and supersedes any State law or decision to the contrary.

(3) Contact either an attorney capable of handling a possible attendance problem or talk to someone who understands home schooling. If your children are part of an umbrella school or guidance center, contact the organization.

(4) You may be asked to come to a hearing. In California, the group is called a Student Attendance Review Board. If the request is by letter, you should probably accept the "invitation." Legal consultation is critical at this point. If you receive a court subpoena, attendance is mandatory. In either case, if you can, arrange for counsel to represent your views. Your own statements cannot be used against you in court.

(5) If you expect a serious confrontation, prepare a declaration under penalty of perjury stating your reasons for home schooling. If any of the reasons are based on religious conviction, biblical references would be appropriate. Become familiar with pertinent decisions from the U. S. Supreme Court and from your state courts. Use these decisions, as appropriate, to support your position for home teaching. Use wording from the decisions as it applies to your situation, and give the references.

The declaration should be typed, signed by both parents and notarized. It could be presented to the truant officer at the first contact. It will become the cornerstone for the entire confrontation.

For more ideas, see the appendix in Christian Liberty Academy's *Legal Manual* (listed in the bibliography of this book—Appendix H).

(6) Unless you have convinced the authorities that what you are doing is all right or that they can't succeed in causing you to change, the next step is being asked to appear in court. The school district, not the state office of education, takes this responsibility. If you haven't already gotten legal counsel, be sure to do so now.

(7) Your legal advisor will want to give information to the school superintendent or to the judge that will help them see that they should drop the case.

(8) The best approach in dealing with an unfair school law may be to challenge its constitutionality. If your attorney takes this route, he will want to do so before entering a plea. Failure to do so in some states waives the right to attack the constitutionality of the statute involved. When the plea is entered, you assume to be responding to an accepted law.

(9) If you face the judge, your carefully kept records and fidelity to the law as you had interpreted it will greatly improve your chance of success. If your reasons for home schooling are religious, be sure you can explain them clearly. You will show that your children are being well educated and that you are being a responsible parent according to your sincere religious convictions.

Additional suggestions for defending your rights

A relatively small number of home school parents are accused of violating attendance laws, and of that group only a fraction—maybe one in ten—are tried in court. In addition to doing your best to minimize the possibility of confrontation and responding intelligently in the scenario Attorney Smith outlined, here are several more suggestions to consider if your home school is threatened:

(1) Ask for all communications from school officials to be in be in writing. Keep copies of all their responses.

(2) You may be contacted by a school attendance officer who is not really hostile but is fulfilling his responsibility to investigate your situation following a complaint. If the inquiry asks for information, or questions the legality of your home school, the Christian Liberty Academy *Legal Manual* suggests submitting a statement of assurance, giving basic information about your school and accepting responsibility for it. Be sure you are on firm footing with the law before submitting such a statement, however. You may want to talk with your superintendent to find out whether such a document would likely satisfy their need. Counsel from someone at your home school guidance center or support group would be wise. Talk with an attorney if your have any questions.

(3) If you should have made a formal application or declaration for a home school, get counsel about the advisability of conforming with the requirement.

(4) I have already mentioned the importance of keeping careful records. If you feel that you may be called into court, records from a school previously attended could be valuable for establishing that your child is currently making good progress.

(5) If keeping your child out of the regular school is a religious conviction, seek help on that basis. Some organizations have policies on religious rights and employ personnel who specialize in providing help.

(6) Consult an attorney. As with a physician, you may have to pay a fee for a visit, but you are still free to refuse to go ahead with the expensive "operation." Contact your attorney as early as you can when you see a problem coming. It's always nicer to avoid trouble than it is trying to get untangled from a confrontation.

Any attorney can help you, but one familiar with school attendance problems will have the advantage of experience and will require less time in study. You can find an attorney by asking for a referral from one of the three organizations listed in the introduction to Appendix Section C which specialize in this type of practice, or by checking your phone book for a attorney referral service. If necessary, contact the American Bar Association (1155

E. 60th St., Chicago, IL 60637, 312-947-3685) to help you find a referral service. If you contact one, specify the nature of your problem. I would talk with several lawyers, asking about their experience and their fees.

(7) Any school that wanted to, could probably enroll your child as an extension student or home student. In California this is called an independent study program. The idea is slowly becoming more popular.

(8) Sometimes families who see no other reasonable solution to the legal restrictions threatening their home teaching plans, move away.

Significant legal decisions and opinions

Statutes and regulations as various states and provinces have decided them and opinions from court cases help clarify the home school position with respect to the law. The most fundamental legal backbone is the Constitution itself with amendments defining basic rights. Several key U.S. Supreme Court decisions have been briefly mentioned and are cited in the notes and references for this chapter at the end of the book. To be thoroughly prepared to defend a serious case, your attorney would want to be familiar with them and with subsequent cases which have considered their results applicable or not applicable. One of the most important of these is the Perchemlides case from Massachusetts.[6] The four quotations which appear in the following paragraphs are of general significance, but are not intended to be comprehensive.

On requiring college degrees for private school teachers

From the partially dissenting opinion of Judge C. J. Krivosha in the Nebraska State Supreme Court decision, *State* v. *Faith Baptist Church*, 1981.

I find nothing either in our statutes or in logic which compels a conclusion that one may not teach in a private school without a baccalaureate degree if the children are to be properly educated. Under our holding today, Eric Hoffer could not teach philosophy in a grade school, public or private; Julia Child could not teach cooking; and Thomas Edison could not teach the theories of electricity. While none of them could teach in the primary or secondary grades, all of them could teach in college. I have some difficulty with a law which results in requiring that those who teach must have a baccalaureate degree, but those who teach those who teach need not. The logic of it escapes me. The experience of time has failed to establish that requiring all teachers to earn a baccalaureate degree from anywhere results in providing children with a better education.

While it may be appropriate for a state to set such requirements in a public school where state funds are expended and, in effect, the state is the employer, I find no basis in law or fact for imposing a similar requirement in a private school. The failure of the private school to have as adequate and as trained teachers as the public school, may be a factor which parents will take into account in deciding whether their children should be enrolled in that private school. I do not believe, however, that it should disqualify children from satisfying the compulsory attendance laws. I could accept a regulation which required instructors in such schools to satisfy the state that they were adequately trained to perform the functions they were hired to perform. I believe, however, that such functions may be adequately performed absent a baccalaureate degree. . . .

The record in this case clearly establishes that the failure of all instructors in appellants' school to hold a baccalaureate degree has not in any manner detracted from the quality of the education being given its students. . . .

Even the State Board of Education has recognized that the obtaining of a degree may, under certain circumstances, be waived. . . .

While it is true that there are further requirements of that rule [to legalize payment of salary in a state school or to legalize employment in a nonpublic school of a person not fully qualified for a certificate] which ultimately may compel the individual to obtain a baccalaureate degree, one must ask the question: If the holding of such a degree is so critical as to affect the education of a child, why does the State Board of Education waive it under any circumstance? Obviously, the requirement of holding such a degree is not so indispensable to the providing of a good and sufficient education that it must be required under all circumstances and at all times.

It may be argued, as the State does, that any other requirements would impose a severe burden upon the State, in that it would then be required to conduct various tests of students in these schools in order to determine whether, in fact, they are receiving an adequate education. No one, however, has ever suggested that the mere fact that action required to be performed by the government may be difficult justifies the government's refusal to perform the required act. . . .

Experience . . . discloses that students taught by teachers holding baccalaureate degrees do not necessarily receive an adequate education in each and every instance. The record in this case supports that view. Witnesses who qualified as experts in the field of education ventured the opinion that the mere fact that a person held a baccalaureate degree did not mean he or she would be a good teacher.

In my view, attempting to strike a balance between the various interests of the parties herein does not justify requiring that all persons teaching in appellants' school can qualify as a teacher only by holding a baccalaureate degree. I believe there are other reasonable regulations which can be adopted for private schools that would permit these schools to continue, thereby striking the necessary balance between the two competing interests. I would have so held.

Deciding exemptions based on religion

From the case notes published with Ohio school attendance laws:

Because Ohio's compulsory school attendance law . . . permits home-based instruction that meets state requirements . . . the law is not necessarily in conflict with *Wisconsin* v. *Yoder,* 406 US 205 (1972), or *State* v. *Whisner* . . . . When confronted with a religiously-based request for exemption the local superintendent of schools must apply the three-pronged test enumerated in *Wisconsin* v. *Yoder,* supra, and adopted by the Ohio Supreme Court in *State* v. *Whisner* . . . namely: (1) are the religious beliefs sincere? (2) will application of the compulsory school attendance law infringe on the constitutional right to free exercise of religion? (3) does the state have an interest of sufficient magnitude to override the claim of the violation of the right to free exercise of religion? . . . A local board of education may prescribe the course of study. . . . A determination that a child may be excused must be based upon a judgment by the superintendent that the program of home education proposed for the child will satisfy applicable requirements. OAG No. 79-056."

A provision to make public officials more responsible

A part of one of the Civil Rights Acts (42 U.S.C. 1983) states in essence:

Every citizen of the United States has a right to sue the federal government, the state, the county, the city and any person individually employed by any of these entities, if those entities or those individuals violate one of our constitutional rights.

On local school board authority in regulating home schools

From Utah Assistant Attorney General Opinion (83-20):

The home instruction exemption to the compulsory attendance law [in the state of Utah] . . . attempts to balance three important interests: parent, public and student. *Wisconsin* v. *Yoder,* 408 U.S. 205 (1972).

The parents of the school child have a fundamental interest in directing the upbringing and education of their child. *Pierce* v. *Society of Sisters,* 268 U.S. 510 (1925). While this interest finds protection in the constitutional concepts of privacy and liberty, it is not absolute or unlimited. Generally, parents can act in good faith to accomplish the proper education of their own child through their own efforts at home; but the public, through the school officials, can set reasonable standards to see that the child is well educated. *Prince* v. *Massachusetts,* 321 U.S. 158 (1944).

The public has a compelling interest to assure that every child is educated in the branches prescribed by law; but it cannot require every child to attend public school exclusively. The public can set reasonable, minimal education and academic standards to accomplish the prescribed education of the child in the appropriate branches.

The student's interest is to become reasonably well educated. He is entitled to become capable, responsible and self-sufficient enough that he can participate in a politically and civilly responsible manner within his ability. At the same time he should not be so independent as to be unable to function in society.

Thus, there arises a juxtaposition of three interests: parent, public and student; a balance hopefully pursued in a cooperative manner to accomplish a common goal with no one interest being overwhelmed by another. . . . With the school district setting standards for instruction and the parents selecting the time, place and manner of instruction, it is imperative that there be a close cooperation and trust between school officials and parents to accomplish the common goal of properly educating the child. The child is benefited by an education reasonably equivalent to that acquired by children in public school, but the school district cannot require the individual child to become "identical" to the children in the public schools. . . .

A question sometimes arises regarding aid to students in private schools based on the establishment clause of the United States Constitution. The objection is that government aid seems to promote or entangle religion, but it has been clearly held that a school district can furnish texts to promote the interests of the individual student, and that such aid is not a significant support to or entanglement with religion. *Board of Education* v. *Allen,* 392 U.S. 236 (1968). However, the question of religious entanglement should not even arise in our situation because under Utah law a private school is clearly different than home instruction and a home instruction program receiving district support is clearly in the interest of a child and would not be questioned under the establishment clause.

Not every home school case is decided in favor of the parents, but most seem to be, so in the unlikely event that your right to teach your children is challenged, you should not be discouraged. And while the legal wheels are turning, you may be allowed to follow your convictions in educating your children. If you do your job well, you may be able to clear your own record and be instrumental in setting precedents that will help other families.

5

Battle for the right to teach

By Christopher Klicka

Every now and then I wonder how the right to teach our own children, one of the most basic of all rights, could be in jeopardy in a free country such as ours. I don't want to believe it is really happening. As I travel around defending home school families in court, speaking at conferences, and testifying before legislatures, I sense the crucial war waging over the control of our children. Families trying diligently to teach their own children are being harassed and intimidated by local public school authorities.

Some families have been charged with truancy or child neglect for following God's call to take a personal interest in educating their own children. Others are even threatened with having their children taken away.

Although the number of parents fighting on the front lines for their First Amendment freedoms is actually quite small compared to the mass of home schooling families, their battle is for all of us. If they lose, Christian schools lose, and ultimately the family will lose. We dare not take this conflict lightly.

The issue

It is becoming increasingly apparent that the issue is not whether the children are being educated, because in virtually every case in which HSLDA (Home School Legal Defense Association.) has ever been involved, the children have performed above average on standardized test scores. The real issue involves who has the authority to dictate how the children are educated: their parents or the public school authorities. This issue can be further divided into two underlying themes: control and money.

In talking with public school teachers, administrators and superintendents, I have found that they often believe that only the system that they (and the National Education Association) represent is capable of educating children. Time and again superintendents have told me that parents who have not had at least seven years of higher education cannot possibly provide their children with an adequate education. Some superintendents have personally asserted that no form of home schooling is adequate. They have refused to allow home schools to operate in their districts.

Other superintendents have denied home schoolers the right to exist claiming that the children, not being with others their age, will not be properly socialized. One outrageous argument was raised by the prosecutor in a home school trial in North Dakota. He stated that home schooling was inadequate because the children did not have the educational advantage of being pushed around by a school bully! In other words, it is harmful for the child to be sheltered from bullies because he would miss an important social experience which would prepare him for life. Of course, this is the exact type of "negative" socialization which home schoolers want to avoid and replace with godly standards and church involvement.

The crux of the matter that I see is that many of the school administrators actually believe that both the authority and the responsibility to teach the children resides in the state. They believe that they are the "guardians" of the children and that their authority surpasses that of the children's parents. They reason that the education of the children should be left to the professionals who have teaching certificates and are specially trained. Therefore, many superintendents operate on the assumption that they have virtually unlimited authority to control the home school program. Resistance from the home schooling family often damages their pride.

Vested interest

This country's largest union, the National Education Association, nurtures the mentality that demands control over home schools. The NEA recommends that its members push for laws requiring home school teachers to be certified or "meet special requirements approved by the state." They want the law to contain annual approval for home schools; monitoring by the local public school; instruction comparable to the public schools; mandated testing; and records showing progress, attendance, and instructional time.* {See Appendix I for reference.}

In every legislative battle over home schooling, the proponents of greater regulation have always been supported by the NEA. They need the tight controls in order to achieve their agenda. They would like to create home schools into small public schools. In fact, I have personally talked with dozens of public school superintendents who have claimed that home schools are "extensions of the public school" thus justifying restrictive standards and tight monitoring. The pervading philosophy held by the public school administrators is that home schooling is a privilege not a right.

The other issue, besides the philosophy of control, involves money. Your child is worth some two to three thousand dollars in tax money which will be designated to the school district if he or she is enrolled in the public schools. It is to the advantage of public school officials to deny a home schooler the right to exist in order to get the child back in public school. The more lenient the laws and policies, the more likely larger numbers of students will leave the public schools. The survival of public schools and the NEA teachers union depends on the number of children in the system. Home schooling is competing with their vested interest in public education.

In several states, superintendents receive state aid for home schoolers. They insist on strict monitoring procedures because they feel they have to provide a service to justify the per pupil state aid they are receiving. This incentive for collecting state aid needs to be cut off because it interferes with the home schooler's right to due process.

One of the elements of due process is the individual's right to have a neutral decision maker preside over whether or not they can exercise a certain privilege—in this case, teaching their children at home. The neutral decision maker must be available at the first instance. Thus a superintendent or school board with a vested financial interest is not neutral and must not be allowed to determine whether or not a home school may operate.

Facing the conflict

From our perspective at HSLDA, we see the battles are intensifying. The spiritual warfare is growing fierce. Around 85 or 90 percent of home schoolers are teaching their own children for religious reasons. They believe God has called them to personally teach their children so they can apply the principles of God's Word to every subject. They want to protect their children from the humanism and from the "negative socialization"—from the drugs, violence and sex—occurring in public schools and in some private schools. They also want their children to have the basic skills enabling them to read God's Word and live in His world. They don't want them to be among the 27 million illiterate children graduating from our nation's public schools.

Home education—one of our most crucial rights—is guaranteed by the First and Fourteenth Amendments of the U.S. Constitution. I think the enemy sees the danger of this growing movement and is seeking to regulate home schools out of existence or into conformity.

The war has two fronts. First, the spiritual, requiring constant commitment and prayer by God's people. This conflict could result in intimidation or even prosecution.

Secondly, it is a legal battle, taking place in the courts and legislatures of this country. The staff of HSLDA needs commitment from its members and from home schoolers in general in support of their ministry. The right to teach our own children, free from unreasonable government restrictions and threats, is too precious to lose.

6

Helping your child learn

An earlier chapter pointed out that teachers don't produce learning; students do. But teachers certainly help it happen. In this chapter, I will make some observations about how you can help it happen in your home school.

Being a parent-teacher

As a parent, you have known your child longer than he or she has known you. From birth, you have fed, diapered, clothed, disciplined, and loved your child. But this child-parent relationship, important as it is, could cover up the realization that each of us is an individual—young and dependent at first, but still a living being, more valuable than all the gold in the world, with tremendous potential for good or evil.

I would not imply that you and your child are peers. You are not. As a parent you have the responsibility for directing and guiding your young charge. He or she has the responsibility to obey. What you must avoid is the subconscious feeling that the child is your property. Adolescent kids have a way of disillusioning their parents on this point, but it is well to understand it much earlier.

Now you face a new role—teacher. Of course it's new only in a sense. You have been teaching all along, even when you haven't intended to. But your responsibility is now expanding to include intellectual and skill development traditionally committed to "experts" outside the home.

What is the difference between a home school teacher who is obviously still a parent, and a more traditional parent who teaches outside of school hours as a normal part of parenthood? Both have tremendous responsibility. The major distinction is that teaching school must be planned and carried out in a serious way. Of course, education before school years and outside of school time is serious, too, but it can have a more casual stride. Your conscious instruction to your preschool or out-of-school child is given whenever it seems appropriate.

The biggest part of casual teaching is being there, caring, and controlling the environment. As your child matures, however, the educational program must be more carefully planned and diligently pursued. Spontaneous? Yes, as much as possible, but directed. And when there is no spark of interest? Stir the fire! We discuss this more in the chapter, "Structure for Learning."

Qualifications for teaching

To be a good teacher, how much education is enough? No research evidence indicates that students receive any better instruction from certified teachers than from uncertified ones. Students in private schools do better, in fact, on standardized examinations even though certification is often not required for their teachers.[1]

How much should a teacher know beyond the level taught? Enough to permit some flexibility. Enough for a degree of freedom in answering unexpected questions. Many parents with only a high school education have successfully instructed their elementary children. In fact, a person with even less formal education who is well-read, studious and organized should be able to succeed. Using preplanned home study materials obviously requires fewer years of educational lead time than are needed for teaching independently.

In addition to knowing subject matter, a good teacher also understands something about how children learn. Here again, formal teacher training isn't necessary for school at home. An intuitive notion of these learning principles may be developed, at least to a degree, by watching children and interacting with them.

A person may successfully teach an idea without having previously learned it in school. True, the teacher who learns just in advance of passing on the knowledge or skill usually lacks the broader understanding helpful in directing the student's spontaneous interests. But teaching new material has an advantage, too. The learning teacher, having just found a way to master the new concept, remembers how it was analyzed, broken down, and made understandable. He or she tends more to see from the learner's viewpoint. This is at least one reason why students often find it easier to understand their peers than their teachers.

I'm not suggesting that teacher training and certification are unimportant. I do maintain, however, that they are unnecessary for the home school.

Your children must like you

Now lets talk about how to teach. I have appreciated a little book by James L. Hymes, Jr. entitled *A Child Development Point of View*. The chapter titles themselves have something important to say: "You Are a Teacher," "Your Youngsters Must Like You," "Your Youngsters Must Like Their Work," "Your Youngsters Must Like Themselves," and "Your Youngsters Can Climb the Highest Peaks."

Approaching our discussion of teaching from the line of thinking in Hymes' book (although with not all the same ideas), let's consider first the importance of your youngsters liking you. Whether child or adult, we all learn from someone else more easily in an atmosphere of confidence than in an adversary relationship. When we trust the one we are with and feel that that person has our best interest at heart, our minds are free to concentrate on the learning task; we can ask questions and test out our ideas in discussion. Children, perhaps even more than adults, perform to please their teacher. The better they like the teacher, the more their energy goes into learning.

As a parent who cares, your relationship with your son or daughter is probably not all that bad, but realizing its influence on learning emphasizes the value of improving it.

More than good learning performance on school tasks is at stake. Children unconsciously want to be like people they admire. This indirect potential for character development is an even greater reason for working to strengthen the bond.

Children need adult support and affection during all their growing-up years. Your child wants to admire you all the time, but expectations are different during different stages of development. Young children until the age of 8 or 10 especially need physical contact. They need to be "mothered." Take their hand now and then. Give them a little squeeze.

As this period merges into the intermediate elementary years, the ideal for the parent or teacher changes. As Hymes puts it, now "they are not looking for a wonderful mother hen. They want you to be a good egg!"[2] This is the time they want to see you do the active things they like to do—play games, run, ride a bicycle.

Then at the junior and senior high school level, young people want you to respect them like adults. They aren't entirely grown up yet, and they know it. But they look to you to admit them to your adult world by the way you relate to them.

This pattern of a personal, caring relationship with your children doesn't mean you let them do whatever they please. Notice Hymes' explanation:

> The meaning is clear for every age. Be friendly, sure. Be warm and approachable. Be decent, but be an adult. Children want you to be. They need someone stronger than they are—more aware, more alert—as a prop to their own efforts to do the right thing.
>
> Youngsters don't want rules staring them in the face wherever they turn. They don't want to be picked up on every little thing they do every second of the day. They appreciate a little flexibility. If the same law is broken time and time again, they hope you will take a second look at the rule to see if it really is a good one.

They want some patience on your part. You cannot pass a law and expect children to be letter-perfect on it the very next second. Children need time to learn how to do the right thing, the way it takes them time to learn to read or to do arithmetic. . . . You have to allow time for mistakes in grammar to straighten out. The heavens must not fall every time there is a slip.

Youngsters like it best, too, when you talk things over and keep talking them over, day after day. If you are harsh, you push children away from you. If you are severe, you push them back. If you are tough, you push them off. When you explain, interpret, discuss, then you draw the youngsters in.

If you have a rule, if it is a good rule, stick by it. Your sensible, reasonable rule joins hands with the friendly talking way you uphold the rule. The two together—your rule and your friendliness—develop strength and security in youngsters.[3]

Your children must like their work

People learn better when their motivation comes from inside. When your child picks up a consuming interest in some special topic—it could be growing tomatoes, or amateur radio, or one of a million other things—learning really happens. An external system of rewards and punishment may support a certain degree of learning—just enough to get by. But even when "getting by" is all you want, the ultimate name of the game with only outside motivation is beat the system.

For children to like what they are doing, the first requirement beyond liking their teacher is having the ability to succeed in what is expected of them. Whether the task is walking, knitting, or working word problems about boats going up-or downstream, success depends on more than trying hard. Until the child has the necessary maturity, the result will be failure, frustration, and a block to learning.

How can you tell when your young student is ready to learn? The calendar won't tell you because each child is different. Maturity is difficult to define and measure, but still, readiness for a specific learning task is clear and obvious. The key is enthusiasm.

Adults can fake it. They can look interested when they are bored. But not kids. When they are ready to learn, you can see it all over them, in their questions, their remarks, their willingness to listen. Of course, you wouldn't interpret an intelligent question about what holds aircraft up in the sky as an indication that your young child is ready to begin flight training. If you attempt more than very simple answers before your child is ready for serious learning, you may be tuned out after the first sentence. Besides enthusiasm, two other indications of readiness are sincerity and duration of interest—qualities almost synonymous with maturity.

I am not suggesting that you just sit and wait for an indication of interest in something, then try to teach it. You and the textbooks provide the material to be interested in. Also, your child will pick up ideas worthy of building into the curriculum.

From a practical standpoint, you may need to push ahead even when your child isn't wild with enthusiasm. But when your boy or girl is obviously not ready, hold off.

At every point of development, a child is ready for some worthwhile learning. As a home school teacher, you have a real advantage. You can observe more closely, and you can alter the curriculum as needed.

Another characteristic of elementary children which affects how well they will like what they are to learn is action. You may enjoy sitting in the summer breeze, watching the world go by. But not kids. They are part of the world that you see going by—at top speed. Learning tasks need to involve physical action, especially for the very young.

Also, for young children, attention spans are very short. Plan activities that are quickly finished. Break longer tasks into short segments. You can easily adjust the length of your assignments and explanations as you teach. Just remember to be sensitive and watch the level of interest.

You have to keep searching for children's interests. Once you find them, don't let the youngsters off easy. They don't want you to. They want you to have high standards, just as long as the learning makes sense to them. They want you to hold them to the grindstone, and they respect you and are grateful when you do. They want your expectations to stretch them up to the peak of their growing powers. They count on you to ask the most searching questions, to check them on details, to open up the next step in thinking or doing. Youngsters want to achieve.[4]

Your children must like themselves

Much of what we have already discussed about getting your young scholars to like you and to like what they are doing contributes also to the third principle in promoting learning: helping children to like themselves.

If you believe that humanity has a higher object of affection than itself, you have a right to question advice to encourage children's ideas of their own importance. You know how easily children show disrespect to elders and are demeaning to other children. We must differentiate between self-worth and self-centeredness. People who have been hurt and hated often place a low value on themselves and try to push other people around. People who feel good about themselves usually feel good about other people too.

The Christian's self-denial isn't a process of depressing the individual worth (Matt. 11:28, 29). It means trusting God rather than going it alone. In view of Heaven's sacrifice at Calvary, each person is valuable beyond measure.

If you remember that children are people and you realize the price paid for their redemption, you can have the kind of respect for them that will help them feel important in the right way. You are still in charge, but you will look for opportunities to help them use all their potential.

Kids like to work; they want to achieve; and they look to you to help them feel good about it.

Teaching techniques

You may have expected this chapter to tell you what procedures to follow to produce learning in various subject areas. In raising cattle, precise feed formulas and specific treatment of the animals have been figured out to achieve optimum results. Educating people, however, is not that simple. Certainly vast amounts of research have been done on teaching techniques. And there are good ways to get ideas across. But more basic than teaching methods is the teacher.

This chapter has been only a brief sketch of a few ideas that can help you be a good teacher. In order that you not get the idea that techniques are unimportant, that you can just be nice to your kids and they will learn, I should clarify. You do need to follow a consistent, steady teaching program using logical methods.

The next block of chapters in this book offers general principles for teaching specific subjects. Textbooks, teacher's editions and guidelines with package programs also offer help. As you get into the process of planning and teaching, the great mystery of what to do will shrivel up.

7

Inspiring motivation

Have you ever tried to build up enthusiasm in a disinterested child, wishing for a "want-to" button you could press? In a broad sense, the previous chapter, "Helping children learn," told you how to foster motivation. Here I want to share with you what I see as the very bottom line—the causes behind why anyone does anything. Then I'll suggest how you might face a problem with a reluctant learner.

Parents' responsibility

Some would advise just letting children do what they feel like—encouraging them to follow whatever motivation they happen to have, as long as they don't injure anyone. The idea is that the standard for right and wrong develops from within the individual and that, in time, good will emerge. I disagree. First, people just don't get better by following natural inclinations. And second, I believe parents have a responsibility not only to love and provide for their children but also to guide them—to help them develop a sense of right and of priorities.

In this guidance, we must realize that children mature. Activities we proffer should, as far as possible, depend on the child. The successful instructor takes advantage of the learner's readiness or, when appropriate, helps create the circumstances to produce it. Also we would not want to violate the learner's creative interest and individuality by insisting on an inflexible learning program that leaves no room for the adventure of exploring.

No one does anything without a reason. The reason may be selfish and based on misunderstanding or it may be right and sensible, but there is a reason. Even doing nothing is an "action" prompted by a reason because it is a decision to reject opportunity.

So the boy who doesn't want to learn about fractions has a reason for dragging his feet. The girl who gazes off into space while you tell about the Civil War, although maybe not aware of it, has a reason, too.

Reasons for not wanting to learn

What reasons might hinder motivation to learn? Here are some possibilities:

1. *Lessons that don't make sense are boring.* Without the maturity to understand or with gaps in prerequisite learning leaving new ideas unclear, the individual may not be motivated to try. Memorizing chemical names, for example, won't likely have much appeal until the uses and behaviors of the substances are discussed and maybe the system for determining chemical names is understood. The more a person can connect new ideas into his or her existing structure of understanding, the clearer and more appealing they become. However, as you can see, something has to come first. So now and then, learning with only a slight relationship to previous understanding is necessary.

2. *Certain learning tasks may be seen as contrary to personal goals already established.* If a boy wants to be considered "tough" and he thinks an interest in poetry might jeopardize that image, then he will avoid the area as much as he can. Peers often influence what children see as desirable.

3. An interesting psychological mechanism tends to protect us from the hurt of failure, and to lead us to "invest" in areas that promise success. Thus *it's much safer not to be interested in a topic than it is to face inability to understand it.* Peer or teacher intimidation strengthen the tendency. Unfortunately, the avoidance this process produces only makes matters worse.

Disinclination and failure through neglect turn to burnout. How important it is then for the parent-teacher to encourage balanced learning and to watch for intentional disinterest in any area.

You have probably read about right-brain and left-brain individuals. Apparently one side of the brain tends to deal with logic and order while the other specializes in feelings or the aesthetic. Our protection mechanism tends to strengthen whichever side is stronger while neglecting the weaker.

Certainly we wouldn't argue that everyone should have the same interests and abilities. For example, we expect men to be logical and women to be sensitive. We like it that way, but how sad to see either essentially devoid of the opposite traits.

4. Mental application may be blocked by an *unsolved personal problem*. This might be a marriage problem between parents, rejection by boyfriend or girlfriend, threat of physical harm, lack of money to meet needs, or guilt.

5. Drugs, alcohol, lack of sleep, or similar *physical problems* could simply put the mind out of gear.

6. Serious *physical needs may be unmet*. Hunger, cold, inability to see well, or other similar problems could be stopping learning.

7. *The teacher's intent may be interpreted negatively* causing a lack of trust.

8. *The mind may be overstimulated*. The source could be, for example, drama from reading or television, sports, or an improper diet.

9. Through spirit possession or hypnosis *the mind may have been turned over to another intelligence*.

Quest for happiness

We have considered factors that impede interest in learning. What encourages it? Selfishness may appear to achieve happiness, but the end result is always disappointment and misery.

What brings deep, lasting happiness? Would cooking or music or building a dog house or whatever you usually enjoy be any fun with no one to share the results? Motivation, then, is the lure of personal satisfaction. And, for most of us, this means the desire to create happiness for someone else. God wants happiness for His children and has given them the drive to seek it.

How the motivating force develops with maturity

As an individual matures, his or her ways of seeking happiness expand. In the ideal pattern for development, the source of greatest satisfaction shifts through four levels:

1. *The personal comfort stage.* In infancy happiness is enjoying the love and protection of parents and having the physical comforts of being warm, clean, fed and so on.

2. *The caregiver-approval stage.* The child's focus of affection turns first to the visible sources of authority and comfort—the mother and father and, in the primary grades, the teacher. The comfort desires of the earlier stage expand to include whatever makes life easy and fun.

3. *The selected friends stage.* In teen years satisfaction often comes from pleasing peers. The individual's desire to look good to these friends influences choices of activities, material possessions, and values, as well as learning.

A person with a religious orientation or with a more balanced outlook may be less influenced by special friends, but will still see them as important. For the Christian, God is seen as Provider, Protector and Source of all good things. Accepting Him gives comfort and security.

Most people never pass this level. Their values change as they get older but are still largely determined by friends. Even those who think more independently usually focus their actions on themselves or on certain people who meet their approval. People are valued because they belong to the same race, the same nation, the same church fellowship or the same side in a dispute.

4. *The unrestricted stage.* Here people are loved who don't necessarily love back. Happiness comes from helping people simply because they need help. Close friends are still selected as people who support similar ideals, but kindness and understanding aren't restricted to them.

For the Christian, God becomes a close companion. Pleasing Him at any cost brings deep satisfaction and is no longer seen primarily as a means to find salvation or to fulfill expectations of Christian friends. The individual identifies with his Maker's interests and objectives.

As I see it, the shifts from one stage to the next are not abrupt. Also happiness for a person at a certain level may often come from a lower level or occasionally from the next higher level.

Planning for motivation

How, then, can understanding the basics of motivation help you encourage better learning? For example, if your child sees good spelling as a means to achieve happiness, spelling lessons may take on new importance. At the caregiver-approval stage, spelling is desirable for clear communication. When selected friends are important, its appeal may be the achievement of better social acceptance. And for the individual with mature happiness goals, spelling as a part of communication is seen as a tool for helping and loving people.

In planning, we would want to appeal to the highest sources of happiness the individual is capable of understanding. Nothing is wrong with wanting to be warm and dry, but appealing to these desires while neglecting their relationship with more mature purposes, would encourage selfishness.

Of course, talk about how to find greater sources of happiness even to young children. You may not see a response. Your discussion may seem like only good theory, but remember to mention it as it seems appropriate. The concepts will crystallize later. Your own example is extremely important in giving the ideas reality and in helping them take root.

Let's not overlook the obvious importance of making learning fun. This means: Show enthusiasm and understanding yourself. Relate learning to established interests. Think of interesting activities. Choose attractive materials and physical surroundings. And give your child a significant role in planning.

Even with high happiness goals established, all learners, especially young ones, also need short-term objectives like preparing for a test, or finishing the chapter before lunch, or even occasionally the promise of a special treat. But these reasons to achieve should be understood as helping reach the genuine end goal.

Solving a motivation problem

Now let's face reality. Everything doesn't always turn out as we might wish. What do you do when your child shows little interest and just doesn't want to get in and dig for understanding? Here are some suggestions for approaching the problem of lack of motivation:

1. Search for the reason for not wanting to learn—for refusing opportunity. It may be a delicate issue. Probably even your child won't have identified the problem. Listen more than talk. Care.
2. Help the learner work it through. This may take time.
3. Show positive interest. Provide appropriate activities that are fun.
4. Help the individual to internalize the happiness goals—to see all appropriate learning as a means of bringing joy to others and to God.
5. Hold high (and reasonably attainable) expectations, but present them in small steps with short range objectives, especially for younger children.
6. Show appreciation. If this doesn't come naturally, practice. It's vitally important.
7. From the Christian viewpoint, lift up Jesus by life and word. He is Heaven's window.

In the end, we recognize that only God, who has given to each a measure of faith can, in connection with that faith, give motivation.

8

Developing
an educational framework

Your interest in home schools may have come from a fairly clear picture of what you don't want for your children. Your purpose should be more, however, than keeping them away from a certain school situation or wanting a particular environment. A person who sets out on a trip with no particular destination in mind generally arrives at no particular place. To a certain degree education is the same way. You can plan some good activities and study some good books with your child, and certainly some good learning will occur. The question you must face is, in the end, will the young person in your care be fully balanced and prepared to function adequately to his or her full potential? Some of the details of your purposes will develop as you go along, but the general directions as well as some of the mileposts should be marked out before you start.

Educators make a distinction between "goals" and "objectives." Goals are more general. The educational goals you establish tell the broad purposes of your child's learning. They are chosen in harmony with your philosophy. An example of a goal is to handle finances wisely and efficiently.

Objectives are more specific and are developed from the goals. The objective of being able to convert between fractions and decimal numbers, along with many other objectives, leads to the goal of handling finances wisely and efficiently.

Wait. Don't get discouraged at this point. Not even professional educators sit down and from scratch write out a detailed chart of goals and objectives. They have help, and you will find that most of your work is already done, too. Books on education suggest goals, and most textbooks or teacher's editions list the objectives they cover. The school system represented in your neighborhood has its list of goals. Looking at them can give you some good ideas.

Your job then is first to think of some of the things you really want for your child. Then see to what extent they are covered by the lists you look at.

The next step in making your educational plan is placing priorities on the goals. Priorities are developed naturally from your philosophy. Keeping them straight doesn't take fancy planning. Just stop now and then and consider what you are doing and whether you are teaching what is most important. If you don't, you could end up with mostly frosting and very little cake.

The final step is determining a sequence for meeting the objectives. Actually, you don't need to worry much about this either, because textbook authors and curriculum committees which influence them have already planned a good sequence for most of the objectives, and the small details of what comes first often don't matter.

Next let's look more closely at the process of setting goals, then at the matter of sequence and of choosing an educational program.

Considering goals

One of the best lists of goals for American schools was prepared by the 1955 White House Conference on Education.[1]

1. The fundamental skills of communication—reading, writing, spelling, as well as other elements of effective oral and written expression; the arithmetical and mathematical skills, including problem solving. . . .

2. Appreciation for our democratic heritage.

3. Civic rights and responsibilities and knowledge of American institutions.

4. Respect and appreciation for human values and for the beliefs of others.

5. Ability to think and evaluate constructively and creatively.

6. Effective work habits and self-discipline.

7. Social competency as a contributing member of his family and community.

8. Ethical behavior based on a sense of moral and spiritual values.

9. Intellectual curiosity and eagerness for life-long learning.

10. Esthetic appreciation and self-expression in the arts.

11. Physical and mental health.

12. Wise use of time, including constructive leisure pursuits.

13. Understanding of the physical world and man's relation to it as represented through basic knowledge of the sciences.

14. An awareness of our relationships with the world community.

Remember that educational goals and objectives must focus on the outcomes we expect for the student, not on a list of what we think we should be teaching. Although you may not sit down and put your goals into words, it's important from time to time to think about the education your children are getting and question whether or not they are being directed in the general way you feel they should go. Lists of goals can help you focus on what you feel is important. Here are goals for the type of education I feel is best: Each individual should learn . . .

To love sincerely. Love and respect for other people grows out of a personal relationship with God and a realization of self-worth. Sensitivity to the value and needs of others built on a stable, caring home life leads to a happy marriage, to good citizenship, and to successful human relationships in general.

To adopt a healthful lifestyle. A healthy mind and body is one of the most important factors in personal happiness and in usefulness to society.

To work responsibly. Time is the essence of life. Each individual should be able to use it efficiently. Each needs salable skills, a sense of dependability, a respect for the property of other people, and an appreciation for the value of all kinds of productive labor.

To communicate clearly. All human relationships and learning depend on skills in listening, speaking, reading and writing.

To enjoy beauty. Beauty is found in the simple as well as in the magnificent. To see it, to receive satisfaction from it, and to share it are part of happiness.

To reason perceptively. Clear understanding, good logic and creative application of knowledge constitute thinking— the highest level of human capability and a necessary element in freedom.

To conduct personal business prudently. Earning responsibly, investing wisely, spending effectively, and careful planning for the future form the atmosphere for efficient human functioning.

To relate intelligently to the environment. Life is supported and enriched from natural resources. Understanding and using them wisely makes a better life for everyone now and for generations to come.

Notice that this list does not directly mention specific school subjects, although you can see if you look back over it that many of the typical subjects lead toward these goals. For example, language arts or English produces communication skills. Math helps conduct personal business, stimulates thinking, and affects working responsibly. Science leads to the goals about health and the environment. And so on. Some of the goals are not typically achieved through studying school subjects. But this should not be surprising since education is a product of an individual's total environment (whether good or bad) and during the entire life span. With a home school you have the opportunity for a few early years to coordinate the total development of your child.

Your own list may be somewhat different from mine. You may want to place major emphasis on some points I have only indirectly assumed. Remember that you are guiding a life that is not your personal property. The effects of your teaching will continue long after you have ceased to be a part of this old world.

I prepared this list of goals to be acceptable to parents with differing philosophies. For those of you who hold a system of priorities similar to what my wife and I believe is important, here is one more goal for your consideration:

To have a right relationship with God. I'll let you expand this concept. My first listed goal relates to it, but the more explicit statement may help keep its importance in view. As a starting point for goals in the Christian setting, consider Luke 10:27.

As you work with your child from day to day, teach for a balanced education. Keep in mind that the subjects and the separate learning tasks are only important as they lead to the final goals. And remember, too, Rome was not built in a day—nor by a single individual.

Knowing what to teach and when

As you begin to think of specific objectives, you will realize that a framework is necessary. What do you teach? and when? Actually the problem is much simpler than you might think. If you use a preplanned home study learning package, this is figured out for you. Even if you don't, textbook companies realize that teachers like help in this respect. They prepare "scope and sequence" charts for each series of textbooks in a subject area. These charts describe what is covered in each grade in each of several categories of objectives. The order in which the various concepts are presented in the books is also shown on the charts. In other words, these charts are like outlines for the books. In most cases, following through the textbook assures you of a good scope and sequence, and gives you good objectives as well.

Appendix section F shows the subjects and general topics typically taught from kindergarten through the twelfth grade.

Perhaps in giving you the theoretical basis for choosing what to teach, we have left you with the feeling that you need an extra six months to do research in order to establish your own special curriculum—to reinvent your own wheel. In practice your task will tend to be finding sources, approving what you see as desirable, making modifications to include or emphasize what you consider high priorities, and adding special items central to your own philosophy.

Improving on tradition

School at home is older than school at school. An increasing number of parents are teaching their own children. Although no one knows how many children are being taught at home, Patricia Lines' estimate for the number in the United States is probably the most reliable.[2] Using 1985-'86 enrollment figures from all the home study guidance organizations she could locate, and assuming that an equal number of children are taught at home in other ways, she estimated 100,000. Or if there were twice as many as that, the number would be 200,000. This is an impressive figure although still less than 1% of the school- age population.

School reformers Raymond and Dorothy Moore and John Holt along with many others have made serious contributions in helping parents know how to make the break with tradition.

The Moores believe, through their study of research, that formal book learning should be delayed until a child is eight to ten years old. See my chapter, "Early Education" for more on this topic.

John Holt believed that schools in general are poor places to learn because traditional educators tend to separate teaching from real life; to feel that only they can teach, that schooling makes people better, and that they, not the students, must decide what is to be learned.

In pressing for drastic school reform, Holt insisted that children should learn whenever and however they want to, guided by their own curiosity instead of at someone else's command; that the "fixed" curriculum should be made open and free; that the system of testing and grading, which he viewed as corrupting, impeding, and without useful function in learning, be abolished; and that children should be allowed to learn without being "taught." He argues that "compulsory school attendance no longer serves a useful function, either to schools, teachers or students, and that it should be done away with or greatly modified."[3]

Choosing a home study program

As you know by now, teaching your own children is a major task. And even if you enroll them in a home study school, you will have more to do than stick on stamps and seal envelopes. You or someone you designate will be responsible for directing the learning day by day at least through most of the elementary years.

If you use a correspondence school program, you can expect the school to set up the curriculum, choose or prepare the learning materials, provide a syllabus of teaching instructions, give counsel and encouragement as needed, and, in most cases, grade tests at several points during the year.

A guidance center or supporting school will not give you as detailed a syllabus but materials will be provided or suggested with general instructions and probably standardized tests.

The factors which follow can help you decide which school or program can best serve the needs of your family—particularly at the elementary level:

First, you would expect the philosophy of study materials and methods to not conflict with your own. This is not generally a serious problem, but still needs consideration. In the elementary grades where you will be the teacher, to a large degree you will be left to make your own interpretations. Even Bible classes in church-sponsored schools will be designed to teach mostly principles of behavior and attitudes you will appreciate. If this is a concern, you may arrange to make omissions or substitutions as you see fit.

Obviously, you want a school which provides an effective and efficient program. "Well educated" is difficult to define, but whatever it means to you, that is what you want for your children from the school program. You can get cues about the quality of what a school offers by studying its promotional brochures. Opinions of parents using the program or specific lists of materials and samples may also be helpful.

If you decide to use a preplanned program, you should still plan to add to it any concepts and skills which seem especially important to achieve the education you want for your child.

Home Study under guidance from a local school

The educational establishment, both public and private, sometimes views home schooling more as an attempt to circumvent good education than as a serious concept to be studied and encouraged. But this picture is changing.

Leaders in church-operated schools have always recognized the home as the foundation of moral strength. Now they are beginning to see the total educational potential of home schools and to be a little less concerned about the threat to their sometimes small enrollments.

Some private classroom schools now offer supervision services for home schools. In California, public schools may also elect to accept enrollments for children studying at home.

Local schools can help cooperating home schools in several ways: (1) provide legal enrollment with grade and attendance records, (2) give supervision through a visiting professional teacher, (3) instruct parents through training sessions, (4) accept extension students into the classroom for special events or for certain classes, (5) loan books and school equipment, (6) evaluate extension students with standardized and other examinations, (7) provide a smooth transition into the classroom school, and (8) in general, hold high standards assuring quality education for even the few students whose parents may be tempted to become lax.

A school planing to accept extension students will want to set up a plan for administering the "branch" home schools. Obviously the degree of control could vary from only writing down a child's name to holding to a duplication of every learning objective and test set for the corresponding classroom. I believe that any school which agrees to enroll a child must also carry a degree of responsibility for the learning that occurs. At the same time, the goals, resources and skills of the home teacher call for broad flexibility.

Here are suggestions to consider: The school will need to plan one or several conferences with the parents as part of the registration process. If the parents already have a well-defined plan, one meeting may be enough. If not, a first meeting would serve for exploring options. At the final conference, the general teaching plans for the year would be approved by the sponsoring teacher and the child's official enrollment would be accepted. Starting the process in June for a fall enrollment would be ideal. General plans would include the school calendar, textbook selection, course outlines and a list of services expected from the supporting school. Using a structured correspondence course may simplify administration and teaching.

Some schools will want to record letter grades. I would suggest only progress reports with yearly promotions noted. Parents, student, and supporting school need to understand that neglecting to follow through with the teaching responsibility or a serious lack of learning progress would automatically call for a re-evaluation of the plan. A contract can clarify plans, conditions and responsibilities.

Establishing an independent home school

Saving money is often an incentive to be completely independent. In addition to paying for books and supplies, parents enrolling their children in a home study program pay a tuition fee to help cover costs of planning and administration.

To go it alone and do a good job you will need somewhat more preparation and skill than you would following a preplanned program. Of course you can do most anything with your children and call it school, but if you are not careful it may not be all they need for a balanced education.

You don't need to be a natural fountain of knowledge to conduct an independent home school. Get help anywhere you can. For example, find a professional teacher to visit your schoolroom and advise you on a regular basis. Also, search out and use community resources. The chapter entitled "Enrichment resources" and the ones by Margaret Savage provide specific suggestions.

If you feel you can do it well, go ahead and try independence. The unknown is always scary, but if you are willing to find out what half a year with a correspondence program or hire a teacher to get you started.

In some ways teaching is easier for the lower grades, but at the same time it is more critical. A well-laid foundation in attitudes as well as in knowledge and skills gives strength to your child's whole future. Subject matter in the higher grades presents more challenge. At times you will find yourself learning as much as your child.

The multifamily school

As we mentioned in Chapter 1, a group of parents may want to join together to hire teachers and set up a private school. You could explore arranging to use children's Sunday School rooms in a nearby church.

A less formal alternative for a group of several families would be for the parents themselves to share the teaching responsibilities. Some have done this by conducting school in different homes on different days of the week. Dividing up the teaching load can work out very nicely if you stick to a well organized, coordinated instructional plan, but moving from home to home is disruptive for the youngsters. Also, responsibility for any particular subject shouldn't shift frequently from person to person. (See the next chapter under the subtitle, "Organizing for convenient operation.")

Choosing a high school level correspondence program

Secondary correspondence study is somewhat different from elementary. Few parents who lack a firm academic preparation will want to establish a secondary home school without using a correspondence program. As you can see from the second part of Appendix A, many state universities and private institutions offer high school correspondence study.

In choosing a secondary correspondence school or an individual course, you will want to consider the quality of the instruction offered, the services provided by the school, and the costs.

Courses vary somewhat in quality and philosophical approach even within the same school just as they do with different teachers in a traditional school. Although there is no way to be completely certain of satisfaction, most of the schools I am familiar with take a serious professional attitude toward the programs they offer, and produce good courses. Most schools will allow you to switch to a different course if you do not like the one you first enroll in. You will probably have to pay a small fee to make the change. The course description in the school catalog will give you clues about whether or not you are getting what you want. Also notice what textbooks are used with the course.

For a half unit—a course in one subject for half of a school year—you should expect ten to fifteen lesson submissions and one or two supervised examinations. Part of each lesson is a printed commentary from the course author representing what a teacher might say in class. This presentation usually ranges from less than a page to half a dozen pages. The amount and type depend on the information already available in the study materials.

In addition to the commentary, most lessons have an assignment to send in to the school for grading. Sometimes lessons include self-check exercises. Often workbooks, cassette tapes, lab equipment, or other special learning materials are used along with textbooks.

The school receives lessons, logs them in, has them graded, records the results, and mails them back.

Transcripts are issued for satisfactory course completion, but not all schools offer diplomas. Most students supplementing their classroom education take only one or two correspondence.courses. Those who do want to complete their studies by correspondence can sometimes get a diploma through a local high school if their correspondence school doesn't offer one.

Examinations are administered outside the home. The student sends in request forms at appropriate points in the study program to let the correspondence school know when to send them. State universities often have designated examination centers scattered throughout the state. Those who study from an out-of-state university or from a correspondence school which is not state-sponsored arrange for an acceptable supervisor, usually at a nearby school.

Correspondence schools do not serve hot lunches or pick up their students in buses, but they do provide services beyond receiving tuition and mailing study materials. Some of the help and guidance a teacher in the traditional school would give a typical student is anticipated by the correspondence school and included in the study guide. The correspondence teacher grades the lessons and tests, and writes notes to encourage students and to help them understand their errors.

At least one university correspondence school expects supervisors of its high school students to do more than proctor the examinations. They are to be "links" between students and school to offer encouragement and guidance.

Although talking with the teacher on the telephone will not often be a great advantage with well-designed courses, occasions may arise when a short conversation could clear up a misunderstanding blocking progress on the course. Some schools encourage direct contact with teachers and will give you their phone numbers. Some will not. To find out about the policy you may need to ask. A few schools have WATS lines permitting students to telephone in without toll charges.

The prompt return of graded lessons is certainly desirable since students not only are rewarded by the results of their work but also learn from their errors. Unfortunately the lesson handling process is generally slow. The typical "turn around time" is ten days. Delays in returning lessons usually come from the teachers who are in most cases employed full time in a typical classroom, and who grade lessons as a sideline for supplementary income. Sometimes graduate students do the grading. If a teacher allows lessons to accumulate for a week before being graded, added to time in the school office before and after, and several days each way for mail service, the student might not see the corrected lessons for several weeks after sending them in.

Several schools use a computer to help grade some courses. This allows them to have lessons back in the mail the day after they are received. Objective type responses such as multiple choice can be handled efficiently by the computer which not only indicates the mistakes but can give information to help the student find the right answers. Computers would not be used for subjective work such as art and English compositions which are better graded by "live" teachers.

May failed examinations be repeated? As a rule, students plan to pass, but being able to retake a test is usually better than repeating the entire course. It is well to find out before enrolling whether or not tests can be repeated, which tests, and under what circumstances.

All secondary correspondence schools we know of handle grade records responsibly. Grades are reported to the student and transcripts are sent as requested.

Mandatory school attendance ages generally cover most of the high school years as well as all the elementary years. Accreditation is important, but the primary issue is your receiving authorization to not send the young person to a traditional school. This problem was discussed in Chapter 4. Credit acceptance may depend more on whether or not the high school you ask to honor the credits feels the student should be studying outside the traditional system, than it does on the qualifications of the correspondence school.

Be sure the courses you choose lead to the goal you want— presumably graduation. If you plan for your young person to graduate from the correspondence school, say so when you enroll and be sure you are getting necessary courses into the program. Verify that the school actually offers a diploma and that your son or daughter can qualify for it. High schools generally have a limit on the number of correspondence credits which they accept toward graduation. In practice, however, if a student has a good reason for being out of the traditional school, arrangements can be made to accept the credits.

Most home school parents who use secondary-level distance education want their young person back in a classroom school for part of the high school years. Unless you are fairly sure your son or daughter will graduate from the correspondence school, it would be wise to discuss your plans with someone at the school to which he or she expects to transfer. Even if you don't know what school may be attended later, a visit with a local school guidance counselor might be worthwhile.

An option you probably haven't thought of is entering post secondary education without ever graduating. Even without a high school diploma most universities will accept students who show a reasonable possibility of succeeding. Scores from the SAT (Scholastic Aptitude Test) or the ACT (American College Test) help them decide. If you are interested in this plan, consult with someone in the university admissions office and, if possible, get written verification of their policies. Bookstores and newsstands sell books to coach preparation for the tests. The universities can tell you when and where they are given.

Charges for courses vary considerably. When comparing tuition, note that most schools include the cost of the study guide in the tuition. A few charge an additional fee for it. Some schools have a "registration" fee which you will need to pay with each course or each time you send for a group of courses.

Know what reimbursement is made if it becomes necessary to drop a course. If the policy is not printed on the enrollment form, you may wish to write it in yourself before you sign. Keep a copy. If a particular course turns out to be unsatisfactory, most schools allow another course to be substituted for it. Check the costs and time limitations.

Also find out how much time is given for completing a course. Most schools give you a year, but for an additional fee they will grant an extension.

The *NUCEA Guide to Independent Study Through Correspondence Instruction* lists courses offered by the National University Continuing Education Association schools. To get the specific information you will need for enrolling, request catalogs from the schools which appear best for your needs. Appendix Section A or the NUCEA guide (listed in Appendix H) will provide ideas about which schools to contact.

9

Teaching in the home school

So far, we have considered some of the basic principles of school at home and have discussed initial decisions important in setting up an educational program. This chapter deals with getting ready to put your plans into operation. We discuss in general terms: selecting books, planning, effective teaching methods, organizing the teaching responsibilities, and evaluation. Subsequent chapters offer advice for specific subjects. Although I write here as if you have chosen the option of an independent home school, much of the discussion will be valuable also to parents using preplanned programs.

Selecting major learning materials

Good textbooks don't teach by themselves, but used wisely they certainly carry a heavy part of the load. Selecting materials which help you meet your objectives is an important consideration unless you are using a preplanned package such as home study schools offer. Even then you can, to a degree, judge the school by the materials it uses.

In the next chapter, Sandy Gogel offers advice on selecting learning materials. If you don't have time to read everything now, you could read her practical ideas and skip the rest of my comments in this subsection.

If your confidence and enthusiasm about home teaching are not already in high gear, they will probably come to life when you begin looking at the great variety of excellent learning materials on the market. Mary Pride's *Big Book of Home Learning* (noted in Appendix H) makes the "shopping" fun. Your problem may be more in choosing what you like best than in being able to find something that will work.

Appendix Section B lists many publishers and gives examples of their products. Several offer quality textbooks and other learning materials for those who prefer a Christian orientation.

Obviously you can't order all the books published for a certain grade just to choose what you like best. To get an idea about what you want, you can do several things: If you have time, you could visit a curriculum library at the elementary or secondary education department at the closest university. Publishers send them materials knowing that their students will soon be teachers choosing textbooks. A day looking through a collection like this would certainly be well spent. You not only can choose what you want to use, but also you will get ideas about what is taught in the various subjects and even how it is presented. Since they wouldn't have religiously oriented books, and such a visit may not be convenient for you, you may also want to look at materials used in a nearby Christian school. State departments of education and school district offices also have curriculum libraries.

A visit with a teacher of the grade you are interested in might be another way to get help selecting textbooks. Her (or his) opinions about the books would give you good clues. In fact, you may even be able to borrow books you want from the school. You will probably still need to buy the teacher's editions, but don't be afraid to ask. While it is possible that you might get a cool reception, you will more likely develop a friendly source of future counsel and support.

Perhaps the nicest way to learn about curriculum materials is to visit a home schooling curriculum fair. The support group in your area could tell you about when one might be planned.

Before you look seriously at a particular textbook, find how you can get it and whether you can also get the teacher's edition. Some of the major textbook publishers, probably as a safeguard against cheating and to keep the schools happy, sell teacher's materials to parents only through school addresses or with school approval. A school name and printed stationery may facilitate a direct order from any of the publishers. One mail-order source for printed stationery is Nebs (500 Main St., Groton, MA 01471, 800-225-6380). Many small publishers and distributors sell books especially for home schools. Of course they have no restrictions based on who you are.

For classroom textbooks, you will want both student's and teacher's books for most subjects, although in a few cases you may be able to get by with one or the other.

Workbooks may be helpful, although they are never necessary unless used as textbooks. Just be sure any materials you use produce more than busywork.

You will be able to order special books for below-average students. Catalog descriptions identify books for special use.

Supplementary materials such as cassettes and filmstrips are often published to accompany major textbooks. They are nice but usually too expensive for one-time use. If your local school uses the books, try to borrow units of the accompanying supplementary materials on a short-term basis.

When you sit down to examine textbooks, here are some principles to consider:

\# First of all, check the book to see whether it covers objectives you believe are important. If you have a list of specific objectives before you start looking at texts, it probably will not be a long one. Here you can expand your vision deciding if what the textbook authors expect is suitable for your use. Look at the table of contents to get a quick idea of the scope of the book. If you don't see anything about some favorite topic, remember that everything is not taught in a single grade. In fact, textbooks usually cover more than the average class gets through in a year so that, to a certain degree, teachers can choose what they like to teach.

\# Compare the clarity of the writing style in the books you are looking at. A number of factors such as the length of the sentences and how often long words are used determine what is called the reading level—the grade in which the material can be easily read.

This and type size are well controlled by most elementary textbook publishers. For your inspection, just look for nice style and clarity.

See if the exercises or study questions seem useful for the student and easy to check.

Look for review and self-check exercises. Skill-building subjects like math, grammar, and spelling need an ample amount of practice. Pick a specific concept like reducing fractions or capitalization that is introduced at the particular grade level, and compare the books you are looking at to see how much work is available on the topic and whether or not sufficient review reinforces the concept. (The beginning of some school books, such as for math, contains a review of the previous year's work, although it is not labeled as such.) You will not use every exercise and question, but a good number should be available to you.

Attractiveness is important. Of course you expect your child to be interested in the basic subject matter, but in reality, nice illustrations and interesting format add a little sparkle to what might be a rather ho-hum school experience from the child's viewpoint. Pictures and verbal illustrations need to appeal to your child whether or not they are interesting to you.

Verify to see that concepts contrary to your philosophy are not promoted. Depending on your ideas, these might be marginal profanity, illustrations of activities you would not want imitated, fantasy, humanism (extolling the greatness of man in and of himself), evolution, violence, deception, hatred, and so on.

Finally, look at the teacher's edition (when you are sure the publisher will sell it to you). Check to see that it will be easy for you to use. The teaching suggestions should be clear and practical for your home setting. Often a teacher's edition will have extra questions and problems that can be used for quizzes.

The school calendar

Setting up a school calendar and a weekly schedule may seem like a formality important only for the efficient operation of schools involving more than one or two families. Not so. Time planning is important for teaching only one child just as it is for operating a large school system. It is important whether your home school is entirely independent or whether your child is enrolled in a preplanned program.

Your school calendar helps both you and your child to know that during school time other nonemergency activities have to wait. It also shows vacation times when the books can be put on the shelf and temporarily forgotten with a clear conscience. By keeping your educational program moving, a calendar helps you get through the grade without having work to finish during the summer months when young friends are enjoying their "freedom."

State laws require around 180 school days each year for their public schools. Often the minimum applies to home schools, too. If your child masters the concepts slated for the grade before the end of the required number of days, you can plan "supplementary" experiences for the rest of the time. Think of the tremendous range of possibilities for worthwhile learning!

Quite naturally, needs will arise to take off days scheduled for school. Making up the time ahead when it's feasible will help your child understand that learning is serious business.

Making a weekly schedule

School laws often call for six hours in the elementary student's day. With half an hour off for lunch, school typically runs from 8:30 to 3:00. Recess time counts as school hours. First graders normally have a shorter day and kindergarten is conducted for even less time each day, usually only three or four hours.

Ideally, school hours should be planned for the time of day your young person is most alert. From a practical point of view, your schedule is also influenced by the pattern of family needs and activities. For example, if the father, whose work keeps him away from home during the day, teaches one of the subjects, you may want to have an evening session. A shorter day on Friday can be arranged by lengthening the other days.

Plan for frequent physical activity. Children in the lower grades need two or three 15 to 20 minute recess periods in addition to lunch time. For upper grades, one or two. You can plan one of the recess periods as physical education.

Even high school students need breaks for physical activity. In the traditional school program the five minutes for changing classes along with physical education periods provide the refreshing shift from brain concentration to body activity. In the home school where changing classes means reaching for different study materials, be sure to plan for active breaks. A brief run in the fresh air invigorates the body and lifts the spirits. One way to memorize material is to summarize it on cards and learn while walking. The mind is alert with good circulation and fresh air.

The subjects normally included in the first six grades are: math, reading, language (grammar, composition, spelling, handwriting, etc.), social studies, science, health, art, music, and physical education. In grades seven and eight, reading and language are modified and become English, handwriting drops out of the picture, and science is more specialized. Often state history or government is required. Appendix F outlines the "typical course of study."

If your philosophy has a Christian orientation, Bible study may be part of the curriculum, and you should consider beginning each day with a devotional period.

An important area to consider adding to your curriculum includes cooking, sewing, mechanics, house maintenance, and gardening. You could plan a period each day for these and call it "home skills" or "practical skills." One or two of the skills would be taught for several weeks or months then the program would change depending on the season and available resources. This would be a planned learning program although jobs that need doing could be part of it.

Other special topics you may think of will probably fit into one of the regular subjects. The environment, for example, would be part of science. Computer language fits into math. Making tiffany lamp shades could come under art, and so on.

The school day normally begins with opening exercises. This short period may be spiritual or secular and could include discussing any special plans for the day, reading from a story book to your child, singing, saluting the flag, and similar activities. The religious opening exercises or devotional period would include prayer.

Most home teachers don't divide the day into short time blocks the way classroom teachers often do, but you may want to. A fifth- or sixth-grade schedule for a 32-hour week with short periods might look like the one on the next page.

Of course this schedule should be modified according to the subjects you teach and the emphasis you give them. The opening period could lead into a Bible class. You could reduce or eliminate the supervised study period since parts of most classes are usually supervised study. All-day field trips, visits to the library, and other such special activities would make exceptions to the schedule.

Instead of the precise schedule just suggested, you may want to plan larger blocks of time for general curriculum areas. The language arts, for example, could be lumped together in your schedule. You could concentrate for several days on a particular subject such as reading, then shift to spelling or writing. You might plan for language arts and math in the mornings and other subjects in the afternoons. Although in a more open schedule like this you could capitalize on natural motivations, letting your child concentrate on one or two concepts until they are well understood, balanced learning would be harder to maintain. You would want to guard against the temptation to neglect areas less appealing to you and your child.

Even if you choose a relatively, unstructured approach, you should still plan carefully to meet certain general objectives and add structure to your program as needed. A definite schedule, even if you don't follow it closely, provides a point of reference. Many parent-teachers mark out each day what learning activities are to be done; and when they are completed, that's it. You may succeed without following a close schedule, but don't forget your purposes. An aimless study plan achieves worthwhile goals more or less by chance and teaches your child to drift through life in the same way.

	Monday through Thursday	Friday
8:00 - 8:45	opening period (Bible)	opening period
8:45 - 9:30	math	math
9:30 - 9:45	recess	recess
9:45 - 10:15	language arts (grammar, composition, etc.)	language arts
10:15 - 11:00	reading	reading
11:00 - 11:30	social studies	science & health
11:30 - 12:00	supervised study	supervised study
12:00 - 1:00	l u n c h	l u n c h
1:00 - 1:15	handwriting: Mon., Wed. spelling: Tues., Thur.	physical education
1:15 - 1:45	science & health	art
1:45 - 2:45	home skills	
2:45 - 3:00	physical education	
3:00 - 3:45	music / music practice	

Thoughts on interpreting a schedule

Raymond and Dorothy Moore of Hewitt Research Foundation have prepared "Sample Program" sheets, one for younger children and one for older for ones. They suggest that the following daily schedule may be helpful if you need to present plans for approval. Their book, Home Grown Kids, explains their recommendations.

    9:00 Bible
    9:40 Music
   10:00 Recess
   10:10 Language Arts
   10:40 Science
   11:20 Recess
   11:30 Math
   12:00 Lunch
    1:00 Story time and rest
    2:00 Social Studies
    2:30 Art

A general note on the sheet "for a child less than 8 or 9 years old" reads: "Adapt and adjust this schedule to your home program and your particular needs. . . . We do not suggest that the child do any reading of books or writing of his own except as he asks to do it or picks it up by himself. Many of the above activities can take place incidentally in connection with your daily household duties, but all may not need to be included in one day."

The following comments offer ideas on how to approach the various subjects for children in this younger age range:

Bible: "Reading or telling Bible stories to the child, finger plays, verses, etc. as in children's Bible School."

Music: "Singing, marching, listening to records or tapes, etc. (Formal music lessons such as piano are not recommended at this age.)"

Language Arts: "This includes reading to your child, playing word games . . . [thinking of words that rhyme or begin with the same sound, etc.] to sharpen hearing skills, and conversation to help him build vocabulary, organize thoughts, etc. Give opportunities for him to tell you a story or an incident. Sometimes let him dictate a story, letter, or incident. A daily diary is good for the parent or older sibling to write."

Science: "Collecting natural things like leaves, rocks, shells, etc., nature stories read or told to the child, a walk in the woods, experiment with an ant farm, caring for an animal, etc. Simple physiology and anatomy, keeping track of the weather, or stories about such things are also 'science.'"

Math: "Measuring in the kitchen or garden, sorting or counting, learning to tell time, learning about money, etc."

Social Studies: "Trips to the market, bakery, post office, library, etc., stories of how people live in other lands, or any kind of simple history or geography stories, or experiences are appropriate."

Art: "Coloring, painting, crafts, etc."

For children beginning at age 8 or older, the Moores suggest a gradual transition "from informal activities to textbook study"—at first 20 or 30 minutes a day, increasing to 60 or 90 minutes with several breaks. "However, all the time you spend in responsive companionship with your child, whether baking bread, or raking leaves is education and can be interpreted in your schedule as 'comparable to that of public school.'"

"List any educational aids which you use. There is no limit to the amount of enrichment you can put into a home program, but be sure to put it all in the framework of consistent discipline and character development which is accomplished best in practical work with you in the daily tasks of the home or your vocation."

Notes on the program sheet for older children suggest what might be involved in teaching the different subjects:

Bible: "Continue to read or tell Bible stories to your child, memorize Bible verses, and look up some of these in a large print Bible, repeating enough so the child will learn to do it independently. You and your child or children could role play appropriate stories."

Music: "Continue to sing, march, listen to records or tapes, etc. Formal music lessons such as piano should probably be postponed another year or two."

Language Arts: "Follow a Teachers' Guide in using reading, writing, spelling and phonics books. Continue to read to your child, play sound word games to strengthen hearing skills, and converse with him to build vocabulary, organize thoughts, etc. Give opportunities for him to tell someone a story or an incident, perhaps on the telephone. Let him write or copy a short story, letter, or incident. Keeping a diary or daily log is good."

Science: "Follow a good elementary science program. Continue to collect and identify natural things, including bird songs and other nature sounds."

Math: "Gradually introduce formal math, following the Teachers' Guide of a good math series."

Social Studies: "Child may draw a floor plan of his house, a map of the neighborhood, learn to be the navigator on trips, etc. Widen his horizons by stories and experiences as much as practical."

Art: "Woodworking, sewing and practical arts are appropriate here as well as other typical creative arts."

In practice, the Moores view the specific program more as a reference guide than a pronouncement of what would happen each day at certain times.

The yearly teaching plan

We have discussed planning the school calendar and deciding when to teach each subject. Now we face the question of what to do with the time allocated. Of course you could just plunge right in and see how much book you have left over at the end of the year. Although teachers sometimes do this, planning ahead has the obvious advantage of helping you know how to use school time most efficiently. Also, instead of achieving objectives that just happen along on your voyage through the text, you can work toward them with intelligently directed effort. And if your right to teach your children is being questioned, neat purposeful plans are evidence that you know what you are doing.

Theoretically, teachers view textbooks only as tools to use as appropriate for meeting particular, independently determined objectives. Often in practice, however, the textbook becomes the principal source for what is to be learned. For the parent-teacher, carefully chosen textbooks are generally the curriculum backbone.

The table of contents provides a starting point for laying out the year's study. Look at the suggestions in the teacher's guide indicating how much time might be allotted for the various chapters or units. If you don't find suggestions of this nature, check the number of pages in each chapter for a clue to which ones might require more and less time.

Even though the textbook will probably be your major learning source, plan to use other resources as well. Some of these can be figured into your year's master plan. Others will become apparent as the year unfolds. You can then modify your plans, always keeping an eye on the overall goals.

For lower and middle grades you will want a day or two each month for review and for unit tests. By the time seventh and eighth grades come along, I would plan two or three days' review plus a day for examinations four to six times during the year.

Thus your yearly teaching plans can be quite simple. They might be only dates and notes written on your textbook table of contents pages. Or, much better but still simple, a chart divided into thirty-four to thirty-six weeks with columns for various subjects. The margin designating the weeks would show specific dates and would take into account vacations and holidays planned in your calendar. In the blocks you could write topics (and objectives), textbook page numbers, and notes about nontextbook learning experiences.

Specific plans

After you have distributed over the school year the principal topics of a particular subject, you can begin to make more specific plans showing what you expect to accomplish each day. Include the objectives you are attempting to achieve, the particular teaching strategies you expect to use (such as discussion, questioning, demonstrating, problem solving, or reading), references to the textbooks and other sources, notes about tests and other evaluations, and, as appropriate, assignments for independent study.

You will find it best to make these more specific plans in blocks of several days or even weeks. Plan a whole textbook section with accompanying special activities as a continuous unit leaving the final details for the daily lesson preparation.

Then, while you are polishing up your daily written plan, think through carefully what you expect to do. The plan on paper is to reinforce the more important plan in your head. You will learn much about the subject from reading the textbook itself as you prepare to have your child read it. Don't let this intimidate you. Professional teachers learn from the textbooks, too. Modify the plan according to the current progress and needs of your student. And add notes as cues for comments, discussion questions, quizzes, and so on.

As you teach, your plan should be adapted to the dynamics of the situation. Your child's reactions, and needs that become apparent should alter your strategies and determine how far you can advance. Incidentally, this shaping of the lesson plans is done in the classroom too, but there only a small degree of individualization is possible. Generally, the whole class is pulled ahead or held back to satisfy the most obvious needs.

It isn't necessary to prepare unit plans for the whole year at once. In fact, teaching your first unit will give you ideas about how to plan the next ones.

Don't be afraid to let your child help you plan, especially when you see alternative ways of achieving your objectives.

To give you an idea of what daily teaching plans might look like, the next two pages show samples for thee subjects.

Notice that the social studies plan is more detailed than the other two. One reason is that no textbook is being used at this point. In most cases you would not need to plan as formally as this. In the simpler plans for the math and spelling lessons, objectives and other details were assumed to have been understood from the text materials.

Spelling

Have him review list on p. 64.
When ready, Quiz over p. 64.
Review missed words & quiz again.
Then fill in exercise on p. 65.

Math

Percents
  Relate to fractions.
    Tell how word helps explain meaning.
Have him read explanation on p. 138.
Then go through sample problem on board.
Have him try samples from p. 138.
Assignment: All of exercise
  17-2. pp. 138, 139.
Have him check with key.
Remind him of test next week.

Social studies

Lesson topic: Work more on family tree.

Objectives: Figure out what information is most significant for family history. Improve sentence formation (language).

Strategies: Have him write to Aunt Alta. Help him figure out what to ask. (should include):

1. Names of relatives she knows of.

2. Relationship to family.

3. Any dates and places of birth she knows.

4. What they did for a living.

5. Any stories (if she has time to tell).

Evaluation: Look over his letter. Talk about what to correct and add.

After class assignment: None this time.

If you use a correspondence or packaged home study program, much of the planning is done for you. Still, every day you must understand the lesson, and decide how far to go. Also, consider enriching the sometimes bare-bones preplanned program with field trips, supplementary reading, extra problems as needed, or other special learning events. Remember, you are essentially the teacher even if someone else plans the overall program, makes the tests, and gives the grades.

Good planning takes time, although not as much as you might think. Some people tend to drift along with little planning. If you are one of them, you might feel a bit scolded as you read this book. (Sorry about that!) At the other extreme, however, are a few valiant souls who busywork themselves into total inefficiency. Learn to plan quickly. Look for shortcuts in identifying textbook concepts, and find fast ways to transfer plans to paper. Remember that your written plans are signposts, not a surveyor's map of the highway.

Planning is important. It not only makes your teaching easier, but well-planned, well-organized teaching inspires the same kind of learning. Interest is maintained and behavior problems are minimized.

Organizing for convenient operation

Meg Johnson, Margaret Savage and Ginny Baker, in the chapters they have written for this book, offer specific ideas about putting theory into practice in organizing your schoolroom. I'll add a few suggestions here.

Designate a special place for school. Standard school desks and a chalkboard are nice but not necessary. Your children can help plan and keep order in your home classroom. Arrange a specific place for the children's school books and for your records and materials. Check lighting and ventilation.

A second person may share the teaching responsibility. Most home schools have one teacher—Mother. As a second teacher, Father often makes an ideal team mate. He may teach a subject for which he happens to be better prepared or that is in an area of his special competence. The second teacher may be a retired professional teacher who also supervises the regular home teacher. For art or music, lessons can be arranged outside the home. Sometimes two or three mothers will set up a school for their children and will each cover certain areas of the curriculum.

Unless one of the instructors is a trained teacher and comes to supervise the home school part of the time, a divided teaching responsibility should be on the basis of subjects or grades.

If you know other home-school families in your area, consider organizing a joint school once a week or once a month. This will require more planning and coordination, but could be very rewarding. You could divide up the children by grades, each teacher-parent taking a group. Students could prepare special assignments at home. Most children will benefit from the experience of studying for someone other than Mom and of discussing in the presence of peers.

For whatever plans you make, each teacher must be fully committed to the task. No subject of any importance can be taught successfully on a when-I-get-time basis.

Frequently, school at home involves more than one child. With a few organizing techniques and careful planning, as Meg Johnson and others point out, one teacher can probably handle several grades.

Except in math and reading which depend heavily on past learning, classes for consecutive grades may be easily taught together. Classes, even in subjects that build on past learning, may be partially combined by studying the same topics but with different assignments. Certainly projects like putting on a play or planning and preparing a meal or making a "museum" can involve your whole school.

In much of your teaching you will want to plan discussion and explanation for one grade while others read or write out assignments. Expect your older students to learn more directly from the textbook without leaning on you unnecessarily so your explanations can be brief.

Another way to simplify teaching several grades is to ask an older child to help teach a younger one. I'm not suggesting that an older student should take the full responsibility for a subject, although in a special case this might work out. All of your children need time to do their own classwork. And responsible teaching takes maturity. The older child can listen to a younger one read, drill spelling words, help explain math problems, read stories, and so on. The secret of success is good supervision and planning on your part.

A foundation for new learning

Learning any concept depends on prerequisite knowledge. For example, a cookbook may provide instructions for making a certain dessert. One of the steps may be to blanch almonds. The cookbook author, in teaching you how to make the dessert, assumes you already know how to "blanch" as well as many other things including how to read the instructions. Without a complex array of knowledge you would certainly fail at learning how to make the special dish.

Now take a rather obvious example from math. If a child is absent when the classroom teacher explains long division, he or she could not expect to do other mathematical calculations dependent on the process. Fortunately, instruction is normally planned by textbook authors as well as by teachers so that essential concepts and skills like this are presented more than once. Succeeding presentations, however, come as review and a shy child that misses the initial explanation may fail to ask the right questions when the concept is reviewed.

For several reasons, home school students are less likely to totally miss an essential concept, but if by oversight the idea is not covered or if it is assumed erroneously to have been part of previous learning, a student might be unable to move ahead.

When a new concept seems unusually difficult to grasp, one of the things to do is to ask what is difficult about the new idea. If your child can't explain—which will probably be the case—start asking about all the component ideas.

For example, you may be teaching the science concept of pressure. Suppose the pressure cooker idea is used to help in the explanation. If your child missed the concept that water expands as it changes to steam, the pressure cooker won't make sense, and therefore the concept of pressure won't be learned, unless by another avenue.

When, with a little probing, you uncover the difficulty, remember that the book and your lesson outline are not in charge of the teaching. You are. Tactfully and without undue fuss go back to the idea that got missed and build through to the concept in question.

Of course, remember also that learning blocks often occur for reasons other than lack of prior knowledge. Your child may be mentally, emotionally, or physically unready for what you are trying to teach. Again, patiently talking it over will help you realize the problem, and wisdom will help you know how to modify the educational plan.

From printed page to understanding

Few people learn thoroughly the explanations they read or hear. Most of the words, as the old cliche puts it, just go in one ear and out the other. For typical students, if a point is emphasized very strongly or somehow captures the imagination, it may stick until the next day. Then if the teacher goes over it again or assigns exercises that use it, or builds more simple ideas on it, long-term learning could occur. Good teachers do emphasize and repeat and reuse ideas, but they also try to help their students become aggressive, active learners.

Of the four major personal characteristics which I see as producing learning achievement, inherited mental ability is for most individuals, the least critical. The other three—time spent, sustained interest in the topic and study skills—make the big difference. You can understand how to spend time. And interest is developed through motivation which we discussed in other chapters.

Here we would add guidelines for developing what is probably the most significant study skill—learning effectively from printed text. The general principles apply also to learning from lectures. Every point on this list wouldn't be appropriate for every chapter and article or for every student. If you understand and practice them, you will know how and when to introduce your child to them.

    # Before reading a chapter or starting a book, leaf through the volume to see how it fits into the overall theme and purpose.

    # Glance through your chapter or article touching down here and there to see how the author organized it—to see where he or she is leading. Ideas make more sense when seen as part of a structure.

    # Then return to the beginning and read carefully. Compare the new thoughts with what you already know. Stop after every few paragraphs to see if you caught what the author said. What were the boiled-down concepts? Often the majority of an author's words are used to convince you that the topic is important, to help you enjoy it, or even on side issues just too good to leave out. Looking for the major ideas helps you sift out what you don't need to remember.

    # Before going on, underline a few key words that can help you recall these ideas at a later date. You could underline large sections of text just to show you liked it, but you won't then be able to quickly find and review the concepts.

    # When you come to the end, reconsider the whole chapter or article, asking what big ideas the author tried to get across. If appropriate, write a note by the title stating the thesis and maybe your opinion of it.

    # Outline the article or chapter if all of it is important and if the relationship among concepts is significant.

    # Write the ideas you want to learn on a card.

    # Review. Even well-understood concepts fade unless reviewed. Going over them say a day later, a week later and a month later will make them more or less permanent.

    # When preparing for a test, try to guess what the teacher might ask and make up answers for the imaginary questions. Then check your responses and fill in the weak spots.

Mastery learning

In the typical classroom, some students naturally learn faster and better than others. They apply themselves devotedly and shed big tears over anything less than A grades. Others plod along at varying paces and only become serious the night before the test. Still others who have not had successful school experiences actively resist cooperation and learning, seeking their rewards in other ways.

In spite of this wide range of ability and interest, most schools achieve an amazing degree of success. Extra projects are assigned to the enthusiastic while the stragglers are pressured and sometimes given extra help.

The general learning pace is a compromise. Usually only the top students experience thorough, complete understanding. If the teaching process is slowed down and intensified in expectation of total achievement for all but the anti-learners, the top students are bored, and even the poorer students become unhappy because they feel guilty for holding up progress, and because many of them really don't consider good grades worth all the effort anyway.

No matter what methods are used, schooling widens the achievement gap between good and poor students. Mastery learning attempts to minimize the problem. Although a class operated by this technique may meet for some group learning experiences such as lectures, audio-visual presentations, and discussion, students do much independent study. The course is divided into modules with specific learning objectives. When the student feels competent in the objectives designated for a certain module, he or she goes to the teacher or testing center for the module examination.

A nearly perfect test score indicates that the objectives it covers have been mastered, and the student moves on to the next module. If the proper performance level is not attained, the student goes back to study more and returns to take a parallel examination on the same objectives.

Mastery learning eliminates the grade competition problem which causes good students to become conceited and low-achieving students to develop poor self-images. It is also efficient, making the best use of student time during the course. However, the most important advantage may be the preparation of a solid base for future learning and future life experiences.

In schools, the mastery concept is not applied as much as it might be because it requires more teaching energy and therefore more expense. Home schools are already geared to the individual student, and applying the principles of mastery learning does not significantly increase the teaching effort. In fact, although the process may at first seem tedious, later learning should require less review and will come easier.

Teaching for mastery doesn't mean you should expect perfect work. Mistakes aren't crimes, and children aren't mature adults. The object is to work patiently and carefully toward short-range goals, clearing up misunderstandings and building skill.

With a single student you don't really need examinations to have a good idea of whether or not goals have been reached, but you may be wise to use them anyway for middle or upper grades and depending on the individual child.

Evaluation

Some people believe that giving grades interferes with ideal learning. I would agree that, *if misused,* the traditional system of accumulating points to be converted into grades good enough to pass at the end of the year could tend to set teachers and students against each other. Teachers can say, in effect, "If you don't learn what I tell you, I'll fail you or at least embarrass you properly." Students' battle tactics include arguing for points, getting the teacher off the subject to avoid a quiz, and cheating.

In spite of the inherent weaknesses of giving grades, most educators agree that abandoning the system entirely would be much worse. Grades are convenient and concise. Their fundamental purpose is to express evaluation. So our interest in grading, whether for school at home or elsewhere, leads us to consider the broader issue—evaluation.

Evaluation (which may or may not include examinations and grades) helps both student and teacher see the results of their efforts. It indicates the extent to which goals and objectives are being reached. It implies directions for continued study. And beyond these purely logistic functions, evaluation is a channel of reward for the fundamental human desire to achieve and to be appreciated.

While tests and schoolwork in general are the most obvious sources for evaluation, students may also be judged by general observation of how they react to instruction. A single student in a home school can be observed more easily than a whole classroom of children. The mother-teacher, faced with the extra effort required for making and grading tests, may be tempted to rely entirely on informal observation for evaluating success.

Importance of testing

Tests would not tell the home teacher much she did not already know about her child's ability, but they are valuable in several ways beyond the measurement of achievement. (1) Tests promote learning by stimulating study. They furnish short-range purposes for learning. Tests help keep students on their toes. The home school's lack of stimulation from competition with other students makes this reason for tests more important. (2) Tests teach. They induce recall which improves remembering, and they may cause new learning by requiring the student to pull ideas together for the solution of problems or the formation of conclusions. And (3) tests are a vehicle for reward. It's fun to find the right answers and to have someone notice. Also, seeing concrete evidence from major tests showing that efforts to learn have succeeded is a little like getting a paycheck.

The frequency and nature of examinations should depend on the subject and the maturity of the student. Young learners need to be observed, but formal examinations, even oral ones, don't make much sense for six-and seven-year-olds. Plan serious tests for older children every few weeks during the school year clearly explaining ahead of time what they are to cover. Quizzes may come in between. Textbook publishers often offer examination booklets with keys to make your job easier. You can use or adapt them.

Now a few words about tests which originate from outside the home. (If this doesn't apply in your case, you might want to skip down to the next section).

Being naturally eager for their children to look good, home teachers sometimes teach for the test. They look at the examinations prepared by the textbook publisher and make sure their children are capable of responding accurately to all the items.

For two reasons this is usually not a good idea: first, tests, as a rule, only sample the student's understanding. An automobile manufacturer could make the reports on new models look very good if he knew which vehicles would be borrowed for the test drives. So an examination measuring only specifically prepared understandings doesn't give an accurate picture of achievement in the broader area. Second, textbooks and printed tests are tools. Good ones have good objectives, but you are the teacher and (unless following a preplanned course) should decide the details of what your children are to learn. Thus you can add or subtract from the publisher's tests or scrap them for your own.

Submission of the examination for grading is a pledge of having followed the instructions for giving it; and the test results for a student who has been specifically coached present a dishonest measure.

Reviewing for the general objectives of a test is honest, responsible preparation. Also, practicing with items similar in format to ones on the test is sometimes a good idea because it can relieve some of the student's anxiety.

During examinations, your child will want to ask questions. Clarifying points unrelated to course objectives is proper, but don't give hints about concepts that might have been learned for the subject being tested. If the test is to be sent in to a correspondence school and you realize you didn't teach the idea behind a certain item, your accompanying note could explain.

Expectations

What is satisfactory achievement for your child? How good is good enough? You may feel a little frustrated by not knowing how your child compares with other children in the same grade. Of course, comparing with goals is much better than comparing with other children. Still, you want to set reasonable expectations. You could ask someone at a regular school to test your child, or if you are associated with a home study guidance center, standardized tests may be available to you. Or your state department of education may require and administer standardized examinations. In any case, as long as the textbook material is fairly well understood, you can feel confident of success.

A special caution is in order relative to the level of achievement you should expect. It's easy to push too hard, especially if your home school situation is threatened. Children need free time to relax. But relaxing now and then doesn't mean low standards. Both learning efficiency and self-worth call for a high degree of success. Also, as we pointed out in an earlier chapter, children want you to expect them to work hard. Just be sure fun time is part of the program.

The most important kind of evaluation is self-evaluation. Talk over with your student what is to be accomplished. When a segment of study is completed, encourage him or her to figure out whether or not objectives have been achieved. With guidance, expectations can be realistic, not too hard, not too easy. Then instead of performing only to satisfy you, learning starts to become your child's responsibility.

Make a conscious effort to expect work to be done completely, done well, and done on time. Work habits can suffer in a home school situation. If you and your child feel that a certain concept is understood, you will be tempted to stop working on it with papers and projects incomplete. Or tasks might be dropped when interest wanes. Of course, there is a time to abandon an unproductive project, but this should be the exception, not the rule. Also, schedules and reasonable deadlines could be easily neglected in the one-student school.

You can help your child build habits of regularity, efficiency, punctuality, dependability, and thoroughness by your own planning and direction of school at home.

Feedback

The kind of feedback you give can tend toward motivation or discouragement. If praised by written and spoken comment for work well done, your child will be ready to reach for the stars for you. Positive reports to others around the house and in letters also encourage good work. Even if the task you are evaluating was a general failure, you can usually find something to praise—perhaps an original idea. If the work was an improvement over past performance, praise the progress.

Praise doesn't mean pretending something is excellent when it's terrible. Kids know when their work is bad. Be warm and sincere. Evaluate in a way that lifts and inspires, rather than crushes. Instead of writing a big red F and saying to your child, "I told you how to do this. You are acting as if you didn't have a brain in your head." your comment would be, "You need a little more practice with this, but you did remember to watch your handwriting this time. It looks nice." Expect good work and don't put up with obvious attempts to circumvent the rules. But be careful not to interpret misunderstanding and inability to perform as naughtiness. Show that you care when something is hard or tedious. Instead of scolding, help your child set goals to improve weaknesses. Don't constantly show an attitude that says, "Not quite good enough—you can do better" or your child miss the joy of work well done.

And one more suggestion that you might not have thought of: In grading complex work, don't try to point out every failing at once. For example, in a story writing assignment, you might focus on making complete sentences and on verb agreement while only briefly noting other flagrant errors. In fact, if your student knows ahead of time what you will consider most important in grading, he or she can better sharpen those specific skills. This approach saves your child from feeling overwhelmed, and it makes your work a little easier, too.

Give written assignments. Use points. Mark the papers. Write remarks or orally comment. Recognize work well done. Show areas for improvement.

Should you give grades? That is, A, B, C, D and F? The answer depends somewhat on how you use them, but in general I would say no. Good grades are good, but bad grades are bad. With the mastery learning concept you won't need bad grades. The choice there is to do well or to try again. The "try again" doesn't need to occur often when the student plans to be ready before trying the test in anticipation of moving up to the next level.

Professional growth in home education

Support group participation provides opportunities to learn from other home school parents and from lectures. You may feel that this book already has more in it than you will ever have time to absorb. I can understand your frustration. It just seems to grow with each new edition. Of course, you can pick what seems most important and then come back to look at different chapters in greater detail when you see needs for them. And it's not a bad idea to check out authors that might disagree with me. You will find a number of other books listed in the bibliography.

Home schooling periodicals are a particularly important source of continued learning. I would subscribe to at least one—maybe two or three. Reading them regularly can keep you in touch with the legal scene, bring you a fresh flow of teaching ideas and inspire courage as you learn how other families face the home schooling challenge.

Seeing sample copies will help you decide which periodicals you might like best. You'll find a list in Appendix H, part 2. Some of the newsletters not mentioned cover specific geographic areas or are planned for members of particular support organizations.

Teaching in the home school is a challenge worthy of the effort. You may not do everything perfectly or as I have described in this chapter, but children are adaptable and with reasonable effort and common sense you are bound to succeed.

10

Structure for learning

While the formality or "institutional" nature of the typical school may not be the primary reason some parents are deciding to teach their children at home, it certainly helps tip the balance. Why should some adult—or even worse, a distant group of them—decide what, when, how, and where children should learn? Wouldn't a child left free to think and grow naturally, do better?

I can understand the reaction to classroom exactions and confinement. When I started teaching, I didn't see any reason why my students should write their quizzes on paper of different sizes and shapes. All will be a certain size, I declared! Everyone must conform! Papers of offenders I threatened with the circular file. I don't remember any reactions from parents, but the importance of such a requirement could certainly have been questioned. I've long since dropped that idea.

From my own childhood, I can remember my third-grade teacher passing out duplicated sheets with pictures to be colored. Robert, one of my special friends, liked to find short crayons with the paper peeled off and color his pictures with the crayon flat on the sheet instead of using the end of the crayon. The teacher did NOT approve. I'm still not sure what could have been bad about that. Most likely, it was simply not the way she had said to do it.

And, of course, unnecessary exactions can creep into the major subjects in the curriculum, too. Instead of helping students think for themselves, a few teachers tend to demand that only their own explanations be learned, or mark papers wrong for not parroting the textbook.

In reaction to such situations it's easy to get the idea that all structure is harmful—that it inhibits "real" learning. Perhaps this is why we see a great emphasis among some home school authors and even parents on a sort of blissful freedom for children to learn if and how and when they feel like it.

You probably have sensed by now my concern that home teaching is sometimes too loosely structured—that decisions and planning should be based on more than what feels good and seems like fun at the moment. Please note also that the opposite extreme—insensitivity to your student's interests, and lack of concern for making learning enjoyable—could be just as bad. The challenge is to help your child achieve full, balanced development in a pleasurable atmosphere. In fact, if schoolwork is bitter medicine, development would certainly be stifled.

Home school parents have many reasons for wanting to teach their own children. The appeal of seeing their children mature "naturally," developing their own interests with appropriate guidance is certainly one of these reasons. Structure could be seen as working against this natural development. The question is, can we help children form the character traits of clear thinking and self-directed, moral behavior expected from an atmosphere of greater freedom, and still teach them such things as how to follow through after a project loses its initial appeal, how to cooperate when their own ideas aren't adopted by the group, and how to stick to a schedule? I believe we can.

"Natural" learning

We've all read glowing reports of children learning everything from Latin to computers in a relaxed home environment on their own initiative. These homes are said to provide an exhilarating environment of such potential experiences as contact with outstanding people, books, and travel. The children seem so happy and well adjusted. How could anyone think of calling for more structure and "regimentation"?

The reasoning which leads to providing only a good environment and letting children learn as they feel like it is similar to the ideas advocated by the 18th century philosopher Jean Jacques Rousseau. He believed that a child's potential is within himself or herself and may be fully realized only in an environment where self-development is unrestricted—where the child can unfold naturally. Parents who see a Source of wisdom and strength outside of humanity and who believe they have been given the responsibility for guiding their children, obviously take a different view of education. And every parent, from no matter what background, can see the problems of the unlovely traits of character "unfolding naturally" as well as the good traits.

Of course, in one sense good learning *is* natural. Kathleen McCurdy believes that "the desire for knowledge is built into every living creature, though often we mistakenly suppress it; that skills are best learned through example and encouragement; that all parents instinctively want their children to be equipped to survive in our society; and that they will be successful at home schooling if they will just practice the art of parenting as it was done for thousands of years."[1] I would see the parent-teacher's responsibility a little differently than she does, but the basic principle is worth emphasizing. Good parenting is good teaching.

Structure as part of freedom

I have learned that people need both structure and freedom. Even though these two concepts seem like opposites, they go together. I don't mean part of the time structure and part of the time freedom, either. To see how the two ideas relate, let's examine what we mean by self-discipline. Imposed discipline is justified only as it helps develop self-discipline. You already know that discipline is not punishment (although punishment or withholding of privileges may have to come into it). But, even beyond nonpunishment ways of inhibiting bad behavior, real discipline is also developing good behavior. So when we set a goal of self-discipline for our children we try to lead them to do right not because we are watching, but because it is right. And that's where the freedom comes into it. Constructive, helpful, achieving behavior by solid, personal choice. Then the structure is self-imposed, or when working with other people it is voluntarily accepted. No one needs to follow this kind of individual around with a paddle (or with tax audits, for that matter).

Notice that I'm not advocating blind adherence to someone else's thinking as is expected by totalitarian governments, or TV commercials, or even often by labor unions. Freedom? Yes, within chosen or accepted unselfish structure.

How is self-discipline achieved? Little children certainly don't have it by instinct. As parents, it is our privilege and responsibility to help mold their characters. Our children depend on us for more than food and clothes. They depend on us to direct their behavior and they naturally feel secure in our guidance. As they get older they start edging toward the driver's seat. And that's good, too. The proper environment for a teenager is not proper for a six-year-old. Parents need the discernment to know how much structure to impose and how much to expect from self-discipline.

A balanced life includes opportunities to dream and relax. But even these times for the really mature individual don't come by the whim of the moment any more than do times for study, work, eating, sleeping, or worship. Unfortunately some of what is written about home schooling (including several of the books in the bibliography) seems not to be in harmony with the concept that character development needs structure, so I will explain.

What do planning and routine have to do with good discipline? The disciplined, mature individual does not act simply to gratify the feelings and impulses of the moment. He or she sees long range objectives. Lasting happiness for this person comes not from current sensations but from the achievement of happiness for others. And happiness for others means becoming and being a caring and productive part of society.

Here is where education comes into the picture. A good education develops useful skills and understandings, and it teaches the individual to be sensitive to the needs and feelings of other people. But beyond knowing, a well balanced education must teach the willingness and internal drive to act. Acting means effective use of time. We have a lot of "educated" people in the world who aren't much good either to themselves or to society because they aren't self-structured enough to be productive.

Can time be used responsibly without routine? Not as I see it. Routine doesn't mean nose-to-the-grindstone every minute. It must include time to relax and refresh. When it becomes obvious that a plan needs to be changed, break the routine or revise it. A planned program of activity should be a guide and servant, not a slave master.

What child has learned to play the piano by practicing only by the impulse of the moment? You may be able to think of a few young Mozarts that have avidly developed their musical abilities, but they are rare and they certainly didn't learn by relying on whim. They worked rain or shine for their self-imposed goal. In fact, they may well have needed a little parental direction to bring balance into their lives. For them, outdoor activities and social graces may not have come so naturally.

Incidentally, I'm not suggesting "force feeding" for any subject, least of all music. Help your child internalize worthwhile goals as much as possible. Then as readiness develops for working toward certain components of the goals, lend your support of adult maturity by encouragement and gentle, appropriate pressure.

Along with other home school enthusiasts, I feel that our lawmakers need to take a more reasonable look at compulsory school attendance requirements. But should children and youth old enough for formal learning attend school only when they feel like it? Here I mean either school at home or school at school. A good home under most circumstances is the best place to learn, but whether at home or in the classroom, should study be determined mostly by current interests? The answer is not hard to find. In spite of school attendance laws, public schools simply have many absent (and not sick) students every day. What are these youth doing? Obviously what they would rather do. Are they achieving? Ask the principal of any school. Their grades are certainly bad, but some people would point out that grades are a measure of what the *school* wants them to achieve. You will find, however, that they are probably not achieving their own goals either. Despite what they might say, normal individuals want to be able to understand the world around them and to interact with it intelligently. The school skippers are rarely achieving their own conscious or subconscious goals. Would they be better off in school? Some might not be if they are really determined not to cooperate, but for many others, the requirement of being there is a real help.

Now let's bring it a little closer home. You and I as adults; if we want to learn something new that takes more than an hour or so to achieve, whether Spanish or computer programming, or how to service automatic transmissions, or whatever, we are not apt to be successful unless we plan and follow through. If we go to our teacher or to our book only when we feel like it, we will soon drop out.

Appropriate structure depends on maturity

You have probably read convincing arguments for letting children learn instead of "schooling" them. Other writers have objected, making more structure appear important. To help you make sense out of this dilemma, let me suggest that it may not be so much *which* is right but rather *when*—under what circumstances.

As already implied, the degree and type of structure should depend on maturity. Much of the educational program described by casual learning advocates is quite appropriate for early, informal years. However, through the ages of about seven to ten, children's learning needs undergo considerable change. An orderly environment is important from birth, but the kind of structure and how parents should apply it changes as the child develops. Also, with increasing maturity, the source of structure or discipline shifts from the parents to the child. Chapter 14, "Early Education," develops these ideas further.

Choosing with reason

We have discussed time structure. Content, or what we teach, also needs structure. Most of us would resist expecting our children to learn something merely because schools teach it. Tradition isn't automatically best, but neither is originality. We need to think through carefully what we want education to do for our children, then be sure we know a better way before abandoning the core of what schools teach. Creativity is good, but creative spelling due to lack of solid study in the subject is a serious handicap. Choosing books to read because they are interesting may be enriching, but a good citizen will, interesting or not, know something of the major forces that have shaped history. Understanding such things as what got our country into World War II and what led to the fall of the Roman Empire lead to more responsible participation in seeking solutions to current government problems.

The mama robin knows by instinct what to teach her young, but people parents face a vastly more complex world. God's gift of individual freedom calls for choice based on application of principle. Learning, after the early informal years, must involve much more than wandering aimlessly here and there exploring experiences that happen to appeal to parent or child. Rather, it's an extremely important preparation for life, here and in eternity. Kids often feel that because they are too young to earn a good wage, too young to vote, and too young to get a driver's license, therefore their time isn't valuable—that to do something important, they have to grow up. What a mistake! And often adults, too, think kids' time is cheap—a double mistake!

Some may feel that structure discourages children from thinking for themselves. Maybe this idea comes from a misunderstanding of what good structure is. We aren't talking about a rigid inflexible formality but about a sensible plan. Children can help work out the schedule and even choose some of what is to be learned. We don't expect to become slaves to the minute hand on the clock, especially in a home school. But we do need an overall daily and long range guide to the learning program that can be altered whenever a change can better serve the goal. Encourage spontaneous discovery experiences as you would occasional pauses to pick flowers. Minor route changes don't need to affect the destination as long as the goal isn't obscured by the daisies.

The primary elements of school structure are: goals, a definite program with suitable materials, a specific time and place to study, and evaluation as appropriate.

Can unstructured learning succeed? For young children with caring parents, yes; and for anyone through brief incidental experiences, yes. But for long-range life skills, not so well. Sometimes we point out that children in classroom schools learn something good in spite of the teaching rather than because of it. They often do at home, too. But why settle for bits and pieces when you can help your children build a solid foundation? Will they grow up like weeds or as well developed plants?

Choosing a structured curriculum

My reason for adding this section is prompted by recent interest in a curriculum structure inspired by the medieval European educational system. Before I go on to tell you what I am going to tell you, I need to explain that some really nice people might disagree with me. In fact, articles I have read contain some good thoughts. You may draw your own conclusions.

In 1947 English writer Dorothy L. Sayers presented a paper entitled "The Lost Tools of Learning."[2] She felt that the concept of mind training which apparently fostered the upper-class system of education in medieval times should guide the curriculum structure for modern education.

In those days, the system for creating "educated" people called for successfully passing through two major steps, the *trivium* and the *quadrivium*. The trivium prepared the scholar for the quadrivium. It was divided into the *grammar, dialectic* and *rhetoric* stages which emphasized respectively a study of particulars, of systems and of interrelatedness—in that order and each essentially mastered before moving on to the next. The idea of the trivium was to build the tools for superior achievement in preparation for the quadrivium which, translated to our day, would begin at the university level or possibly before. (The quadrivium originally meant music, arithmetic, geometry and astronomy.) Together, the trivium and the quadrivium made up the seven "liberal arts."

The trivium has recently been adopted by a few well-meaning home school advocates as a structural model for elementary and possibly secondary school. Some of the principal ideas in the adaptation are: (1) Small children are thought to be able to memorize better than older ones making the early years especially suitable to learning isolated facts. (2) As in other subjects, the facts of history and geography are learned first, then applied to systems and finally to a whole in the three trivium stages. For my opinions on this, see my chapter on teaching social studies. (3) Classical languages are emphasized, vocabulary first. Latin would begin in early or middle elementary. Greek would be introduced soon after. Then Hebrew or modern languages would follow. The Christian parent might see some value in learning Greek if Biblical Greek were substituted for the classical Greek which is typically studied. (4) Mathematics is studied rigorously and, in part, with some of the same rationale as modern math. (5) Chemistry and physics are particularly important. (6) Grammar, composition and literature are taught perhaps as they would be in a regular school, except that importance would likely be given to classical literature. (7) Logic and debate, studied near the end of the trivium, are considered good training for thinking skills. (8) Theology was a part of the ancient study system. This would take on a different form in the modern adaptation for a Christian school but would still stress early learning of particulars.

To put these ideas in perspective, it would be well to see why they aren't being followed in modern educational systems.

Learning to learn

Until as recently as fifty years ago, a set of formal courses such as Latin, Greek, and advanced geometry dominated the American high school curriculum. The elementary school had already broken away from a similar pattern, and high school educators were eager to try out new ideas, too. But college entrance requirements dictated most of the curriculum. The strict set of courses was thought to prepare the mind for advanced study. Adventurous educators disagreed, and from this frustration developed what became known as the "Eight-year Study."[3]

Thirty high schools were chosen and agreed to set their own graduation requirements. Between 1936 and 1939 about 2000 of their students entered colleges and 1475 of these were matched one by one with students having similar backgrounds and abilities but who had graduated from traditional schools. The college success of both groups was carefully checked.

When the massive accumulation of data was finally sorted and tallied, the experimental group from the thirty schools was found to have achieved more in every scholastic area except foreign languages where the comparison group did a little better. Also, personality and social attributes of the experimental students were rated slightly better. Even in memorization ability, they were 3% ahead of the comparison group.

We must take care in drawing conclusions. College success wasn't shown to be improved by just following natural interests and inclinations in secondary school. The experimental students had challenging graduation requirements to meet. But the results certainly did strip the ivy from the traditional curriculum tower which had been considered so important for building learning competence. The thirty schools taught to prepare their students for life, and that goal proved also to be the better preparation for continued learning in college.

Returning to the question of the trivium, even if it did produce better learning, I don't see how it would justify such an austere curriculum with no life science, no health education, no fine arts, and no physical or practical skills education. It's easy to agree to add some of these, but how can you with such a demanding program already? Remember, too, that a balanced education means development of more than the intellect.

Reasoning from particulars to generalities is known as *induction* or inductive reasoning. The opposite, reasoning from accepted general principles to particular outcomes, is called *deduction*. The system we have been discussing seems to imply that most precollege learning is by induction. It's true that the carpenter learns his particular tools, but in real life, he doesn't learn all of them and master every skill before considering the whole job and seeing which tools need more attention.

Young children do learn by seeing particulars and putting them together to make sense out of their world, but they also develop their reasoning ability by sorting exercises—looking at a general mixture of objects and classifying them into particular groups. The Suzuki music method owes much of its success to a strong emphasis on interrelatedness—actually making music—with learning the particulars to come as the need is felt. The point is that both in learning and in life functions, deduction and induction occur together.

Since the trivium idea (training in stages of particulars, systems and interrelatedness) is thought to promote learning, maybe it would be well to ask how people really do learn. I'll tell you how I understand the process. You can compare with your own experience and with what you have observed in your children. New ideas are generally acquired as follows: (1) A need to know is sensed. (2) If, in trying to understand, certain elements are unclear, the main object is postponed while the necessary communication transmitters, such as word meanings, are defined. (3) The new idea derives meaning as it is related to prior knowledge through both induction and deduction. (4) Final possession of the concept occurs when it is applied and found to work. The process is successive and stops if any step fails. This pattern describes learning all through life.

It doesn't hurt to examine how the medieval upper class were educated. We might pick up some helpful ideas. But, loving God with heart, soul, mind and strength and loving others as ourselves (Mark 12:30, 31) implies a much broader education and a very different base.

So we face two opposite dangers: learning without direction and following possibly wrong directions. Although no teaching is perfect, your children's future is a solemn responsibility. Do all you can to assure its success.

11

Selecting learning materials

By Sandy Gogel

Deciding on a curriculum for your child should be an individual matter. If you are willing to let someone else choose for you, then you may wish to join a plan where the organization sends you a set of books with a program to be completed within a prescribed length of time. In a classroom situation, the teacher survives only by having all children, or at least groups of children, learning from the same material. To my way of thinking, one of the joys of home schooling is in providing an individualized curriculum for each child.

When choosing materials, consider your child's preferred learning style. Is it visual, auditory or kinesthetic? If you don't know, I recommend the book, *Growing Up Learning* (listed in Appendix H). The author also offers help in choosing activities for each learning style.

Does your child enjoy a sense of accomplishment from finishing a written page or does he (or she) hate even to write his name at the top of the paper? A child who doesn't enjoy workbooks will do better work and learn better orally or with hands-on materials. Keep in mind that every child over the age of eight should do some written work each day. But if it is difficult for your child to get much writing done, you may want to write some of the answers as he says them to you.

Choose books that appeal to you as well as to your child. Your enthusiasm (or lack of it) will rub off. No doubt some subjects are more interesting to you than others are. Pray for new enthusiasm for subjects you do not enjoy.

Preparation time varies considerably from one type of approach to another. Some curriculum programs, like Alpha-Omega, require very little teacher time because the workbook format includes most or all necessary instructions and explanations for the student. The weakness of this type of program is in not naturally encouraging much teacher-student interaction. Although the who, when, what and how are efficiently taught, the child might miss out on the why and on developing skill in analytical thinking. If you choose workbook-type materials, be sure to plan time for discussion.

Do you enjoy research and detailed projects? Then I might recommend a unit-study program such as Weaver; Konos; or Sing, Spell, Read and Write. As an alternative to both the workbook-and the unit-type programs, you might want to consider traditional textbooks with teacher's manuals. Lesson plans would be easy to prepare following guidelines in the manuals.

When you consider materials, try to discover whether they require relatively mature learning skills. Curriculums from Rod and Staff and from A Beka would come in this category. Although they teach excellent concepts, immature students will have difficulty with them.

Some publishers label their materials for children younger than I would recommend. The Little Patriots reading program, for example, is advertised as being for a kindergarten child. Some children at that age do very well with it, but many are not ready to read this early, and could profit from it more at a later time.

If cost is a factor preventing your purchase of everything you need at once, get materials for reading and math first. You can supplement from the library for social studies and science using the *Typical Course of Study* (See Appendix F) as a guide until you can afford more. But do purchase regular learning materials for these subjects as soon as possible. This is especially important by the time your child is in the fourth grade.

Since programs for teaching Bible differ widely in scope and sequence, you can feel more at liberty to organize your own plan, choosing topics as well as methods of presentation. You may find it easier to maintain consistent quality in your Bible program, however, by choosing one of the many fine sets of materials which are available.

Books are not the only items that help children learn. You may use games, puzzles, flash cards, art media, music, globes, microscopes, science equipment and even toys. You might suggest to relatives and friends that some of these items would make appropriate gifts. The cost burden for supplying your school could thus be lightened a little.

Finally, remember that your program is a tool. You are the one in charge. If you find too much practice prescribed on a concept your child has already mastered, feel free to delete part of it. Do a project for one of your social studies units instead of going lock-step through the book. In short, use the curricular materials as tools to achieve your desired end—the education of your child.

12

Enrichment resources

Wherever you are, teaching resources are all around you. This chapter will help you recognize them and give you a few ideas for using them. Margaret Savage's two chapters, "The Lovely Game" and "The Redwooded Headpecker," also offer suggestions on finding people, places and things to enrich your teaching.

It isn't that your textbooks will lack enough good material to keep your child busy, but learning achieved from other sources can enrich your teaching in several ways: it can brighten up your program; it can help your child see how school is related to real life; it can give the learning an up-to-date aspect; and it can help your child develop observation skills and be aware of his or her surroundings as sources of learning.

Making activities worthwhile

To help keep activities which use resource material from becoming useless busywork, consider three cautions. First, Insist on active finding out. Tracing the borders of a map of your state or province may teach little more than tracing, a skill your child may already have mastered. To make the activity worthwhile, ask questions which help develop useful concepts. For example, if one boundary is a wavy line, help your child discover why. Have him or her know the neighboring states, where on the map your home is located, and so on. Collecting wild flowers is nice, but don't stop with collecting. Learn their names and something about where or how they grow. Information will need to be looked up. Use an encyclopedia or check in a nearby library.

Of course you can easily run a project into the ground by expecting too much. Ten questions to answer about the map, if they all take looking up, could seem to a young scholar like a major research project. The younger the child, the simpler the project must be. The activity should end while it's still fun. We discuss other aspects of teaching with projects in the chapters on reading and social studies.

The second point to remember is, Relate the new concepts learned through resource material to your basic curriculum. Choose, or guide your child in choosing, projects or materials with potential for complementing what you are studying in your textbooks.

The third caution is, Don't let the tail wag the dog. An experienced teacher might be able to build a whole year's social studies program around Eskimos or the local newspaper and keep it balanced, but you may find it easier to arrive at your goals by following a good textbook for the major part of your time, keeping your projects as sidelines.

Projects do take time—often more than you anticipate. Don't be afraid to skip minor topics in your textbooks if you feel your students will gain more from the outside project and you need the time. You can still cover the major textbook concepts, keeping a logical plan and sequence in your teaching.

Before discussing how specific items might be used to enrich your teaching, we need to remember that a child's developmental level changes rapidly and extensively in moving from kindergarten up through the elementary grades and into high school. Perhaps the best way to get an idea of how much to expect in planning an assignment is to compare what you want your child to do with activities suggested in the textbook and teacher's guide as well as with your assessment of your child's abilities. If you judge wrong and make an activity too simple, you can add new projects on the same topic or simply adjust your planning for the next time. If your assignment is too hard—a more likely error—you can help with it yourself, making it a joint endeavor. Guidance of a teacher who has had experience at your child's grade level can be very valuable on this point.

A number of developmental factors determine readiness. For example, attention span, movement skills, reading ability, reasoning ability, and prior learning. These all, to some degree, affect interest which we discussed in an earlier chapter as the best indicator of readiness.

Most of the problem of seeing that a particular learning task is matched to your child's abilities will take care of itself if you let him or her plan the project as well as do it. This assures a good deal of motivation, too. You can discuss with your student in general what is to be gained from the experience; then make only necessary suggestions as your young adventurer plans a course of action. Help him be realistic—to not bite off too much. If a simple goal is reached, further work could be considered.

Now let's consider several different categories of materials within easy access of most homemakers. These ideas can start you thinking about many more. As topics and concepts come up in your study materials, let your mind search around the home and into the community for resources to reinforce or expand the learning.

Print materials

Such a mass of books and printed matter of all kinds floods our world, and so much of it is degrading, that we sometimes forget about the great amount of good reading matter also available. Your home school library may not count thousands of volumes, but with careful planning, you can surround your child with a rich environment.

Magazines and newspapers contain readily usable material. Pictures, articles, and even advertisements can provide a great variety of good learning if managed right. You will want to subscribe to several magazines. Consider: a children's magazine if your kids are young, a teacher's magazine, and others such as *Ranger Rick's Nature Magazine, National Geographic World, Reader's Digest,* and maybe *Popular Science.* Appendix H lists a few of the many worthwhile periodicals claiming the interest of home-taught children.

To decide which magazines you want, visit your public library. For magazines you want but can't afford, your librarian can help again. She can check out magazines to you on loan, and may even give you copies of discarded older issues.

Periodicals and books can be used in many ways. The best ideas for your students depend on many factors. I can give you only some general suggestions, hoping you find them helpful in expanding your own ideas.

First of all, even though direction and keeping on target with the textbook objectives are important, a certain amount of free-time reading can be very worthwhile. It's wrong to teach children like you would control a nuclear reactor, deciding exactly what goes in when and precisely measuring the output. Your job is more to provide the atmosphere of time, appreciation, physical comfort, and good reading matter. And don't hesitate to allow time in your program for learning for the fun of it without being tested and measured.

To add just a little structure, you can talk to your child about what was read. Discussion encourages more alert reading and reinforces the learning.

Taking another step in structuring the situation, you may talk over the objective with your young scholar and let him or her choose an article or book to help meet it. Material is easy to find on broad topics like controlling the relationship between people and wildlife, or seeing how authors use active verbs, or energy conservation.

At times you will want to assign specific articles or books to achieve particular purposes, and you may even wish to provide specific questions to answer.

Children can demonstrate their learning from special reading projects in many ways. You may ask them to underline a sentence that gives the author's key thought. You may have them choose ideas they feel are important or that they disagree with. They can write a summary in their own words. And, for advanced learners, occasional formal reports are appropriate.

Scrapbooks are fun. Children too young to read may not have the fine motor control for cutting either, but they can tear and tape. A collage, or composite of several pictures glued to the same paper, gives opportunity to exercise creativity while learning from the pictures. Advertisements with prices and other numerical data can help connect math skills with the real world.

Weekly Reader and Xerox offer periodicals for students which provide articles and activities in particular subjects at various grade levels. This extra study material coming every week or month can add interest and be a helpful supplement to your regular textbooks. Their catalogs will give you an idea of how school periodicals can help your teaching. (Addresses in Appendix H).

The daily newspaper has more good instructional resource material than you can imagine. In addition to following news events in a selected world area or on a specific topic, and learning math from the advertisements as already mentioned, you can clip news items and have your child make up headlines, then compare with what the paper used; you can follow the weather forecasts and make a notebook comparing expectations with what actually happened. You can graph the temperatures (not for lower grades), and on, and on.

Books are obviously important print resources even though you may not want them cut up and marked as much as your magazines and newspapers.

Your home school should also have reference books. A good dictionary is a must for every home with children growing up, even if they go to a classroom school. And, if at all possible, get an encyclopedia suitable for children, like *World Book* or *Book of Knowledge*. Bibles in various translations, a Bible dictionary, a concordance, and accurate Bible story books are also important reference material for Christian home schools.

Nonprint materials

Beyond books and other printed information sources, the home surroundings abound in valuable learning possibilities. Before discussing this potential, let's notice two more principles that apply to supplementary learning.

<u>Learning sources should be appealing.</u> Since interest probably influences success more than other factors do, students should choose their own projects as much as possible. But children's interests are scattered and changing. Starting a serious project every time an interest surfaces would spell failure and frustration. How does a parent know which ideas to encourage? Before you spend a thousand dollars on amateur radio equipment only to find that your child's interests have turned to horses or stamp collecting, it's wise to plan a "cooling off period" like the Federal Trade Commission requires for contract sales. Taking the time and effort necessary to learn the code, theory, and laws for passing the novice radio test would indicate more than passing curiosity in ham radio. Two weeks' delay in purchasing a skate board or a camera could help your youngster's judgment mature and might save money, too. I don't mean that you need to keep your foot on the brake all the time. Occasionally you will want to follow through right away. But whether slowly or quickly, encourage those interests that will help your young person build solid character and be prepared to live a full, productive life.

Sometimes children will follow your interests. But not always. Don't be surprised if their preferences are not exactly like yours. Be open minded, and judge from principle. Then when a project is chosen, you can double the fun *and* the learning by joining in. Of course, avoid the temptation to take over even when you know a better way. Be a consultant, not the project manager. When appropriate, ask questions to stimulate thinking.

<u>Learning sources should nourish balanced development.</u> Parents can easily let learning pursuits become unbalanced. For example, music is important, but we should not be so set on seeing our children show off our own high culture that we neglect their opportunities to learn to use tools. Or we should be careful that sailing or basketball or clothing construction doesn't crowd out the quiet time for aesthetic spiritual experience and the time to just relax. As your child grows and matures, stop now and then to check on what is happening. Do you see a good balance of mental,

physical, social and spiritual development—a balance between heart and head and hand?

Now let's explore the gold mine of teaching resources around your house. Your own kitchen is a first class science laboratory. You know it's good for teaching home economics, but with some simple equipment, most of which you can make or purchase inexpensively, it can also be a fantastic one-student lab. Follow the cues in your science textbooks to know what to do when, and how.

The sewing corner can become a learning center. Find a good sewing book, perhaps one for children. Spend time on clothing repair as well as on making new things. By the way, boys like to sew, too. And without the stigma of what classmates might think, they can pick up a very useful skill.

What fun the workshop can provide! Here safety rules are extremely important. Hair grows back and cuts heal, but sawed off fingers and eyes with metal chips in them don't have such good chances. If you are a mother and not used to working with tools, this safety caution may frighten you. Don't let it. Shops are safe when you make them that way. Safety is an important lesson in life. I would say, no power tools for children in lower and middle elementary years. Small electric tools like a drill, a saber saw, or a sander could be used at the junior-high level or possibly sooner. In addition to ensuring greater safety, using muscle-powered hand tools helps develop good manual skills and coordination. A good rule for any sharp or heavy tool is, anticipate where the instrument will go if it slips. Then keep hands away from that place. During senior high years, major power tools are safe after training and *with supervision*. And as with sewing for boys, don't underestimate your daughters' potential for craftsmanship.

Next let's look outside. Digging in the dirt, stretching muscles, planning, can be great fun and in the end, much more rewarding than sports. To plant a garden, patiently cultivate it (with your encouragement and insistence), water it, and weed it, then to prepare the harvest for the table can bring your child real satisfaction. Making the yard look nice involves more than cutting grass and picking up papers. The greatest beauty is created by individuals and is shared.

Consider giving your child complete control of a spot of ground. Provide counsel and help, but let his or her decisions stand. Learning comes from mistakes as well as from success.

Television

Television's impact on our society claims special attention. The typical American child spends more time watching television than attending school. If the TV is managing your whole household, I suggest you sell it, give it away, or let the trash man haul it off. Where home is school, control of the television is imperative. We also discuss the topic as it relates to learning to read, but have more general suggestions here.

Television is an effective teacher. Conservative parents who understand its potential and want good education for their children don't want them to watch violence. But if Mom and Dad watch the stuff, what can they tell the kids? Let's say you switch to "off" when the shooting programs start. But have you considered the effect of the other programs? What makes the comedy programs interesting? Deception. Selfishness. Sex. Think about it. And the commercials? Not much better. What motivates the quiz shows? We could go on.

For several reasons I don't recommend *Sesame Street* and similar preschool programs. Young children need to be chasing butterflies, or sorting clothes for the washing machine, or helping Mommy make bread—not sitting in front of the TV. Flashing numbers and rocky music are hard on delicate nervous systems. Fantasy is no help in preparing children to enjoy the real world. Too much close focusing damages developing eyes. And the quick shifts from one thought to another designed to keep the interest keyed up tend to dull enthusiasm for real-life learning which requires gradually lengthening attention spans.

Now before you throw a brick through the TV screen, let's look at the other side of the coin. There *are* good programs, especially on noncommercial stations—programs that can enrich your teaching. How can you take best advantage of them?

First, plan. Don't just turn on the TV to see what is on. Choose programs that seem to offer the most desirable learning.

Some television programs pack a great amount of information into a short time. For your youngster, learning from them may be like trying to get a drink from a fire hydrant. You can do several things to help. Before watching the program, learn what you can from the program guide. Look up background information in the encyclopedia, or even in a dictionary.

Note taking is a great learning aid, but this skill which involves watching, sorting out what is important, condensing it to brief coded statements, and writing, all at once, is too much to expect from younger kids. They can *begin* to learn in the junior high years. You take notes. Then as soon as the program is over, discuss it. If you don't, not much will be retained, and some significant points may be entirely missed. If you have a video recorder, watch the program again. Plan a quiz.

Field trips

Field trips can provide outstanding learning experiences. If managed well, these educational visits to places outside your home classroom will not be time off from school, but one of the best kinds of school. In addition to brief field trips to places not far away, plan learning experiences in connection with your family vacation. Even weekend outings can be partly school time. But keep careful records if you are fulfilling state requirements. Incidental learning that occurs in routine travel would less likely be considered as school work by attendance authorities.

Teachers in regular schools would probably take their classes on field trips more often than they do if it were not for the extra work and supervision required. Handling 35 children on a field trip is not the same as teaching them in a classroom. Here again home schools have an advantage.

Planning and follow-up are even more important for field trips than for educational TV programs which are already designed for teaching. Relate learning trips to the rest of your study program. Read about where you are going or about what you expect can be learned there. Help your students make a list of questions to answer from the trip. For several children in different grades, the questions can be different depending on maturity. Information should be recorded on the spot in a notebook.

A camera makes the trip more fun. Notes should be written about the pictures as they are taken. Also, if your camera has an adjustable focus (and you can afford it) shoot pictures of plaques explaining what you are seeing. This is a quick way to get accurate information for a review at home. A portable tape recorder can preserve tour guides' explanations and answers to questions asked, or your child might use it in place of the camera for dictating posted information.

When you return from your trip, your child may profitably spend as much time as your visit took making a booklet about the whole experience. Where you choose to go depends somewhat on the maturity of your student. Very young children typically visit places in the local community such as the fire station, the power plant, a bakery, the hospital, the police station or a dairy. And don't leave out the place Dad works every day.

Risk of lawsuit for injuries and the nuisance of kids running everywhere handling things causes people in charge of some manufacturing plants and other interesting places to say no to field trips. A parent-teacher with one or a few children might be able to get in where a large group could not. You may need to point out this better control factor. And if you go, set strict rules ahead of time!

Here is a list to help start you thinking about where you might take your "student body" for a field trip:

Museums. There are many types. Some are at colleges and universities.

Historical sites. Get information from your travel bureau, a tourist information center, or from your state historical society.

A zoo. Have your child write down animal names and match them with photos taken.

Birding. Find someone who knows birds to take you out. Identifying birds is more fun than you might think.

Looking for minerals. Find a rock hound to take you to collection sites and to help identify what you find.

Ecology sites. Go to the seashore, a mountain stream, a desert, a swamp, or any specific wildlife habitat. Don't just run in and out again, but sit down, watch, compare, think. Take a notebook for drawings and observations. See what your child can discover about the plants and animals that live there. Read about them and add names and other information to your notebook.

An amateur radio station. Your child can talk to someone by radio and maybe get a QSL card to prove it.

A TV or radio station. Call ahead to arrange the best time.

An airport. Try to get permission to visit the control tower and to enter a plane to talk with the pilot.

A construction site. You might arrange two trips, first to see the action from a safe distance, then after working hours when the boss can take you through the site to explain what is being done.

A boat excursion.

A courtroom.

A legislative assembly.

An office.

A garage.

A printing press.

An art shop. Or the studio where an artist is working.

Resource guests

Sometimes instead of taking a trip to help your children learn, you can arrange for the outside information to come to them. Invite interesting people to share their special knowledge. They may be able to bring pictures and objects to demonstrate what they are talking about. Occasionally a resource guest may not understand the level of the audience, or may try to use the opportunity to advocate a special hobby horse or political position. It is well to talk with the person ahead of time. You can prepare him or her for the thinking level of your children, and knowing more about the topic, you can do background study with them.

Children learn from everything around them. Their learning is extremely important, but it also comes naturally. Your biggest job as a parent-teacher is to create the best learning environment. Then get help from textbooks and experienced people and teach faithfully. You will never regret the privilege of watching and helping your child develop. Your teaching means more than providing intellectual knowledge and skills. You are guiding the formation of character. And character is permanent.

13

Support groups

By Cindy Short

To write the article* which has been slightly abridged to become this chapter, Cindy Short studied questionnaire responses from many support group leaders. From the wide variety of purposes, activities and people in these groups she found a wealth of ideas—ideas that give you reasons to join a group if you don't already belong to one, and ideas to make your group better if you do.

How do support groups get started?

There are several possibilities. Sometimes two home-schooling families find each other and start meeting together for fellowship or to meet specific needs. Sometimes one person with a vision advertises an informational meeting or get-acquainted potluck or calls on other home schoolers to find those interested in starting a group. Some groups that have large memberships or that cover large areas will subdivide into smaller groups or refer newcomers to a newly forming group. Contacts made at a home school seminar or at church sometimes lead to the formation of a support group.

What purposes and objectives do support groups have?

Surprisingly quite a few. A primary goal is usually *support and encouragement*. This can take two forms. The first is spiritual support and is accomplished by Christian fellowship, Bible teaching or study, memorization and meditation, and prayer.

In some groups, the fathers and/or mothers take turns preparing a devotional or Bible message for each group meeting. This is sometimes followed by a sharing time for prayer requests and a time of prayer for the needs of each family and of the home schooling movement. This kind of support is maximized in an all-Christian group, especially when all have similar doctrinal positions.

The second form of encouragement is moral support and is accomplished by just being with other home schoolers as well as by sharing common experiences. Needs and problems, as well as victories and solutions, are shared for the benefit of all. This occurs during group discussions or in one-to-one conversations. Friendships are formed between both parents and children, and children are encouraged by the attention of other adults.

A second goal of many support groups is the sharing of *information* about home schooling with each other and with those interested in getting started. This includes information about curriculum, methods of teaching, legal options, and seminars or books that are helpful.

A third goal, which is emphasized by some groups more than by others, is to provide *educational opportunities* that would be difficult for parents to provide by themselves. Some groups have been successful in arranging a skill exchange between families. One parent may be an excellent teacher of higher math or science and be available to tutor children whose parents have difficulty with those subjects. Another parent may provide coaching in creative or artistic skills. One group publishes a phone number in its newsletter for a "Grammar Hot-Line" to answer the questions of stumped parents.

Many groups arrange special one-time presentations such as science experiments or craft demonstrations for the children at their meetings. Almost all support groups play some role in arranging field trips of an educational or enrichment nature. Some groups have well-attended regular classes on subjects ranging from art to science. Social and expressive skills for both parents and children are also taught or encouraged in many groups, directly or indirectly.

Another goal of support groups is to visibly *represent home schooling* to the community, to their relatives or friends, to local churches, to government and legislators, to a state home schooling organization, or to school officials.

A few groups have incorporated as a school or satellite program, and one includes families who want to supplement their children's public school education.

Who is involved in support groups?

Some support groups consist of members who are very similar to one another and others include families with great differences between them. One factor that can greatly affect the activities and atmosphere of a group is its policy about including or excluding unbelievers. Groups that have a written statement of faith may require that it be signed either by all members, by those who vote or participate in certain activities or only by the leaders. Other groups are all or mostly Christians by common consent. Some groups include activities such as Bible teaching and prayer that give the group a definite Christian emphasis. Others take a neutral position or even deliberately appeal to non-Christians and seek their cooperation and participation. Some groups consist all or mostly of families from one church or denomination and report very close fellowship and an absence of conflicting beliefs. Others find unity in their common faith in Christ and avoid doctrinal discussions.

Support groups may include both new and experienced home schoolers or all beginners. Experienced home schoolers can give valuable help and guidance to those just getting started. On the other hand, enthusiastic beginners often pitch in and help each other and organize innovative activities when they realize there are no "old-timers" to tell them what to do. They usually find by trial and error what works best for them.

Some groups tend to have only families with young children; others have some with older children or teenagers. The unique needs of these different age groups are sometimes difficult to meet in groups that do not have several in each age group.

There are various policies on the attendance of children at group meetings. Some groups hold meetings for parents only, some include children in all functions and some have planned activities or supervision for children separate from adults during meetings. The responsibility for supervision of children in the latter case is either delegated to one or two volunteer parents or taken by rotation of all parents. When children stay in the adult meetings, the parents are expected to keep them from distracting others or else take them out. Many groups have separate planning meetings for adults and include children in other meetings. A few have special meetings for mothers of toddlers or for families with teenagers to meet their unique needs.

Some groups encourage members to invite friends, relatives or school officials who are curious or skeptical about home schooling to visit their regular meetings. Others hold special meetings for the purpose of answering the questions of those interested in home schooling.

Support groups can include home schoolers from several counties or from just one community. One large group subdivides by zip code for some of its meetings to provide closer contact between members.

How are support groups organized?

There are two basic patterns for support group organization styles with some overlapping. The first is the small informal group. It is usually fairly new and is loosely organized. Leadership is provided by volunteers, by one or more members who see this as their ministry, or by rotation of responsibilities among all the members. Decisions are made either by the leader(s) or by consensus. There are usually no official memberships or dues. Funds are provided as needed by collection of donations, by one or more members' ministry of giving, or by equally dividing the cost between participating members.

The second type of organization is the larger, more formal group with a tighter structure. Leadership is provided by the group's founder(s) and/or by elected officers. Decisions are made by these leaders or by voting members. Sometimes a written constitution is adopted. Membership in the group may be associated with certain requirements such as signing a doctrinal statement, participating in a minimum number of activities, or paying dues. Privileges include voting, receiving a newsletter, and participating in certain activities. Some groups have different levels of membership, each with its own requirements and privileges. Membership lists are usually for members only and to be kept confidential. Funding for these groups' usually extensive activities and services comes from dues, newsletter subscriptions, and/or user fees.

As mentioned above, there is quite a bit of overlapping of these two styles. Some small groups are more organized and some large ones are less. Large groups often subdivide into smaller ones, at least for some activities. Some groups deliberately limit their size for more efficient operation, dividing in half when the group exceeds the limit. Some groups have experimented with formal organization and found that it caused a loss of fellowship and sharing. Large or formal groups find they need to counteract this tendency by providing ample opportunity within their total program for individual contribution and interaction.

How do support groups communicate with their members?

In small groups the leader will often contact each member personally by phone to announce meetings and activities. As the group grows beyond a few families, however, this becomes too time-consuming for one person to handle. At this point a phone chain or phone tree is usually started with each person calling the next person on the chain or with certain members each calling 3-5 others. Another use of the telephone is to have one or more members available to answer questions, channel newcomers to those who can help them get started, or refer requests concerning specific needs to volunteers who can help in those areas.

Sooner or later many if not most groups find mailing more efficient than phoning. This can take the form of occasional flyers announcing meetings and activities or of a regular newsletter. Newsletters are published with varying frequency—from weekly to quarterly. They can contain announcements of group activities or community events, articles on home schooling or scriptural topics, or creative contributions from members of the group—both adults and children. The newsletter is produced by an editor, by a team, or by each member taking a turn in rotation. Costs of printing and mailing are covered by dues, subscriptions, or donations from the whole group or individuals. Sometimes members provide self-addressed stamped envelopes for mailing.

Other printed material may include a welcoming letter or brochure for newcomers describing home schooling in general or the support group itself. Sometimes the support group prints its statement of faith in these materials to clarify its stand. Some groups print a questionnaire to identify the needs of members and evaluate the success of various programs. Membership applications sometimes provide the group with specific information about each family, such as names, ages, birthdays, curriculum used, experience level, hobbies, skills, interests, needs and availability to help others. Some groups distribute reprinted articles or brochures obtained from outside sources which they feel would be helpful to the group.

A few groups have advertised their existence in magazines or local papers and have gained new members in this way.

What do support groups do?

There is a rich variety of activities and services provided by the support groups we have heard from. The most basic activity common to most groups is the regular *group meeting*. These meetings are held from weekly to monthly, usually in someone's home unless the group is too large. Larger groups or those that include children often meet in churches, schools or rented halls.

Some groups open with prayer, Bible reading, and singing and include a devotional by one of the parents and a time of group prayer and requests. Others are conducted as business meetings using *Robert's Rules of Order.* There is often a speaker on some topic of interest to home schoolers and sometimes a workshop or discussion period centered on a specific topic or question. Some groups have a time for book reviews or the presentation of helpful articles, sometimes distributing reprints of these. Announcements are made regarding the group's activities as well as state and national events or news of interest to home schoolers. Sometimes a legislative crisis will call for discussion and action by the group.

Educational presentations are an important part of some group meetings. One group chooses a subject area such as American history, science, geography or literature as the theme for the year's meetings, and then subdivides the subject into smaller sections, covering one at each meeting. Families present material in various interesting and creative ways such as reports, plays (with costumes), poetry recitations, games, demonstrations, arts and crafts, songs, Scriptures, and even simulated radio or TV programs. Small children are involved in these presentations as much as possible with their parents and older brothers and sisters. Follow-up learning is included in the form of printed handouts and suggested activities.

Many group meetings include a time for free sharing between members, either as a group or in one-to-one conversations, and end with refreshments. Other meetings are held either before or after a picnic, sack lunch, or potluck dinner for fellowship. Sometimes the children make and bring the refreshments. A few groups have one person in charge of bringing food bought with group funds; others rotate the responsibility of contributing refreshments.

A common feature at many group meetings is a resource table including printed information, books and magazines on home schooling or curriculum displays for parents to take home, browse through, buy, borrow, order or trade. Some groups also have lending libraries.

During meetings that are not geared for children, some groups have planned and supervised activities for them in a separate room. These can include informal play, games, stories, crafts, entertaining or educational movies or even regular classes. Responsibility for these activities can be taken by one person or several either permanently or by rotation.

In addition to the regular group meetings, some support groups have special meetings for parents only or for parents of preschoolers or teenagers only. Another common kind of meeting is "Mom's Day (or night) Out," either for relaxation or business or both. Dads or baby sitters keep the children during that time.

Some kind of *planning* is usually required to make the group meetings go smoothly. Planning meetings may include leaders only, dads only, moms only, or the entire group. Or planning can be done by individual volunteers or by rotation, one or two families being responsible for each meeting.

Group *field trips* are a primary activity of many support groups. Responsibility for planning these can be one person's job for the year or taken in turns by one or two members at a time. Some groups have no official field trips, but individual families make their own arrangements, sometimes inviting the group or another family to join them. The lasting value of field trips is greatly enhanced by prior study of the topic as well as by follow-up activities.

Field trips can be of several different types. *Cultural* field trips can include symphony or other concerts and visits to art museums. In the area of *community services* there are public utilities, police and fire stations, courts, libraries, and hospitals, as well as private charities and nursing homes. Some support groups visit nursing homes regularly as a ministry to the residents. Various *occupations* can be explored by visits to businesses, factories, bakeries and newspapers or to the home or shop of a self-employed farmer, artist, or craftsman. The subjects of *science* and *history* can be enriched by trips to museums, exhibits, planetariums, and local events such as rock and mineral shows. *Nature* walks or hikes with or without a knowledgeable guide help children appreciate God's creation.

The ideal number and age range of children to be included in any given field trip depend on several factors and require careful consideration for best results. Many groups have learned by trial and error that smaller groups of children accompanied and well supervised by their parents learn the most from field trips. Some field trips are of more interest to one age group than another. Sometimes there are rules or requirements made by the place you are visiting that determine the size and age range of the group.

Support groups have field trips with varying frequencies—from two each week to one each quarter.

Several groups go beyond field trips or occasional educational presentations and provide *classes* in various subject areas for their members. Arts and crafts classes are sometimes taught by working artists and explore various media. Projects created may be displayed in an art show. Music, drama or puppetry classes may produce a musical or play or go Christmas caroling. Regular periods of sports or exercise are provided by some groups using public parks and gyms or church facilities. Sometimes home schoolers participate as a group in classes provided by the local park and recreation department. One group held science courses in entomology and chemistry, taught by a public school teacher. The entomology class collected insects and the chemistry class was centered in the kitchen observing chemical reactions commonly occurring there. One group had a parent teaching beginning readers in a phonics program. Sometimes groups will meet regularly but vary the subject from time to time to include enrichment in many areas.

Classes are usually held weekly and continue for a period such as six weeks or for the entire year. They are taught by volunteer parents with or without expertise or by outside professionals. Some require tuition; others ask for fees just to cover costs of materials.

Social activities are important to many groups. Potlucks and picnics are commonly enjoyed at regular intervals. Holiday celebrations may combine a special dinner with an appropriate program at Christmas, Thanksgiving, Harvest time (Oct 31), or Valentine's Day. Another type of special dinner is the International Fair, which includes dishes and costumes from many countries.

Parties are given regularly by some groups, either for everyone or for a certain age group such as teenagers. A favorite is roller skating. Usually the support group or several groups together will reserve the rink strictly for themselves and provide their own music and supervision.

Many groups have park or sports days in the summer with games and contests or just general playtime.

Annual events that can be anticipated and prepared for all during the year are planned by some support groups. A program of various presentations by home-schooling families or individuals is one option. A variation of this is the talent night. Another is open house, which can include displays of the children's school work or special projects. Science fairs are another possibility. Some groups prepare a play or musical every year. Parts can be practiced mostly at home and then put together in a few rehearsals or worked on weekly in a class. Graduation or award assemblies give parents an opportunity to recognize their children's achievements. Each child can be recognized for something, whether it is academic progress or excellence in a certain subject or development of a character quality.

Support groups often hold or participate in *book and curriculum fairs* once or twice a year. These include displays by many different publishers and give home schoolers an opportunity to buy, sell, rent, trade, give away, or examine materials.

Seminars or workshops on various topics of interest to home schoolers are either hosted or planned by some support groups.

Several groups have *lending libraries* containing a variety of material helpful to home schoolers, and some even lend children's textbooks.

One group keeps a scrapbook of its activities throughout the year and produces an annual *yearbook*.

Such *services* as health screening and standardized testing are provided by some support groups. Others include consultations with certified teachers which meet legal requirements, or even a full-fledged umbrella school.

Support groups give home schoolers enhanced opportunities to help and encourage one another in accomplishing their common goal—to train their own children in every area of life.

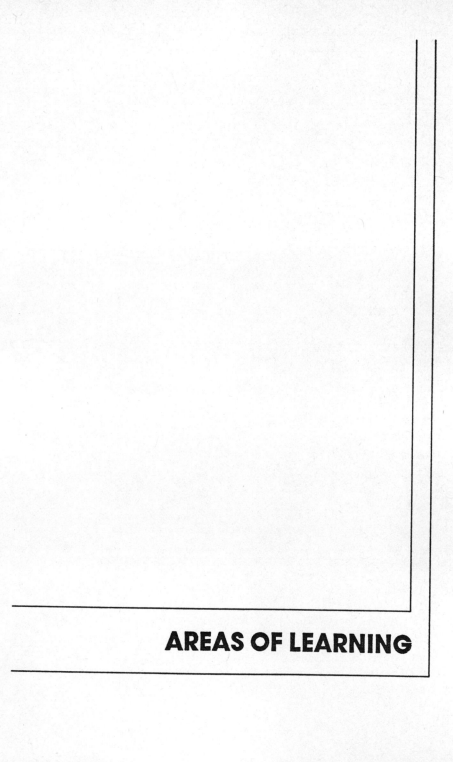

AREAS OF LEARNING

14

Early education

Human infants begin the journey of life with but little intellectual baggage. They are preprogrammed to know certain things, but only a meager fraction of what the normal preschoolers somehow classify and store behind bright little eyes. Consider the complexities of walking and talking—all mastered without the help of a certified teacher!

Why not give them an early start?

It seems only reasonable that instilling young fertile minds with the foundations of reading, math and similar bridges to general learning would be a great advantage. In fact, an increasing number of parents are evidently interested in special early training for their kids. The portion of three- to five-year-olds in the United States in nursery school and similar prekindergarten programs has been rapidly increasing: 37% in 1970, 52% in 1980, and 55% in 1986.[1] As the trend is going, I expect a continued increase not only in numbers but also in the emphasis on intellectual development.

But the push to get ahead by starting early raises certain questions. The principles of learning, for young children, are a little more complex than it would at first appear. For example, let me remind you that preschoolers who learn a second language apparently as easily as you and I learn half a dozen telephone numbers, also forget it unless they continue using it past the age of six or eight. Melvin, my own youngest, was conversing fluently in simple Creole and French when he was five, but knows almost nothing of either now.

Although the answers aren't always simple, we dare not take education for granted in the first crucial years of life. And it's not enough to accept the conclusions of skilled speakers or writers without examining the evidence on which they base their ideas.

In this chapter we first discuss research studies which can help you decide what "education" should mean for your young child. Then we look at some specific teaching principles for helping preschoolers think and develop. And finally I'll suggest how a child for whom you have delayed formal instruction can be integrated into the stream of classroom education.

Delayed formal instruction

Raymond and Dorothy Moore have examined research studies on characteristics of young children and the effects of early schooling.[2] They conclude that children are not ready for "formal" instruction before they are eight to ten years old. Formal instruction requires sustained eye work, fine hand muscle control, confinement for seat work, coping with peer social interaction, logical thought processes, and so on.

Just from this description and from what you know about your own children, you probably are beginning to see reasons for delayed school entrance.

Some of the most convincing reasons to wait come from studies comparing children who actually began earlier and later. For example, the following report from *USA Today* mentions two studies indicating that children who wait a year to start school get higher grades than those who attend first grade as soon as they are eligible.[3]

A seven-year study of 70 children in the Cincinnati school system found:
* 81 percent of boys who waited had above-average grades, while only 47 percent of the younger boys did.

* 100 percent of girls who waited had above-average grades, compared to 60 percent of those who started early.

The added maturity may allow development of coordination, vital to reading and writing skills.

A study of 278 Nebraska pupils found those who began school as soon as they were eligible were more intelligent than their older counterparts, but got lower grades.

Let's consider a few characteristics of the typical first or second grader. Young eyes can focus at close range, but certain evidence indicates that early close work might cause later nearsightedness. Frequent confusion between similar letters and words means extra strain on an immature brain. Auditory perception—the brain's accurate interpretation of sounds—isn't mature. Ability to see a spatial arrangement and predict what certain changes would do to it, comes at age eight to eleven. Young children are more susceptible to respiratory and other diseases, thus hardly braced for recycled classroom air. Because of the way young children reason, they have little defense against unwholesome peer influences. Without the ability to weigh issues for understanding right and wrong, little children in groups too large for good adult supervision hurt each other emotionally and sometimes physically. And young learners thrive on action—running, jumping and climbing—not desk work.

Results from preschool experimental programs

While information and ideas from the Moores seem to tell us not to begin so soon, results from two recent major preschool experimental projects would appear to imply that school isn't starting soon enough. Let's take a closer look.

Each year between 1962 and 1965, three- and four-year-olds were selected from among disadvantaged children in Ypsilanti, Michigan and admitted to a specially designed preschool program. Another group from the same community and with essentially the same backgrounds and characteristics—called the control group—was not admitted to the program, but was studied as a comparison. Eleven years later, tests and questionnaires showed the group who attended the special preschool program to have greater school achievement, more commitment to school, a more positive student role and decreased delinquent behavior.[4] But I haven't told you the whole story. Here is part of a letter I received from David P. Weikart, project director:

> The Ypsilanti Perry Preschool Project, which was reviewed in Monograph #7, reported the results from a group of children who attended an early childhood education program (the High/Scope Cognitively Oriented Curriculum) and a group who did not attend, but who were just like them. In the group that attended preschool education, each one had a home visit each week for approximately 90 minutes to assist the parents in understanding the child and to help him in the home setting. This mutual parent/teacher involvement allowed the teacher to learn a great deal about the home, and the parents learned a great deal about the teacher and their own child in a learning setting. In our opinion, this involvement of parents was essential for the long-term outcomes which we have obtained. We have some data from a later project where it appears that children without home teaching who only had center-based experience, did not do as well as time passed.
>
> You noted that the experimental group achieved more than the control group at age 14. Upon testing functional achievement at age 19, we found that the difference continued to be significant in favor of the experimental group. We are not going to test achievement at age 25, but secondary evidence . . . [indicates] that it will be even more likely at that age. . . .
>
> . . . I conclude that preschool programs are an important benefit for children who come from low-income homes. They are the families who do not have

the resources, either personally or financially, to provide the stimulation that children need. That situation is perfectly understandable given the pressure and conditions under which these families exist. Families with more financial resources and who have benefited from education, etc., are able to provide that to the children. Thus, in the disadvantaged child's case, the public needs to provide the experience and resources while in the middle-class case the family provides it. In both cases development occurs because someone cares.

Another interesting experiment—the Brookline Early Education Project—had a similar research design.[5] The investigators tried to develop the "school competence" of a group of Massachusetts children by a program of health and development monitoring, parent education and children playgroup or prekindergarten sessions. Children who had been in the experimental group and who were evaluated during second grade, tended to have fewer reading problems and also showed more skills such as following directions, working independently, completing work, and getting along with other children. Observations during kindergarten were less encouraging.

Although the implications are worth considering, they are somewhat shaky because all the children in the experimental group had parents who were interested enough in the types of help the program offered to voluntarily sign up for it. In other words, these parents whose children appeared better would naturally do more for them, program or not. Children for the comparison group were selected and tested several years before the program started. We must assume that some of their parents would not have been interested in program participation had it been available. The question then arises, to what extent were the better results of the experimental group influenced by having more concerned parents and to what extent by the special treatment they received? We don't know. Also, only 60% of the experimental group was available for second-grade observation. To what extent were the good results influenced by having more stable parents (stability indicated by not moving away)? We don't know.

More significant than weaknesses in research design is the fact that both projects not only brought their experimental groups into their classrooms but also had home training programs to show the parents how to foster their children's learning. I suggested to Donald Pierson, director of the Brookline project, that the parent involvement phase of their program might have caused most or all the improvement. His response is significant. "We think the parent involvement and support is crucial. The other areas are helpful."

From these projects, we can conclude that preschool programs very likely do make a difference, especially for the disadvantaged. We cannot, however, say that school is a better early learning place than home, because the experimental programs involved strong home education components. We don't know what undesirable side effects the schooling might have had or for how many of the children. None were evident from the research reports.

The day-care option

The experimental programs we have described were certainly different from the typical preschool day-care services where you find less-qualified personnel, more children per adult, and little if any deliberate, planned learning or parent participation.

Working mothers of the approximately four million American children not cared for by other family members find a variety of solutions for their child-care problem. Some arrange for baby sitting, some leave their children with a neighbor who watches (or tries to watch) a flock of children for supplementary income, and some can afford services from a licensed day-care center. But even among licensed preschools, probably only a small fraction, for financial or other reasons, compare in quality with the experimental preschool programs I have described.

Research comparing children from day-care services to those who can stay at home raises serious questions about social development. The day-care children in one study were found to have worse peer relationships, more aggression toward other children (shown by hitting, taking possession without consent, and abusive language), more hostility toward teachers, and so on.[6] Although a few preschools or day-care centers may, through well-planned effort, help their children avoid most of this negative social influence, we would expect most to be as bad as the negative reports declare or worse, since centers with obviously poor care would not be expected to submit to research studies. Reports of child abuse at a few day-care centers don't paint a fair picture of the vast majority, but if my children were still small, I would want a good reason before leaving them with someone I didn't know very well.

How does all this relate to home schools?

A good early education program involving both classroom and parental guidance is evidently better than no program. But contrary to what some promoters would like to imply, evidence does not support the idea that little children from ordinary functional homes should be sent off to school as early as most of them usually are.

Responsible home education was not tested in these research projects, but evidence discussed in this book and the experience of numerous families support it as the ideal plan for young children. A good out-of-home early education program is better for kids than having them unguided, but an organized nurturing home is best of all.

Montessori and Waldorf Education

Montessori and Waldorf schools are increasing in popularity and are beginning to claim the attention of home school parents. While their methods apparently achieve certain good results, I have some concerns about their philosophical backgrounds which quietly influence the developing perceptions of young children. From reading this book you will realize that these educational systems don't harmonize with my own understanding of truth.

Let's look at a few of their basic ideas. Then you can judge for yourself.

Maria Montessori was an innovative Italian physician who turned her attention to children's education in 1907. Her "science of the human spirit" proposes to free the child from its ordinary limiting weaknesses such as laziness, disobedience, violence, etc., and to reveal its true nature of joy, and harmony with the environment.

The method taught to Montessori teachers "expresses an intangible inner commitment to certain absolute principles, the source of which lies completely within oneself. The realization of such an inner commitment with children creates a psychic condition within which the 'normalized' child is compelled to emerge."[7] The teacher's job is to observe, to respect individual liberty, and to stage the learning environment. The child is seen to be "the true creator of its own 'normalized' nature—a spontaneous expression of the mysterious creative power of the universe springing from life itself."[8]

You might contrast these beliefs with what the Bible says about the natural heart and the source of our strength. (See Jer. 17:9, Rom. 8:7 and Phil. 4:13.)

Rudolph Steiner, founder of the Waldorf School, was a German occultist who promoted his belief in "knowledge produced by the higher self in man" and in "spiritual perception independent of the senses." Beginnings of Waldorf Education date from 1913. The "essence of education," according to this philosophy, is a "releasing and freeing of forces and capacities that live in the child."[9] By properly relating to these changing forces, Steiner considered the child to be prepared as a citizen of both the earth and the spirit world. The young child is thought to be still charmed from its "pre-earthly origin," with objects and sounds around it echoing the "spiritual world." Children "awakened" too early from the dreamy experience are considered deprived of "spiritual strength" in later life.[10]

Steiner applied his ideas to more than education. Titles of some of the books transcribed and translated from his lectures are: *The Fifth Gospel, The Reappearance of Christ in the Etheric, Occult Reading and Occult Hearing, Metamorphoses of the Soul.*

For evaluating these ideas you might want to look at Bible texts in Heb. 9:27; Eccl. 9:5, 6; Rev. 22:12; Ex. 19:31; Is. 8:19, 20 and Eze. 18:20.

Early academic emphasis in question

In a second experiment of the Perry Preschool Project, 68 impoverished children were randomly assigned to three different preschool programs. One taught academic skills reinforcing frequent responses from the children. The second took the opposite approach of the "child-centered" nursery school allowing children to initiate their own play activities, with guidance from teachers only as requested. The third program used the project's High/Scope curriculum which combined child-initiated activities with teacher interaction in planning and discussing with children.

Interestingly enough, intelligence and school aptitude for children from all three approaches turned out to be about the same—near the national average. The three groups didn't appear different in other ways either until 1986, when the participants were evaluated at age 15. Then those in the group directly instructed for academic skills reported having engaged in delinquent acts at a rate of about twice what was reported by those in either of the other two groups! In other terms, 44% of the direct-instruction group were classified as high-rate offenders compared to 11% of the nursery school group and 6% of the High/Scope group.

Although the groups were small, the children were all disadvantaged and no stay-home-with-Mom group existed for comparison, we must wonder whether the early strong academic emphasis might have interfered with the process of character formation. Might the child-initiated approach promote it? Perhaps so.

Ideas you can use from High/Scope

In my opinion, principles from the High/Scope plan may be adapted for home education without the dangers of early formal schooling. Very briefly, I will sketch out the methods as I understand them. In appendix I, you will find more information about how to get a more complete explanation.[11]

Although children in the program initiate their own activities, adults remain in charge. They provide activities from which the children choose. They help them plan, follow through and evaluate. And they stimulate the thinking process. A balance is maintained between adult-suggested and child-initiated activities.

In *providing a secure atmosphere,* teachers set and maintain limits. When it's necessary to say, No, they give a reason and offer an alternative activity. They calmly deal with problems when they arise and show that they mean what they say by following up commands with actions.

To *support children's actions and language,* they join in their activities while respecting their purpose and initiative. They use physical contact. They give them time blocks to work on their projects. They talk with them, and get them to talk with each other. And they save adult conversation for later.

Leading children in making decisions guides them to think for themselves. Adults can help children be aware of making choices. Of course, they should not offer alternatives when only one behavior choice is appropriate. For instance, when it's time to come in from play, other options aren't considered.

Adults *help children solve their own problems* by not doing for them what they can figure out how to do for themselves, and by allowing them to make a mistake without saying, "That's wrong."

Probably the toughest part of following this plan is restraining your own impulse to make the decisions and solve the problems, thus countering the creativity and initiative you are trying to help your child develop.

Now let's put this in the context of a Christian home. Isn't our response to God's invitation based on the freedom of sanctified reason (Isaiah 1:18; Joshua 24:15)? As you encourage and join with your children in their projects of making and doing, you help them learn to think clearly. By word and action you hold up before them the beautiful plan of happiness God has given in His Book. And as you help them explore the wonders of creation, you ask for the Holy Spirit to influence their choices and plans ever leading them to reverence the One who made their minds.

Early home education

Of course you teach your young children in other ways than those just described. We have explained some of them in other chapters. See especially, "Teaching values," "Teaching reading," and "The lovely game." Basically, be a loving parent. Spend time with your children. Talk with them (not just to them). Go places and do things with them. Read to them. Provide challenges to stimulate their intellectual and physical skills. And set a good example.

School learning or book leaning is not to be stoutly forestalled until some magic age, then started all at once. In the right environment children's natural curiosity will lead them to ask how things work. They will want to go and do and make and find out. The most important learning subject for early years, as we explain in the next chapter, is values. The advantages you can give your own child are a home environment and learning appropriate for young minds and bodies. Start slowly. Introduce activities as readiness becomes apparent.

Preparing your children to begin traditional schooling

As children mature, they become ready to handle a more formal learning program, whether you continue to teach them at home or send them to the classroom. By the time most children are around eight years old they need to begin more concentrated study in order to achieve the extent of education for which they are capable. Children can advance in numbers and reading while they are younger and less mature, but the learning is often slow and tedious. Avoid both extremes—pushing too early and relaxing too long.

When your child is mature enough and you have evidence to believe that the time has come for a more serious look at the 3 R's, you have the choice of school at home or in the traditional classroom. In either case, I recommend that your child begin formal schooling with the grade children of his age are usually in. That means you would start an eight year old in third grade, not first grade. Why? (1) Learning materials for each grade are designed to appeal to the interests of children expected to be at that level. (2) Your child will probably already have covered much of the previous grades' curriculum. (3) When your child eventually joins the traditional classroom, peers will relate better if he or she is not too different. And (4) classroom management depends on the general age level of the students.

If you plan to begin formal schooling with the third grade, I suggest you borrow sets of first and second grade books two or three months before formal school is to start. If your child really knows very little about reading and math, a gradual introduction beginning six or eight months earlier might be better.

I suggest a pick-and-choose approach to topics in the grades below your child's age level especially if you will be continuing to educate your child at home. A superficial understanding may tempt you to move too lightly over some areas. By checking carefully you will know. Some points are indeed less important and can be skipped. Concentrate on the foundation blocks. Small errors in choosing what to teach in your get-ready program can be amended later. Also, the review of essential ideas that appears in the beginning lessons of sequential subjects textbooks, and an understanding teacher help fill in small missing areas.

If the idea of going through several grades in a few months seems unrealistic, remember that an older child beginning formal study will usually learn in an hour, concepts that would have taken days during younger years; and that he or she has already informally mastered many of the goals for the early grades.

A solid early preparation, a good home atmosphere, and thorough study year by year will give your child a tremendous advantage.

15

Teaching values

Let's stand back and take a look at what we really expect from the education we plan for our children. Do we want people to be impressed by where they inherited all their intelligence? Or what good providers their parents are? Oh no, at least not at the conscious level. We want our children to be able to function well in the world they face. We want them capable of making a good living at something they enjoy.

And we really want even more from a Christian viewpoint. We want happiness now and in the hereafter. We want our children to relate unselfishly to people and to honor God. Most Christian parents expect their children to learn the three R's in school and religion in church, but in too many cases it just doesn't work that way. Peers and entertainment during the week teach a lot more values than the preacher can unteach in church.

Of what worth are skills in math, reading, writing, foreign language or playing a musical instrument compared with solid principles for living? If you had to choose for your child between wealth and beauty of character, which would it be? Often parents are so eager to gain an advantage for their child that they start to train the intellect too early, ignoring the idea that values are taught at all.

Values are learned just as certainly as knowledge is. All learning falls into three categories named by psychologist Benjamin Bloom and associates:[1] (1) cognitive—factual information and ways to handle it, (2) affective—values and appreciations, and (3) psychomotor—body movement skills. Practically all schooling is directed toward cognitive development. Spiritual and moral values, our particular concern in this chapter, would come under the second area—the affective.

Often, well-meaning parents or teachers plan to teach values and end up changing only the cognitive. The ability to repeat a set of words isn't the same as believing the message they expound. For example, a child can repeat the Pledge of Allegiance to the flag without changing his patriotism, or the twenty-third Psalm, without knowing the Shepherd it describes. Learning words, however, can play a role in changing the feelings if we combine values (affective) teaching with the factual (cognitive).

You may have heard of "values clarification." Be careful. Its focus is more on choosing values logically and applying them than it is on considering a specific set of values. From a Christian education viewpoint, I see this as the wrong emphasis. Clear, perceptive choice is important, but basic principles of right and wrong must be presented as absolutes. The topic is discussed more in the chapter, "Teaching Social Studies."

How to teach values

Teaching the heart isn't complicated. The first element is personal example. If you teach in your health class that sugar clogs up the body's defenses and then make a sweet roll the main part of your breakfast, what have your children learned? If you tell them that spiritual commitment is important without holding it in your own heart and actions, are you teaching any more than empty words?

Your own way of life is the most important method for teaching values, but it's not enough. Good values have good reasons. Talk it over. Young children like to do what Mommy and Daddy do, but adolescents want to think for themselves. Childhood habits are easy enough to carry into adulthood if they have been backed up with clear thinking.

The third factor in teaching values, in addition to example and logic, is control of the environment. We learn though all our senses all the time, and we learn from all our associates. Talk to your children about the principles, then help them choose what they feed their minds—what they read and watch on TV, the places they go, and their friends. As a parent, you have potential for a greater influence in your children's choice of friends than you might think. Find other families with high ideals and invite them over for special occasions; plan outings together. Your children will quickly become friends with theirs. And the cross-family friendship will help them develop socially far better than classroom associations.

Finally, values are learned from beginning to end by spiritual strength—yours and your children's. Paul says that the natural man cannot accept or even understand the things of the Spirit of God "because they are spiritually discerned" (I Corinthians 2:14). Proverbs 3:6 admonishes, "In all thy ways acknowledge Him, and He shall direct thy paths," and Psalm 119:105 says, "Thy Word is a lamp unto my feet and a light unto my path." Spiritual values are learned from opening the heart to God through prayer and listening to His voice through the Scriptures.

To teach values: appeal to your child's reason; follow through with your own example of enthusiasm, earnestness and consistency; shape the environment; and direct mind and heart to the Source of all wisdom.

Development of spiritual maturity—an ideal pattern

Psychologists have described in some detail the typical developmental characteristics of individuals as they grow from birth to full maturity. But development involves more than physical, mental, social and emotional growth. God's plan of education includes another dimension—the spiritual—growing "in grace, and in the knowledge of our Lord and Saviour, Jesus Christ." "Till we all come in the unity of the faith, and of the knowledge of the Son of God, unto a perfect man, unto the measure of the stature of the fullness of Christ" (2 Peter 3:18; Eph. 4:13). In Peter's second epistle, he lists areas of spiritual growth as faith, virtue, knowledge, temperance, patience, godliness, brotherly kindness, and charity (chap. 1:5-7).

Although the following list of stages in spiritual development may be expanded or modified according to your own understanding, it can help as you plan strategies and choose materials for teaching values. These stages are not automatic. Children need guidance for spiritual growth just as they do for physical, mental, social, and emotional development.

Ages 0-1. Learning God's love through parental example and control. Trust is developed and nurtured through loving care and guidance from parents. Self-control in later years has its basis in behavior patterns set from the earliest time in life. At this stage and for the next several years, parents stand in the place of God to their children. Habits of obedience to parents makes obedience to God's will a natural trait in later life.

Ages 1-3. Learning what God is like. As the imagination develops, the child learns about God through stories of Jesus. Impressions are made through songs and a growing, trusting relationship with parents. Simple Bible stories plant seeds of knowledge which mature later in the behavior patterns. Character is basically set.

Ages 3-6. Bible principles taken for granted. The child learns the basis of what is right and wrong but expects parents to be in control. Good behavior is by habit and obedience rather than from principle. Verses of scripture reinforce later growth. Object lessons from nature make lasting impressions.

Ages 6-9. Guidelines for right living accepted as reasonable. Specific do's and don'ts begin to make sense and are often observed scrupulously, while other behaviors are sometimes overlooked. It is easy for the child to see problems in other children and to expect them to be treated according to his or her own sense of justice. More of the Bible stories are learned. In addition to stories, principles for right behavior begin to make sense.

Ages 9-12. Principles begin to be integrated into the lifestyle, rather than being just acceptable isolated rights and wrongs. The controversy between good and evil begins to make sense. Even though a somewhat fuller picture is formed, the focus still seems to be more on behavior than on a relationship with God. Skill is increased in comparing scripture with scripture.

Ages 12-16. Biblical principles applied to a growing personal dependence on God. The prayer life grows to be more of a connection with God. God's word takes on deeper importance and significance. Opportunities to share God's love in simple ways are taken advantage of. With increased adolescent independence in thinking, parental values are no longer taken for granted. Disparity between church members' lives and church or Bible standards provides a new kind of temptation—to excuse personal misbehavior. This crucial time in life when the emotions call for independence is often a turning point. A previous trust relationship allows the youth to accept parental counsel, and principles learned can help form the new value structure. The new-birth experience marks an abrupt change for the person who turns to Christ from a life deep in sin. In the more ideal spiritual growth pattern, as I see it, the child, ready to accept responsibility for personal decisions, renounces sin and makes the new-birth commitment at around the age of 10 to 14. Terminology and theological understandings differ.

Ages 16-20. Total dependence on God, living by faith. New spiritual concepts enrich the relationship. A reasonably good command of the Scriptures prepares the individual for serious witnessing and leading others to a decision for Christ.

Ages 20 and onward. Settling of convictions. Searching and testing of God's way subsides. Major questions about Christ's being both Lord and Master have already been decided in the thinking. Gradually, as the years progress, the faith becomes unshakable. Growth continues in understanding God's will and in relationships with others. People are seen as those for whom Christ died. Each is valuable. The burden of being a representative responsible for the souls of those who need to be warned becomes serious. Divine providence is accepted, and faith holds onto the continued, ever-growing relationship with God and confidence in His Word.

Bible Study

The Word of God should be the major source of study for developing values because through it we understand our Creator and Redeemer, and we see how God relates to people. From Bible study we can expect (1) to think more deeply through the guidance of the Holy Spirit, (2) to be safe from deception, (3) to build a personal value system, (4) to develop a sensitivity to people's needs, and (5) to grow in our personal relationship with God.

Scripture study deserves more than incidental consideration in the curriculum. For young children, read and discuss Bible stories written for their level of understanding or review the stories yourself from the Bible and tell them in your own words. Add stories showing how God leads people in our day, too. Get children busy acting out the Bible stories, making felt or sandbox representations, writing about stories or principles, and so on according to age.

Older children need to learn to dig out life principles from their own Bible reading. Have them choose an interesting verse and concentrate on its meaning. Then discuss it with them. Study Bible topics systematically.

Youth can learn to find Bible answers to their problems and to share God's love with others.

At all levels, have your children memorize scripture. For small children just a few simple words from a chosen verse will suffice. Older children can memorize more.

Always pray before reading the Bible. Not to open our minds to divine help is to be led into misunderstanding and doubt. The same Spirit that inspired the Bible writers is needed to help us understand them correctly.

Home grown Bible learning (by Mary Pride)[2]

At the risk of sounding old-fashioned, I would like to suggest using that great old standby for teaching Bible. It's called *The Bible.*

What with all the puppet lessons, flannelgraphs, Bible stories, Bible videos, Bible dolls and so on, sometimes our Bible programs end up missing the mark. For some reason, Bible curriculum designers have been really heaping on the fun 'n games lately. The kids love it, of course, but the Bible ends up moldering in the corner, or even gathering dust under the TV Guide.

You don't really think it's too hard to teach Bible straight from the Book, do you? Whether we do or not, curriculum designers *think* we think it is too hard. So they load us up with "easy activities," like finding the puppet figures, dragging out flannel pieces 22A-24F, or correcting a Friends of Jesus Crossword Puzzle. That's OK for fun once in a while, but it does get rather old after a few school weeks.

So how about just reading the Bible to your children instead? They are going to pay attention because, after reading, you will have each one tell you the passage in his own words. Alternatively, the children can act out the passage (with or without costumes), draw pictures that explain the passage, model it in clay (quickly, and you don't have to save the results forever unless you want to), or write it out.

With a little creative imagination, your children can be actively listening and retelling all of Scripture to you in their own words.

Numerous spiritual leaders from Moses on have urged parents to not only share, but apply, God's Word to our youngsters. The easiest time to do this is when the family is all gathered together listening to Mom or (better) Dad read the Bible.

Commenting is just as easy as sharing your thoughts out loud. You can comment on the passage as you read it, making your own applications and explaining the difficult parts, or connect it to other portions of Scripture. The children will see the difference between your reading the Word and talking about it, while benefiting from both. This is more than can be said for many Bible programs that substitute Bible stories for the Bible and give comments on the the Bible equal weight with the Word itself.

Are you weak in some areas of Scripture, like just about everyone else? Good for you for being honest! Then you can use a good commentary, and let the children help you find answers to some of your questions. Also teach them how to use a Bible dictionary and a Bible encyclopedia.

Bible storytelling (by Gregg Harris)[3]

A child whose heart is filled with accurate accounts from the lives of people in the Bible is able to make right moral decisions much more consistently than a child who has only been given a list of rules and a lot of spankings. Current events in the church today warrant a return to this kind of Bible storytelling.

Rules are important. The Ten Commandments are still the basis of all God-given law. But only 15% of God's Word comes to us as commandments. The other 85% is recorded as history.

Storytellers tend to distort the Bible stories freely for the sake of younger children. Distortions come in various ways. We can add ideas for which there is no basis in the biblical account. Some publishers have Noah giving altar calls like a modern day preacher. Other publishers distort some stories by editing the plot to achieve a "G Rating." The story of Samson comes to mind. In other words, accuracy is being sacrificed to modern tastes of what is appropriate for children to hear.

Beware of this tendency in your own storytelling. Don't say that something happened if it didn't happen. And don't skip over something that the Bible includes as part of the story. If you feel a particular story is inappropriate for a very young child, just don't tell it yet. But for the child's sake don't distort the story when you do tell it.

Handled accurately each Bible story will accomplish God's purpose. Study each character's life story as God recorded it, then, at the right time, tell it like it is, warts and all, to your children.

I'm convinced that a child raised on accurate Bible stories would know that people, even God's people, (himself included) are still people.

The Bible told him so!

PS:

Mary Pride and Gregg Harris have suggested making the Bible real to children. I would like to just add one serious concern to expand their thoughts. The cartoon approach, popular in Bible materials for children, is a "quick fix" to get kids interested, but the end result may be disaster.

Suppose you are a little child, growing up again. In the pictures and stories you hear, Jesus and Noah and especially Jonah are presented at the same level of reality as Garfield or Cinderella. The songs often match the pictures. You have tried to believe in Santa Claus. But in a year or so that becomes "little-kid stuff," and pretending doesn't get you more presents anyway. As an adolescent, social life appeals to you, and this becomes the big thing in connecting you with religion. Later you are interested in making money and getting ahead in the world. Why then God?—except as a sort of eternal-life insurance just in case there was something to it.

Then what about Abraham, Jesus and Santa Claus? You will teach them to your children. Have they not become part of your cultural tradition?

Coming back to present reality, I think you can see my point. Certainly we need to use bright pictures and happy songs. Friends are important, too. But let's focus our search for happiness on the reality of eternity.

16

Teaching reading

As soon as children begin to realize that information and ideas and stories are locked up in visual symbols, they want to be able to decode them. Learning to read is like working on a puzzle. It's a key to the grown-up's world. And as you and I know, reading is an essential tool for all serious learning in practically any area.

Although I can't tell you in one chapter all the important things about teaching reading, I do want to give you some ideas about what to aim for, how to give your child a running start, how to teach, and what to watch out for.

In the lower grades, reading is generally considered the number one objective, and math comes closely behind. Reading is part of the broader area of language arts which includes spelling, grammar, writing, speaking and listening. At first, most of the teaching-learning effort goes toward reading. In the middle grades, the other language arts areas begin to get increased attention. And at the junior high level and beyond, the class is called English. In senior high literature becomes more important while study is continued in grammar, composition, and sometimes speech. Then when the "cream of the crop" enters college, half of them still can't read and write well enough for serious scholarship, so they take composition courses which re-teach what should have been learned in elementary and high school.

When you consider that only a fraction of people go to college and that few of them finish, you can see why so many are functionally illiterate, or can't read enough to fill out a job application form, and why many more find it too much of a struggle to plow their way through a book or to write a résumé. Are these people just too "dumb" to learn? I firmly believe not. Most everyone has ample intelligence. I think you see the point. Your child's future depends to a large extent on reading skill.

What do we mean by being able to read? Can a person who is able to pronounce a variety of words read? Is knowing word meanings reading? Having in mind what we expect gives direction to our learning. I suggest you consider the following goals:

\#   Recognize words in an ever-expanding vocabulary and be able to pronounce them.

\#   Make sense from blocks of reading material. Be able to analyze and evaluate.

\#   Read fast and accurately.

\#   Gain proficiency in both silent and oral reading.

\#   Choose reading in harmony with life goals.

\#   Remember what was read and be able to apply the new learning.

\#   Enjoy reading.

How people learn to read

No one really knows for sure how anyone learns anything, but we do understand enough to choose reasonable teaching strategies. The steps which follow are not teaching levels, although teaching may be implied from them. They are stages of an individual's development in learning to read. The process starts long before the child begins to decipher the printed symbols we call words and letters, and it continues on through the achievement of mature reading ability.

1. Develop spatial-visual perception. That is, make sense from what is seen. Distinguish sounds and associate them with people or events.

2. Associate spoken words with physical objects and with simple ideas. Figure out the muscular process of producing words. These, by the way, are utterly complex skills based on practically

no prior experience and little if any conscious teaching. Yet they are learned!

3. Understand the time relationship of sequences of events, and be able to conceptualize a sequence from its narrative description. This means stories make sense because stories depend on a time sequence. Then later, complex trains of abstract logic may be understood.

4. Begin to recognize visual (printed) words—which are symbols of spoken words which, in turn, are symbols of objects and ideas. This complex process is different for each individual and relies on a mixture of decoding keys: some shape recognition, some letter-sound cues.

5. Recognize more words by: linguistic cues (comparison with similar words or root meanings), contextual cues (seeing what word would make sense in the sentence), and phonetic cues. Linguistic cues would lead to words not yet in the speaking vocabulary.

6. Perceive meaning for groups of words as reading speed picks up.

7. Understand meaning from a flow of printed words often completely bypassing the sounding-out process, even mentally.

What about phonics?

The place of phonics in teaching reading is a hot issue. And, as with most volatile topics, intelligent answers aren't quite as simple as the questions. Although we don't have space—and you probably don't have time—to review all the arguments in what has been termed "the great debate," I hope to help you make sense (or nonsense) out of what you hear, and give you a basis for sound planning in teaching your own child.

By *phonics* we mean the process of sounding out words according to a set of rules describing the sounds made by letters and letter combinations. No one is really *against* teaching phonics, but some believe that early, very strong drill and practice with the rules will save the child from reading problems and thus unlock a brilliant intellectual future. At the other extreme are those who say that children learn from a variety of methods and who practically omit sounding-out skills from the whole reading program.

One popular trend among home schoolers who are concerned about giving their children a solid reading foundation is to use reprinted editions of the old McGuffey readers, feeling, evidently, that in the "good old days" educators really knew how to teach reading with phonics and that the textbooks then hadn't yet been affected by the humanistic influence. Both points have validity, but there is more to consider. A quick history review will help give the phonics question a little more meaning.

At the turn of the century, elocution—or public speaking employing gestures and vocal delivery—was considered an important art. Thus the reading program in schools employed oral reading with inflection, distinct pronunciation and, of course, phonics.

A change occurred when good methods of standardized testing were developed, and educational measurement promised to find scientifically accurate answers to every problem. Researchers discovered that students well-trained in oral reading tended to read slowly. Silent reading then became a primary concern, and teaching techniques began emphasizing quick word recognition. The new challenge was "see and say," rather than "sound it out."

Then the project method came into vogue. Instead of the various school subjects taught one at a time in isolation, projects were chosen that required application of math, reading, social studies, science, and so on. Learning had a purpose beyond pleasing the teacher and getting good marks on a report card. Tests showed better achievement from schools trying the new method.

Teaching through projects is still a good idea and works well for home schools. That is, it's good if you are alert and avoid its pitfalls. First, one project can't teach everything. Some study not related to the project needs to go on. Second, projects don't tend to foster the reinforcement of basic skills so essential to thorough learning and remembering. To be a little more specific, I mean drill. That's an unpopular word because drill without meaning is pointless and uninteresting. But just remember, meaning without drill may not stick. Basic skills take lots of practice. You need both.

Now back to the history lesson. As the project method was adopted far and wide, basic skills, including reading, began to suffer. Neither word recognition nor phonics drill was getting much attention.

In the 1930's and again after World War II, schools were loudly criticized—even though achievement was good—and they turned back to more basic skill-building. Then in the 60's the cry became, "We want it relevant," and drill wasn't. In the 70's national test scores slipped steadily downward and the watchword was "back to the basics." Now scores have shown a little gain but are still far from ideal.

I don't believe that a lack of basics was our real problem. Drugs, sex, alcohol, tobacco, violence, TV, broken homes, and similar influences are certainly more prevalent now than in the past and can't help but interfere with learning as they destroy the usefulness of our youth.

That's the picture. The educational pendulum swings back and forth, but good school teachers have always worked for both skills and meaning. Home teachers should, too.

To return more specifically to the phonics question: In 1956, Rudolf Flesch's book, *Why Johnny Can't Read,*[1] appeared. Flesch deplored the prevalent poor reading skills and outlined for parents (and teachers if they would listen) a plan for teaching reading by an initial basis in phonics. The title of Flesch's 1981 book, *Why Johnny Still Can't Read,*[2] is a clue to its message. Most textbook publishers and schools aren't living up to his expectations. He lists five publishers that do.

Before his subsequent book came out, *Family Circle Magazine* published what essentially became its first chapter. The tremendous reaction provided plenty of material for the rest of the book. Flesch has some important ideas but spends most of his wind blasting the "look-and-say establishment" and relating stories that tend to support his views.

After the *Family Circle* article appeared, the International Reading Association board of directors adopted a position statement. Flesch quotes it as an attack on his good work. But even if you feel that it could have favored phonics training a little more, it certainly calls for an open-minded look at methods for teaching reading.

In the light of recent public statements that suggest that reading can best be taught by using a single method through strong emphasis on a specific skill or through the use of a specific set of materials, the Board of Directors of the International Reading Association emphasizes that learning to read is a complex process requiring not only the ability to recognize words, but also the ability to comprehend and evaluate the meaning of written materials. The most important factor related to success in learning to read is the teacher. Differences in the learning styles and abilities of children emphasize the need for a variety of approaches to meet those individual needs. No single method or approach nor any one set of instructional materials has been proven to be most effective for all children. Furthermore, to learn to read well, children must read a substantial amount of material for useful purposes both in school and at home.

Therefore it is resolved that the Board of Directors of the International Reading Association recommends that parents and teachers exercise caution and judgment when considering statements or selecting materials that advocate any single method or set of materials as being the best one for teaching reading. Moreover, the Board expresses concern about those who use scare tactics and oversimplification to support their own easy solutions for teaching children to read.

Later in this chapter we discuss using phonics in your teaching program.

Laying the groundwork for reading success

Scholars have identified an impressive array of prerequisite skills a child needs, to be ready to learn to read. The suggestions we offer here for guiding your child's development are simple and important. Most of these experiences you would provide for your child as a caring parent anyway. Still, understanding what promotes good development will make your caring more purposeful and probably more successful.

The first question to address under reading readiness is how to know when the preparation stage is sufficiently completed so you can begin teaching your child to read printed words and sentences. Elsewhere in this book we discuss the concept of waiting until a child has achieved the degree of physical, mental, and social development necessary for success before beginning formal instruction. Here let me just remind you that most of us are tempted to jump too fast in our eagerness to convey what seems so simple and natural for us. As we discuss factors, you can see that full-blown readiness takes more years than are usually allowed.

From experience and from looking at the results of a few research studies, it appears to me that early reading skills instruction may not help in the end. Perhaps, for normal homes, the massive preschool impact of Sesame Street and The Electric Company blossoms early like a desert flower, then fades away.

Serious educators have been concerned about the damage structured reading instruction can have on children too young for it. Seven national professional organizations directly or indirectly involved in fostering good reading instruction published the following statement:[3]

A growing number of children are enrolled in pre-kindergarten and kindergarten classes in which highly structured pre-reading and reading programs are being used.

In attempting to respond to pressures for high scores on widely used measures of achievement, teachers of young children sometimes feel compelled to use materials,methods, and activities designed for older children. In so doing, they may impede the development of intellectual functions such as curiosity, critical thinking, and creative expression, and, at the same time, promote negative attitudes toward reading.

Aside from providing love and protecting life and limb, probably the most valuable help parents can give their children toward becoming good readers is to read to them. Jim Trelease's book, *The Read-Aloud Handbook*,[4] can tell you all about it.

Children need to hear the comforting and controlling sound of their parents' voices even before they can understand words. Read or simply talk to your infant. Your words may not make sense, but your tone of voice does. And you are establishing a communication channel. As your child becomes old enough to understand words, avoid the natural tendency to use only words you think he or she understands. The result of such limited communication not only stifles vocabulary building but tends to severely limit talk, reducing what you say to a few simple command words—hardly a basis for a growing relationship. Although you don't want to talk over your child's head, he or she can mature best as you explain and describe and share the small joys and sorrows. Reading to your child helps build vocabulary and concepts.

Also, sing. Your child's sense of melody and rhythm can develop naturally. And music conveys feelings of love, security, and inspiration while it teaches words and concepts. Some parents like to sing religious children's songs to begin preparing their child for a trust relationship. Resist the temptation to consider yourself a nonsinger. This is your chance to practice. Get a record or tape of children's songs as a guide.

As parents, your own skill with words will greatly influence your child's learning. An extensive vocabulary heard at home will make reading growth easier especially for your middle-grade child. When familiar words pop up in print, they are recognized and reinforced. You don't just switch on rich vocabulary, but you can build slowly. Of course, reading itself can expand vocabulary for both you and your child.

Another skill you need—one not automatically fostered by reading—is clear, correct enunciation. The reason is obvious. Words incorrectly pronounced get incorrectly spelled and aren't easily recognized in print. Have you ever heard anyone say something like, "Gimme sump-em te-eet"? Words mumbled and slurred are bad teachers.

Children who read early and who begin learning well in school generally (1) have been read to regularly, (2) come from homes with a variety of printed material, (3) have had paper and pencil readily available, and (4) have experienced interest in their reading and writing from people at home.[5]

Reading to your children can help build their vocabulary, expand the horizons of their big new world, build memory patterns as stories are repeated, and increase capacity for time sequences and cause-and-effect relationships. Reading time, unlike TV watching, is a time for physical closeness and sharing between child and parent—a time to reflect and discuss. And while children are being read to, they pick up information such as how words are arranged on the page, how the pages turn, and they even begin recognizing some words by sight.

Let me suggest some guidelines for reading to your children. Most of them you can find in different form and explained more fully in Jim Trelease's book which I already mentioned.

Set aside a regular time for reading each day. In fact, you might want a devotional reading time as part of your daily program. Then you could read more at other times, too.

Allow time for questions and discussion. Expect interruptions. Ask some thought questions from time to time.

Keep the length of your reading time and the choice of material within the maturity level of your child. But don't be afraid to try something now and then on the difficult side. You can interpret and simplify as appropriate.

When you read to several children at once, remember that older ones still enjoy picture books, but younger ones might not appreciate the longer, more involved stories.

\# Most people need practice reading aloud. Don't read too fast, and use expression and emphasis letting your tone follow the story mood. To make your reading better, read the story first to yourself.

\# Fathers should read to their children (and to themselves in the children's presence) as often as possible to help avoid the idea that reading is for girls. And, of course, Dad shouldn't miss out on this opportunity to help build friendship bonds.

\# Control the TV; don't compete with it. It shouldn't be a matter of which the child prefers. Offer to read during times already designated for the TV to be off.

Readiness factors

Language development: Plan opportunities that encourage talking and listening. Your child can develop by playing with a toy telephone or a tape recorder, acting out stories, describing an object for another person to guess, or giving directions to a blindfolded person. Ask your child to follow directions to find special gifts you have bought. Stop in the middle of a story and ask what might happen next. Also, being a good listener yourself helps your child to develop meaningful talk.

Visual perception: In order to read, your child must see clearly and have the mental capability to interpret what is seen. Both come naturally as time passes and they can't really be rushed much. However, watch for eye strain, focusing problems or one eye not getting used. Being able to interpret partly symbolic pictures indicates readiness to understand the printed symbols we use for words.

Auditory perception: As with seeing, both the ability to hear and to interpret and differentiate between sounds are necessary for reading. This is because reading is understanding printed symbols by comparison with previously understood sounded symbols. Hearing problems are usually easy to detect. For a simple ear test, rub your finger against your thumb and see how far away from each ear your child can hear it. Compare the results with your own hearing.

Motor development: Here motor means muscle control. Writing is an important part of reading, and writing takes fine motor control—being able to accurately use a complex array of hand and arm muscles. Before that, the visual impulses and the muscle control must be coordinated in the brain, and before that, or with it, the large muscles need to be controlled. All this takes lots of time, and activities like running, jumping, climbing—things done best with loving parents or caregivers.

You can do much to prepare your child for reading, but don't rush it. Some of the most important preparations are the simplest. Find interesting activities to share; read and talk together. You will find workbooks offering reading readiness preparation, but they aren't helpful until your child is practically ready to learn to read anyway.

When your child wants to know what certain words say, tell him (or her). Show him how to write words when he asks. Let him watch as you read. One day he will be reading without hardly ever having been consciously taught. If this is earlier than the ideal age for serious study, don't worry. You can't make the river run backwards. The only cautions I would offer are: (1) Don't push before your child is mature enough. Answer questions; be open; but don't get out the books and set up a reading program too early, and (2) If reading starts early, limit reading to 5 to 15 minutes at a time. If you don't, your child's eyes may not develop right, possibly causing nearsightedness; and your boy or girl curled up with a book for long periods will miss out on too much of the active part of life needed for balanced development.

Organizing your reading program

Now suppose your child is mature enough to begin a serious attack on reading skills. Probably he or she is already familiar with most of the alphabet and recognizes a number of words by sight. What's the next step?

In setting the directions for your reading program you will want to keep in mind both goals and backgrounds. Now let's look at three general ways you could tackle the teaching itself. Then we will go over some important components to expect or plan for in your program. And finally, I'll suggest how you might put it all together.

You have several different routes to choose from for organizing your reading program. (1) You can use a variety of materials building all the principles and practice needed into your total curriculum. (2) You can select a reading textbook appropriate for your child's ability or grade level. Or, (3) you can use a course of study planned especially for home teaching.

Option one—teaching from "scratch"—obviously requires the most skill, and the correspondence school or packaged program option, the least. Of course, the program you put together wouldn't just come out of your head. You could use textbooks to a certain degree along with other resources. A little later, I'll tell you about one way to build your own program.

The second option would be to use standard reading textbooks. Teaching materials in the main elementary curriculum areas are either basal or supplemental. The basal textbook is part of a series—usually one or two books for each grade level. And it covers explanations, exercises (which means stories and such, if it's a reading series), reviews, extra challenges for students who tend to finish their assignments ahead of the rest of the class, more drill for those who need it, and so on. Teacher's manuals, tests, and often workbooks are available to go along with the textbooks. The whole series is planned to cover and review a progressive and comprehensive set of objectives which the authors have traced out on what they call a scope-and-sequence chart.

The supplemental materials emphasize special information and skill practice which might not be covered adequately by the main text series or which a few people would consider important and which might have been omitted from the main textbooks. Nonbook materials would also be supplemental.

The advantages of following a major textbook program are obvious. Just remember that the suggested way isn't the only way (although the publisher may have tested and revised the program for several years in actual classrooms). And remember that no one child or even one class is usually expected to do everything in the book (although skipping most of it wouldn't be advisable either). What you leave out should be determined by its relative importance, whether or not your student already understands the principles involved, and what alternate activities you include.

Several reading textbook series place a strong emphasis on phonics.

A popular variation of the follow-the-textbook option is using books selected and sold by organizations established specifically for serving home school families. A number of these institutions are listed in the appendix.

The third option would be a program preplanned for home study. This may be a package you buy and use on your own, or it may be a program administered through a correspondence-type organization. The organization would provide detailed teaching plans and possibly periodic tests as well as textbooks and other materials. Generally, but not always, tests and specified samples of student work are sent in for evaluation.

Parents without training or experience in teaching or without fairly good organizational skills are much more likely to provide a full, balanced program if they choose this third option. We discuss choosing a providing organization elsewhere in this book.

Your choice might be a combination of these options. You could use the main parts of a preplanned program with the key-word idea explained later in this chapter. You could use a textbook and have a tutor help some. Or you could even have your child in a classroom for certain activities. Whatever you do, make a plan and stick to it as long as it's reasonably successful. Change smoothly at appropriate points if you need to.

Next, let's consider some components or characteristics to plan for in your reading program.

Reading for Fun

People who design a reading curriculum and write textbooks consider the various skills good readers need and plan to cover them with adequate explanation, practice and review. They try to make their reading selections appealing. Some students, however, seem to see all the reading they are expected to do as hard work for learning specific skills.

To learn to read well, more practice is needed than is provided in the normal school program. So, what can be done to get children to enjoy reading so they will read more and become really good readers? Success here depends more on the teacher than on the materials. I have a few suggestions.

First, enjoy reading yourself. If you don't read much, make a change. Do you think you could help your child build sustained interest in camping or sewing without getting involved yourself? The same goes for reading.

One proven method for encouraging more reading is known as SSR—Sustained Silent Reading. Here is the plan:

1. A special time each day is set aside for silent reading. It should be relatively short—often ten or fifteen minutes—and may be increased with maturity.

2. The child selects a book or article to read. It is to be chosen before the SSR time begins. And switching isn't permitted during the period.

3. You read, too. This is important.

4. No reports are required, and no records are kept.

Keep good books within reach. Occasionally read the first chapter of a book as an enticement. (I will never forget the day my mother polished just one of my shoes.) Make fun trips to the library, and buy books to keep.

Television is the biggest enemy of making reading fun. In fact, for whatever value it has, TV is an enormous threat to mental health, to character development, and indeed to every noble pursuit requiring the time it absorbs. According to Harry F. Walters, by the end of kindergarten the average child has seen 5,000 hours of television![6] That's more time than it takes to get a four-year college degree. While you want your children to develop impulse control, television is teaching them that they should have what they want *now*. While you plan for your children to become loving, caring people, television tells them that dishonesty is funny, that loyalty and purity are only a game, that hatred and the violence it inspires bring satisfaction, and that constant excitement makes life worth living. Television cheats your child out of direct experience with life, it short-circuits creativity and thinking things through, and it essentially eliminates your influence through family togetherness. Although by careful selection an occasional program may be worth watching, the liability of access to a TV set is probably too great for your children who have not yet developed the maturity and judgment of adulthood.

If I haven't convinced you to get rid of your TV set, let me suggest a way to help keep it under control. Instead of arguing with your children and running to turn off objectionable programs all the time, make specific rules. Decide what hours during the week the set may be on and what programs may be watched. Permit each child to suggest one special program each month (or oftener). And require all chores to be done well and schoolwork to be up to date before any TV watching occurs.

Teaching for Comprehension

Poor comprehension may well be the most serious reading handicap in today's society. According to examination results reported by the National Assessment of Educational Progress, students in American schools tend to understand the basic ideas in what they read but don't do as well as they might in seeing the deeper meanings.[7]

Scholars connected with the NAEP describe a four-step model for the comprehension process:

1. Initial comprehension (Read with understanding).

2. Preliminary interpretations (tentatively see the author's idea).

3. Re-examination of the text in the light of these interpretations (look closely to see whether or not the initial idea fits).

4. Extended and documented interpretations (establish the author's total meaning).

Although this process is more than we would expect of a first-grade reader, it is certainly a necessary skill for anyone who expects to achieve serious learning from reading.

If the instructional emphasis favors isolated skills, a child may not learn well to read for meaning. Decoding and word recognition are certainly important, but your child also needs to be able to make sense from and to analyze reading material. Good readers constantly analyze what they read by asking themselves questions. They compare the new information with their own knowledge; identify the main points, relating them to the overall theme; and anticipate what the author might say next.

To help your children develop comprehension skills, encourage them to think about what they read as it relates to what they already know and to other information in the text. Before the reading begins, talk about what your child already knows about the topic and tell him or her that the text will mention something similar. Then, after the reading, discuss the author's ideas. Children can become aware of what they read and they can learn to draw inferences and to make comparisons. In a subsection of the chapter, "Teaching in the home school," I discuss understanding from reading.

Phonics in your program

Next let's consider what we know from research and observation to guide us in our approach to teaching phonics. First, some characteristics of young learners.

They learn informally rather than consciously trying to reach abstract goals. Teachers need to put the important ideas into the fun activities they plan.

Their attention spans are short.

They have a natural curiosity. They love to hear secrets and to play guessing games related to their world.

Knowing makes them feel good.

They set their values by what they see others doing. Role modeling is very important.

From the developmental stages mentioned earlier in this chapter, it's obvious that mature individuals don't read like children do. On rare occasions, you or I might stop to sound out a word, but we certainly read by sight recognition and not phonics. So the question becomes, does phonics help children?

According to Jeanne Chall, who made a careful study of research through 1965 on reading teaching methods, "a code-emphasis method—i.e. one that views beginning reading as essentially different from mature reading and emphasizes learning of the printed code for the spoken language—produces better results, at least up to the third grade."[8] Also the 10th research finding listed in Appendix G supports phonics instruction.

The relationship between spelling and pronunciation in the English language is not very consistent. While it's true that practically any word can be pronounced by phonetic rules if the rules are complex enough, it's also true that most of the exceptions to the general rules are common words. For example: a, again, against, answer, beautiful, been, breakfast, buy, catch, choir, come could, do, does, dumb, eye, friend, girl, gone, have, laugh, money, neighbor, none, of, once, one, only, ought, people, pretty, put, ready, said, says, sew, shoe, some, should, the, their, there, to, two, was, Wednesday, were, where, who, whose, women, and would.

It's interesting to note that many, if not most, children recognize some rather complex words by sight before they are ever taught any phonics. These are usually words that have a special impact on their thinking.

On the positive side, phonics really works. It gets kids to take a close look at words. Spelling and pronunciation become easier because most words are seen to fit patterns. When the structure makes sense, it's easier to remember and build on. Decoding skill builds confidence, and confidence inspires more reading.

In her book, Fact and Fiction About Phonics, Roma Gans helps us put phonics teaching into perspective. She describes a good reading program as one that develops in children: enjoyment of books, stories, news, etc; ability to recognize words in several ways; skill and wisdom in reading choices; and depth of understanding. Then she expresses an important concern:

> The teaching of phonics, in a program of this breadth,
> is absolutely essential. To concentrate on phonics,
> however, even for a period of six to eight weeks, to the

exclusion of the continued challenge of reading for enjoyment is unpalatable educational fare. Such procedure forces a child to dedicate himself to the narrow success of learning word elements, words out of context, and rules, rather than to experience the excitement and rewards to be gained from the whole process of reading.[9]

So phonics training is important, but children do learn in other ways, too, and reading means a lot more than decoding letters into sounds.

Reading with minimal phonics instruction

Children in one of the most difficult New York City school districts, many of whom don't hear English at home, are showing remarkable success in reading.[10] They are part of the Open Sesame project which uses large numbers of ordinary children's books instead of the typical basal readers.

In this method (1) the teacher reads systematically to the children; (2) they are encouraged to read from many library books displayed in the room; (3) activities such as dramatization, discussion and illustrations make the books that are read to them more memorable; (4) key words (at the kindergarten level) are chosen by the children and displayed on cards around the room; and (5)—the most interesting characteristic—phonics is not stressed. It is taught as children ask for help with their writing, and in quick crash courses before taking standardized tests.

I'm not recommending that you throw out your phonics books, and I expect that the children in this project could profit from a little more phonics instruction. But we should realize that this decoding skill isn't necessarily the whole lifeblood of reading ability.

Reading as part of a broader educational view

Reading can't be taught well in isolation from the total language arts program. Writing, spelling, speaking, listening, literature, and grammar along with reading are best learned as they relate to each other. Integration isn't as hard as it might seem. Your structured textbook program might already do this to a degree. To help tie the concepts together, just comment on what you see important about one subject while teaching another—spelling in reading, grammar in literature, writing down spoken words, phonics in spelling, and so on. Then make reading important in studying other subjects, and encourage general learning from reading class.

The key-word method

Two early-grade teachers, Pam Palewicz and Linda Madaras have developed their own way to teach reading. It makes sense to me, although it might take a little more skill than following a textbook. I'm not sure I would depend on it for the whole backbone of a reading program, but it could certainly work for a period of time or for an added help.

The idea in brief involves getting children to learn from words they choose and copy, and stories they tell or write. The plan requires more individualized work with children, but that's the way you teach in home schools anyway. The points or steps which follow have been condensed from the book, *The Alphabet Connection,*[11] and filtered through my thinking:

1. Teaching with the key word plan begins after the alphabet is mostly learned. You ask your child to choose a word for you to write on a card. Work with several words at a time, but don't start them all at once. It would be all right to add more words before all are learned, but not too many. If your child doesn't think of a word, prompt with questions.

2. You will write the words at first. Your skill in printing isn't important, but size is. Make them big.

3. While you are writing the word, sound out the letters.

4. Repeat the word and ask the child to say it. Then go over the letter sounds again.

5. Depending on your child's writing ability, either hold the hand with a finger extended to trace over the letters, or ask her to

trace over the letters with pencil or crayon. Touch and movement are important in teaching young children. If you have delayed the beginning of formal schooling as we discuss elsewhere in this book, muscle coordination won't be a problem.

6. As abilities permit, ask your child to copy the word in space you have left at the bottom of the card.

7. You can ask the child to draw a picture of the word, but not on the word card itself to avoid remembering the word by the picture.

8. Ask your child to tell you a story about the picture. Three to five sentences are enough. You write the story from dictation on the card with the picture. Children won't think of simple words like articles and prepositions when asking for new key words, but they can learn them from seeing the stories on their picture cards.

9. The authors of the program suggest not judging what the child asks you to write in order not to interfere with the learning to read. While avoiding scolding is certainly important, I believe we teach our children more than reading.

10. After the story is copied down, read it back. Your boy or girl will probably hear grammar mistakes as you read. Correct them. If mistakes aren't noticed, you can correct serious ones.

11. Then you can ask your child to look at the story and find all the words that are the same as the key word the story is about. Other words might not be recognized yet.

12. When your boy (or girl) is mature enough, ask him to copy the story word-for-word below the words you wrote on the card.

13. Have your child think of new words. Start new cards and new stories.

14. The stories can be shared with other children or family members as the child begins to read them.

15. Begin reviewing after a few words are on cards. Also review sounds made by letters and letter combinations. Review and add new words about three times a week. If the list gets too long to learn effectively, discuss which less-special words might be eliminated from the ones to be learned.

In thinking over this technique, we need to ask whether it might not take on a more casual approach with children for whom formal reading instruction waits for a little more maturity and natural interest. Then when the child is older, key-word cards won't be apt to play a very big role. The method does sound like fun and might be worth trying a time or two even when using another basic plan.

Choosing what to read

For parents who view education as character development, reading instruction must deal with the question of *what* to read as well as with how. We often lament the evils of television, forgetting that the printed page can produce many of the same effects.

Many parents and educators today seem to feel that our youth should have access to whatever they want to read, and great protests arise whenever parents want certain books removed from school libraries. Christian parents and all concerned parents need to remember that children are a responsibility, that they are by nature dependent, giving us the privilege of guiding their moral as well as their physical development.

Everyone would agree that young readers need material that is interesting, intellectually stimulating, a little challenging, and a model of good writing. But if we recognize that values and attitudes are more important to learn than math and reading, and if we consider relationships to be more important than knowledge, we will want to take a close look at the material we provide for reading practice, to see whether the risk from side effects might outweigh the therapeutic value.

In the next chapter, we look at purposes and dangers of teaching literature, and I will suggest a list of criteria for judging reading material or literature. Instead of creating a dull existence, high standards in reading and viewing lead to deep satisfaction, unshakable mental stability, and lasting happiness.

As you consider what your children should read (and watch, and hear) you may sense the importance of your own reading and television habits. Children learn values from their parents. You can't fake it. If you need to make a change, now is not too soon.

In conclusion

As we stand back and take a wide-angle view of teaching reading, we see several major ideas.

Good reading ability is important. Doing a good teaching job will pay off in later life.

No single teaching technique is a unique solution. Don't get off an a tangent.

Preparation for reading begins long before the child concentrates on words in print.

When it's time to learn, follow an organized program. You don't build a house by browsing through the lumber store. And occasional visits to the library won't likely be enough to develop good readers with a breadth of language skills.

Make reading both a science by teaching specific skills, and an art by making reading fun.

Get rid of the television set, unless you can control it very well.

Teach for comprehension by getting your children to ask questions about what they read.

Integrate reading into other subjects, especially writing and spelling.

Education in its deepest sense is character development. What children read is even more important than how.

Your children's future probably depends more on learning to read than on any other traditional school subject. Do your best, ask for help when you need it, and check your progress every year or so with standardized exams.

17

Teaching literature

To know how to relate to the teaching of literature, we first need to ask what good literature is and why it comes into the curriculum in modern schools.

We might argue that literature is anything that can be read. But what is "good" literature to those who are supposed to know? And why do certain selections find their way into textbooks?

From my observations, three characteristics qualify reading matter as literature worthy of study.

(1) Meaning. A selection must provoke thought. Even if the thought is not serious, the words must do their work well to get classified as literature.

(2) Good writing. Good literature shows excellence in writing skill.

(3) Wide recognition. For writing to be classified as "great" literature its quality must be recognized by many people.

Objectives for studying literature

From these three characteristics of important literature we find three reasons for studying it:

(1) To learn from the thinking of renowned people of the present and past.

(2) To improve self-expression by being exposed to and by analyzing good writing.

(3) To be able to communicate by referring to ideas from commonly known literary works and authors.

The hook

Christian parents are influenced by what the rest of our society considers important for education. We have always heard that Shakespeare and Poe and Emerson and a long list of others were the "greats" of literature. And we believe our kids must learn from these supposedly great men and women. To do otherwise would seem as uncultured as going barefoot to a formal dinner. But if our values are set in the framework of eternity, we recognize that some people whom the world considers great have, in reality, worked against the glory of God and would teach us, directly or by inference, to do the same.

Then what about the purposes for teaching literature? All the authors found in popular school literature for children and youth show at least the first two of the three characteristics I have listed. And it's right that they should. Certainly we want meaningful reading matter. We also should demand the demonstration of good writing skill, and there may even be value in the third objective—an introduction to the authors. But in addition to these criteria, those of us who are looking for wisdom from above for ourselves and our children expect more. We want literature that lifts, that builds character.

Suppose we do recognize some wrong ideas in certain recognized works. Shouldn't we be be able to read for "literary value" even though we disagree with some of the ideas? Can't we read all the famous authors and get the spiritual "more" from our Bibles? Here's the problem: "Good" literature is philosophy skillfully expressed. Writing without significant art and purpose is just not good writing. Whether in a story or an essay or a poem, if it's good literature by the standard of the world, the author writes with power. He drives the message home. He teaches his philosophy. And, although we use different terms for it, philosophy amounts to the spiritual essence at the heart of religion. Philosophy defines values. It decides purpose for life. For this meaning, I look to God as revealed in His Word, and I think you do, too.

Influence

For the Christian, the whole basis of child training rests on the idea of learning through influence (Prov. 22:6; 2 Cor. 3:18; Heb. 12:2). Alexander Pope, sixteenth-century English poet, expressed the problem of evil influence very well:

> Vice is a monster of so frightful mein
> As to be hated needs but to be seen;
> Yet seen too oft, familiar with her face,
> We first endure, then pity, then embrace.*

The Apostle Paul put it in the positive:
> ... whatsoever things are true,
> whatsoever things are honest,
> whatsoever things are just,
> whatsoever things are pure,
> whatsoever things are lovely,
> whatsoever things are of good report;
> if there be any virtue,
>   and if there be any praise,
> think on these things (Phil. 4:8).

As adults, we are influenced by what we see, otherwise there would be no advertising. How much greater then is the power of influence on children who have not developed the ability of discrimination and on youth who are novices at it? Literature which the world considers great, generally has certain enduring qualities. But when laced with distorted values, we teach or study it at great risk.

For the unavoidable evil that surrounds us, we can claim strength from the admonition of Isaiah 33:15, 16:
> He that walketh righteously,
>   ...

that stoppeth his ears form hearing of blood,
and shutteth his eyes from seeing evil;
He shall dwell on high.

Also remember, as parents, that what you feed your own minds opens the door wide for temptation for your children even years later, after they have flown from the family nest.

We are addressing the question of reading matter, but in our world of VCRs and satellite TV, the total mass of sensory input—even private conversation— must stand up to the quality of heaven.

Standards for choosing

Consider the following criteria in deciding what should be read:

(1) *God's character may not be distorted.* It has been Satan's purpose since the beginning of sin to obscure the true character of God. To some he tries to give the idea that God is unjust and selfish, or that He is unmerciful and capricious. Others are led to believe that God doesn't care how they behave or that He really doesn't exist at all, leaving them to be their own gods.

(2) *Any people the reader is led to identify with, whether story characters or authors, must be worthy of emulation.* Flaws in character justified by the author are probably the most dangerous. Consider, for example, the lie which achieves apparent good, or deception to create a laugh.

(3) *Words or phrases that dishonor God's name or His attributes should be avoided.* The major problem in exposing ourselves to profanity is that, by repetition, these emotional expressions become engraved in the thought patterns. Then when the emotion occurs, the words tend to surface.

(4) *The mind must be kept receptive to the impressions of the Holy Spirit.* Prayer and the study of God's Word are the Christian's lifeline. Reading that feeds the appetite for excitement, and stories that lead to a dream world dull the spiritual perceptions and tend to leave the mind indifferent to communion with heaven.

(5) *The emotions and attitudes developed toward other people must lead to respect, sensitivity, valuing human life, and in brief, love.* Too much of what we read and see tends toward hatred, suspicion, prejudice, and the poisoning of vibrant, fulfilling relationships.

(6) *The reader must be left a better person.* Asking what is wrong with a selection is not enough. There must be something right about it before we can expect time and interest to be spent on it.

Then what can be studied?

When you look closely, many famous literary works don't pass the test. (For me, most don't.) Of course, some do. Certain selections from an author may be good while others are objectionable. And many works that aren't famous still teach good value and writing quality.

Of course nothing equals the Scriptures for literary quality in depth of truth. To see them as literature in the secular sense, is good. But when you examine the deeper meaning of God's love letter to us, the words of inspiration become a treasure beyond value.

In the final analysis, "Where is the wise? where is the scribe? where is the disputer of this world? hath not God made foolish the wisdom of this world? . . . He that glorieth, let him glory in the Lord" (1 Cor. 1:20, 31).

18

Teaching writing

You already know why writing skill is important. It's a vital tool for the interchange of ideas necessary for developing human relationships. But beyond communication, writing reflects and reinforces thinking. The ability to write well requires instruction and practice. You can help your children learn this essential skill even as your own ability grows.

In preparing the first and last parts of this chapter, I have leaned heavily on ideas from a brochure available from the National Council of Teachers of English entitled, *How to Help Your Child Become a Better Writer*.[1] Some material—as indicated—is quoted directly; some has been adapted; and some ideas are my own. Five subsections in the middle of the chapter, which show the by-line of Jessica Hulcy, are from her article written for *The Teaching Home*.[2]

Encouragement for writing

To lay the foundation for writing and other communication skills, "Build a climate of words at home." Talk with your child about places you go and things you see. Intelligent discussion of shared experiences helps younger children develop ability in using language.

"Let children see you write often." Write letters to friends and businesses. You might even write stories to be shared with the children. As appropriate, ask their opinions of your writing. If you can, use some of their ideas to improve it. Thus they can see revision as a natural part of writing.

In guiding your children's writing, you help most effectively by getting them to think for themselves. Instead of being a literary critic, help them discover what they want to say. Instead of trying to correct every mistake, be available as a resource for spelling, punctuation and usage. "Rejoice in effort, delight in ideas."

Gifts like pens, pencils, a desk lamp, stationery, and stamps help make writing fun. A booklet for a diary or journal may begin an rewarding experience, especially if it can be kept private. The gift of a dictionary provides spelling help as well as other interesting information about word origins, synonyms and pronunciation. A typewriter—even an old one—is fun for special purposes. And a computer with a word processor can be an important learning tool once keyboard skills are adequate.

Because, with a computer, text can be easily moved around and changed, more of the energy goes into thinking and creating, and less into the mechanical effort of getting words to look good on paper. One unexpected side effect of using the computer or typewriter, however, is getting less practice with handwriting. You will know how to work for a balance. If I had waited for perfect handwriting, I might still be scribbling (or I should say *only* scribbling).

Look for reasons to write

Real purposes make writing (or any other kind of learning) much more interesting. For this kind of opportunity, classroom schools can't match homes. If you are following a textbook or packaged program, look for every chance to substitute activities touching the real world for less realistic ones (with similar objectives) in the book.

One such real-life activity is letter writing. Share appropriate letters you get—especially parts your child might be able to relate to. Ask your friends and relatives to write special letters to your child, or to include notes in letters they write you. Writing is more fun when people respond. Pen pals provide more letter-writing opportunities.

Your child can also write for free and low-cost items. (Check your library for *Freebies* magazine.)

Other writing "jobs" include grocery lists, taking telephone messages and preparing invitation notes.

The greatest writing joy may be seeing your work in print. But selling (or even giving) writing to a publisher is not easy for the vast majority of would-be adult writers. For children, it's usually only a dream. But there's a bright spot in the picture for home schooled children. Ron Brackin edits *Home School Gazette* featuring articles submitted by children (Appendix H). *Hostex News* (Appendix H) and *Wordscape* (P.O. Box 6426, Salt Lake City UT 84106) also publish work from children.

You might also help your children publish their own booklet of poems and stories. My first publishing venture at age 15 or so was on a toy cylinder press using rubber type. I "printed" a sort of family news report and sent it to all the relatives. It even featured the first part of a still-unfinished nature story—all of three or four sentences. Now in the days of photocopy machines, good typewriters, and computers, homemade publishing is easy.

Set aside time by Jessica Hulcy

How do children learn to write? The answer is WRITE, WRITE, WRITE! Practice makes perfect. Just as four weeks of intensive piano practice will not yield an accomplished pianist, so four book reports a year will not produce a writer.

One family I know spends an hour or more each evening writing letters, poetry, short stories, or diary entries.

In our own home school, we set aside large blocks of time each week to compose. Each Friday we devote three hours to writing. This is not a solitary three hours of grinding pencil to paper. We have brainstorming, goal setting, dialoguing, organization strategy, plus exercise breaks to keep the blood flowing to our brains.

Developing good writers, takes a consistent investment of time.

Write from Experience by Jessica Hulcy

Children, and adults as well, write best about firsthand experiences. This is where the hands-on experiences in our KONOS unit study curriculum provide motivation for writing.

It is easier to write about that which we know or have experienced. For example, a paper entitled, "From Fleece to Frock," will flow more easily if a child has visited a sheep farm, bought wool, then carded, spun and weaved it, than if he merely copies the steps out of the encyclopedia.

Have your children write what they know and feel. The more informative, hands-on experiences you provide them, the more their writing will flow.

Know the Standard by Jessica Hulcy

What constitutes good writing? We must know the principles and share them with our children. The rules listed below are part of the generally accepted standard:

1. Use the active voice: *The boy hit the ball.* (active), vs. *The ball was hit by the boy.* (passive)
2. Put statements in the positive form.
3. Use specific, concrete language: *orange* vs. *fruit*
4. Be concise by omitting needless words: *hastily* vs. *in a hasty manner*
5. Use verb tenses consistently.
6. Choose more descriptive nouns and verbs instead of adding a multitude of adverbs and adjectives: *ambled* or *strutted* vs. *walked*
7. Vary your writing by finding similar words in a thesaurus: *quarrel, fight, rift, squabble, feud*
8. Keep related words together: *She saw a stain in the middle of the rug.* vs. *She saw a stain in the rug that was in the middle.*
9. Place emphatic words at the end of the sentence.
10. Use an appropriate mixture of descriptions, explanations, facts, statistics, reasons, and comparisons in each paper.

11. Hang ideas together with conjunctions or by repeating a word from sentence to sentence.
12. Use transitional sentences to bridge the gaps between paragraphs.
13. Follow the natural order of events in the paper.
14. Stick to your subject.
15. Develop your point by using extras such as humor, quotations, questions, and examples.
16. Use a mixture of simple, compound and complex sentences.
17. End your paper with a clincher.

Use Formal and Informal Writing by Jessica Hulcy

Your child needs both informal and formal writing exercises. Informal writing emphasizes the process—the flow of ideas. Formal writing emphasizes the product—both content and form (punctuation, capitalization and spelling).

Informal writing may be looked over for mistakes, but is not rewritten because it is usually for one's own enjoyment. Letters, diaries, inspirations and poems lend themselves to informal writing.

Formal writing, on the other hand, is always edited, revised and recopied, since it is primarily written for an audience. Papers a child would hand in, such as book reports, essays or term papers, would require formal writing. As a child's ability matures, more of his writing will be formal.

Assist with the writing steps by Jessica Hulcy

Frustration can occur when parents send Johnny to the other room to write "a paper," and 30 minutes later find he has two crummy sentences. Good writing does not just happen. It is a three-step process that involves assistance from you.

Step One: The prewriting or rehearsal phase is the most important, yet often neglected, step. Prewriting involves choosing a topic and letting it incubate.

I assign topics for my children's papers on Monday to be written on Friday. They have two days to think about them. On Wednesday I arrange a firsthand experience for them related to the topic. Then two more days of incubation. On Friday they come prepared to talk through or rehearse their paper and to get help with expressing and organizing their ideas.

If too broad a topic has been assigned, choosing pertinent information is difficult. Therefore, make assignments specific. During prewriting, outlines are made, notes are jotted down, brainstorming takes place, and the paper is talked through or even dramatized—whatever helps your child organize his thoughts.

Step Two: Now it's time to write. Writing does not have to be a solitary or even quiet activity. Some writing can take place in groups of children helping each other. A child may hum or rock back and forth as he writes. The rough draft should be exactly that, with frequent stops to read what has been written, seek further parental input, and continue.

If your child gets stuck while composing and begins to despair, help him by taking dictation. Try to help him see his problem. Is it sequencing of events, or problems with sentence structure or what?

Step Three: Editing is the final step. After the paper is written, encourage your child to check his own work to find errors. This is where knowledge of grammar is applied to composition as grammar, punctuation, capitalization and spelling are corrected. Rewording and rephrasing occurs. If necessary, move entire paragraphs around by cutting and taping. During editing, refer the child back to the standards, and help him see specific ways to refine his paper.

More principles for teaching writing

In two sections of Mrs. Hulcy's article not quoted here, she deals with recognizing stages of development in writing skill, and she lists methods appropriate for them. KONOS (the organization offering the curriculum she has helped develop) offers a cassette presentation, *Building a Good Writer.* In Appendix A, we list

KONOS and several other good programs being marketed for home schooling.

You will need more than the ideas I have gathered for this chapter to teach writing beyond the early preparation years. Unless you are following a packaged program or a correspondence course, I suggest you use a language arts or English textbook for general direction.

As I have implied in the chapter on teaching reading, language arts skills aren't learned in isolation. Learning to listen and talk prepares children for both reading and writing as well as for speaking. And these communication skills need to be practiced while studying science, history, math and the other school subjects.

Writing skill develops slowly. The program you use should introduce concepts and activities in progressing complexity. Being sensitive to your child's level of ability, you can adapt your instructional material to his or her needs.

Expect your curriculum to include a wide variety of writing experiences. People learning to write need to practice with different forms (letters, essays, stories, etc.), different purposes (to inform, persuade, describe, etc.) and for a variety of audiences.

Quoting from the NCTE pamphlet: "Check to see if there is continuing contact with the imaginative writing of skilled authors. While it's true that we learn to write by writing, we also learn to write by reading. The works of talented authors should be studied not only for ideas but also for the writing skills involved. Good literature is an essential part of any effective writing program.

"Watch out for the 'grammar trap.' Some people may try to persuade you that a full understanding of English grammar is needed before students can express themselves well. Some knowledge of grammar *is* useful, but too much time spent on the study of grammar steals time from the study of writing."

Keeping your child's writing (or samples of it) in a file folder allows you to assess progress. Also, in case you are questioned by authorities (or relatives) a collection like this shows that your child is really learning. And it's a source of keepsakes for remembering childhood experiences. Date each article.

As your young writer develops, she (or he) may begin pressing the limits of your own competence.[3] Then consider asking someone with advanced ability to mark occasional writing assignments and to discuss them with her (him).

My comments under the subheading, "Feedback," at the end of the chapter, "Teaching in the home school," are particularly appropriate for teaching writing.

In your own response to your child's writing, concentrate more on content and creativity than on technique. Both are important, of course. But if your interest emphasizes the flame, then finding and chopping the wood will have its own purpose.

19

Teaching math

Monroe Morford is the best math teacher I know so I asked him to share some of his wisdom with you. The dialogue which follows was transcribed and edited from a cassette tape we made just for this book. Many people aren't successful in math. Monroe doesn't believe failure is necessary for normally alert people, and I agree. The textbooks you use will give you good ideas about what to teach, but as you "listen" to our discussion, try to learn how to help your child avoid the dead-end math street that has been the final destination for so many people.

An interview on success in mathematics

Morford> The major thrust of what parents need to realize is that they cannot *teach* their children mathematics in the way that that word is usually used. The best they can do is to provide the experiences from which the child will learn. In other words, they can't teach successfully by telling the child, "Now, this is what you are supposed to know." It isn't going to happen. At least not in a beneficial way. Children may remember what they've been told for a day or two, but that is not going to develop mathematics. What parents or teachers must do is provide the materials, the kinds of experiences with which the child may interact, and as a result, add new concepts to his previous understandings.

Wade> What pattern do parents or teachers sometimes use that doesn't result in genuine realistic learning?

M> Most textbooks start out very nicely by developing concepts with groups of items to be counted. Children get the idea that when they see four items that this means four, and that the word four is an abstraction, not of four apples or four oranges or four balls, but an abstraction that relates to all of those things. Then they start building on this. Kindergarten or first grade exercises ask children to draw circles around items or mark every group that has four items in it, for example. And this goes fine on over to a certain point when the children have been shown through these exercises that when they have a group of three and a group of four, then they end up with a group of seven. And this is written down for them: 4 + 3 = 7. Then most teachers just leave all of this concrete experience behind and feel, "Well, the child has seen it once. Now he's supposed to know it."

I think the teacher, and in your situation the parent, must take the position that whenever the child does not come out with the seven having been given the four and the three to add together, that he not be told, "It's seven. Now remember it." This wrong answer is merely a signal to the teacher or the parent that the child has not grasped that reality yet. You must go back and go through the reality again, until the child gets the abstraction established. When he sees four objects and three objects, he must get through to the seven, by whatever mental processes it takes for him to tie them together. In other words, if he can't look at four and three and come through with a short-term seven, there's no point in just telling him the answer. You will then only transfer him over to trying to remember, which is not going to build his understanding.

W> Would you say then that teaching needs to be for the purpose of understanding meaning?

M> All teaching must make sense, and providing practice must go along with explaining. Whenever you recognize that the student is not able to do the exercise—to put into practice what you thought he had learned, go back and provide the realities to go through the learning again.

W> This sounds like what we called new math a few years ago, where the designers of the mathematics curriculum were very theoretically oriented and wanted the children to know the fundamental meanings of mathematics, feeling that that was much more important than all the drill and exercise. They caused a great revolt which is still going on in the back-to-basics movement.

M> Knowing the fundamental meanings was the intent of the modern mathematics concept but it isn't what the movement produced. It produced some very precise mathematical language stuck back into first, second, third, fourth grade which the teachers didn't understand and only gave as more stuff that the kids had to remember rather than as a set of activities through which they were to learn the concrete ideas. That's what went wrong with new math. Many teachers like me were teaching modern mathematics or new math ten years before it got out in books, and are still teaching it today using now the more fundamental—as the word is used—back-to-basics textbooks. We just continue to do what we have always done—to teach kids to look at reality and think and know why.

W> Do you see any danger in the extreme position of the back-to-basics movement?

M> Oh, yes. Because it will merely give the people who have always said drill-drill-drill more chance to beat kids over the head. This will produce in children who have enough determination on their own to find out why, a little faster action. They will come through with a little more precise reactions in their work. This will be true for maybe the top twenty percent of kids who will think in spite of the teachers rather than because of them and will come up with their own reasons why they are able to see it through. And it will also produce at the other end a lot more frustrated kids who are just anti-mathematics because they get totally frustrated with trying to remember what they are supposed to remember but can't. The drill is supposed to be producing more results, and it's producing less for all but this top group. For the majority, it's only more confusion and more frustration.

W> Would you say that too much drill is probably not a good thing—learning number facts and so forth?

M> First, I want to pick apart your words. Too much drill without understanding merely causes frustration. Not enough practice after understanding will leave it not well enough developed. There's nothing wrong with practice. Practice is good. But drill without understanding is debilitating to the mind just like bad food is to the stomach.

W> That makes sense to me.

M> Let's say that an individual has a set of cards—multiplication facts, addition facts, or whatever—and he's holding them up giving the child one or two seconds to respond. Maybe he has a ticker set up and every time it ticks he lays one down and picks the next one up. The person giving the drill may be keeping track by laying them into separate piles—the ones the child knows and the ones he doesn't. Nothing wrong with this. I do it with my grandchildren. I do it regularly with children I'm working with. Whether you are helping develop concepts or giving meaningless drill is determined by what happens when you've gone through and you've given them their second or two seconds or whatever it is that you're allowing them per card. And you have your stacks of the ones that they knew and the ones that they didn't know. Now what do you do afterwards? That's the critical issue.

Suppose you pick up the pile the child didn't know and start going through them again, and the child isn't able to respond within the period of time. You can see him start counting on his fingers, or whatever else you don't want to happen. Now what's your action? If for example, one of these cards you hold up is eight and seven, and the child doesn't know eight and seven are fifteen. So you say, "Fifteen." Nonsense! You haven't helped him. You've only frustrated him. He may remember now that you told him it was fifteen, but that doesn't help. It only creates more fear and frustration. He's going to forget it again next time.

W> All right, what would you do instead?

M> Instead, I would go back to whatever basic concept I had been using with the child to help him gain a reality. Up to ten probably you deal with looking at objects and counting them up. The child who can conceptualize combinations up to ten, will do so through some reality handling of the situation. When you get above ten, he's got to move to some kind of an abstraction or else count fingers. And thereby, he must move into a two-step process of some sort. If you're back at the three-and-four stage, you lay down again the three and the four and let him look at them and count them up and establish whatever reality he makes of it. This is something you can't establish for him, although you may help him a little bit.

If, for example, you know he knows what five is—he can see five all right without having to count it up—then maybe you take one of the three and stick it over with the four, completing a five and leaving the two from the three. Then with the two and five he comes to the seven. This is one way of helping him establish his reality of whatever the problem is. In the end, he will probably do it on his own, because most children do. The reality situations up through ten they figure out some way in their own little minds—putting things together that they understand, and it comes through because they can see it.

But now, let's go back up to the eight-and-seven situation. Instead of saying "The answer is fifteen," you ask the child, "How many more do you need with the eight to finish up a ten?" He will say "two more." All right, where are you going to get that two more? From the seven. OK, take the two from the seven and what's left? Five. What does that make? He'll come up with the fifteen.

If you feel he didn't follow that through too well, maybe you want to go back and ask him the series of questions over again. If he lets this turn around in his mind three or four times, he now has a reality in his mind, so the next time he sees seven and eight his mind takes that cycle, in maybe a second and a half. The next time he does it, it may take three-quarters of a second. The next time it happens in a tenth of a second. In other words, after several cycles of that set of thinking he comes out with it as though he had memorized it. But he actually has built up a mental pattern that works for him to develop it.

W> Would you say that some of the number combinations, for example, the ten and the five, are more easily conceived and therefore remembered than other number combinations such as the seven and the eight.

M> Oh, yes. It always is, because the child has ten fingers, five on each hand. He has gotten used to that; that's a reality with him. He doesn't have any trouble with ten and five making fifteen because he's done that with his own fingers.

W> Of course, he's counted by tens. That's the same as counting by one's except with the zeros.

M> Exactly. And this is, of course, what he deals with. These are the realities. And you don't have him memorize ten, twenty, thirty, forty. You have him look at it and get a connection between the words of two and twenty, three and thirty, four and forty, and let him build up his own meaning of counting by tens.

W> Then are you saying that, because some number combinations are more easily understood and remembered than others, we might best teach those more complicated number combinations by relating them to the simpler ones?

M> Always. This is the whole issue, I think, in mathematics instruction, if you want to call it that—carrying out some kind of experience that a child grows from. And to me, you see, this is where teaching methods are quite different. Some people—in fact, most people—would say when you're teaching them you tell them what the answers are and they're supposed to remember. Or you tell them how they're supposed to think. Mathematics instruction is not telling them how they're supposed to think, but finding out what they do think and helping them tie in new ideas. You may choose what you supply to them as the next thought of development so that it will lead them into patterns of thought that you want, but you don't tell them, "Now this is the way you think." Because then you have started taking them out of reality again and told them, "Now you do it my way." You've got to lead them if you want them to do it your way; you've got to lead them to right understanding from where they are through some logical thought of their own.

If the teacher does not understand the child's physical and emotional maturity level, he may try to toss ideas to the child that are like his own, but the child may not yet be ready to work with them. So knowing the child's viewpoint is very important in tying new learning to already established reality.

This is where the whole idea of the psychological development that Piaget's research has shown us, fits in. You must recognize developmental levels as important steps and not try to jump ahead of them with your instruction.

Up to this point, early learning—learning number combinations—basically is all we've talked about. But the same idea carries on throughout. Any kind of experience the parent or teacher provides for the child to do should be connected with some kind of reality. For example, as we move on, instead of just saying to the child, three times four is four three's added together or three four's added together, you give him pennies or dimes or something else in a pile on the table. Then you move out four, then four more, and four more beside them, thereby having a group of twelve in the combination of three groups of four. Then moving on through other multiplication facts he continually repeats this idea until, whenever he sees any two numbers multiplied together, he immediately thinks of them in terms of groups. He won't be working through this concept of adding groups his whole life, but he will make the move over to simply seeing the numbers.

W> It seems like much of mathematics is learning to do things easier. Perhaps if we try to help our children see math as fun ways to achieve easier results, that might help them see why it's important. For example, in multiplying four times three, it's a lot quicker to add by groups of three's than it is to count to twelve.

M> Before the child goes, for example, to multiplying seven times three, he has probably gone through the experiences of learning to add groups. Let's say he cannot remember three times seven but knows that three times four is twelve. And he knows that three and four are seven. And so his seven can be broken up into a three and a four. Then he can see how three times three is nine and three times four is twelve. Adding the nine to the twelve gets the twenty-one.

Now to the person who is saying, But that's a lot of work, why not just know that three times seven is twenty-one, I agree at the end result. But in the growing experience that going through those steps of thought is building up what I call electrical circuits in the brain. This is programming the computer so that it will do it instantaneously for him at a later point. And sure, that takes longer to go through than it does to tell him that three times seven is twenty-one. But, having that experience several times establishes a circuit in his brain which works for him. Many children, just counting by threes adding three to each number in their minds as they go along, will automatically build these electric circuits.

So the next day when you say to a child with this background, "What's three times seven?" his eyes roll a second and his mind retraces that counting. He doesn't go through now and count up, three, six, nine, twelve and so forth and add each time to do it. His mind established a pattern of thinking the previous day, and he says, "Twenty-one." He doesn't remember in the sense that we usually use that word, pulling it out of memory from having been told. His mind retraced the pattern of thinking and came out with the result. The child who has not established that kind of thinking doesn't have a memory pattern to turn to.

W> I think in my own experience, I understood the concept of what multiplying meant having seen it in some rudimentary examples such as three times four. Then I extended that and took the more complex combinations for granted and memorized them.

M> Well, I don't think you actually memorized them. I think, in your play time or whatever else as a child, your mind went back through those things and you just established those realities for yourself. The teacher didn't have to do it. In other words, people who have developed their mental capability just do these kinds of things. We plan our teaching assuming that everybody functions like these individuals who have had basic understanding built up for them.

My main point here is, everybody doesn't function like that. Some get to a certain level, and the pattern breaks. We keep teaching, assuming growth is going on, but it isn't. When we discover a problem we have to look for the point where learning stopped. As long as the child is moving on his own, fine, just let him grow. Keep tossing out new ideas for him to think about. But as soon as you see he isn't grasping an idea, that he's striving to pull it from somewhere because he's supposed to, this should be your signal to stop. Move back for him, trying to find out where his reality or clear understanding actually is and where you can tie in to begin building up the structure of understanding you assumed he had.

Of course, encourage him to make these realities all along. Suggest to him, for example, that maybe while he's going somewhere today he can look around at windows of a building and count them trying to see groups of two or groups of three, so he can begin to see certain reality patterns that you are trying to help him build.

W> Maybe we should bring in a point of how people learn. It's very possible for a person to understand something superficially—just understand it without having it internalized so that he thinks, yes, it looks reasonable. If the teacher doesn't recognize this difference between superficial assent to the reasonableness of a concept and understanding the concept well enough to be able to explain it, he could misjudge what learning is taking place. When the child says, "Yes, I understand," we are tempted to move quickly on to something else without going over the idea or coming back to it enough to establish it well.

M> An important thought in this is that instead of asking the child, for example, to go back to the multiplication tables when he doesn't remember that six times seven is forty-two you can say, "Well, how do you think?" Don't ask him what's six times seven again. You just found out he doesn't know. Or maybe even after you told him it's forty-two, you turn around and ask him to see now if he remembers two minutes later. That is not helping the mental patterns. Ask him how he could get at six times seven. Let him verbalize to you what he understands. And if he can't come up with any logical thought process, then you know you're certainly in the dark to tell him what the answer is. He needs to come up with a way to work toward it. You've got to go back and help him build the pattern over again. Don't tell him what the pattern is, but have him build it. Because as soon as he's built it himself, even though he doesn't realize it, he will have a much better learning experience.

It's the teacher's job to seek real things in the student's daily experience that can be handled, drawn and seen to which new ideas may be attached. For example, scores in a game are ideal for developing the concept of positive and negative numbers. Pick a game that your children know how to play and that has situations where they lose points for doing something wrong and can even "go in the hole" if they do wrong things often enough in comparison to doing right things. Then start watching the score. You gain four points this time; next time you gain three points; next time you lose five. Where are you? They know how to add up those scores. They have experienced it in their reality development; and when the idea of negative and positive numbers is tied to that game reality, they have no trouble remembering what to do with figures on paper.

W> Would you like to talk about asking questions?

M> Well, only to re-emphasize that, as far as possible, to help a child with a problem he can't attack you should use leading questions. You can ask, "What is it talking about? What have we done with that before? Can you make any sense out of the problem situation you're seeing?" So that rather than telling him what's going on or asking him to give specific answers to a problem, try helping him relate to his own thinking process so that he can conclude what he's supposed to do. Of course, I think this is important for any subject, not just for mathematics.

Going on then to another idea, it's very important that the teacher realize the sequence of topics which builds the structure of mathematics. When, for example, a child doesn't know the multiplication facts, you should question whether or not he knows the background items required to get them. You realize that before you can multiply, you have to know how to add. Before you can divide, you must understand the concepts of multiplication, and you must be able to reverse that concept. The best test to find out whether a child knows his multiplication facts is to ask him to tell you what possible numbers he could multiply together to get a certain number. For example, "What numbers would you multiply to get thirty-six?" Of course, the child should be able to come up with six times six, four times nine, two times eighteen—not immediately, but with some dwelling on the idea. He arrived at the fact that thirty-six was the result of multiplying four times nine. If he can do this throughout the multiplication tables, then you can be very confident that he knows his multiplication facts, and furthermore, that he now is ready to do division.

W> Then you can say, given thirty-six, if two is one of the numbers, what's the other one?

M> Then he is ready. Then division makes sense to him. He has no problem knowing what he is doing or why he is doing it. And when you go to fractions, if division has not been established as meaningful, then to talk about dividing by four or about finding a quarter of something won't make sense either. Or it will make sense only as far as he can mechanically cut up a whole into equal parts. A child can usually look at a thing and divide it up into six parts and so he can handle one-sixth. But when it comes to combining that one-sixth with two-thirds, unless he has this concept of division as being a dividing up into parts and then taking a certain number of those parts to formulate a fraction, there's no hope that the fractions are going to work correctly for him. The concept that division comes out of multiplication must be understood.

W> What part to you think that frustration has in math learning disabilities?

M> Frustration is probably ninety-nine percent of everybody's problems in mathematics. It's the frustration of not being able to remember and not having any way to go back and build.

W> Do you think perhaps frustration leads to a desire to avoid the topic in order to avoid some of the problems expected?

M> All human beings are animals biologically, and we respond as animals except as we consciously decide to do otherwise. We know from research on animal learning or animal deterrence, that desire to achieve a goal is completely canceled by frustration. The quickest way to stop a rat from wanting to run a maze is to formulate some kind of frustration in the maze. If he's frustrated, he will stop trying, even though he's half starving to death. Learning is the same. A person may want very much to learn, but he won't have the courage to get at it unless the frustrations can be eliminated.

Of course, my point of view is that anything not meaningful that you try to remember only frustrates because it immediately builds fears that you will forget. Fear causes frustration and frustration creates more fear and more desire to not come in contact with the subject.

Building foundations

I would like to add just a few thoughts to the discussion with Monroe Morford. First, on building foundations. In other chapters I have written about not pushing formal learning too early. This advice is certainly true in teaching mathematics. If you have time, read about how the work of Piaget applies to learning math, but if you don't have time, just remember to be sensitive. If your child isn't understanding, and he or she is under eight years old, slow down. Young brains don't find it easy, for example, to see how something can change shape and still have the same total value, and they can't easily imagine abstract things. Serious abstract study such as is required for algebra is difficult before the adolescent years.

Physical objects are important. Kids need to touch, see, count and move around. One of the best ways to teach place value (the concept that digits are worth more the farther they are to the left in a number) is with money. Get a variety of coins. The pennies, dimes and dollars will show that one is worth ten of another. You can make up the exercises. For example, looking through a catalog and laying out the money necessary to purchase some treasured item is both fun and educational. You can also buy or make sticks for teaching place value and understanding quantities. Get lots of them. They can be bundled in tens and in hundreds, or used to explain other ideas.

Visit a school supply store or look through educational materials catalogs to get other ideas. See the appendix in this book.

Math deficiencies found in home educated children

Standardized exams have shown deficiencies in math computational skills for a significant number of Washington home schooled children.[1] More research is needed to know why, but I have two ideas to suggest:

An advantage often claimed for teaching children at home is that your children (always the brightest, of course) don't have to sit and be bored while the teacher drills and repeats to get the rest of the dumb class to catch on. As Monroe has told us, drill without understanding is debilitating, but it does take practice (with understanding) to get the idea nailed down. In my teaching and learning experience, knowing how to work a problem doesn't mean it's safe to go on. Computation skills just take more practice than seems necessary.

The other thought on avoiding this weakness involves the unit or project method of teaching. We talk about it elsewhere in these pages. Keeping track of expenses and profits in a home business is fine, but it's not enough to assure the broad foundation in math experiences needed for continued study and efficient living. Of course, in the natural, study-by-impulse plan, who would expect to do pages of just plain old problems?

Problem solving

In 1980 the National Council for Teachers of Mathematics issued what they called *Agenda for Action; Recommendations for School Mathematics in the 1980s.*[2] (Shortly after this book gets into print, the NCTM will have generated another such list which I rather expect will reflect many of the same concerns.) Two points from this list are worth noting because they bring out needs you will want to be alert to in teaching your children to be ready for the world today and tomorrow. The first deals with problem solving and the second with computers.

Problem solving is at the top of the NCTM list. Even kids who can accurately manipulate figures in long division and fraction exercises, often don't get to first base with simple word problems. Let's face it. Our society (mostly though TV) teaches kids to be absorbers more than thinkers.

One thing you can do is to be sure concepts are understood all along. To line up figures in certain ways and to put digits in various places may get the answer, but the "why" is important, too, as Monroe Morford told us. When word problems come in your textbook, go through them slowly enough for your child to make sense out of what you do. Children are tempted to feel (sometimes by the way we teach them) that when they get the result of their calculation, they have somehow achieved success in math. Just remember to press the idea that knowing why is even more important than getting the right answer.

I read an article not long ago by someone who felt that word problems were irrelevant. You may wish your teacher had thought so, too. "If the stagecoach leaves Mosquito Junction at 4 p.m. going 28 km/hr, and . . . ." Who cares how long it took to catch up with the wagon train? And stage coach drivers didn't know about kilometers, anyway! Well, maybe there are some magic new ways to learn how to make numbers work for you in complex situations, but I don't know what they are. Figuring out costs and quantities for lemonade your child is really going to make is an excellent learning experience. Home life, however, just doesn't happen to provide for exercising some of the abstract thinking or the repeated application that apparently builds continuing competence in math.

I should qualify my concerns. Any time you can find a good live situation for practicing math, by all means put it to work for you. It will be more appealing and better remembered than the book problems. Just don't imagine that you can toss the book out the window unless you are sure you have taught and reinforced all the skills needed for a good mathematical foundation.

Perhaps even more important than learning mathematical processes which certain word problems teach, is developing skills for tackling complex situations—for analyzing them and using what is known to find out what isn't.

Following are steps in the logical process of solving word problems. As you can see, they are more appropriate for upper grades or high school. If your concern is lower grades, however, study it anyway. Understanding the principles yourself will help you get the right approach to guiding your child. Not everyone will use this same attack. Sometimes steps can be skipped. But seeing a sensible plan will help you help your child conquer word problems.

1. Understand the situation without much concern at first for the numbers.

2. Identify the question. Know what you are looking for.

3. Think backwards if the problem is very complex. Remembering what you are looking for, ask yourself what you would need to know to find that answer. Then look at your problem again to see what information you actually have.

4. If some of the needed information is missing, see if you have other facts that would, in an added step, lead to the missing information for the basic solution.

5. If you are in a "blind alley," back up and look at your question again. Does the given information prompt you to think of a different way to get to your answer?

6. Draw a sketch of the situation. This can help you visualize relationships in the problem.

7. If you think you have found a plan for solving your problem but aren't too sure, try it using very simple numbers—numbers you can think through to a solution without getting bogged down in the calculations. If your process works, you likely have a good plan.

8. Carry out your plan, with careful attention to calculation accuracy.

9. Compare your solution with the "question." Is what you came up with actually what was requested in the problem? Have you used the correct units of measure to express your answer?

10. Examine the numerical value of your solution. Does it make sense in terms of the reality of the problem situation?

11. If you can, use a check method to verify your solution.

Computers

First let's talk about calculators. They are really special-purpose computers. And they are now a permanent part of our world. Kids should know how to use them, but that doesn't take long. Although your children may have less need than your generation has for pencil-and-paper calculation, that skill is still important. Your children won't learn it if they use calculators all the time. You need a firm policy. I suggest you permit calculators to check exercises already worked (with mistakes corrected by hand) and whenever you or the textbook specifically calls for them.

Computers are becoming more prevalent and less expensive. They aren't taking the place of books and they won't. Your child will need to know something about them to face the world he or she is preparing for. "Computer literacy" is a topic which falls into the school subject category of math. Newer textbooks will deal with it. If yours doesn't, get some information from your library or a local bookstore or from a computer store. I won't try to tell you about them here except to say that most information you will run across will come under categories of (1) knowing what they can and can't do, (2) knowing how to operate them, and (3) knowing how to program them. The first two aren't difficult to know something about. The third—programming or telling them how to think—although not as important as the first two, is worth adding to your curriculum. Only a few people in our society need to be experts in this area, but many need to know enough to work intelligently with a programmer and to write simple programs or to make minor modifications.

As teaching instruments, I don't believe computers will take over the job of textbooks, although we are beginning to see some real changes. More and better software is appearing. For most home schools, however, learning by computer is still somewhat limited by its expense.

One lady told me how excited she was about home schooling. She felt that she would just get a computer to do the teaching while she went off to work! Sorry, it doesn't work that way. Even if finances aren't a consideration, computers can teach efficiently only a fraction of what kids need. If you have access to a computer and the appropriate software (programs) by all means use them, but view them as a supplement to your main program.

A computer could be an asset to your home school in several ways:

Teaching programs in many areas (not just math) provide interaction and feedback.

First hand experience would better prepare your child to face the world which uses computers extensively.

\# Word processing software (prepared instructions you can feed into your computer to tell it how to receive and handle words) is a convenient writing tool as long as your child still has ample practice in handwriting neatness. A spelling checker (now a part of the word processing package) may also teach if used conscientiously. The one I use has an option for making a record of which words were misspelled.

\# Computer programming (the writing of coded instructions to tell your computer how to manipulate information you will give it) is an interesting challenge and provides practice for organized, logical thinking.

\# The novelty of thought interaction with a machine brings added interest to your home school.

Computer games may subtract more than they can add to your child's education. Consider the hours they absorb and what most of them teach about kindness to others. I'm not making a blanket condemnation but would like to encourage you to think it through.

Goals for teaching mathematics

Your textbook series will list appropriate expectations for your teaching. Take time to look at them and to discuss them with your students. Mathematics is important for several of the general goals I list elsewhere in this book. I just want to point out that although math appears to be the least likely subject for expecting moral values goals, there are several. Don't forget to tie them into your teaching. I would list: honesty, accuracy, respect for property (your own, other people's and God's), a sense of the value of time, and responsibility for providing and using resources wisely.

We referred earlier to recommendations for mathematics learning. Here is the whole list of skill areas important in the elementary school years: problem solving; applying mathematics in everyday situations; alertness to the reasonableness of results; estimation and approximation; appropriate computational skills; geometry; measurement; reading, interpreting, and constructing tables, charts and graphs; using mathematics to predict; and computer literacy.

20

Teaching science

Children in our modern society face a mostly artificial environment—from Big Bird and cartoons, to junk food, to competitive sports. Science can open the door to the real world, and kids usually enjoy the experience.

My older son, Tim, was five or six when I took him down into the mechanic's pit where I had been changing the oil in our car in Africa. We talked about how the engine turned the drive shaft which turned the axle to make the wheels go around. We traced the path of the exhaust and talked about what the muffler did. He was totally interested, and absorbed more than I thought he would.

What is Science?

Science is observing and explaining nature. It's looking for interesting situations and events, then trying to explain cause-and-effect relationships or checking out someone else's explanations.

We study science as *process* and *content*. Process describes the ways of exploring science. Content tends more to be the facts and explanations—the end results of the process. From process, we learn how to think. Content is what we think about.

The process skills are: observing (measuring, testing); interpreting (reading between lines, explaining); classifying (organizing, comparing); communicating (getting and giving information, using numbers to express and analyze values); and predicting (explaining, making theories, testing hypotheses, judging importance).

The content part of science is most obviously descriptions of objects—maybe the different kinds of blood cells or the metals that can be easily magnetized. It also includes purpose and relationships—What do the white blood cells do in the body? Where do they come from?

Then considering the process aspect, we see that the science class has more to offer than information. The process skills are important for perceptive thinking. They are ways to learn and understand the facts of science, they are skills used by the scientist, and they provide skills for relating to knowledge outside the area of science.

Why science belongs in your home school

A study of science can help develop attitudes of enjoying and conserving earth's natural resources, and a respect for the One who provides them for our happiness. In studying nature we see the hand that made and guides all things. We already mentioned the importance of developing rational thought processes. Knowledge is important, too. Knowledge includes specifics, processes, concepts, generalizations and unifying principles.

Deciding what to teach

You can teach smorgasbord style, just bringing in interesting things whenever you find them, but after the preschool or early grades I recommend using textbooks. Get ones you like. If evolutionary concepts are objectionable to you, look for them before making your choice. Then use your books as a general guide, but don't feel you need to cover everything. Add learning from field trips and explore questions that come up. Invite people with knowledge in science areas to come in.

The study of science content (natural science, not social science) may be divided into the general areas of: (a) life science or biology (botany, zoology and health), (b) physical science (chemistry and physics), (c) earth science (geology and weather) and (d) astronomy.

The process part of science is more prominent in the elementary grades. Beginning at the junior high level, the laboratory and special exercises cover process skills without identifying them particularly.

Through the sixth grade, textbooks are generally divided into units featuring topics from the various general areas. Often the three junior high years will cover the areas of life science, physical science, and earth science; although biology sometimes comes into grade 9. Students not headed for college often take only "general science." Physics and chemistry are usually electives in the senior high years.

How to teach science

We have already suggested using textbooks as resources and for part of what you cover. As a busy teacher, you won't have as much time as you would like for adventures such as finding bird's nests. But do make science more than reading the chapter and answering the questions at the end.

Kids enjoy laboratory time. For elementary school, this is much simpler than what you might remember from your high school or college chemistry class. Your textbooks will give you ideas. Don't try to perform every experiment suggested. Just have your young scholar help you pick a few that seem especially interesting. You may have to buy a candle or a magnet, but most experiments won't use exotic equipment. And remember that labs are for exploring. Refrain from explaining too much. Ask leading questions. Direct your child to where to find the answers.

Projects are worthwhile if they don't run away with too much time. Help guide their design to avoid unproductive busywork. Plan to have your child participate in a science fair if a nearby school is having one.

News magazines include a science section. Add appropriate reports to your study sources. Consider subscribing to a science periodical published especially for schools.

Field trips are great for teaching science. We discuss them in the chapter entitled "Resources."

Science for preschoolers

Small children are naturally curious. Teaching them science means providing things to investigate and asking questions to keep them from wandering off too quickly. For instance, where do ants go? what happens to ice when it melts? Go for nature walks and watch for interesting things. Find nature books in the library. Your older children will like the nature adventures, too. They can help plan them.

Object lessons

Jesus, the master teacher, used parables effectively for adult audiences. Spiritual truths were associated with the common things in nature—sheep, weeds, grapevines, flowers, even the weather. Later as the people saw the objects again, the lessons would come back to their minds. As you work with your children, be alert to opportunities to draw parallels between nature and life principles. For example, think what might be taught from an experience with poison oak or poison ivy considering the delay between contact and reaction. Such lessons don't require long discourses, just a sincere comment at the right time. Your child, if old enough, will enjoy discovering object lessons. You can discuss them together.

Success

You don't need to know all about science to be a good science teacher, although preparation is certainly recommended. The most important way to get kids to learn is to get them interested. For them to be interested in a topic, you must be, and you must show interest in their discoveries and projects.

21

Teaching social studies

If we define education as preparation for life, then social science education is that part of the preparation involving an understanding of human relationships. For example, consider what is studied in several of the major social science branches: history—the development of civilization; government—the process of control and cooperation of social groups; economics—exchange of goods and services; and geography—how people relate to the land.

Social science education in the elementary and secondary schools is called "social studies." The object is to expand children's understanding of how people live and relate to each other. It also lays the groundwork for continued study in the general knowledge area of the social sciences.

To the extent that teaching social studies helps prepare our children to resolve tension and misunderstanding in our troubled world, its value is obvious. And for those who feel a responsibility to share the Christian's good news with all the world, this area of study is even more important.

Standardized tests cannot reliably measure grade-level learning progress in social studies for lower and middle grades and, therefore, are not used much in this subject as an indication of overall scholastic achievement. This is because values (important learning for social studies) aren't measured with pencil and paper, and because understanding the concepts of the subject depends very little on sequence and thus not on grade level. Therefore, the fact that key testing for achievement focuses on math and language arts, does not imply that social studies is unimportant.

In this chapter we will (1) look at the development and rationale for the modern social studies curriculum, (2) discuss how you might plan for this area of learning in your home school, (3) consider the use of resources, and (4) express concern about some recent approaches to teaching social studies.

We discuss more directly preparing children for good social behavior in the chapter, "Social Development."

The social studies curriculum

Traditionally, schools have taught geography as lists of cities, countries, mountain ranges, rivers, climates, exports and stereotypes of how people of other cultures lived and dressed. History has been mostly key people, wars and dates to relate them. By request of legislatures, classes in government were added to geography and history.

Not many years ago (in the 1950's and early 1960's) the "new social studies" took over—or tried to take over—with the purpose of teaching concepts instead of disconnected facts. Of course, concepts had always been important, but few teachers or textbook authors had seen beyond the easily measured memorization of names and places.

The new course material was prompted by ivory-tower experts in the various social science disciplines and turned out to be a little tough and also seemed irrelevant for many elementary school kids.

Now, since the late '60's, educators have gone a step further by teaching how to use the basic concepts. Thus, the end purpose of social studies has become decision making. Discrimination, drug abuse, crime and war are irrational. The new emphasis promised to help oncoming generations use better judgment. Although "perfect" social studies teaching won't bring world peace, the goal of learning to make rational decisions based on understanding is certainly better, in my opinion, than the traditional emphasis.

Decision making has meaning only in the context of concepts; and concepts are derived from facts. To take it a step further, understanding factual information requires certain skills. In social studies, these skills are: finding information in books, distinguishing between reality and opinion, interpreting maps, and so on. Putting all this together, you can see that to reach the goal of rational, informed decision making involving societal issues, our curriculum needs (a) instruction for developing information skills, (b) key facts of what is and what was, (c) concepts that make sense from the facts, and finally, (d) guidance in forming rational decisions by applying a set of values to the facts and concepts.

Of course, all this is a big order—too much to master in the first six or eight or twelve years of school. But by tipping the balance early toward concepts and skills, the foundation is hopefully set for the learners to apply information wisely in their life roles as members of family, business and social groups and as responsible citizens.

The study sequence in U. S. schools

The general areas covered in grades one, two, five and eight are usually the same across the country. We will list them and fill in with a typical pattern for the others.

Kindergarten: Self-discovery, people who help us, health habits. (Similar to first grade.)

First grade: Family, school, other cultures, safety, courtesy.

Second grade: The neighborhood, the local environment.

Third grade: The community, cities, business and industry, pioneers.

Fourth grade: State government and history, regional geography, world cultures.

Fifth grade: The United States: history (including recent history), geography, culture (including cultural problems), relating to neighboring countries.

Sixth grade: The Western or Eastern Hemisphere. Usually selected examples and then generalizations.

Seventh grade: The hemisphere not taught in the sixth grade or, more likely, world culture, world geography and nation groups.

Eighth grade: U. S. history.

Ninth or tenth grade: World history.
Eleventh grade: U. S. history.
Twelfth grade: U. S. government.

Social studies in your home school

I've sketched the usual curriculum approach and sequence of topics for teaching social studies, not because you have to do the same things in your own program, but rather to let you see what seems important to professional educators, and to broaden your consideration of goals you will want to keep in mind as you teach from day to day.

If your program is Christian oriented, you will probably feel that the religion class provides a better framework for the majority of your study of attitudes toward people and principles for decision making. Later in this chapter when we discuss values and moral development, you may form more opinions along this line.

As I think about the whole curriculum for the elementary school, I feel that social studies would need less emphasis than some other subjects. It might best be "taught" informally for the first several grades. In fact, even the typical classroom program is very low key for the early years. I suggest you center your teaching through grade two or three on experiences like field trips, learning to relate to relatives and friends, and discussion. I do feel you need to plan, actually spend purposeful time, and keep a careful record. Your child will enjoy thinking of it as "school" but formal evaluation beyond progress notes in your log book would seem unnecessary.

By planning, I mean schedule a field trip or cultural television program every week or so on a somewhat regular basis. Then after each event, sit down and discuss it. A scrap book, souvenirs, or drawings could help make the experiences more meaningful. Read about field trips in the chapter on educational resources, and leaf through some lower grade textbooks to get more ideas of what to do.

After these early informal years, I suggest you follow a textbook or planned program but actively look for reasons to deviate from it.

The reasons might relate to: (1) Unique characteristics of your community (a military base, a tourist town, a foreign country), especially if you are apt to move away. (2) Special needs of your child. (A death in the family could prompt a study of dying.) (3) Opportunities that arise. (Dad may need to attend meetings where your child could learn new things.) (4) Interests that develop. (An uncle may be elected judge, or friends may leave for mission service.) If you expect to omit part of a supervised program, you will want to remember to arrange for the substitution.

Planning a unit on a special topic

Exploring a topic away from the path marked out by your textbook or guided learning program could turn out to be of little value unless you plan and follow through carefully. Work with your student to develop a project or unit plan. Consider including the following elements:

A *title* to express the general topic or the initial point of interest. Your title might be the last part of the plan to be finalized.

Questions to be answered. Some preliminary investigation may help you know what you might want as outcomes. Questions could be added or dropped as work progresses.

Skills to be developed.

Attitudes expected to emerge or be reinforced.

Resources you expect to be used.

A brief description of the planned *culminating activity*. This will probably be a simple written report, but could instead be a slide show, a play, a map, a lecture or whatever seems appropriate. Some written record is especially important if there is a chance it may be needed to substantiate the validity of your home school.

An expected *completion time*. Be realistic.

An *evaluation,* particularly if attendance officials are breathing down your neck. Even if they aren't, your child will appreciate your appraisal, and expecting it will help him or her see the project as serious learning. Your evaluation may be very brief. It could be a note on the student report mentioning how well objectives (expressed as questions, skills and attitudes) were met and recognizing good work in particular areas.

Current events

A study of current events could add a little life to your social studies program. But as you can probably imagine, world watching without purposes in mind could easily become an exercise in gathering information pack rat style.

To make current events provide valuable learning, here are several possible outcomes to keep in mind:

★ Issues and actions in history become more meaningful when related to similar situations today.

★ Knowing what kinds of information the media offers and how to find them, opens channels for future learning.

★ Careful guidance can bring a young learner a better perception of bias and objectivity in reporting. Ego-supported opinions, financial reward, political pressure and cultural background can be seen to affect all kinds of information provided for the public.

★ The process of government operation can be illustrated by noting media reports of current activities.

★ Variables that influence the ever-changing atmosphere of our society could be identified. These might include supply and demand, group or individual self-interest, protection of freedom, oppression from the strength of numbers of other sources of power, withholding or distorting information, possession and allocation of natural and financial resources, and so on.

★ Value judgment may be practiced.

★ Following a particular story over a period of time helps clarify the complex factors that influence human action.

Of course, the media also provides interesting information in areas other than social studies. You can think of ways all the subjects of the curriculum could be reinforced with attention to selected media excerpts. Especially consider how news events and reports can give meaning to your spiritual instruction by illustrating

Bible prophecy, interaction between good and evil, and principles of justice and mercy.

I really haven't listed these possible outcomes to impress you with the complexity of teaching. The idea is that you should plan for meaning and purpose in your use of media reports. You probably won't use this list as a starting point. I see current events more as resources to reinforce important ideas from your teaching plan than as a separate subject to be studied. As concepts come up in your school program, look for reports of recent events to reinforce them. Occasionally you may also want to discuss principles not related to what you are currently studying when news items illustrate important lessons especially well.

In addition to radio, TV, newspapers and news magazines, several current events sources prepare material specifically for school use. World News of the Week is a poster-type publication dealing with a range of topics including: people, issues, careers, arts, science and recreation. Both Scholastic and Xerox publish weekly magazines for social studies (and for other subjects). See the bibliography for addresses. New York Times and Newsweek also publish materials for school use (although the Newsweek materials may be unsuitable for lower grades).

Notes of caution:

★   Being true doesn't make an event worthy of contemplation. Be selective. Give priority to character development. Material published for schools would be less objectionable than the public media in this respect.

★   Current events may sometimes offer lessons of more importance than some of your regular program. Just keep your objectives in mind, and don't let essentials get crowded out.

★   Media sources alone cannot provide the structure of fundamental concepts you would expect to find in social studies curriculum materials published for school use. In other words, a subscription to a news magazine would hardly constitute a social studies program.

Other resources

In both my chapter on educational resources and Margaret Savage's "headpecker" chapter, you will find lists of resource suggestions. More could be added. As you consider a particular concept you want to teach, think also about where you might go to learn more about it.

If decision making is important in your curriculum as I have suggested, then seeing the process in action on real issues would be valuable. You could visit a legislative assembly or a city council meeting. Attendance at a public hearing may be worthwhile since it is a vehicle for citizens' voice in government decisions. Business and church board meetings probably wouldn't welcome visitors, but some church or civic committees might.

Also, it would be well to create the opportunity for your child to experience the role of committee member. Family council time teaches early lessons along this line, but for older children, it would be well to arrange for peers to help make group decisions. For example, the group could plan a joint family picnic. Supervise as appropriate, keeping quiet except to head off really serious problems and to help get everyone involved.

Values and moral development

Intelligent decisions are based on facts and concepts but also depend on value judgments. Thus in teaching young people to make wise decisions, educators have felt a need to help them choose moral principles and apply them to the factual information. The training emphasis stresses the importance of choosing and not what the choice should be (apparently because morality is the realm of church and not state).

According to the popular concept known as "values clarification," values are carefully selected after considering alternatives, then they are prized, and finally established by consistent application.

Sensing the importance of learning to make wise decisions, you will want to remember the idea of identifying values as you discuss societal issues with your children. For example, it is easy to decide what is right or wrong about the "equal rights" movement, but upon what value principles is the judgment based? Learning the historical facts about dropping the atomic bomb on Japan is of relatively minor importance without personally relating to the moral decision involved.

For those who recognize a source of authority—a standard of right and wrong—outside of humanity, I see several dangers in the values clarification process as it has been commonly understood: (1) choosing values in an atmosphere of neutrality teaches implicitly that the choice of particular values is unimportant as long as it is clear. (2) Even when teachers don't conceal their own values, students are urged to choose freely, and the teacher's bias could be an objectionable influence. And (3), although a child or youth may bring to school a good set of values from home training, peer pressure in a secular environment is often too great for the expression of values much different from the group norm.

Another recently popular concept related to decision making is Kohlberg's theory of moral development.* According to this idea, an individual moves through six stages to arrive at full moral maturity. Briefly summarized, they are: (1) Decisions depend on obedience, prompted by fear of punishment. (2) Personal benefit influences decisions. (3) Approval from authority becomes a motivating force. (4) Respect for authority and rules govern behavior. (5) Action is governed by a system of rules seen as reasonable. By cooperative agreement, the rules may be modified. And finally, (6) decisions are based on what the individual considers to be high ethical and consistent principles. Personal judgment, rather than exterior standards, guide behavior.

Kohlberg sees higher levels as better and believes children should be helped to advance from one stage to the next.

For the person who feels no particular responsibility to God, or for someone who believes that a relationship to God is independent from relationships to other people, this theory of moral development is a reasonable explanation. However, I see a subtle element of humanism. To me, the theory says that we gradually mature until, in stage 5, we intelligently conform to a standard we see as just. Then, as I understand the intent of stage 6, we "advance" to become our own standard of behavior.

The development of ideas I shared with you in the chapter, "Inspiring motivation," is a response to Kohlberg. I have related moral development to motivation or purpose. The first stage I call the *personal comfort stage*. Next is the *caregiver approval stage,* then the *selected friends stage,* and finally the *unrestricted stage,* which the majority of individuals never fully reach. Instead of developing to the point of independence from imposed standards, I see individuals as developing ideally toward unselfishness.

Bible in the context of social studies

If your school has a religious orientation, notice that many of the principles discussed in this chapter apply to teaching Bible (also discussed in the chapter on teaching values).

For example, Bible facts have meaning as they illustrate concepts, and concepts must lead to rational decisions. You might want to consider concepts in the areas of: (1) God's character—how He relates to us, (2) where we came from and how we arrived at our present condition, (3) His present and future purpose for us, (4) how we may choose to relate to Him, and (5) how we relate to others.

Then, returning to social studies and other subjects after studying the Bible, the values required for good judgment are clear and need not be pumped from a dry well.

22

Teaching art

By Sandy Peterson, with Kim Solga

Like pieces of a puzzle, each area of learning has its special place. And art is an essential piece in the balanced education picture. The arts and crafts you teach your children will provide excellent opportunities to polish their personalities and help them find life more meaningful. Each child has unique talents. Experiencing fine arts offers discovery, use of creativity, and enjoyment of beauty. It helps develop the special abilities God has given.

Teaching art in the home classroom also allows you as the teacher to participate in the creative learning experiences. It can be a beautiful growing experience for both you and your child. With your involvement, remember that your child will be doing the work. If you tend to be a perfectionist and do it for him, you lose the most important things you are trying to teach. You should, of course, teach for neatness and carefulness, but remember that children work according to their age and experience.

For success in teaching, be genuinely interested in art yourself. Then spark that interest in your child. Visit galleries, craft stores, and museums. Talk over the types of things he or she would enjoy learning and doing. Then together plan the art projects you have chosen.

Planning

To begin, you might plan your art area layout and decide how to decorate it. You will want a place for pictures, a bulletin board, and some shelves for storage and display. Even if you need to teach art in the same place the other school subjects are studied, you will want to make it as suitable as possible. Kim Solga will share some ideas about setting up an "art center," after we finish looking at the basic ideas of planning.

Prepare for your art classes in advance. First, choose a general area of interest. Then:

(1)   Decide when and how long you want your art classes.

(2)   Make a list of possible projects.

(3)   Plan according to seasons and events, student abilities, resources and materials available, and practicality for your situation.

(4)   Organize your materials in advance so that you are sure to have everything you need.

As you plan and teach, keep the following suggestions in mind:

(1)   Teach your child to enjoy looking at, touching, and making pretty things. Wherever you are, you can teach him or her to observe and appreciate the surroundings. In the home, at church, outdoors in nature, and even in the grocery store, you can help your child notice simplicity, beauty, organization, and neatness.

(2)   Choose projects within your child's capabilities and interests. For each project in this chapter I have suggested appropriate grade levels. The projects appear in order of increasing difficulty. As you become better acquainted with your child's potential, you may wish to expand into more difficult projects. Flexible instructions allow opportunity to use imagination. Plan projects to be more than just busy work. Use them to help your child build a positive self-image. If you begin a project for which your child shows positively no talent, change projects rather than apply pressure. Always offer appropriate encouragement and appreciation, while at the same time promoting thoroughness, carefulness, and the importance of doing one's best.

(3) As already mentioned, do *not* do your children's work for them. Sometimes in a joint project, you can do one part, such as a frame, while your child makes the picture. But don't redo his or her handiwork.

(4) Choose activities that are practical for the home classroom. Many nice art activities use materials you already have on hand or that are easy to buy. You don't need to choose elaborate and expensive projects that require a lot of materials you will use only once.

(5) In developing your art program, use all the resources around you that you can think of. For instance, take advantage of your local library for art and craft ideas that will expand beyond the suggestions given here. Look in bookstores and school supply stores for good books. Find an older person in your church or community who will be willing to teach you and your child an artistic skill that is new to both of you such as knitting, quilting, crocheting, ceramics, tatting, etc. Or enroll your child in special art classes.

The art activity area by Kim Solga

I suggest you designate an area in your home as an art center. It should be near running water, have a washable floor or protective rug covering, and be stocked with all kinds of art materials as suggested in the paragraphs that follow. Above all, it should be easily accessible to your children so they can come when they have free time, and work on projects without adult direction.

Teach the necessary skills of cleaning up after projects. Even preschoolers can learn how to clean brushes and set them on their handles to dry, put the covers back on the felt pens, set the crayons in the box and throw away paper scraps. Children should wipe up their own paint spills and put the clay back in the bags. Only by being patiently taught to take care of their art tools and materials will children develop responsibility in working alone on their art projects.

Art is learned from more than the projects you assign and the techniques you introduce. Really creative work takes place when children decide for themselves what to make—what to do with the art skills they've learned. Encourage your students to work on their own, give them the time freedom for it, and praise their creations!

Suggested general materials

Arts and crafts materials may be purchased at most discount stores, office supply stores, and some supermarkets. Stores that sell only art supplies are nice, but often charge more. I would use them only for specialty items that cannot be purchased elsewhere.

Basic tools and space needs: pencils, scissors (blunt ends for the very young), tempera paint, string, glue, paper of various types, ruler, ink, crayons, tape, water color felt pens, and a special table.

Materials to save: oatmeal boxes, magazines and catalogs, small glass jars (with lids), empty spools, foil, cloth scraps, ribbon scraps, seeds, old pictures and cards, talcum powder, old crayons, old toothbrushes (sterilized), old candles, newspapers, old aprons or shirts, hair spray.

On selecting materials by Kim Solga

Children, especially young ones, should be given nontoxic art materials. Many items sold in art stores, even some made for children's art, are not safe! To be sure, look for the official "CP" or "AP" nontoxic label on paints, glues, inks, clay or anything that might end up on a child's fingers and in their mouths.

Children's scissors should cut as easily as your best sewing scissors. Nothing is more frustrating than trying to cut paper with cheap tin scissors. Several companies manufacture very well-crafted embroidery scissors with blunt ends—perfect for youngsters.

Art materials for very young children are often over sized—fat crayons, wide handled brushes, giant felt pens. These jumbo tools may be harder for tiny hands to grasp and use than the normal sized items. Be sure to provide both large and regular sized pencils, crayons, brushes and chalk for preschoolers so they can experience both and choose tools they are comfortable with.

Materials to gather from your community by Kim Solga

Paper trim scraps: Print shops often have boxes full of "trim scraps"—the edges of paper trimmed off in commercial printing jobs. These papers are in many weights, textures and colors—luxurious papers you could never afford to buy for kids, and in the tiny sizes they love. Ask if you might have a few of these throw-aways now and then.

Hardwood scraps: Ask a cabinet maker. Use these with glue to create wood sculptures and mosaics. Nailing hardwoods doesn't work well, especially for kids. Paint and draw on them.

Softwood scraps: Find these by asking at a construction site. Use them with glue, nails and paint. Carve them to make woodblock prints. Wrap needlework and pictures around blocks to make plaques. There's no end to what you can do with wood scraps. Even sawdust can be glued to paper or sculptures for great textures.

Posters: Hardware stores, supermarkets, card shops and other retail stores often discard advertising posters. These can be folded and stapled to create big sculptures. They can be cut into interesting areas of color, letters and shapes; or they can be painted and glued. You may even be able to find full-sized billboard papers from an advertising company. These are heavier than wallpaper and have truly giant figures and shapes.

Manufacturing leftovers: Visit small manufacturers and craftspeople in your community. Find out what child-safe materials they might be tossing away. Dressmakers or tailors would have scraps of fabric, lace and cords. A tile store might discard discontinued or broken tiles and linoleum scraps. A shoe repair shop might give you bits of leather. A newspaper publisher would have thin aluminum printing plates (not best for small children).

Big cardboard cartons and Styrofoam blocks: Check with an appliance store or just drive around behind now and then to see what they have set out for trash pickup. These materials can be cut with a hacksaw which is less dangerous for children. The big cartons might make nice playhouses if used with adequate supervision.

By asking you may receive art materials in abundance while making friends and educating your students on commerce in your community.

Projects

In the rest of this chapter you will find suggestions for projects to get you started. Change and experiment with them as you wish. And by all means, don't limit yourself to just the ones listed here. These are just to spark your interest and imagination. Don't view them as a series to be dutifully completed.

For each project I have shown: a title, a suggested grade level, the general type of project, materials needed, and directions and ideas.

CARD MAKING

Suggested level: All levels.

Project: Designing and making all types of greeting cards.

Explanation: Card making is fun for everyone and simple to do. Handmade cards with that "personal touch" mean so much more. You can make cards for: birthdays, Christmas, Valentine's, weddings, Mother's Day, Father's Day, graduations, get well, friendship, and special family occasions.

A variety of techniques may be used. Some of the other art project ideas work well for making cards. For example, see: leaf prints, pressed flowers, potato prints, rubbed prints, scratchboard, and spatter painting. And you can also use ink drawing, pencil drawing, water color painting, pastels, silhouettes, and even crayons.

Materials: Choose any heavy paper such as index stock, tagboard, construction paper, bristol board, or lightweight cardboard.

To fold the cards consider: (1) a regular book fold, (2) a top-down fold, (3) a top-down fold with the top shorter, (4) a three-panel fold with sides folded in, (5) a regular fold with a window cut in the front. Before folding, you will want to plan the card to fit an available envelope or one you make.

Special materials you might want to use: paper lace; bits of ribbon; dried flowers, leaves or ferns; border designs; glitter; foil; metallic paper; soft fabric; wall paper; stickers; gummed stars; or doilies. To deckle the paper edges for your cards, use a heavy paper (construction or water color). Draw a line along the edge to be deckled and paint a water strip down that line on one side of the paper. Turn it over and do the same thing on the back of your first water line. When the paper is saturated, place a ruler along the line and tear the paper *upward.* Smooth down the edge and let it dry.

To make parchment-like paper, dip a soft cloth into salad oil and rub both sides of any kind of paper. Let the paper dry for two days, and it will look like parchment. Typing paper works well for this.

STRING PAINTING

Suggested level: Preschool and lower grades.

Project: Painting with string on construction paper.

Materials: For this project you will need sheets of light-colored construction paper (12 by 18 inches is suggested), two or three pieces of string (18 inches or longer), two or three colors of liquid tempera paint, a large magazine, bowls for the paint, and some newspapers.

Directions: (1) Fold the construction paper in half in either direction. (2) Unfold the paper and lay it open on the newspapers. (3) Pour the paint into a bowl. (4) Carefully dip a piece of string into the paint. (5) Take the string from the paint and lay it on one side of the paper in an interesting pattern, leaving a bit of the string showing at the bottom. (6) Fold the paper over land lay the magazine on the top. (7) Press down lightly on the magazine with one hand and quickly pull the string out of the paper. (8) Remove the magazine and unfold the paper. (9) Let the picture dry and then repeat the process, using another piece of string and another color of paint.

This will produce an interesting and unique painting. Using more than three colors will usually make the picture unattractive.

MILK PAINTING

Suggested level: Preschool and lower grades.
Project: Painting.
Materials: One-half cup of milk powder, one-half cup of water, dry tempera paint.
Directions: (1) Mix the water and milk together and stir until dissolved. (2) Add the desired coloring. (3) Use as you would any paint.

This is an excellent paint medium for the little ones to use. Give them a specific assignment to paint. For example: a day at the beach; when the family goes camping; winter fun; a day at Grandmother's house; springtime in my front yard; my favorite pet; a birthday party; Christmas fun.

Mix only the amount of paint to be used at one time. This paint dries to a glossy finish and is not dusty.

SCRATCHBOARD PICTURES

Suggested level: Preschool and lower grades.
Project: Scratching through ink-covered poster board to make pictures.
Materials: In doing this project, you will need heavy paper such as tagboard, poster board, or light cardboard. You will then need crayons, dusting powder and black India ink (which may stain clothes), or black tempera paint. You will also need something sharp to scratch through the ink. For the younger children, the best thing to use is a mechanical pencil with no lead. A straight pin or sewing needle can also be used with caution. You will need newspapers to put under the painting.
Directions: (1) Choose the size of picture you wish to make. A good size for little ones is 8 by 10 inches. (2) Using the crayons, color the entire page heavily with wax. Be sure to use the lighter colors, as the dark ones will not show up when they are scratched.

(3) Check the picture to make sure the child has filled in the entire sheet. (4) Dust the picture with talcum powder. This will help the ink or paint adhere to the wax. (5) Cover the entire board with India ink or black tempera paint. (6) Allow the picture to dry. (7) When the paint is thoroughly dry, let the children begin to scratch through the ink and watch the colors show through. (8) Have the children scratch a particular subject such as a family picnic, a fall scene, winter fun, etc. (9) If the child makes a mistake, it can be blocked out by touching up the picture with a bit more ink. Be sure to let it dry before they start scratching again.

FINGER PAINTING

Suggested level: Preschool and lower grades.
Project: Painting.
Materials: To do this activity, you will need newspapers, old shirts or aprons to protect clothing, paper (typing paper or butcher paper, or regular water color paper), and finger paints.
Directions: (1) Cover work surface with newspapers. (2) Wet the paper and choose one or two colors of paint. (3) Spoon about one tablespoon of one color of paint onto the paper. (4) Smear around with the fingers. (5) Using one finger like a pencil, draw a pattern or picture. (6) The surface can be worked with for several minutes, but soon the paper will begin to tear, so encourage your child to work in a short time. (7) Set aside the picture to dry.

Finger painting is best with only one or two colors because the paints mix together and more colors will result in a brown. Two recipes for finger paint are given later in this chapter.

PUFF BALL ART

Suggested level: Preschool and lower grades.
Project: Sculpting with cotton balls.
Materials: To do this unique and fun project you will need a bag of cotton balls, a cookie sheet, some small bowls, food coloring, a cup of flour, and a cup of water.

Directions: (1) Mix the water and the flour together until you get a smooth solution. (2) Divide it into the bowls and add a few drops of the desired food coloring to each bowl until you get the color you want. (3) Drop in the cotton balls (one at a time) and twirl them around with your fingers until they are completely coated with the solution. (4) Carefully lift out the balls and place them on a lightly oiled cookie sheet. The cotton balls will retain their shape with a little puff. Don't squeeze them or you will lose the air that is inside. (5) Create any shape or design that you wish, making sure that the cotton balls touch one another. This will make them stick together as they dry. (6) Bake in the oven at 300 degrees for one hour. (7) Let the shapes cool before removing them from the cookie sheet.

If you wish to have brighter colors, do not add food coloring to the mixture, but rather paint them with tempera paints or water colors after they have cooled. You can use the shapes to write mottos, your name, or a favorite saying. You can make animals and bugs (caterpillars are favorites). And you can make many attractive flowers, too. If you wish to make smaller parts for heads, tails, ears, etc., just pull the puffs apart before you dip them in the mixture to make smaller puffs. They will become hard like beads when they bake.

SPATTER PAINTING

Suggested level: Preschool and lower grades.

Project: Spattering tempera paint on paper.

Materials: For this art project, you will need tempera paint, art paper, a stiff toothbrush, scissors, a blunt knife (a table knife will do), straight pins, and newspapers.

Directions: (1) Draw some designs or interesting shapes. Silhouettes would be pretty. (2) Cut out the patterns. (3) Lay your drawing paper on some newspaper and pin the shapes on top of it. Be sure to leave margins around the edges of the paper. (4) Mix your paint. (5) Dip the toothbrush in one color of paint and hold the toothbrush slightly above the picture bristles down. (6) Draw the edge of the knife *toward* you across the bristles making the paint spatter. (7) Repeat the process with one or two more colors, removing some of the shapes if desired. (8) Put aside the picture to dry.

WAX PAINTING

Suggested level: Preschool and lower grades.

Project: Washing paint over a waxed surface.

Materials: This art activity requires drawing paper, tapered candles, crayons, tempera paint, a paint brush, and a pencil.

Directions: (1) Decide on a pattern or picture you wish to paint. Lightly sketch or trace it on your drawing paper with a pencil. (2) Using a sharpened candle, or a white crayon, draw over the sketch, leaving a heavy coat of wax. (3) Thin the paint with water. This is called a wash. (4) Brush the paint over the design, and your picture will appear. (5) Let the picture dry.

For a different effect, use a light-colored crayon to make contrasting colors in your picture. (Darker colors don't show up well.) For example, you could use a bright yellow crayon and deep blue paint.

MURALS

Suggested level: Lower and middle grades.

Project: Painting, cutting, pasting to make very large pictures.

Materials: A large sheet of butcher paper or newsprint, lightweight colored construction paper, scissors, glue, pencils, and water paints.

Directions: (1) You might want to begin this project with a discussion of plant life and ask the children what changes they notice in the fall. (2) Let them bring, show, and talk about the leaves, flowers, seed pods, and insects which they have gathered. (3) Decide what kind of mural you wish to make, and have the children draw a small sketch of the picture they wish to create. (4) The parent-teacher might prepare the background for the mural (hills, trees, roads, sky and such background objects), and let the children arrange the ideas. (5) Show the children how to arrange the shapes attractively. (6) When they have decided on a particular arrangement, begin gluing the objects or construction paper cutouts of them to the background. Continue with this until you have the desired picture.

A mural is a very large picture. Parents should plan its size to fit the space where it will be displayed. I suggest at least 2 by 3 feet.

For an autumn mural, you might want to use leaves, flowers, ears of corn, pumpkins, birds, frogs, cats, a big moon, etc. For a winter scene, you could use cotton, artificial snow, cut-out snow men, snowflakes, houses with snowy roofs, children playing in the snow, and so on. For a spring picture, flowers and springtime activities would be appropriate.

CRYSTAL GARDEN

Suggested level: Lower and middle grades.
Project: Watching nature's designs.
Materials: Pieces of coal, rock, charcoal bricks, or anything porous; a shallow bowl (a glass pie dish works well); 6 tablespoons of salt; 6 tablespoons of laundry bluing; 1 tablespoon of ammonia; food coloring if desired.
Directions: Lay the pieces of porous material in the bowl. Mix the salt, bluing, water and ammonia together. Pour it over the pieces in the bowl. In about fifteen minutes, crystals will begin to form and you will have a beautiful garden in just a few hours. If you wish to have the crystals colored, just add a few drops of food coloring to the pieces after you have poured on the mixture. The garden will last a long time if you add a little ammonia and salt water to the dish every few days.

Don't touch the crystals because they are very fragile. Keep your garden out of reach of small fingers.

POTATO PRINTS

Suggested level: Lower, middle and upper grades.
Project: Stamping pictures with a carved potato.

Materials: Several large potatoes, tempera paint, paint brushes, a sharp knife, drawing paper, and newspapers.

Directions: First plan your picture or design and make a sketch. Make it very simple. Cut one of the potatoes in half with a straight cut. (If your potatoes are too soft, you can soak them in water.) Cut your design into the surface of the potato digging down to remove materials from all but the areas you want to print. Mix your paint. Brush it onto the cut surface and press the potato on the paper. Repeat the process using different colors or designs to get the effect you want. A stamp pad will work to apply the color if you don't mind getting potato juice on it.

This is an excellent project for making your own gift wrapping paper.

RUBBING PRINTS

Suggested level: Elementary and secondary grades.

Project: Learning to understand textures.

Materials: Medium to thin paper (typing paper is good); crayons, pastels or charcoal; hair spray or spray varnish.

Directions: Lay your piece of paper over a rough surface and rub it with the desired medium. Crayons work best for your first try. When using charcoal or pastels, spray lightly to seal the finish to avoid smearing. Cheaper hair spray seems to work better than the more expensive brands.

Surface ideas: Bricks, rough wood, screens, sidewalks, wire fencing, manhole covers, etc.

Cut the prints into interesting designs and put them together on a larger piece of paper to form a picture or pattern. You can use the idea to make a game. Cut several different patterns and place them on one side of a piece of construction paper. The person playing the game then tries to guess what the prints are made from.

A similar art project would be making pictures of objects like coins by placing a piece of paper over the surfaces and rubbing over them with the side of the pencil lead. A child can make his or her own math problems by tracing various combinations of coins and figuring the totals.

TIE DYE

Suggested level: Upper grades and high school.

Project: Design from uneven dying.

Materials: Fabric (clothes, scarves, ties, etc.), fabric dye (one or several colors).

Directions: (1) Prepare the dye as directed on the package. (2) Tie several knots very tightly in the fabric to be used. (3) Dip the fabric according to the dying instructions. (4) Remove the fabric, let it dry partially, then untie the knots and continue the dying process. (5) If you wish to dye it again, retie the knots in different places, and use a different color of die. (6) When using more than one color, begin with the lightest first. Use colors that go well together. If you mix red and green, yellow and purple, or blue and orange, you will get a brown color.

BATIK

Suggested level: Upper grades and high school.

Project: Fabric design with dye.

Materials: Fabric (scarves, ties, table cloths, clothes, etc.), fabric dye (one or more colors), paraffin wax, half-inch flat bristle paint brush, newspapers, iron.

Directions: (1) On scratch paper, draw sketches of designs for your fabric. You could make swirls, large flowers, different sized dots, squares, fruit and vegetable shapes, etc. Plan for the color to soak into the areas you won't be coating with wax. (2) Melt the wax in a double boiler—a pan of boiling water with another pan inside it with the wax. (3) Spread fabric out over the newspaper. (4) Using the paintbrush, apply the wax following the chosen design. Don't spread the wax too thick. (5) Let the wax set. (6) Mix the dye according to the directions on the container. It should be warm, but not hot, because hot dye would melt the wax. (7) Wad up the fabric and dip it into the dye. Soak it for the directed time. (8) Remove the fabric from the dye and hang it up to dry. (9) When the fabric is dry, place it between layers of clean paper and iron with a medium heat to remove the wax. As soon as the paper becomes saturated with the wax, change it for fresh paper.

You may repeat the process, using a different color of dye for a variety of effects. The wax will crack when you put it into the dye. This gives a pretty marbled effect. Experiment for fun.

STRING ART

Suggested level: Upper grades and high school.

Project: Making designs with string run from point to point on a board.

Materials: Pencil, poster board (8 by 10 inches suggested for beginners), large needles, several colors of embroidery floss.

Directions: (1) When you have an idea of how designs can be formed with string, make a scratch paper sketch of what you want. (2) Draw your design very lightly on your poster board. (3) Choose a beginning point and make a dot. Follow all around your sketch lines placing dots evenly. (4) Using a needle (darning needles work best), go back and poke a hole through each dot. (5) Now choose a color of floss, and thread an embroidery needle using two or three strands of floss. (6) Tie a knot in the thread and pull the needle through from the back side of the board to the front. (7) Cross back and forth to opposite points on the board, making a pattern. The longer strokes should appear on the front of the card to form the pattern, with the shorter segments on the back. (8) You can use one hole several times to get an interesting effect.

Alternate idea: Instead of making holes in cards, you can cut a small piece of three-eighths or half inch plywood. Sand the edges. Cover the board with a piece of thick, solid color cloth wrapping it around the edges to attach to the back. Draw your sketch on paper. Lay the paper on the board. Then following the points on your sketch, drive small finish nails through paper and cloth into the board. Your pattern is formed by running the thread from nail to nail. Patterns with lots of long straight lines work best. If you wish, you can get painted nails used for paneling.

NATURE'S ART

Suggested level: Middle grades, upper grades and high school.
Project: Using leaves and flowers to make prints.
Materials: Drawing paper, writing paper, card-type paper or any desired work surface. You will also need water paints, drawing chalk or pastels, pencils and glue. You will then find leaves, flowers and other objects in nature that can be flattened or pressed.

Directions for making leaf prints: (1) Gather different leaves from your yard, or a public park. (2) Choose a color and paint one side of the leaf, covering it well. (3) Lay the painted side of the leaf down on the paper which will become the finished picture. (4) Place another piece of paper on top of the leaf and press firmly over the entire leaf. (5) Put special emphasis on the center vein and the edges of the leaf. (6) Remove the top paper and the leaf, and allow the print to dry.

You can use this idea for making stationery, pictures, or even greeting cards. If you wish to have more than one leaf on the picture, wait until the first print is dry, then make another impression using another color. If your leaf is green and you treat it gently, you can wash off one color of paint and use the leaf for another.

Directions for making pressed flower pictures: (1) Collect leaves, flowers, ferns and other small plant items all year. (2) Press them between pages of a book for several days until they are thoroughly dry and flat. (3) Choose your paper or board material. (4) Arrange chosen pieces into an attractive design. (5) Lightly sketch a guideline if necessary. (6) Remove the pieces and begin gluing them back on, going from the background to the foreground.

Dried flowers can be painted with water colors for brighter colors.

BASIC DRAWING

Suggested level: Middle or upper grades and high school.
Project: Introducing the basics of drawing techniques.

Materials: Sketch pad or drawing paper (typing paper is good for beginners), several drawing pencils, kneaded eraser, hair spray or spray varnish.

Concept: Many people believe that they just don't have the magic touch to be able to draw, but in reality most people can learn to draw well. The ability to draw is a basic for learning to paint pictures. It does take time, but the skill is well worth achieving.

Directions: (1) Begin by helping your child see basic shapes in real objects. Look for squares, rectangles, circles and triangles. Then study what happens to these shapes when they are tipped—when the viewing angle is changed. Talk about parallelograms, ellipses, and so on. (2) Have your student practice drawing the basic shapes and the tipped shapes. (3) Look around your home for shapes to draw. For example, the clock face, the refrigerator, a tent and so on. (4) With an understanding of shapes, detail can be filled in. (5) A full description of drawing techniques involves more than we can deal with in this chapter. Purchase some good drawing books. By copying the pictures in them and trying out the ideas they present, drawing can improve.

WATER COLOR PAINTING

Suggested level: Middle and upper grades and high school.

Project: Painting.

Materials: A pad of paper suitable for water colors; three round brushes—small, medium and large; a set of water color paints—black, white, red, yellow, blue, orange, purple and green; a container for water; and a pencil.

Directions: (1) Choose what you would like to paint. (2) Very lightly sketch areas to be painted. For example, draw a line to separate land from sky, block out grass, mountains and so on. (4) Paint from the background to the front of the picture. (5) Let each color dry thoroughly and add any fine details last.

You may also want to experiment with washes (thin paint). Get your paper wet and using a large brush, paint in several areas. If you want a special effect, you can let the paint run where it will. Be careful not to use too many colors or everything will turn an ugly brown. As the paper begins to dry, paint in the details to make the areas look like flowers, animals, birds and so on.

Paint recipes

FINGER PAINT RECIPE 1 (Yield: 2 cups)

1/2 cup white flour
2 cups of water
1 tablespoon of glycerin
1 teaspoon of borax
several small jars with lids for storing the paints (Baby food jars are excellent.)
food coloring or poster paints

(1) Mix the flour with 1/2 cup of water to form a paste. (2) Add the rest of the water and cook over low heat until the mixture is thick and clear, stirring constantly. (3) Cool the mixture and then add the glycerin and the borax. If the mixture is too thick, you may add a little more water. (4) Divide the mixture into the jars and add the desired color. This recipe dries to a matte (dull) finish.

FINGER PAINT RECIPE 2 (Yield: 2 1/2 cups)

1/2 cup of cornstarch
3/4 cup of cold water
2 cups of hot water
2 teaspoons of boric acid
1 tablespoon of glycerin
several small jars with lids
food coloring or poster paints

(1) Mix the cornstarch with 1/4 cup of cold water and make a paste. (2) Add the hot water, stirring quickly and vigorously to prevent lumps. (3) Cook the mixture over low heat and stir it constantly. (4) Remove the mixture from the heat and add the rest of the cold water and also the boric acid. Stir until it is well mixed,

then add the glycerin. (5) Divide the mixture into the jars and add the desired coloring. This paint dries slowly and has a glossy finish.

Modeling mediums

Following are recipes for doughs or clays that can be made right in your own kitchen with common ingredients. They work very well for modeling and sculpture projects in the home school. Just follow the directions carefully and let your child's imagination go as he (or she) creates objects with his own hands. Remember that gentle guidance and help may be needed, and it is even more fun if "teacher" participates too! The most important thing to remember, especially for the preschoolers is DO NOT EAT THE DOUGH!

Here are a few suggestions for using the modeling mediums (or "media" if you prefer to call them that): (1) Roll into long "ropes" and write names, mottos, greetings, and so on. (2) Make braided baskets. (3) Make your own flower pots. You will probably want to bake your pots. (4) Roll into "ropes" to make picture frames, round as well as square. (5) Make wreaths. (6) Roll out to about 3/8 inch thick and cut out decorations for Christmas. (7) Make flowers, statues, 3-D pictures, animals and so on.

Where directions call for shellac, you might try a spray varnish. Look for it with the spray paints. Just get a clear color.

MODELING DOUGH (Yield: 1 cup)

3/4 cup of flour
1/2 cup of salt
1 1/2 teaspoon of powdered alum
1 1/2 teaspoon of vegetable oil
1/2 cup boiling water
food coloring

(1) Mix the dry ingredients in a bowl. (2) Mix the oil and water together, stirring quickly. (3) Add the oil and water to the dry ingredients and stir until blended. (4) Add the desired color of food coloring.

Use the dough as you would any commercially available dough. It will dry overnight if left out in the open air.

PLAY CLAY (Yield: 1 1/2 cups)

1/2 cup salt
1/2 cup hot water
1/4 cup cold water
1/2 cup cornstarch

(1) Mix the salt into the water and bring it to a boil. (2) Stir the cornstarch into the cold water. (3) Add the above two mixtures and stir vigorously to avoid lumping. (4) Cook the mixture over low heat, stirring constantly until it thickens. It should become like pie dough. (5) Remove the mixture from the heat and let it cool. (6) Knead the mixture until soft and pliable.

This is an excellent dough to roll out and use for flat items and Christmas decorations. It can be dried in the air overnight, or in the oven at 200 degrees for one hour.

SOAPSUDS CLAY (Yield: 1 cup)

3/4 cup of powdered soap (Ivory Snow)
1 tablespoon of warm water
an electric mixer

(1) Mix the soap powder and the water in a bowl. (2) Beat with the electric mixer until it forms a clay-like consistency. (3) Mold into figures and objects. The mixture dries to a hard finish.

HARDENING CLAY (Yield: 1 1/2 cups)

1 cup baking soda
1/2 cup cornstarch
2/3 cups of warm water
food coloring
shellac

(1) Mix the soda and the starch in a pan. (2) Add the water and stir until the mixture is smooth. (3) Cook at medium heat and bring to a boil. It should look like mashed potatoes. (4) Remove it from the heat and let it cool. (5) Knead the clay well when it is cool. (6) Add food coloring to the clay, or use it as it is, to be painted later. (7) Let the objects dry. (8) Cover them with shellac.

This mixture hardens rather quickly, so it is not good to use if you just wish to play with it for a while. You should have project in mind before you make it.

BREAD DOUGH CLAY (Small yield)

1 slice of white bread
1 teaspoon of white glue
1 teaspoon of water
food coloring
shellac

(1) Cut off the crust of the bread. (2) Pour the glue, then the water, into the center of the slice of bread. (3) Knead the bread until it is no longer sticky. (4) Add the food coloring as desired. (5) Shape the clay into flowers or objects as you wish, and then let them dry overnight. (6) Finish the pieces by shellacing them. If you want to make more than one small object, you will want to prepare larger quantities.

BASIC BREADCRAFT

4 cups of flour
1 1/2 cups of warm water
1 cup of salt

(1) Mix the above ingredients. (2) Cover and refrigerate for half an hour. (3) Roll out and use as "ropes," baskets, writing, or decorations. (4) Use cookie cutters to make ornaments, if desired.

GINGER DOUGH

2 cups of flour
1 cup of salt
5 teaspoons of cinnamon or instant coffee
3/4 to 1 cup of warm water.

Follow the directions as shown for "basic breadcraft."

BRICK BREAD

1 package of yeast
1/4 cup of warm water
1 1/4 cup of scalded milk
1 tablespoon of shortening

2 tablespoons of sugar
2 tablespoons of salt
5 cups of flower
2 eggs

1/4 to 1/3 cup plaster of Paris

(1) Mix the yeast in the water. (2) Add the shortening to the scalded milk and let it cool. (3) Add the sugar to the yeast, then add the milk mixture with the salt and one egg. (4) Mix. (5) Start adding the flour, one cup at a time. (6) Mix with a spoon, then knead with your hands, adding the remaining flour until the dough is no longer sticky. (7) Set your oven on warm. (8) Grease a bowl and set it inside the oven to warm. (9) Then set the mixture in the warm bowl, cover it, and let it set for ten minutes inside the oven. (10) Let the dough rise for one hour, punch it down, and let it set for another ten minutes. (11) Punch the dough down again, and knead in the plaster. (12) "Flour" a board with plaster of Paris, and shape your dough into desired forms or objects. (13) Let the shapes rise for one-half to one hour. (14) Bake on a foil sheet at 350 degrees for fifteen minutes. (15) Brush with a beaten egg and bake another fifteen minutes. (16) Reduce the oven temperature to 150 and bake the projects for eight hours. (17) Turn the pieces over after about six hours. They should sound hollow. (18) Varnish the objects several times, letting the varnish dry thoroughly between coats.

23

Work education

We teach our children an impressive array of academic subjects. We also church them, vacation them and sports them. But preparation for practical, responsible living which common labor teaches best we somehow take for granted. The home school family environment is excellent for work education, but it takes more than being home.

Work education doesn't fit the neat little boxes we use for math and spelling. And neither is it mastered simply by having a job and making money. Let's consider what we expect work education to contribute to the total development of our children. Then we will look at how work might teach at various stages of maturity.

The objectives I see for work education may be grouped into three major areas: job skills, applied knowledge and attitudes for success.

Job skills, specific and general

The first thing we think of that might be learned from a work experience is skill development. Yard work, for instance, teaches plant and lawn care. It teaches operation and maintenance of yard equipment. But how much help are these specific skills for later work as a cab driver, then as an accountant? More than it might seem. The unrelated skills provide the ability to work at a different job when employment in the preferred field is not available. And there are less apparent values which we discuss later.

Work experiences can also teach general skills important for future employment and for efficient, intelligent living. These general skills can be grouped into categories of: (1) caring for personal needs, (2) dealing with people, (3) caring for plants and animals, (4) working with ideas, and (5) handling materials.

Here are a few examples to show what we mean by general skills: keeping skin clean and fresh, using common hand tools, making people feel at ease, using a stove to prepare food, applying paint evenly and quickly with a brush, delegating responsibility in organizing people for a large task, using a typewriter or computer keyboard, arranging objects for visual appeal, and remembering instructions.

The difference between general and specific skills is somewhat arbitrary. The reason for making a distinction in our discussion here is to bring out the idea that even uncommon tasks are accomplished by a combination of more general skills, and that these abilities transfer to other jobs. Thus using a phillips screwdriver in the job of hanging kitchen cabinet doors improves the ability to work with the same tool on the instrument panel of an automobile, and the sensitivity to damaging the screw by too much force even transfers to tightening screws with a wrench. When we analyze just about any task, we find skills or skill components that are general and thus may be applied in many other tasks.

Applied knowledge

In the second category of objectives—applied knowledge—jobs teach factual information, although not as efficiently as books do. A person isn't apt to take a job on a cargo ship to learn the names of a few major seaports.

On the other hand, knowledge seen in application, especially for young children, is easier to learn and remember. Keeping track of money earned for little jobs teaches more accounting to a second grader than careful explanations, even in simple words.

Attitudes for success

What we have said so far is more or less obvious and similar to what you would have expected as benefits of practical work. Now we come to the most important value of work education—the development of attitudes. Consider this list of character traits that might be expected from work experience. Many more could be added.

☆ Perseverance
☆ Responsibility
☆ Sensitivity to people's needs
☆ Respect for authority
☆ Cooperation
☆ Adaptability
☆ Balance: physical, mental, social, spiritual
☆ Setting priorities
☆ Sense of purpose
☆ Contentment: protection from covetousness and envy
☆ Integrity
☆ Sense of value of resources: time, effort, money
☆ Patience, deferred gratification
☆ Self-worth

Of course, factors other than work also contribute to the development of these attitudes. The example of parents or friends, and good reading are fundamental and inescapable influences. But observation is still theory. Only through the experience of personal application can anyone actually claim possession of an attitude.

As they mature

★ For the young child, work and play are the same. It's all fun. To keep work enjoyable, begin guiding toward responsibility while your child is still a toddler. As understanding develops, teach responsibility. Regular eating habits, potty training, keeping quiet in church and putting toys away are important early training objectives.

★ A little later, expect your child to "help" make the bed, bring clothes for the washing machine, fix lunch and do similar tasks you could perform much easier by yourself. Plan activities for developing attitudes of fulfillment through helping meet the family needs, and of acting by principle rather than feeling. At the same time you will be teaching skills in muscle coordination and in following instructions.

★ As time goes on, expect your child to assume more regular responsibilities around home. At this third stage, the child may also fulfill personal needs such as room orderliness, grooming and clothing care. Following through on responsibilities, however, doesn't come naturally for most children. You will need to supervise and encourage. And when progress dwindles, your talk will be heard best while you help (not take over).

Also don't expect so much that no time is left for relaxation, personal creative pursuits, and spiritual growth.

By the way, try to imagine how your children could learn all this if you pack them off to a child care service so you can work during their tender years. I wouldn't argue that it's impossible, but it's certainly not likely to succeed as well.

★ At the fourth stage, after your child has shown a reasonable degree of responsibility at home, it may be time for an outside job. Most children are optimistic and try to swim the English Channel as soon as they can paddle across the pool. They need your counsel. Also, children are easily influenced. You will want to know that your child's working environment is a good one for character development and for physical safety.

Appropriate jobs for children include delivering papers, doing yard work and baby sitting. Some parents feel that such jobs need close supervision. Baby-sitting, for example, could be done in the child's own home with parents present. A parent could go with the child on some jobs.

Also investigate volunteer service work. In addition to such activities as helping in hospitals or nursing homes or in community clean-up projects, your child might enjoy the learning experience of working without pay for a business person.

Being responsible to someone outside the family gives working a sense of seriousness. Someone other than Mom or Dad expects a good use of time and energy. To make the experience more meaningful, take time to talk things over now and then. Talk with the employer, too. You will probably hear more positive than negative comments because, from my experience, home schooled kids tend to be excellent workers.

★ Young people of high school age are ready for more serious employment commitments—perhaps even a full-time summer job. When a new job begins, you and your offspring should make a list of learning objectives for both character development and job skills. Then every month or two you can discuss progress, thereby keeping those goals fresh in mind.

Parent teachers who work side-by-side with their children and youth can build trust relationships that open channels for communicating life values. Making bread or chopping onions together builds a different understanding than other types of encounters. Christian living is seen as real and practical, and academic responsibility becomes a natural extension of the relationship. The adult supervises, but with sleeves rolled up.

★ After high school, work education continues as youth in the spirit of adventure explore their world with new freedom.

Throughout life, useful labor molds and preserves the person who has made God first. At the age of forty, Moses fled to the desert of Midian to learn humility herding sheep and in communion with His Creator. The broader an individual's early base of experience has been, the easier it will be to face the changes that come through the years.

Choosing work experiences

In looking for jobs that educate, useful experience and environment count more than high pay. The biggest job "bargain" for an individual at any level of maturity is a task that involves physical exercise, health-stimulating fresh air, a relaxing emotional atmosphere, and a closeness to God's creation.

Gardening may best answer that description. Digging, cutting, and hauling provide varied exercise; gardens are generally outside; plants don't talk back; effort of mind and body produce predictable, noninstant results; and the work is a partnership, because, as in the spiritual garden, Paul may plant, Apollos may water, but God gives the increase (1 Cor. 3:6).

Character quality, the end purpose

Our complex society offers a vast array of good learning opportunities that compete for our children's time. Christian parents would agree that the formation of a Christlike character is of more value than any other learning. But why is practical labor so important in shaping lives?

Character is values built into the life as governing principles. Reading about values and being able to explain them are important; but *values touch the heart when they are seen in Christ and in the lives of parents and others; and they are firmed up as internal principles when they are put into practice.* Cutting grass, helping sick people, and carrying cement don't by themselves insure good character. But practical work experiences like these provide opportunity for our children to take actual possession of the principles they have seen and read about. Jesus learned the Scriptures from godly parents. He also was "subject unto them" (Luke 2:51). He spent many hours at Joseph's carpenter bench and in helping with the daily family chores. And He "increased in wisdom and stature, and in favour with God and man" (verse 52).

24

Social development

Relatives, neighbors, school officials and sometimes even judges frequently express concern for the social development of children whose parents have made a break with tradition and are teaching them at home. It seems conceivable to these advisors that just perhaps some parents might be intelligent enough to teach their own children, but how could a child shut up at home all day away from agemates possibly develop socially? A parent's first response to such a concern may well be another question. "What do you mean by socialization? Do you think school peers should be the guides and models for my child's social development?" The answer is too obvious. And for further clarification, home schooled children, as a rule, aren't really isolated either. They can, in fact, have a better quality contact with the world and with other children than they would have in school.

Of course, whether taught at home or not, adapting to other people *is important*. Home is the best place to learn the give and take of social adjustment, but only with the right kind of parental direction and through interaction with good friends. I personally know students who have had extensive home education and who adjust very well; so the place children learn isn't the difficulty as long as parents realize the child's need to know how to fit into a social environment.

It's not enough, however, to say that we believe "there's no place like home" assuming that social development will take care of itself. The question deserves a closer look. Avoiding the bad—removing a child from an undesirable school influence—doesn't necessarily guarantee the good.

I see two somewhat opposite character traits that need balanced development. First, we want our children to think independently. We want them to be creative and free from social pressures that violate principle. And second, we want them to get along with other people. School at home easily fosters the first trait—independent thinking. Can it also help develop abilities to become wholesome contributing members of society? I believe it can, with concerned parents.

Characteristics of good social development

If we want our children to develop socially, it might not be a bad idea to stop and determine what characteristics we expect to see as a result of our guidance. What do we mean by social maturity? General goals like "to love sincerely," come into it but are too vague for specific planning.

Here are the social characteristics I propose. Maybe you can add more: (1) Social graces—courtesy and good manners that make an individual pleasant to have around. (2) The ability to make and enjoy friends. (3) Respect for authority—parents, adults, superiors, government, and Creator. (4) Sensitivity to the needs and feelings of others, and the ability to transmit gracefully one's own unselfish feelings. (5) Conversation and correspondence skills. (6) The ability to give and take in a normal relationship with other people, to respect the opinions of other people, and the grace to cooperate when things don't go one's way. (7) Skill in defusing tense situations—generally by cheerfulness mixed with sensitivity to the cause of the problem. (8) Prudence in developing business or social relationships. This means faithfulness, avoiding misunderstandings, and tactful precautions against being dealt with dishonestly. (9) Development of leadership, a skill which includes good followership and the ability to share decision making, helping everyone feel like a part of the team.

Home school is appropriate

From this list of objectives we can see that a good home environment must certainly be important. The primary qualification for a home that can be expected to nurture social development is a good parent-child relationship. People tend to treat others the way they were treated as children.

The parents' role changes as children mature. You are probably familiar with how children change at adolescence. What you might not have thought about is another change that usually occurs at about the same time—age ten or eleven (although I believe it happens earlier in homes with high morals and caring parents). The period before this change Jean Piaget calls "moral relativism." Consequences more than motives are considered in determining what is right and wrong. A child tends to be more concerned about getting caught, or even about compliance with the rules, than about who might be hurt by a wrong act. In "moral realism," the stage introduced by this change, circumstances and motives determine moral judgments. The purpose of a rule is considered instead of just dealing with the letter of the law. Note that we are talking about a maturity change, not good and bad behavior. For social development, the point is that young children who have not yet made this change are obviously in much greater danger from peer influence than are older ones. Without purpose seen behind the rules, the parental behavior code can quickly be replaced with peer standards.

During preschool and early grades, home with close guidance from parents is ideal. A substitute home environment with loving caregivers is next best. Young children learn to share toys, for example, only because you say they should and mostly when you are watching. Interacting with other little children under your supervision helps them develop patterns of sharing and some other social skills, but Mom and Dad are the most important influences.

During middle grade years social interaction with peers seems to me to become important for social development, but still it requires supervision. Instead of restricting your children to being only where you want to be, plan fun things to do together as a family. Get together with other families who have children the ages of yours. Take your children to church where they can be with agemates. Send them to vacation Bible school. Enrolling them in a regular school with the kind of atmosphere you approve is satisfactory under most circumstances. So is teaching them at home.

In adolescence your children start trying their wings. You must treat them differently, but they still need you very much. School social pressures can almost overwhelm some young adolescents especially if they are trying to do right in the face of more popular lifestyles. Home study for a year or less can help them regain their self-confidence enough to face the world again.

If your high-school or junior-high youth is in home school, I suggest encouraging organized activities with peers. After the eighth grade, a suitable Christian school close to home is sometimes hard to find. From experience with my own children and from observing many others, I believe home correspondence study or a good, small day school is much better than any boarding school up through about the tenth grade. At that point the young person's value system is somewhat established, and he or she is usually ready to face peer pressure. Also classmates have become more serious, and adjustment away from home is easier.

Social skills are obviously taught differently from math or spelling. And school subjects classified as "social studies," usually make little contribution to social maturity. Here are a few ideas for helping your children grow socially:

1. *Act socially mature yourself.* This is the most important. Speak with kindness. Never raise your voice.

2. Social grace is part of character development. *Start expecting good social behavior as soon as your child is capable of any social behavior.* Be gentle, loving, understanding and firm.

3. When your child is old enough, *make a simple list of social skills and talk about ones that need improving* or developing. Revise your list as appropriate with input from your boy or girl.

4. *Think through the list once a month or so* and sit down privately with your child or go for a walk together and talk over any of the skills that need improvement. Refer to occasions when poor

manners or selfishness was evident and ask your child what he or she thinks about the situation. If you speak understandingly, not condemning the behavior, your boy or girl will probably see the problem rather than try to justify the poor behavior. You might need to probe a little, asking your child how he or she would feel if the circumstances were reversed, or you might simply need to point out the problem. Then you can ask what should have been done or said instead. Talk it over. As a Christian parent, you will want your child to be familiar with the life of Jesus. You can refer to His example.

How you relate to the issues of social development and home schooling must depend on more than what you read from a book. Watching your children mature year by year should influence your guidance. Your decision to send your children to a classroom school might depend on their social development. I suggest not committing your family to home school for more than a year at a time. You might decide to teach some of your children at home and to send others to a regular school.

Research evidence

As a doctoral research project, John Wesley Taylor, V, asked the question, How does the self-concept of home-schooled children compare with that of other children?* Surely if kids studying at home were as deprived as some people think, their self-concept would be very low. Not having the opportunity to develop a glowing personality from their school friends, they would show up in any social context like embarrassed mice running for cover.

Taylor used the Piers-Harris Children's Self-concept Scale to evaluate 224 home-schooled children. As you would expect if you know home schooling families, he found them to be anything but mousy. Half scored above the 90th percentile, and only about 10% were below the national average.

The Dating Game

I expect that most of you who read this book agree that the marriage union is a serious responsibility and a privilege, and that it should remain firm until broken by death. You no doubt regret to see so many marriages fail where love seems to mean feeling more than principle. I've become convinced that the groundwork for a good marriage is laid in the social atmosphere of childhood and youth. One of the primary elements of this groundwork is a wholesome behavior pattern for boy-girl relationships.

Jon Lindvall, in a newsletter to home school families under the guidance of his "Pilgrims School," has outlined dating principles that call for a rather drastic change from the routine social atmosphere of even conservative youth. I have recently come to some of the same conclusions.

Lindvall begins by describing a typical experience of two teen-age couples who seek security in "going together." Then, under the pressures of envy and manipulation, they break up and form other partnerships. He makes the point that typical doesn't mean normal or right. From a Christian standpoint he refers to Romans 12:1 and Ephesians 4:31, 32.

The pattern, as he sees it, "lends itself to disunity and distrust in present and future relationships. It creates stress as teens view their self-worth in terms of whether or not they are 'going with' someone. It leaves emotional scars from the many rejections experienced by all but the most popular ones. Even these envied and wanted popular teens learn to protect their 'beautiful people' status out of a dread of being left out. . . .

"Even if teens live up to the scriptural standard of sexual abstinence outside of marriage, when they are encouraged to . . . [give] themselves emotionally to one and then another, they develop social relationship patterns that are contrary to the foundation of a good marital relationship. . . ."

Lindvall makes "a distinction between the infatuation dating typical of young American teens and the serious dating, or courting, practiced by those who are seeking a spouse. . . . [The typical teenagers are] driven by their hormones and peer pressure to be 'going with' someone."

He recommends first that youth unready to consider marriage, not form couples, but that mixed groups associate in a variety of activities. This is not an easy stance to maintain considering the force of natural inclination.

Then he explains that "Probably the most important issue related to teen social life is the honoring of parental authority." Counseling with understanding parents brings in more than greater wisdom. It helps place the issue of social contacts in a mature atmosphere, protected from the pressure of youth culture expectations.

I have observed youth who have set a priority sequence in meeting life goals. First, for Christian oriented individuals, is to develop a working faith relationship with God; next they achieve the basic preparation for their lifework; and finally, they form a relationship culminating in marriage. By the time major educational goals are essentially mastered, narrowing affections to one individual leads rather quickly to a well-reasoned decision for marriage.

Being unattached while pursuing an education permits (1) a better understanding of character traits desirable for a life partner through wide association, (2) the free growth of a spiritual commitment, (3) efficient, unrestricted learning, and (4) protection from immoral behavior.

I have shared these concepts to help you begin to see the pitfalls of the modern dating pattern. Your conclusions may differ from mine, but you will want to prepare your children for wholesome relationships before the pressures of the teen society begin to influence them.

A success story

Good social development of home schooled children is certainly possible, but it takes parents who care. The experience in the following letter should give you courage and ideas:

April 23, 1980

Dear Dr. Wade:

In response to your recent letter, I will try to answer some of your questions concerning our experience with home school.

In 1966 we moved to a country home that was 26 miles from the nearest church school. Our main motivation was to take our children back to the joys of nature and away from some of the pressures that are inherent in modern suburban neighborhoods. At that time our oldest son was just entering sixth grade, our second son was ready for fourth grade, our daughter was a third grader, and our youngest son was three years old.

We decided to try home school for a year, since the miles seemed very long to a Christian school. We talked to the regional education officer, who was willing to make us a part of the school system operated by our church. Both my husband and I were professional teachers—he in math and science and I in music. In order to obtain an elementary certificate, I took the required courses by correspondence.

We checked the laws of our state in regard to schools and complied with the requirements.

For the most part we followed the curriculum that the church education department recommended and obtained our books and other materials from them. Music became an important part of each day. Practice periods and lessons were built into the school schedule for each child. In addition, we spent half an hour each day playing together in a "family orchestra."

Yearly, each child was given the choice of home school or "regular" school. Always the reaction was the same—they preferred to stay at home.

In 1970 we decided to build our own schoolhouse—a 14' X 20' building in back of our house. (Up until this time we had devoted one room of the house to our school, where we had a blackboard, school desks, and the usual trappings of a schoolroom.) The children helped in the building of this structure and learned quite a lot about everything from wiring to putting on shingles.

As the older children reached high school age, they took courses from Home Study Institute in Washington, D.C. and from the Independent Study High School at the University of Nebraska. We feel that their correspondence work not only taught the subjects well, but also taught them the value of an organized study program.

For a couple of years two nephews and a niece lived with us and attended our school. On occasion we had one or two others. But our school was mainly for our own children, and we declined to take most of the other students who expressed a desire to attend.

As a person who has spent nine years teaching home school, I can testify that teaching one's own children can be the most rewarding experience available to a parent. No one else can ever understand or care so much for a child as does the parent. However, the responsibility resting on the person who assumes this task is tremendous. She holds in her hands the whole future of these children for this life and the life to come. (I use "she" because in most home schools the mother is the teacher.)

The groundwork is laid in the cradle. The well-disciplined, much-loved child responds well to a teacher-parent. Disaster awaits those who have not established a strong parent-child relationship.

I can also testify that this job is full-time, hard work. When parents go the route of teaching their children at home, they should strive to give them a better education, a closer walk with God, and a more interesting life than if they were in a regular school situation. That is a challenge that takes prayer, effort, organization, and study!

We tried to teach our children to study efficiently and well so that they could finish their assignments faster and better. With the time thus saved, they were encouraged to work on areas of interest to them such as bird-watching, building a radio, sewing, etc. We had no interest in pushing them through school faster, but we were very interested in seeing them broaden their knowledge in different fields.

We tried to emphasize the importance of courtesy and thoughtfulness within the family circle, feeling that a person who can relate to his own family will have little trouble in the wider world of people. Respect for and friendship with older people, along with activities involving others of their own age was encouraged. Camping, all-day bicycle rides, and membership in an orchestra were activities in which the whole family could take part along with friends.

Recognizing that one of the most precious gifts that God has given to the human race is the privilege of choice, we encouraged the children to make their own decisions on the level of their ability, especially in matters relating to religion. We had family worship, Bible study in school, and attended a small church regularly, but we taught the children that it was a privilege, not a requirement, to worship God and serve Him.

I certainly do not want to give the impression that everything was always perfect and that we had all the answers. Far from it. We were all too human for that!

Perhaps you would be interested in how children who attended home school for so long adjust to the world. Our oldest son is a college graduate and is presently in medical school. While in college he was president of his senior class, president of the language club, and president of the biology club. He served as president of his freshman class in medical school and also plays in the orchestra there and in a string quartet. In his church he is the leader of the Young Adults' Ministries.

Our second son will graduate this year in computer science. He was principal violist in a very fine orchestra for nine years. His interests are in electronic and mechanical lines. He is active in his church. He and his lovely wife, who is a registered nurse, especially enjoy boating, water skiing, and photography.

Our daughter was concert master of the orchestra at her college, along with her special interest in biology and ornithology. Unfortunately, she became ill and had to drop out of school. She is now the wife of a minister.

Our "baby" boy, who is now 17, is a student at the Academy of Music in Vienna, Austria. He has always loved people, old or young, and has a host of friends there in Vienna. His teacher tells us that he is her best student and has invited him to appear in an international piano competition in Italy this summer.

God has blessed our efforts, and we give Him all the praise for leading us into a situation where we could get to know our children *so well and in a way that we could be a major influence in their lives.*

At present I teach in a Christian secondary school so still stay very busy. Consequently, I have written this letter very quickly, because I presume you want just a "peek" at our school. If I can be of further help, feel free to contact me.

Sincerely,
Velma Woodruff

To bring you up to date (1988) since Mrs. Woodruff's letter: Roger has been appointed director of the Family Practice Residency at Loma Linda University. Gilbert died in a drowning accident in 1982. Paula has her own accounting business. And Douglas, after graduating with honors from the Academy of Music in Vienna, taught music and German for a time and is now preparing to study engineering while teaching developmental math.

THEORY INTO PRACTICE

25

The lovely game

By Margaret Savage

A story of preschool home education

"Mommy, I learned a new game. Come and see!" Anne-Margot, not quite two years old, tugged impatiently at my hand and led me from the kitchen to the rocky outdoor terrain of our creek-side home in the foothills of the Sierra Nevada mountains. There, beneath the great pines, she directed my attention to a row or small sticks. Warming to the occasion, her brown eyes sparkled and her little hands grasped the edges of her red dress eager to share an exciting discovery. "Families, Mommy," she explained, "stick families. See the daddy stick and the mommy stick and the baby stick? Three in a family. And look, Mom, one, two, three, four families—twelve sticks. See, Mommy? Four families of three make twelve! Isn't it a lovely game? Do you like it?"

A precious challenge

Yes, Anne-Margot, it was a lovely game. After appropriate remarks of interest I left my little daughter all hops and skips and jumps—and sticks, and returned pensively to the house. My mind seemed to spin as it began adjusting to the fact that this busy, eager child had been blessed with a keen intelligence and a self-motivated learning ability which would be an ongoing challenge to those who would carry the responsibility of her education.

Through many other "lovely games" which followed, I observed, evaluated and considered. Would I regard the priceless privilege of the early years with this darting, effervescent sunbeam youngster as simply a maternal fulfillment—a time for taking snapshots and for comparing growth and development with other parents? Would it be a time for teaching meaningless rhymes, a time for plastic toys and the "electronic baby sitter"? Would these bright infant eyes be directed to the unreal and often ugly sight of cartoon-like pictures in garish colors? Would the alert ears be filled with the throbbing rock beat? Would wondering observations of the great world around her be reciprocated merely with adult laughter at her "cute" words and discoveries? And how would I relate to the wondering innocence of a tiny sister just beginning to sit up and look around at the water splashing over the rocks in the creek, the stately step of the deer in the woodlands, and all the sights and sounds of nature around her?

No, these treasures entrusted to my care would be educated and trained to recognize the real values of life. From their earliest days their energies would be directed toward service to God and man. My years of teaching experience would develop and ripen as, with reliance upon more than human skill, I would accept the challenge of building characters fitted to stand firm and to bless others through the stresses and strains of our age. This would become my greatest priority. The golden moments would last but a short time. The opportunity was mine to grasp now.

My philosophy of education emphasizes the balanced development of the physical, mental, social and spiritual areas of life toward the formation of the whole person. The values needed for growth are sadly warped in much of our society. To help our daughters learn good values would require new directions in our lives. I knew that accomplishments begin as concepts in the mind and, if cherished, become life goals. My little girl's "lovely game" had triggered such a goal. It was time now to lay the foundation blocks for character development. What were they to be? Obedience, self-control, respect and reverence.

The avenues of influence

We had started already. From birth I had held tiny hands in morning and evening devotions. A brief prayer of thanks mentioning the infant's name and a simple sweet song. Before ten months of age there were noticeable responses to the first notes of the song. At one year small lips were commencing a recognizable, "Happy, happy home."

How did we educate during those earliest of years? By using our wealth. Were we a moneyed family, then? Oh, no. But we were rich in the possession of delight in our children's ability to learn and in our quiet acre and a half far from town or city. The dawning of intelligence was not ushered in on harsh strains of popular rock or with a jungle of plastic ornaments and gaudy clown faces. It came quietly and naturally with consideration for the development of each of the senses.

Sight

The sense of sight promotes physical as well as practical and emotional development. An infant's visual input is a kaleidoscope of objects, movements and colors. By and by the marvelous mechanism of the brain absorbs, sorts, replays and relates these observations into sensations of pleasantness, harmony and beauty; or those of disharmony, unrest and fear. For our girls we chose loving, smiling faces; bright flowers; green grass; trees moving in the breeze; the view from Daddy's shoulders; the whiteness of winter snow with bright red berries; the comical expression of Hilda, our basset hound; funny, furry catkins hanging above the water's edge in springtime; and the heavens heavy with brilliant stars on a warm summer night.

Hearing

What about auditory input? How easily the sounds that speak to the soul are drowned out by the noise of traffic, angry voices, the power mower or the vacuum cleaner. Is there such a thing as a "still, small voice" any more? Oh, yes! "Daddy, what is the water saying when it goes all bubbly over the rocks? Oh, Mom, listen to my tinkley tune on the piano! If I'm very quiet, I can hear the bumble bee humming my name. Whatever *is* the donkey trying to say, Mom? Ooooh . . . my feet make the leaves say, 'Crunch, crunch'; they sound like cereal when my teeth bite it! Do stars crackle as they shine, Mommy, do they? Listen while I sing the new pretty song from church. Can smoke talk? Hear the grass rustle? Which birdie sings in that nice way, Mommy? Are we going to sit in the rocking chair and hear the quiet now?—are we Mom?"

Touch

The senses make the lessons of life real. Through them the physical, mental, social and spiritual can be merged into full maturity. A few of our younger daughter's early experiences illustrate learning through the sense of touch.

Little Ruth-Kyrie is coming into her own. She hasn't yet learned to talk or walk. We fix up a pup-tent of restful green and prop her just inside its shady doorway in her infant seat. Plump and content but with growing interest, she stretches out curious fingers to the many offerings brought by her faithful "big" sister. Another "lovely game" now is to "teach Ruthie." "Look, Ruthie, this is a pretty rock. Feel the big rock. Feel the little one. This is a stick. It's a rough stick. See how funny it feels on your finger? Touch it, Ruthie. It is a *rough* stick. And here is a smooth stick. See how funny it feels on your finger? Stroke them like this."

And so the "lovely game" goes on. I hang out the washing to Anne-Margot's soft crooning and I wonder. How does she know how to teach when only a year ago she was still learning to talk?

Taste

Ruth-Kyrie follows her preschool heroine's every sound and move. Small wonder that her first word is "Annie," and for the next two years a great portion of her comments will be prefaced by "Annie says." How important, then, that Anne-Margot learn to be a good example. And no better area to practice than in tasting! Here we see Ruth-Kyrie out in sunshine as usual; old enough, now, to be seated in the highchair for lunch. Her legs are pulled up high so that she can see her bare toes beyond the feeding tray, and on each toe she is carefully fitting a large, black olive. Anne-Margot gleefully trots back and forth from a tray, bringing one olive at a time. I emerge from the house with the rest of the food in time to hear, "And one more makes nine, and one more makes *ten*. Ten olives, Ruthie, and ten toes. One olive for every toe."

"See Mommy. See the olives on Ruthie's toes? How do toe olives taste? Do they taste the same as finger olives? Do they, Mom? Have you ever eaten toe olives? Have you, Mommy?" I have to admit that this is a gourmet experience which I seem to have missed. I see Anne-Margot staring pensively at my toes and glancing at the olives on the table, and I hastily change the subject. "How about the blessing?" "Oh, yes. Dear Lord, thank You for the toe olives. Amen." In my thought I'm picturing first grade workbooks teaching one-to-one relationships with such instructions as "Draw a string for each balloon." And here the lesson is learned in the freedom of childhood innocence.

Feeding Ruth-Kyrie, another "lovely game" is capably played by our busy brown-eyes standing on her toes to gently reach little sister's mouth as we talk about sweet tastes, sour tastes, red sweet tastes, yellow sour tastes, salty tastes and more.

We feed the fluffy kitten while Anne-Margot lies on her stomach and twists her head at strange angles as she stares at the lapping pink tongue. Kitty fails to reply to the stream of comments and questions about how the milk tastes, how this cat food tastes and whether he likes the taste of water.

Anne-Margot contemplates Mother's statement that we can help our sense of taste to enjoy foods that are good for us. Later we pick up a magazine to look at. Anne gleefully shows Ruthie and Kitty pictures of foods that we declare to be harmful to our bodies—hardly feeling it significant that they are both taking naps.

Smell

What does the olfactory sense have to do with the training of character? A scent is imprinted upon the memory so firmly that fifty years later when smelling a rose of the same kind, one can recall the perfume and even the occasion associated with it. Then just think about assailing the delicate nostrils and developing lung tissue with tobacco smoke, stale alcohol breath, stuffy, airless room odors or unhealthful fumes! Sometimes I have groped for tactful words in an effort to avoid these pollutants without offending the adults concerned. Frequently a humorous approach works effectively. The problem involves more than inhaling harmful substances. Years later, when confronted with a similar foul odor, will your child remember that Mother didn't allow precious little bodies to be damaged, even a very small amount, without objection? And how did Mother voice the objection? With courtesy and gentleness? With annoyance and irritation? With a frown, or with a hopeful smile?

Social development

As we have seen, physical, mental and spiritual development requires constant guidance through the right sensory inputs. What then of social development? I'm frequently asked, "In home education, how does your child get social experience?" I'll illustrate again.

Watch as Ruth-Kyrie helps to tuck the red and white checkered cloth over the crusty fresh loaf. She and Anne-Margot helped mother pat and knead the bread. Peeping and exclaiming with delight and surprise they watched the bread rise and eventually emerge from the oven. While we walk slowly down the road taking the bread to Mrs. Neighbor, we practice greeting her. Both little girls want to press the doorbell. We talk about taking turns. This time Anne-Margot will press it. The door opens. "Hi, Mrs. Do'bell." Whoops, let's try again! "Hi, Mrs. Neighbor." And Ruth-Kyrie adds, "Good afternoon, Mrs. Neighbor. We brought you some bread. We all *made* the bread." Both little ones sit quietly while Mrs. Neighbor and Mother visit briefly. After we have said good-by and are out on the sidewalk, Ruth-Kyrie announces, "I like Mrs. Neighbor." We talk about making others happy. Anne-Margot jumps and skips all the way home. She says she has a "happy, sharing something inside." Ruth-Kyrie say she has "happy inside, too," and Mother isn't missing a classroom full of thirty fourth-graders reciting multiplication facts at all!

"School" time

The girls were still quite young when an hour of more structured instruction was introduced each day. We had opened our home to accept developmentally disabled children. Anne-Margot and Ruth-Kyrie loved them all and learned to relate well to their special needs. A little bell heralded "school" time and the children came to sit in small chairs arranged in a semicircle. The sixty-minute program included such activities as:

Greeting song. "How are You Today?" (5 minutes). Each
child's name is mentioned in the song as a mirror is held
for each to see his or her face; and we shake hands.

Simple prayer. (1 minute)
Thanks for birds, flowers, trees happy day and so on.

Color song. (4 minutes)
The children are called in turn to stand by "Teacher."
For each, a color is chosen, and as we sing, I help him or
her point to a garment of that color. "Who's a red bird?
(Mark's) a red bird, (Mark's) a red bird, to-o-o-day!"

Follow the leader. (5 minutes)
"This is the way we *walk* along,
walk along, *walk* along,
This is the way we *walk* along
On this nice, bright day."
We sing to various body movements (jump, run, tiptoe,
etc.) as the children follow and imitate a leader.

Drink time. (5 minutes)
Drink in small colored cups is actually poured and served by two children selected daily. We expect spills and the children learn to clean them up.

Outdoor time. (10 minutes)
Pointing out various natural phenomena such as leaves, rocks or birds. Children help bring back objects for the nature table.

Foot-wiping procedure. (3 minutes)

Placing items on the table. (2 minutes)
An old TV tray covered with paper.

Bathroom and hand washing. (8 minutes)
A real "lesson" on proper hand washing and drying.

Observing and discussing items on the nature table.
(2 minutes)

Story time. (5 minutes)
I read or tell a short, simple story with a character-building lesson such as sharing, obedience or care for animals. We usually use a felt board, nature object, picture or other visual aid.

Activity time. (8 minutes)
For example, shoe tying, dusting chairs, raking leaves, piling blocks, learning to use a can opener, folding table napkins, brushing the dog, rhythm band, marching to music or action songs.

"School time is over" song. (2 minutes)
> "We had fun. School is done.
> Now we go and work and play.
> Good-by, good-by,
> See you all another day."

The structured hour—varied from time to time—seemed just enough to teach several needed skills and values. In the children's understanding, they were "going to school" and, by way of learning, so they were. Their minds, however, were not taxed or pushed. The remainder of their time was spent in outdoor activities, work experience (small, simple tasks in house and yard), eating, naps, walks, grocery shopping trips, play on the equipment for large muscle development (including bars of graded levels, a tire hanging from a tree, swings, slide, tether ball, balls, tricycles and seasonal equipment such as wading pools, a sand pile and snow saucers).

Preschool learning experience

During their preschool years before the girls were six and seven, they had numerous family-centered learning experiences. To give you ideas for activities you might plan, I will share some we found worthwhile:

Going for hikes and picnics; attending church programs for children; taking trips to parks, zoos, museums, historical sites.

Working with yarn, clay, scissors, finger paints, paper, crayons, paints and many other collected items. Spools were welcomed. Old wallpaper books were hailed with great rejoicing. Many happy winter hours were spent making things. Guests were sometimes rather surprised with gifts of nondescript appearance but not one failed to rise to the occasion and express warm appreciation for the effort!

Riding the pony; exploring a "dress-up box" (a large box of clothing geared to please small children); playing in the sand or water; enjoying a playhouse with table, chairs, shelves, stocked with "treasures" bought by children from local yard sales.

Helping father in the garden, helping Mother cook and prepare food, caring for the pets, working from a pictorial job list reminder of daily responsibilities with places to check off the jobs as they are done.

Beginning piano lessons from Mother; listening to character-building stories and records; helping work on a jigsaw puzzle; purchasing, wrapping and sending socks and small gifts to an Indian reservation; buying a game and taking it to the children's ward of a local hospital; making food and gift box for and taking it to a needy family; putting on plays for senior citizens and inviting them home for a holiday meal.

Such experiences as these, the continual close family relationship and interesting, stimulating devotional periods each day, provided a start for my two little learners. "A lovely game," Anne-Margot would have said. Yes, Anne, it has all been a lovely game—the game of learning—the game of living life with eagerness and expectancy undimmed and undaunted.

A foundation to build on

An early home education with parents actively interested, working, relating and sharing life's experiences with their children builds a solid foundation for future learning. Some parents consider this preparation for life too important to entrust to any other person. Then, as the age for more formal learning approaches, home may naturally be school, and book learning is not mysterious but merely a continuation of what has gone before.

Whatever approach you choose, remember that the family educates first and most effectively. Fortunate is the child whose parents are aware of their responsibility during preschool years, and doubly fortunate are children privileged to continue home schooling into more formal learning, free from the tensions and influences which damage so may young hearts and minds.

26

The redwooded headpecker

By Margaret Savage

A story of school years at home

The concept of fulfillment and reward in home teaching had not entered my conscious thinking until one day when the door burst open and wide-eyed, breathless, six-year-old Ruth-Kyrie ran in exclaiming, "Mommy, Mommy, I just saw a redwooded headpecker!" We all laughed, including Ruth-Kyrie as she became aware of her verbal mix-up.

What a golden "teachable moment"! Even through the mirth I sensed the joy and reward in being present during my child's learning experience. Had this not been my constant privilege during the early years? Why then should it cease at our state's decreed compulsory school attendance age?

Several years passed. Both daughters had learned at home until almost eight years of age and were now attending a Christian school with an enrollment of approximately ninety students. Anne-Margot was in the sixth grade and Ruth-Kyrie in the fourth. They had fine teachers whom they loved and respected. Their grades were very acceptable and, in many ways, they enjoyed school. Since the time I described in my chapter of "The Lovely Game," my husband had terminated his distant employment and was now able to stay home through the week. But, for several reasons, we began to wonder whether home education might be better for us than even desirable away-from-home learning. At last, following much thoughtful discussion, we set up a home school which, over a period of three years, included eleven other students from five to sixteen years old.

Why we chose home education

We decided on school at home (1) for the general well-being and physical health of our children, (2) to meet special learning needs, (3) for a schedule geared to family travel plans, and (4) to allow more time for many ongoing home learning projects.

The girls had frequently been kept at home with bronchial ailments and illness related to the control of blood-sugar levels. They would thrive at home, but upon returning to school they would become fatigued and lethargic and before long they would be sick again. Also, frequent holiday and birthday celebrations created social pressures when rich party foods were declined. Although the girls maintained high scholastic standings, the arrangements were difficult for everyone concerned. As we studied about health, we made lifestyle changes. We began to spend far more time outdoors. Our diet improved with the elimination of almost all refined foods. We took more time for the exercise and satisfaction of practical work. I was on hand to establish habits of frequent drinks of water, deep breathing and good posture. We took brisk midmorning walks, and the study area was moved to a spot in the sunshine by open windows or often outside. These practices obviously could not be followed in a school classroom.

During the time spent at home through bouts of illness we became well acquainted with the school curriculum. We felt that most of it was helpful and positive, but in many ways insufficiently challenging to our older daughter. We invited the county school psychologist to administer a battery of tests. He recommended that we arrange for Anne-Margot to be enrolled in the first year of a college program. We didn't agree. I believe that good home education can be an excellent alternative for gifted as well as for ordinary children.

We also found that our home "wellness" program was time consuming. We came to believe that our girls' physical health, their health education, and learning to prepare nutritious foods were more important than some of the more traditional areas of study.

The most urgent and winning factor in our decision for home education was the need to visit aging relatives overseas. A two-month stay in the United Kingdom could be arranged only by intruding on the school year.

How to use the advantages of home education

If you are still wondering whether a home school would be the best plan for your family, the outstanding advantages we discovered may help you decide. If you have already opted for teaching you own children, our experience may give you ideas for making the most of your opportunity.

A family-centered start to the day replaces the typical morning scramble and rush for the school bus. Your early morning program planned with consideration for the needs of each family member will bring cheerful faces to the breakfast table. Allow time for your children to begin their day with prayer. A glass of water purifies the blood stream. Outdoor chores promote deep breathing and good appetites. In our home, Father starts his meal first. He is then ready to read to the rest of us from a beloved series of books while we enjoy the main meal of the day. We frequently discuss home needs and plans. We also share family letters and check the jet plane on our family savings chart.

A home education program allows flexibility. Both our Sierra Country Home School and now Pine Acres School have had daily time schedules. But we have felt free to alter them to accommodate unexpected and nonroutine learning opportunities. For example, you may want to deviate from your schedule before a local science fair, for your daily science periods or during the arts and crafts period. Even some of the practical work periods might be used to complete an exhibit needed by a certain time deadline. We often appreciated the freedom to change our program. For instance, one day the house cleaning lady brought her guitar. During her break and ours, we all participated in a pleasurable experience in music enrichment. Another time a sick neighbor needed leaves raked.

Visits from county agency employees, interested parents, physicians and ministers provided fine opportunities to practice social skills and to learn about the work of our visitors.

Once after an early-morning visit to the pond, Ruth-Kyrie announced that it was "tadpole-time." On only one day of the year were the pond edges that black with tadpoles. Seeing them fascinated our boys and girls. By adding our arts and crafts period to our lunch hour and packing along our sack lunches, we were able to fit the excursion into our school day even on the spur of the moment.

Another unscheduled activity occurred a little later in the year as small toads by the thousands appeared on the mud flats of the rapidly shrinking pond. A well-watered rock wall at home provided housing for as many of these interesting amphibians as eagerly cupped hands could transport. The experience gave real meaning to our study of toads from the encyclopedia in our home-school classroom! And what fun to run out to the wall, to "toad city," on our breaks to see them settling in!

At short notice our little group of students was able to respond to an invitation to participate in a "Disability Day" at a local public school. Anne-Margot and Ruth-Kyrie had been asked to share their knowledge in the area of the deaf-mute handicap. They set up a booth. We all took interest in visiting it along with other booths giving informative knowledge concerning major disabilities. Anne-Margot and Ruth-Kyrie addressed several assemblies on the subject of American Sign Language, demonstrating with their hands and delighting several hundred elementary students by teaching them a few words on their own fingers.

Local news has always been a feature in our home learning approach. When we read of a woman in our community who had been the victim of an attempted arson, the children were motivated to express their sympathy and encouragement in a letter-writing exercise. It was not the language lesson I had planned, but it presented the same skills in a far superior way. And the young writers received the unexpected surprise of an appreciative reply.

Since we spent more time on research papers than on workbooks, sudden needs for material at the public library would occur. Although the library was some miles away, no long-term scheduling was required. We took our sack lunches in the car, worked at the library and fitted in a lunch-hour at the local park with a "go" on the swings. Once we even had a great time on roller skates.

One day thirteen deer filed down through the woods across Sullivan Creek. Watching wildlife called for special breaks from the school schedule. Sometimes an extra-handsome squirrel family would perform outside our schoolroom windows, or the little hummingbird "boss" would come flashing his colorful jewels, introducing a new family to the nectar feeder. We watched new visitors come to the bird feeder and observed Mr. and Mrs. Wood Duck making their annual debut. We saw a solitary great blue heron swoop down in front of the canyon wall. Sometimes students would go to the windows for a few moments just to gaze at the rushing, splashing waters below or at the steeply wooded canyon bank beyond, or to feast their eyes on the transforming beauty of snow in winter. For these special moments of contemplation, it was in order to quietly leave one's seat. And the children understood that staying too long would abuse the privilege. One troubled child who had previously known only scholastic failure came to visit and sat for a while at our table. "I could learn here," she announced simply. She came and she did!

The art of conversation

How do children learn conversation in the traditional school setting? You can imagine. In the home school children may hear interesting and stimulating conversation in which they are naturally included. Introduce your young learners to vocabulary-building experiences. Tape recorders let them experiment with their own voices. Vocabulary building records, reading aloud and listening to family members read, word games, singing together, family members expressing their feelings about life experiences, all aid in building skills.

Organization

Some individuals are handicapped throughout life by poor organization and planning skills. Large school classes offer little individualized help for naturally poor organizers to master their muddled confusion. Of course, all youngsters need to learn neatness and order. Growing up aimlessly whether in a home school or in the traditional school can be devastating later in life. To teach organization to children who have a serious problem you may want to write out little lists with simple steps showing what should be done. Organizational reminders may be written at the top of work papers. Children appreciate decorations with small pictures cut from old catalogs or magazines.

Appoint a classroom monitor to assist the disorganized or younger child by helping him or her check for neat work areas, clean hands, properly wiped feet and so on. Even for a one-child home school, take time for the several tasks required to keep up an orderly learning program.

Maintaining discipline

You will probably want to use the same discipline system for both home and school hours. We have tried several ideas: "grapetime" (actually gripe time) in family meetings, a fine/reward system, a check list, a privilege card operation and, sometimes, just "go to your room." For whatever methods you use, success demands consistency.

Peer pressure

I question whether many children below the ages of eight and nine can successfully resist peer pressure. Very small groups of different sexes and varying ages don't tend to produce pressure to conform to a popular behavior pattern. Certainly we would not expect it in the close and fairly constant presence of the home teacher. As peer pressure is but an aspect of cultural pressure, the answer to withstanding cultural pressure in later adult life may well be to have the young children removed, as much as possible, from *all* pressures they are too immature to control. Your child will be better fitted to gradually meet the demands of society through a wholesome home environment with much time out of doors learning that which is appropriate for his or her level of maturity. In company with experienced and, hopefully, wise parents, children learn appropriate attitudes and responses.

Personal habits

Sheer force of numbers hampers even the best-intentioned classroom teacher from helping children develop some most needed habits for good learning. The small home school can provide oral reminders from the teacher, attractive charts and notices, well-trained monitors, encouragement to cooperate, and checks to make sure that students understand reasons for requirements. Success in learning requires: good posture and breathing, ventilation, frequent movement, fresh water intake, proper rest room hygiene, avoidance of fatigue, coping with distraction, correct pen or pencil position, neat and careful work, consideration and concern for fellow students, a sense of responsibility and consistent study habits. In the small group arrangement you can practice eye contact, clear diction, gentle tones, the close-range smile of encouragement and the assurance of a touch on the arm or shoulder.

Balance in learning

The four main areas of learning—physical, mental, social and spiritual—must be kept in desirable balance to meet the complete needs of each student. Maintaining constant development in all areas is an ongoing process for each child. In a large classroom it is extremely difficult to know much of the day-to-day occurrences in the life of each student. In home education with your own children and possibly a few others, you can be sensitive to this sense of balance. At certain times Peter may need more academic encouragement than Johnny. Or Mary's life at home may cause such stress that, more than anything else, she needs your counseling time.

You might be asked to teach someone like a little girl who came to our home school. She showed symptoms of a learning disability generally called dyslexia. Did she need more exposure to the printed page? We thought not. From infancy Beth had spent an average of fifty hours a week indoors in front of a television set. Her brain was overtaxed and weary. She needed an improved diet and much outdoor activity. How she enjoyed the bread-baking lessons and the dog running! Later we cautiously introduced her again to academic learning. Her problems abated. The following year she entered a larger school at only one grade behind her chronological age-level expectation.

Space, equipment and materials needs

The space, equipment and materials considered necessary for operating a home school vary from family to family. We know of one family which checks out a large supply of books from the public library each month, takes in most of the free community concerts, films and plays, permits its teenagers to sleep until noon if they so desire and is active in may areas of dramatic arts. This is their home school program. Our opinion of balanced learning is different, and we obviously need different materials. The following list we recommended as essential:

A study area with adequate lighting and ventilation.
Activity space.
Outdoor areas for work and play.
Adequate rest room facilities with fresh towels.
A place for lunches and belongings if nonfamily children attend. (Plastic storage bins serve the purpose.)
Area for the teacher. (Part of the table top will do.)
A table and upright chairs or school-type desks. (We presently have both.)
A national flag.

\#   Water (not ice cold) and drinking glasses.
\#   Paper, pencils, rulers, erasers, crayons, scissors, glue.
\#   A wastebasket.
\#   A filing cabinet. (Cartons will do.)
\#   A globe and/or atlas.
\#   Teaching manuals or books in language, spelling, math, science, social studies, and we include Bible.
\#   A large-print Bible for each student.
\#   A current dictionary.
\#   Basic gardening tools (for the best physical activity).
\#   Basic cooking utensils.
\#   A clock.
\#   A calendar.
\#   Loose-leaf binder paper.
\#   A pad of newsprint.
\#   Construction paper.
\#   A large bulletin board. (A sheet of wall board or even cardboard will do temporarily.) Pins for attaching paper to it.
\#   A ball or Frisbee.
\#   A good jump rope.
\#   A notebook for lesson plans.
\#   A notebook for student evaluation and attendance records.

A second category of materials we label "helpful and desirable." We use too large a variety to list all of them here. The following have proved the most useful:

\#   Space for gardening.
\#   A sand play area.
\#   A water play area.
\#   Large loose-leaf binders, one for each student with dividers and index tabs for papers in each subject.
\#   A chalkboard, with chalk and eraser.
\#   Felt-tip markers, large and small tips, many colors.
\#   Student textbooks and fill-in workbooks in most subjects. (We use many materials in addition to or instead of workbooks, but workbooks are very helpful for the inexperienced teacher.)

Old magazines and mail-order catalogs.
Several educational periodicals.
A picture file.
Resource files. (These are for maps, charts, booklets, magazine articles, teaching aids, resource lists, ideas, and information on many subjects to be accessed by teacher and students.)
A science equipment box. (Might contain a microscope for intermediate or high school level, simple chemicals, slides, litmus paper, beakers, test tubes, a prism, a magnifying glass, magnets, several types of thermometers, etc.)
A geometric kit.
Old mechanical and electrical devices to take apart.
A visible man or visible woman, kit or model.
Jigsaw puzzles of varying degrees of difficulty.
Map puzzles.
Flash cards.
A bowl of goldfish for school work table.
Milk cartons of various sizes to teach measuring.
Old wallpaper books.
A large box of materials for crafts. (This might include yarn, cardboard tubes, clay, spools, cloth scraps, wooden clothespins, jar lids, interesting containers, shells, driftwood, etc.)
A record player and records. (Our record categories include marches, inspirational music, orchestra, organ, cultural music, instrumental, suitable folk songs, vocal, character building stories, a foreign language course, a typing course, vocabulary building materials and phonics.)
A tape recorder with earphones, blank tapes and tapes for some areas suggested above.
Encyclopedia sets for various levels.
Many books including reference books.
A piano.
Rhythm band "instruments."
Programmed instruction materials (for remedial and enrichment).
Crocheting, knitting, or rug-latch materials.

    #   Simple woodworking tools and soft good-grade lumber scraps.

    #   A typewriter.

    #   Calculators.

    #   A box of coins and frequently used bills.

    #   Snow saucers for winter.

    #   A tether ball and rope.

    #   A tire suspended securely from a sturdy oak limb.

    #   Exercise bars at three different heights.

    #   A tree house with a well-anchored ladder.

    #   A play house (possibly heated for winter lunches).

    #   Balls of various sizes.

    #   One longer rope for group jumping.

Our greatest resource has been a pond some fifteen-minutes walk from home. It has been an ongoing source of exercise with cattails, dragonflies, ducks, frogs, salamanders, fish, weeds and much more.

Resource people

Many people have contributed to the total educating process in our home school. Among them have been family members, members of the community with particular skills, people suggested by the county schools office, small business owners, and those whom we have contacted through local newspaper articles featuring some particular experience or area of knowledge. So far no one has refused. A courteous note, a telephone call or a visit from one or two of our students has resulted in one interesting learning experience after another.

One usable idea from the county schools newsletter led us to contact an exchange student returned from Belgium. The young lady enthusiastically showed us her slides and answered questions about her experience living with a family in another culture.

The greatest human resource in our home school has been the input of knowledge and skill from retired people. Unanimously, those approached have warmed to the concept of home education and to the opportunity to share and teach.

Our girls' own grandmother has given careful mending and sewing lessons. A retired nurse gave skillful instruction in first aid and presented Junior Red Cross certificates at the end of the course. An elderly gentleman taught many different knots. A lady who had majored in drama imparted valuable tips on public speaking and methods of enhancing musical and vocal presentations. A retired physician conducted a special series of devotional meetings for the children, helping each one to develop a sense of security and self-respect. Visits from our church minister encouraged a sense of value in each child. Retired missionaries and others who had traveled in distant lands showed slides and shared many interesting experiences in our home.

One day a 4-H Club instructor provided a lively demonstration and practical experience in making applesauce. Another young woman came along to boost our knowledge of the American Sign Language. Authors, artists, poets, builders, fishermen and musicians have added to this group of wisdom sharers.

Field trips and travel

As a teacher, the term "field trip" brings to my mind stressful memories of bus scheduling; rest stops (especially the unscheduled ones); odors of orange peel, egg sandwiches and wet jackets; startled sensations on counting heads and discovering that Johnny is missing—again; and the familiar frustration of pointing out the trip to the backs of students' heads, and realizing that they are riding too high on waves of group stimulation and excitement to have more than passing interest in the subject at hand. While a small proportion of children eagerly absorb knowledge in spite of distractions, many more become emotionally triggered with escape from the classroom, the presence and noise level of peers and undeveloped self-discipline. Feedback on what was learned is frequently disappointing despite careful preparation before the trip.

In contrast, the small home school venture directed by parents who can explore the learning territory with their children has a relaxed home atmosphere. The goodwill of togetherness and the subdued sense of adventure create a comfortable learning climate. In our family experience, bursts of questions and comments alternate with quiet periods of looking, listening and considering.

Whether with only our own two daughters or with an additional half dozen of their schoolmates along, we have found field trip ventures to be most rewarding. Picture taking, postcards, giveaway brochures, maps, charts and occasional souvenirs refresh memories for reports and letters. Our girls have several large notebooks which tell of trips taken since they were six years old.

A whole book could be written about our field trips and travels. Instead we have compiled a list of suggestions trusting that they may stimulate your own ideas.

Field trip suggestions:

Shopping: With guidance, your child can shop for groceries after menu-planning and studying newspaper ads. You can also involve children in purchases of everything from postage stamps to a new home.

Museums: science and industry, art, American Indian, maritime, logging, gold mining, rock and mineral, natural history, marine life, pioneer, butterfly, archaeological, medical and many more.

National and state parks and monuments.

State capitol buildings.

Tour of a mine.

Famous bridges and harbors, historic ships.

Forest ranger programs in local parks.

Fairs on special topics or with special displays.

A fish hatchery.

Offices and work areas of selected professional people.

Cultural programs.

A bakery.

Family picnics and blackberrying excursions.

Ocean beaches, camping.

Special exhibits or programs in public or private schools.

Places of scenic beauty.
A hospital tour.
County offices, with interviews in various departments.
Airports.
Prisons or jails.
Rock collecting trips.
Amateur radio or computer demonstrations.
A farm, fruit orchard, cattle ranch, or food packing plant.
A construction site or machine shop.
Ski slopes.
An aviary.
Zoos.
Science fairs.
National Aeronautics and Space Administration base.
An ambulance and life support service.
An aquarium.
Concerts.
Historical sites.
Caves and caverns.
Travel abroad.

Supplementary learning and service activities

In addition to the usual classroom activities, children learn from many experiences. Here are a few that we have tried and can recommend:

Reading many books and periodicals each month.
Correspondence with friends, relatives and pen pals.
Physical activities: gymnastics, skiing, hiking, bicycle riding, swimming and lifesaving.
First aid course.
Scrapbooks, diaries, trip books.
Crafts: leathercraft, making cards and gifts, ceramic painting, woodwork, rock tumbling.
Art: oil painting, pastels, drawing and water colors.

\# Domestic skills: cooking and baking, needlecraft household management.

\# Music: voice and instrument lessons and practice.

\# Gardening.

\# Nature: ant watching, camping, flower collecting and pressing, observing a pond year-round, using a telescope to observe eclipses, making science topic notebooks, making weather charts.

\# Family nights: discussion, plays, games and activities.

\# Projects for income: operating a home pet care service; growing alfalfa sprouts for the neighborhood; collecting discarded cans.

\# Planning surprises to help the unfortunate. (For example, in company with a schoolmate, our girls took part of their school time to cover boxes with wallpaper and fill them with groceries purchased with money they had saved. They delivered the boxes to a young couple in need and enjoyed seeing their gratitude.)

\# Monthly contacts with elderly friends: phone calls, handmade cards, personal notes with drawings and poems, baked and handmade gifts and personal visits.

\# Visiting shut-ins: with similar activities plus musical presentations for groups in the day room; and making tapes with musical presentations, poems and words of encouragement.

\# Jail visits accompanied by a parent.

\# Helping slow learners in school.

\# Annual service at a camp for the blind: working as junior counselors, being "eyes" in hiking, riding, archery, water play and swimming, boating and excursions.

\# Collecting roadside trash.

\# Gathering firewood.

\# Occasional baby sitting in our own or a close friend's home (after instruction, discussion and demonstration).

\# In church, assisting young mothers or sitting with the elderly.

\# Helping neighbors and parents with yard work.

We feel that experiences in the real world of work give children important advantages. Academic studies take on new meaning.

The young helpers begin to understand employment relationships. They observe adults busily engaged in tasks they enjoy. This kind of experience is certainly superior to an atmosphere of large scale peer pressure in a society where diligence and excellence are usually not coveted. Thus children develop a sense of the value of their small accomplishments. Here are weekly volunteer jobs our girls have done over the past school years:

\#   Employment in a local pet shop: cleaning cages, stocking aquarium tanks, bathing puppies, tidying shelves, constructing bamboo bird cages, cleaning floors and equipment, etc.

\#   Employment in a pet-grooming parlor: making small ribbon bows for animals ready to go home, cleaning up clippings, dusting, shampooing and brushing dogs, etc.

\#   Employment in a public library: organizing and replacing children's books, assisting young borrowers, dusting, replacing adult books according to code numbers, checking out books, using microfilm, answering the telephone, typing notices, making posters.

\#   Employment in a veterinary office: filing cards, feeding and exercising animals, pricing and labeling medicines, cleaning floors and cages, washing instruments, assisting in small ways in surgery, answering the telephone, accompanying the veterinary doctor on large-animal work at a dairy farm.

In securing work-experience situations for our children we have met with the operators of the establishments which have seemed to have suitable experiences and atmospheres. We have described our school program as well as our students' previous work experience. Employers have expressed appreciation and in some cases have given gifts to the girls.

The school plant

Plan and organize your physical teaching space indoors and out. Consider the work area. The teaching should occur where there is good lighting, near windows, and close to the supply area.

A school name

A name for your school means much to students who may be asked where they go to school. "Greenview" or "Parkend" is a much more satisfying reply than, "I just learn at home" or "I don't go to school." Choose the school name in advance. Let the children help decide.

Planning for equipment

Supplies should be on hand long before the first day of school. Organize and examine them and become well acquainted with teaching guides, books, and so on. Especially in the area of science, collect your equipment ahead of time. Then put most of the supplies away out of sight to provide a little element of freshness as new items are brought out to use from time to time throughout the year.

Curriculum and time planning

What to teach and when are discussed elsewhere in this book, but you might like to see a general outline showing how we divide up our week.

	Monday	Tuesday	Wednesday	Thursday	Friday
8 - 12	study	study	work	study	study
12 - 1	lunch	. . .	. . .	. . .	. . .
1 - 3	study	art/ crafts/sewing	study	domestic duties	study

The actual schedule shows the specific classes beginning with Bible, each lasting 55 minutes with some variation for particular children. We also study on the weekend and add music lessons and practice. On Thursday afternoons the girls clean through the house and assist with cooking and baking for the weekend.

A monthly breakdown of the year's plan is helpful. My custom is to work by subject categories: Bible, language, math, social studies, science, health and nutrition, practical experience skills, arts and crafts, and music. A curriculum guide or outline may be borrowed or purchased from your county schools office. You could also write to other counties or ask about the curriculum from a private school you know about. Even though you might not follow any one outline, they will give you a concept of what is generally introduced at each age level. You will also get an idea of how much is usually covered in a school year. If you are starting without experience or lack teacher training, a home-study course will be helpful.

Next make up weekly plans, and after that, daily plans—even for one student. It's not necessary to make long complicated plans. A few notes on which topics will be presented and what you want to accomplish for each is all you need.

The first two days

We have started each school year with a two-day planning session with the children. On the first day they write down all the suggestions, reminders, hopes and desires which they can think of for the school year. They help unpack boxes, set out the reference books, arrange the schoolroom and put up cheerful bulletin boards. On the second day they set up their own goals and aims for the year and assemble their notebooks, papers, crayons, markers and other supplies. We do a great deal of discussing. Their input is most valuable to me as I plan the year ahead.

We work together on schedules for home and for school, considering the needs of the whole family. Father lets us know when he can teach math and science. After careful work, we put the two schedules up on the bulletin board or on the wall.

Closing the school year

Our school year does not run beyond the end of May. By then we are ready for the more informal summer learning and time out of doors. Last year we had an end-of-school program and an eighth grade graduation complete with printed programs.

Philosophy

We believe children are whole beings with development potential in physical, mental, social and spiritual areas. We teach our children broad values helping them understand the reasons for learning from the out of doors, working with their hands, service for others and making religion practical. Life in itself is education. We expose our children to its many good facets, sharing our impressions and feelings. We teach attitudes and stress that the ability to learn is a priceless resource to be developed with care. We trust that the lives of our children may be channels of helpfulness and blessing to others and an honor to the One who has lent us the gift of life.

Real education, we believe, is the balanced development of character and the grand achievement of love to God and to people.

We like home school

Three years of home education have convinced us that we are doing the right thing. We are seeing the results— two service-oriented young people, already an asset to their home and community. Although our girls are successful learners, we enrich rather than accelerate, keeping a balance among the various areas of development. Home education has helped our girls acquire individual responsibility in planning their time, both in academic and practical areas. They are truly self-motivated and love to learn.

27

Teaching several children

By Meg Johnson

Teaching children of different ages naturally takes a great deal of planning and time. We become very concerned about school lessons, but children need time with their parents for more than schooling. They also deserve personal care and attention, opportunities to help Mom and Dad with projects, and so on. Meeting all these needs can be quite challenging. This chapter offers suggestions for organizing your school program to teach children at different levels without neglecting your preschoolers or other home responsibilities. Because we are deeply concerned about our responsibilities for educating our children, trying to meet all the needs at once creates most of the strain. We teach our children more than academics. Let's examine other areas of guiding and nurturing them.

Meeting individual needs

Children are all different. Even siblings may differ greatly in readiness and learning styles. Be flexible. A program or learning environment which meets the needs of one child may simply not fit the next child's abilities, interests, or aptitudes.

Because home schooling families enjoy close relationships, parents can easily capitalize on their children's individual readiness—and more importantly they can adjust to accommodate each child's differences in readiness among various learning areas. Take time to find out what your children can, should, or wants to be learning at each age or grade level. Then provide materials and an environment to help each child learn as he or she is ready.

Now let's look at a few ideas which might help in organizing activities so that you can be available to teach your older children and still have time to spend with the younger ones. Start by planning space for your "school room." You need a routine place to work and to localize the mess that results occasionally from art projects, crafts, or science experiments.

Using space efficiently

You need to be able to change easily from working with one child to working with another. Positioning desks or tables so that you can move around and sit between children often works well. You need to be able to work with one child while being right there to answer the questions of the others. Encourage children not directly involved with you during this time to do something they are interested in or give them something to do that will occupy them so they are not disruptive. Make a place for toddlers and young children to play adjacent to or in the working area. This may cause a certain amount of disruption, but if each person realizes that he must work and pay attention, lessons can continue and progress will occur. When a quieter atmosphere is needed for concentration, individual children can go to another room temporarily. This arrangement may not be ideal, but most of the time it works better than you might expect.

Teamwork

Younger children pick up quite a bit of basic knowledge and skills from being exposed to the learning environment of older siblings and by imitating their behavior. Far less explaining may be needed for these younger children when it comes time to learn some of the concepts already taught to their big brothers and sisters. But remember that while getting ideas across to the younger children may be faster, each child deserves quality time with his parents investigating the world, and working and doing things with them. Bonds of love and understanding formed between parent and child during early years generally hold when adolescent counseling is needed and, in fact, throughout life.

Older children, especially if they have always been home schooled, should have developed good independent study habits. Setting a goal of getting work done without being prodded can teach responsibility. Make reasonable assignments, and require that each day's work be done even if it means continuing after your regular "school" time. When a child has reached a point of independence in his own work, he can be relied on as needed to take care of very young siblings—changing diapers, keeping an eye on them, and so on. He can also learn to assist younger siblings with their learning by answering questions, explaining directions, or teaching concepts he himself has mastered. This helping can be part of the child's own school program. From the very beginning, each child should understand that he is responsible for getting his work done, and that siblings and the home teacher are there mainly to assist. Also teach your children always to give others consideration when interrupting or asking for assistance.

Being a "teacher's assistant" to younger children can be a valuable learning experience for older siblings. It reinforces their own learning and develops more of an awareness of others' needs. Younger children pick up concepts and facts by listening to discussions of older siblings, and older children understand better by teaching the younger. Because of this cross-over learning, a great deal of reinforcement occurs. This strength of family cooperation and a usually calm environment lead to good learning and thinking skills.

Using time efficiently

Challenges do arise, however, when you will wish you were several people at once. For instance, older children might need to have new concepts explained or to do research or experiments which require adult assistance; infants or toddlers may need to be watched and cared for; and a six or seven year old may want to learn about some unit which requires an adult to read or help him get started. Each child needs time and attention. In such situations, just evaluate as quickly as possible how to most effectively distribute time and attention. Usually in a few moments older children can be guided in the right direction to work until you can get back to them; someone can meet the youngest child's need; and with little delay, time can be devoted to your less mature scholar. Under your organized management, your children will learn to do what they can on their own so you can meet the needs of whoever cannot go ahead alone.

To help make your teaching easier and efficient, plan as many units as feasible which involve all your students. A general topic like airplanes can have many teaching activities. Some, of course, will be too easy or too hard for part of your children. If you remember the varying abilities of your listeners and hold different expectations, they will understand and your teaching will be surprisingly successful. You may want to write your study questions in order of increasing difficulty, assigning work for a specific student up to a certain item number. In other instances you can plan team projects with roles assigned (or permitted to be chosen) according to ability.

Of course, it isn't always possible or easy to have all your students learning about the same subject at the same time with children of different ages working at different levels. Often, although not as frequently as we would like, the younger children will learn from and be interested in the activities of the older ones. Most of the time, however, your children will need to do completely different activities. Experience and trial and error will help you plan wisely and see when to change your plan. If all this sounds like it could easily lead to confusion, try it. Usually you will find that despite some confusion, activities can continue and good progress will be made.

Good planning can limit the amount of your time each child will need. On the average, a child may need one to two hours a day. Your contact time may overlap considerably if two children work together, or if you can supervise more than one at different activities. However, when home schooling involves more than one child, the entire morning or occasionally even more time may have to be devoted to directing learning activities and to meeting the school needs of your children. On many days the time you spend solely in teaching may be much less than this, but plan to commit a good portion of each day to your children. You must be available when needed and must provide guidance and supervision.

Parents don't actually have to spend as much time formally teaching their children as you might expect. Many subjects, such as science, history, geography, social studies, and religious education need discussion, practical application, experimentation, and/or outside trips. Try to provide opportunities and materials so your children can explore these areas. Take time to investigate with your children. While this demands time and energy, and housework doesn't always get done, it really can be a lot of fun. Of course, books are valuable tools too, if used carefully. They provide an efficient way of sharing accumulated knowledge and facts. At home a good balance can easily be achieved between book learning and application.

Some specific ways to teach efficiently include simple ideas such as a daily routine (which should be flexible, but fairly consistent), yearly and daily goals, written guidelines for the children to follow so they know what it is they should be doing, and a place to work which is as conducive to "school work" as possible. In order also to give older children time to be helpful, their learning should be designed to fit their needs. Limit unnecessary repetition of concepts and skills they have already mastered. Use materials with clear instructions and explanations of concepts.

Building character

Help your children develop a sense of personal responsibility for their school work and for helping around the house.

The home school learning environment lacks the classroom atmosphere with pressure from peers and teachers to enforce performance and discipline. The various demands and activities of the home environment give children a more immediate need to develop self-discipline, self-motivation, and initiative. Because these character traits are not easy to form, parents must help their children realize the need for them in their work and study tasks.

As much as possible, let the needs for responsible behavior lead to its natural development. Children may take advantage of disorder or a brother's or sister's demand for attention to fool around or disrupt the schooling. It may then be wise to discuss what each child should contribute to a more pleasant environment for everyone. Such correcting experiences help build character. As a child realizes that out of consideration for the needs of his siblings and parents, he should be responsible for tending to business, he becomes more motivated to work on his own. Self-direction takes time to develop, however, so be willing to oversee your child's work. Check regularly to see that he understands and completes his tasks.

As a teacher, be with your children during their learning activities, even if you must sit between two of them guiding their schoolwork with a younger child on each knee! Each of your children deserves time and loving attention. Even though you are only one person, if you are close by, you can give each child as much as possible.

Remember that although your home school may be less than perfect, its consistent environment, the demands it makes on each family member, and your children's achievement of self-worth from contributing to everyone's welfare, make it the best place for developing good habits of learning and helping. Leading your children to good behavior is an essential part of their education. Just as children who attend classroom schools may get up in the morning and say they don't want to go, home schooled children may refuse to do their school work cheerfully or to cooperate with chores. You can discuss with them the importance of cooperation and consideration for others. The intimacy of the home dramatically emphasizes the effects of each person's actions. Although occasionally a day of school lessons may seem to be "lost" to character building efforts, over the long term a definite maturity will evolve in the children's attitudes about working independently and assisting each other. They will gradually be able to work on their own and become valuable contributors to the household operation.

As you watch this development, your children's contributions to the family's life will balance the burdens of parenting and of home schooling. You may spend a lot of time and effort, but you will be pleased and thankful with the results. It is a most rewarding challenge!

28

Fitting school to four children

By Ginny Baker

The beauty of teaching your own children at home with your choice of materials is that you can work your schedule to suit your needs. If one child needs more hours per week of arithmetic instruction, it can be arranged. If mother needs to attend to an infant at a certain hour, class can be suspended for a few minutes and the students can take their outdoor break.

We even had a "magic clock" in our school room. If something delayed the start of classwork, we reset that clock to the time designated for the beginning of school. It certainly took the pressure off, and class was always on schedule! If interrupted, we could unplug the clock and start it again.

When I began to home school thirteen years ago, I had three school-age children and a toddler, but only one of me. It took several weeks to adjust and rearrange our morning school schedule to fit this situation. We worked out a schedule that allowed me to spend time with each child in each subject. Although our schedules appeared extremely structured on paper, we always were rather flexible. We remained organized, however, as organization is the key to it all.

While I worked with one child, the others did seat work. Sometimes I worked with two children at once, such as in arithmetic. I found it easy to shift mental gears from one level of math to another, so I tried to schedule all the math at the same time. This wasn't as easy in other subjects.

At times I gave a spelling lesson to one, a timed typing test to another, and instructed the third in diagramming at the chalkboard. I wasn't always that busy, though. Sometimes one child listened to phonics records with earphones, another silently read his history, and the third practiced her cursive writing. This freed me to grade a few papers.

When the older children, who were a year apart, got into the higher grades, I scheduled many of their courses at the same time. For instance, they took the same geography, history, and vocabulary courses. All four children always shared the same Bible lesson, although assignments and homework usually were on different levels.

In essence, I often taught three levels of "school" to four children. In many subjects it really doesn't matter at what grade level the child receives his instruction. By the time he "graduates," he will have had all the required courses. Some courses should be presented sequentially for clearer understanding.

I rarely followed a publisher's manual, because I wanted flexibility. We advanced as fast as the child could handle the material and skipped some chapters entirely. If I didn't like the way one textbook presented a lesson, I used another. If an idea seemed unclear to the children after we had spent a reasonable amount of time with it, we would often study it from a different textbook. It didn't make sense to advance if the child hadn't fully understood the current lesson.

Generally our week resembled a college schedule: some subjects were taught on Monday-Wednesday-Friday, others on Tuesday-Thursday. This provided adequate time to properly teach the subject matter, give the child time to work some problems at the board, discuss the subject and discuss the homework assignment. Exceptions to this schedule were English grammar, elementary arithmetic, phonics and reading.

The younger the child the more necessary it is to teach him a little bit every day. But the older high school children do not need to study the same subjects daily. Consequently, our college-type schedule allowed us to have longer discussion and instructional time to cover the material.

Combining two subjects sometimes facilitates teaching. Why not go over the arithmetic or geography lesson in the foreign language your children are learning? One can do all sorts of innovative things! And if you find yourself bogged down and overworked, have an older child forgo his lesson and teach a younger sibling. The younger ones love having an older child for their "teacher."

I wrote all assignments in one book—The Wilson-Jones Page-a-day Daily Reminder available at office supply stores. I wrote each assignment in the space for the day it was due, and each child knew where to look for his homework assignment. They had no excuse for forgetting.

I continue to use this method with our one son still at home. It works smoothly, and I can go back to any day in the past and compare the assigned lesson with the grade (which I keep in a separate grade book) and know how each student did on a specific assignment.

With our magic clock, we kept close to our time schedule. I had a master schedule before me, and each child had his own schedule taped to his desk. When the time rolled around to change subjects, we did, with few exceptions. Occasionally I let one child continue with a particularly interesting reading selection or finish a math problem, while I started another child with his lesson. Before long the kids knew which subjects they must start promptly and on which ones they could take extra time.

Except for timed tests, I let the children take as long as was reasonably practical to finish a test. I was more interested in what they knew than in how fast they could complete tests.

Our goal in home schooling was for them to absorb the material and build a strong academic base in each subject. We believe learning should be chiefly concerned with the building of a man or woman, in which education is a means but not a goal.

So, moms, relax and be flexible. You don't have to finish every workbook. You don't have to finish the end of the year at the end of the book. Fit your school to your child, and enjoy your children. It worked for us!

29

Getting everything done

By Meg Johnson

One of the most frightening aspects of home schooling is the question of how to get everything done. The days never seem long enough even without home school. Then when the teaching responsibility is added on top of it all, how can a person adequately meet all the family needs? The ideal is no doubt impossible, but with careful planning we can do much more than we think.

Home schoolers have generally decided that personal needs of each family member are top priority. These include communication, physical care, opportunities to enjoy individual interests, and educational guidance, to name just a few. As we discuss personal needs let's consider three categories. Most demanding are the needs of the children. Second come the needs of the spouse. And last, the needs of the person responsible for the home teaching, usually the mother. The whole family should contribute to satisfying these needs, but often the major burden falls on the mother and teacher. One person can't do it all, however, so the entire family must be committed to the goals home education. Individuals occasionally will need to forgo personal gratifications.

Meeting children's needs

Adequately caring for each child's needs can be quite a challenge, especially if two or more are under eight years of age. But even if the mother must divide her attention among several children and her other responsibilities, she still gives each child much more time and individual loving attention than could ever be received in a classroom school. Also, sharing and taking turns and waiting for attention are best learned in a family. Such goals require effort from both children and parents, but proper social behavior learned at home will be valuable to your children when they are on their own.

Planning doesn't dictate every move. Actual decisions about who needs attention minute by minute are usually obvious. The baby needs a diaper change; a young learner can't go on until a concept is explained; the telephone rings (some home schoolers ignore this); and so on. Three- to six-year-olds are probably the most easily neglected when there are several children in the family. They tend to need less guidance in learning than older children and require less physical care than the younger ones. They will often go and play quietly when you ask them to, but they still need and deserve your undivided attention for a part of each day.

Have you ever felt at the end of a long day that all you have done is run from one need to another with no time for your own interests? Remember that those who have children around all day often feel this way. Just balance these frustrating times against the days when you do see significant progress. Even though your accomplishments may not be obvious like shiny quarts of apple sauce lined up on the shelf, you have had the opportunity to provide an atmosphere of self-worth and love for each family member. As you work with each child, you can plant seeds for positive character building in a way that could not possibly be matched in a classroom. Even if you don't see much change day by day, when you look back over several months or a year, you should see significant accomplishments spiritually and emotionally as well as intellectually. Your children's real needs will be met.

Being a good spouse

Here you face another great challenge. As both mother and teacher, your children's needs often demand your first attention, but never satisfy them at the expense of your marriage relationship. You might not have as much time as you would like to be with your husband (or wife) during this period in your family's development. But allot special time for communicating. Discuss responsibilities and roles. The husband is the focal point of your family's activity and the foundation on which your home school rests. Usually he must make significant sacrifices to provide a home environment so the mother can devote large portions of time to her children instead of to him, to home making or to helping earn the family income.

Mother is usually teacher, but the roles may be reversed or not so clearly differentiated. While the father may spend little time in actual teaching, his contribution is of paramount importance to ultimate success. His participation in raising his children enhances their learning and enjoyment. His patience while the mother must devote a great deal of her energy to home schooling, considerably lessens her burden of having to meet everyone's needs while all too often no one seems to be interested in meeting hers. The father also provides a model for his children to emulate. In discussing home schools, much is often said about cooperation between parents, but all too often if they are not united, it doesn't work at all.

Dad, as I see it, the environment you help provide adds a dimension to your life. Both you and your children can certainly be enriched. Even though you may feel you are giving up personal time, you reap great rewards. When out with your children, you will have many reasons to be very pleased with them. Home schooled children tend to be calmer, more considerate, more independent, and more thoughtful than many children who spend large periods of time with their peers.

The home teacher

Mom, you are not likely to find much time for personal interests and relaxation until the children are old enough to help take care of themselves. But do set aside some time to relax. Ask the rest of the family to help out. And, just remember that this heavy schedule is temporary. The rewards will more than compensate.

Using teaching time efficiently

In addition to responsibilities for the personal needs of each family member, planning your school program and teaching demand large blocks of time. We never have all the time we would like, to do things with our children. Even letting them explore and learn on their own takes a lot of time. Take a good look at what you do, not on a daily basis, but over the long term. Set goals, of course, but avoid getting despondent when the days just aren't long enough.

If you use structured home study courses you may sometimes feel overwhelmed by what is expected. Remember that because you work closely with your children and have a sense of the learning appropriate for their level, you are the best judge of what they know and need to study. As an alternate to regular enrollment, consider using a preplanned course as a learning resource for your child, and to help you know what children in a particular grade are generally expected to learn. If you enroll your child in a course, make every effort to help him or her learn the course material. Just be sensitive to individual needs and abilities. Use tests to make sure your child is grasping the course material. Many home study courses are based on programs used in schools with children of differing abilities, and they often provide more material than may be needed for a particular individual. Try to work out a plan with the school which fits your children's needs. Good programs offer a selection of ideas and materials so that the home schooler may draw on the knowledge, experience and efforts of many people. Let your home study courses enhance your teaching rather than create pressures which might interfere with it.

For a time-efficient home school, encourage your children to develop independent study habits. Older children to a large degree must learn to teach themselves and to assist each other as well as younger children.

Household demands

Children can develop the skills and initiative to contribute a great deal to the life of their family. They can care for younger siblings, help in the kitchen or with other household chores, and work in the yard or garden. Gradually your children's attitudes about work will change from seeing chores as tedious to feeling that they are helping you and contributing to the family needs.

Teaching your children how to work thoroughly and cheerfully is worth the time and patience. Although maturing children cannot do things as well or as quickly as you can, accept their efforts in contributing to the comfort of the home, and your life together will be rewarding.

The home school routine

In our family, the days are divided informally into time blocks. Mornings belong to book learning, and Mom is available for teaching and assistance during these hours. For us, "schoolwork" must be done first. Afternoons are devoted to other activities which· may include baking, household chores, sewing, home maintenance, community service, individual projects or visits with other home schoolers. Although we have found home schooling to be a full-time demanding lifestyle, it becomes easier as the children grow up. As they mature they become aware of what needs to be done and can help around the home on their own.

In addition to having flexible daily time blocks, we generally follow the regular public school vacation schedule. While home schooling really involves constant learning and growing, our normal program is limited to the school schedule of the children's peers. Vacations and weekends offer good breaks to relax and catch up on unfinished chores and projects. We all enjoy our vacations, but we also find it a relief to return to our regular routine, even though it's quite flexible.

In addition to routine and unavoidable chores, it may sometimes help to accomplish or work on one special project a day. On some days you may simply want to make learning more meaningful. On other days you could take time out to do a family or household project, go somewhere special, do extra shopping, make a doctor visit, or just get ahead in schoolwork. Each family defines, however flexibly, its own patterns and goals as home schooling is integrated into the family lifestyle.

Specific planning and record keeping makes working independently easier for the children. At the beginning of each day, we usually make an outline of what is to be done. The students can then go on and do their work even if no one is there to watch them every minute. And I can tend to other household and child care demands, as necessary, during school hours. Of course, children cannot always be left unsupervised as they may dawdle and bicker, but they become more responsible as time goes on. Eventually they realize that they must do their work. When older children work on their own, you have time to meet some of the needs of the younger ones. Then, in addition to writing out what is planned for the day, we keep a record of what has been accomplished.

Although home schooling family lifestyles tend to revolve around the children, there is more to be done than teaching. Housework and meal preparation demand attention too. Well-organized home school families function efficiently but still face limitations of time and energy. In many families the first thing to slip is the housework. Until the older children can responsibly help with this, it is difficult for the mother to manage all her responsibilities. Some may have children around all day and still keep the house spotless. They are exceptions.

Our family finally had to set a few basic goals. We try to clean up before Daddy gets home to make a little room for him in our small house. We do try to keep our living room fairly neat—a challenge with a toddler. Major cleaning is done when possible but never on the weekly basis that once seemed so necessary. We seriously try to keep up only with dishes and laundry, and we make time to plan and prepare good meals. Someday we may have everything under control but, for now, housekeeping is low priority.

In our hectic struggle to do everything we think we should, let's remember that our lives have purpose. Days devoted to raising children who will have firm character and moral values are days well spent.

30

Making home school special

By Sue Welch

School at home could seem rather ho-hum to your children when their friends are excited about beginning a new school year in the traditional classroom. In many creative ways home school can be made special. Here are some starters. You can pick up more ideas from other home schooling families.

We are not alone

Just as you need support from other teaching parents, your children need the assurance that they are not alone.

\# Being included in your support group, even if not at every meeting, is extremely helpful. Children may not look like they are taking in as much as they really are at these times.

\# Hearing you talk with others about home school helps them see that the idea has wide acceptance. Sometimes, when I finish a phone call, I tell Heather, "That was a mother who wants to teach her children at home, too!"

\# Field trips with a couple of other families or a larger group help. Fifty parents and children went on our first field trip. When we got home our five year old said, "Mommy, almost everyone is teaching their kids at home!" She was impressed.

\# When we pray during our school time opening exercises, we remember other home schooling families. Realizing that friends and relatives are beginning their home-school day the same way brings a sense of encouragement and togetherness.

Talk it up

Both what you do and the words you use to describe your school help your children realize its importance. Your child's age and whether this is your first year home schooling will determine how appropriate some of these suggestions are.

Name your school together. Consider just what you want your school to be, and reflect this in your name. Then make a banner with the school name on it.

Set up a schoolroom. It may be a corner of a room or an entire room. Bookshelves, globe, flags and desks make an impressive array. This will require budgeting for school expenses, although many pieces of equipment can be picked up at garage sales or secondhand stores. Procuring all of these special things will be almost as exciting as Christmas to your children. Help them understand that this is all possible because you are home schooling. Incidentally, I don't recommend substituting school supplies for gifts at regular gift-giving times.

Desks symbolize school. They make a good place to keep supplies and look important for learning even if children end up sitting close to Mother on the couch for reading or sitting at the kitchen table to do math while Mother is working.

Look forward to the first day of school. Buy school supplies, even a lunch pail for trips. Don't just buy new shoes in the fall, buy "school shoes."

For the opening day of school, plan a special "kickoff" such as a field trip a little distance from home. Let your child know that this would not be possible if your were not home schooling. To a child's perception these concrete things make home school very special.

Father may not have any teaching responsibilities—or so he and the family may think. But when you (correctly) name him the Bible teacher and identify Bible as the most important subject, things can take on a new perspective.

Have "school" pictures taken to send to grandparents.

Plan holiday parties with another home schooling family.

\#   Have different classes in different rooms or areas in your house. Say, "Let's go into our math room now," instead of "Let's go into the kitchen."

\#   Take clues from the public schools. If the neighbors are having a big deal wearing a different color to school each day for a week, copy the idea for your children. Tell them, "We are going to have blue day tomorrow, then red, yellow and green."

\#   During school time, occasionally have surprises such as a lesson-related activity, an unexpected field trip for your family, a visiting home schooler to share a science experiment & anything to make and keep school exciting.

\#   Get a school mascot, such as a fish or some gerbils.

\#   List on a chart classroom duties such as care of the school area.

\#   Don't just "take a break," have "recess." That's what your lower-grade child's friends are talking about.

\#   If Father is given the title of "Science Teacher," or "Science Consultant," when questions come up at odd times, Mother can say, "Let's ask your science teacher about that. I'm sure he knows how to find that answer." This gives credibility in a child's eyes to the parent as his teacher.

\#   When teaching a new household chore, call the time Home Ec.

\#   Give report cards. These do not have to show letter grades, but can praise and encourage work that is being done and character that is being developed.

Making your home school special to others

Your children will view their home school, to some extent, the same way they think others view it. Peer pressure is hard to completely eradicate. Also, to help other people accept your home school, you can build bridges for communication and educate in love and patience. The following ideas might help satisfy both needs.

\#   Have an open house when your schoolroom is all ready and you have spent enough days in school to have some work and projects to display. Invite neighbors, friends and/or relatives. They are probably curious about what goes on in a home school and will be impressed when they see your school atmosphere, teaching materials, and the completed work.

\#   Invite grandparents on field trips with you. Send them schoolwork samples and brag up your children's progress. They want to be proud of their grandchildren and their fears can be alleviated when they see that your children are achieving and not "being ruined."

\#   Ask your children's friends what they are doing in school and tell them what you are doing.

\#   Let your children hear you praising their progress in school.

\#   Put on a Christmas or school-closing program. Have your children help plan, invite guests, make refreshments and entertain. A bashful child may record a poem, a song, or a story he or she has written.

\#   The school-closing program could be a graduation, complete with formalities.

Making your home school special will take thought and a little effort, but it should amply reward you and encourage your children.

31

Educating
for superior achievement

When one mountain-grown family seems to be sending all their children to Harvard, it's worth a few minutes to stop and ask why. The father, David Colfax, has a Ph.D. degree. His wife Micki is an English teacher. That sounds impressive. But it's not just a matter of genes because Reed, the third son to follow the scholarly tradition, was adopted. And the parents say it's not a matter of their own education, either.

We must also concede that the roots of success go deeper than merely learning at home. After all, the home school movement is quietly producing thousands of "graduates" that aren't catching the attention of the media for any great feats of intelligence. And people go to Harvard who haven't been home schooled.

Of course heredity does have a part in achievement, and studying at home does, too, but I'm convinced that attitudes, skills and opportunities make the greatest difference, and that these are mostly produced by the home. In this chapter I will share what I see as success factors from two families with track records and then add some thoughts of my own.

The Colfax way

In their book, *Homeschooling for excellence*, David and Micki Colfax identify their educational goal as the development of intellect and character.[1] From their experience with the public school system, they see its educators as professing interest in individual needs of children while "in reality, their primary objective is that of moving the product—school children—on down the line with a minimum of interference from subordinates, parents, the public, or the children themselves."[2]

The Colfaxes do not expect home schooling to change the educational establishment or to "make classroom life any more meaningful for the millions of children whose parents cannot or will not take them out of the assembly-line schools." Teaching at home, they see as a response to the public system. At home, parents can control the education of their children in several ways, provide more efficient learning, and foster the development of autonomy and creativity.

The home schooled child can choose projects and invest time developing them, thus moving toward autonomy by taking responsibility for his or her own education.

"If only by virtue of the freedom it affords, homeschooling promotes creativity. It is an almost inevitable consequence of a program in which self-directed boys and girls are encouraged—and given space—to devise their own programs, to explore, and to experiment at their own pace."

Three of the chapters in the Colfaxes' book imply levels that would take the place of preschool, elementary and secondary education. The chapters are entitled: "Before basics," "The three R's," and "beyond basics."

The environment recommended for the before-basics years is similar to the ideal many educators would envisage. The emphasis is on providing rather than pushing.

On the surface, the three-R's level also appears similar to other solid, individualized approaches to fundamental learning. But here we begin to see what I consider the "secret ingredient" of the whole program: keeping learning interesting so it happens at a fast pace. The Colfaxes have apparently achieved this by: (1) a challenging physical work program which provides both the diversion to make book learning a refreshing change of focus, and the physical exercise to keep the brain alert, (2) waiting for readiness, (3) using materials and methods that concentrate more on the end results of the learning than on drill and busywork, (4) encouraging independence and critical thinking, and (5) expecting achievement and providing an atmosphere for the joy of its accomplishment.

In the beyond-basics level, the young scholar is ready to explore personal interests. The doors to continued learning have been opened by a groundwork of information-processing skills and by general knowledge from wide reading. Subjects usually covered in the high school curriculum are studied—some to greater depths than others. Parents help locate resources to facilitate extensive learning in a few chosen project areas.

The Archer family, another success story

The three sons in the Archer family attended Princeton, Yale and Harvard, and have become intellectual leaders in their professions—paleontology, social psychology and medicine. In contrast to the Colfaxes, they all attended public primary and secondary schools in a small town in upstate New York.

The sons don't attribute their success to the schools, however, but to achievement-oriented parents who supported their personal goals even in childhood. The boys were allowed to establish their own ideals regardless of what peers thought, and parental expectations inspired their self-confidence.

The Archer parents emphasized character development over academic achievement. Made-up stories at bedtime and "thoughts to fall asleep by" written out and tacked to the wall were part of this emphasis. Team sports were discouraged.

"At the time," writes Jules Archer, "it did not occur to my wife and me that we were doing anything out of the ordinary in raising our sons. We believed that we were simply normal parents whose concentration was on the quality of the school curriculum and teaching. In retrospect, and only after exploring the question with my sons, I recognize the importance of the home environment in the learning process.

"All of which raises the question: Does the reputed poor scholastic achievement today reflect a failure of adequate parental support and cooperation more than a failure of the school system?"

Archer's analysis of the achievement of his sons is worth underlining: "In looking for explanations for their success and comparing their educational experiences to those of children today—a quarter of a century later—I have been led to the conclusion that the most important ingredient for improving our educational system lies in the home. Parents are the principal catalysts in their children's openness to education, fascination with learning, and spur to achievement."[3]

True life success

I see success as more than intellectual achievement. In fact, adding good physical, social and emotional development wouldn't spell true success either. Only in seeking a saving relationship with the One who has created all things do we find a context for total development in every area. Talents multiply as they are wisely invested.

Most of the energies of youth in our society are spent in either worthless or harmful activities. From my own experience as a parent, I have learned the importance of helping children avoid those things that would weaken and destroy their potential. Even children with ordinary natural ability can accomplish the extraordinary when their energies are protected and channeled in wholesome directions. Here are safeguards against threats to excellence:

■ Quality sensory input: reading, watching and listening that inspire both intellectually and morally.

■ Learning to act by principle rather than by the feeling of the moment.

■ Emphasis on cooperation—lifting others—rather than on competition.

■ Balanced development. As the individual matures, more attention to some areas is appropriate, but no aspect of learning related to efficient living should be neglected.

■ Choosing friends with high ideals.

■ Making God first and last and best.

APPENDIX SECTIONS

Home school organizations, U.S. based, national / international

Classification of home schooling organizations is not always simple because many of them offer several types of services. You may want to browse through applicable parts of the appendix to find what is available.

We have listed only organizations for which we have received confirmation—for the most part by response to our questionnaires. Other good ones exist and new ones pop up continually.

Listing here does not imply endorsement. We have endeavored to provide information of interest to families with differing philosophies and needs. We don't expect you to be disappointed with the service or integrity of any of these organizations, but if you do have a problem, write to them first to try to find a solution. Then if the difficulty is not resolved, contact the Better Business Bureau in their locality.

THE ALPHABET CODE

To provide the most information in limited space, strings of code letters with the listings give various characteristics of the organizations. An apostrophe after a letter indicates that the respondent noted modifications in the characteristic as we showed it on the questionnaire.

A portion of the items relate to educational beliefs. These were suggested to allow easy identification of philosophical ideas. Please understand that this tends to oversimplification. Letters (items) missing in the list for a particular organization *do not necessarily imply complete rejection.* And no organization would subscribe to every belief on the list. Many of the items do not reflect my beliefs or those of various other contributors to this book.

This interpretation of code letters applies to all organizations except the secondary correspondence schools shown in part 2 of this appendix section.

Primary educational beliefs

A   Children need extensive freedom for natural development of the good within them.
B   The more formal aspects of education should be delayed more than most schools do.
C   Minds are best developed by a formal program of memorization, languages, math, etc. advancing from particulars to interrelatedness, patterned after an old European system.
D   The modern curriculum is good if adapted to the needs of the child.
E   Basic elements of the modern curriculum are good if approached without teaching certain concepts such as evolution and by adding Bible.
F   Character development is the purpose (or a primary purpose) of education and all learning should be related to it.

G The Bible reveals an adequate and essential philosophy for life; practically every lesson should refer to it.

H The Bible is the standard for all truth; it should be studied carefully and frequently, but Bible principles may be taught without reference to particular stories or passages. And direct reference is often appropriate, too.

I Phonics in beginning reading is basic for success in learning; it is inadequately taught in most schools.

J Children should be encouraged to discover their own values.

K Self-expression and creativity should be a dominant purpose of learning.

L Loyalty to God, church and society are primary qualities to be achieved by education.

M Keeping God (prayer, etc.) out of the classroom makes public schools bad.

Services

N Counsel/guidance for parents provided (but not legal defense)

O Legal counsel and defense offered

P Children studying at home are accepted or enrolled

Q Periodical provided for home schooling parents

R Periodical provided for home school children (could be same periodical)

S Meetings on home education sponsored yearly or oftener

T Lectures available on home schooling (for outside groups)

U Information available in print or other media (not including learning materials)

V Learning materials furnished (or sold) to parents who enroll or join

W Learning materials sold to anyone

X Standardized tests provided

Y School work and/or tests (other than standardized) graded by the organization

Z Tests provided for parents to give and grade themselves

a Grades and promotion granted by the school

b Evaluation of student work by other than major examinations

c Grade records maintained by the school

d Grade transcripts issued upon parent request

Staff qualifications (for one or more persons)

e Has taught in a home school

f Has taught in a classroom school

g Holds or has held a teaching certificate

h Has a four-year (or graduate) college degree

i Has taken credit course(s) in education (but no one has been certified)

How to get more information

j A long self-addressed envelope would be appreciated. If no number follows the "j" affix a stamp for one ounce. Otherwise affix postage for the number of ounces specified by the number or just send the stamps.

k Information is available without sending postage.

Part 1. Educational service organizations for families who join or enroll (except secondary correspondence schools)

A Beka Correspondence School, P.O. Box 18000, Pensacola FL 32523. 1975, (904) 478-8480, CFILNUVWXYZacdk. A Beka offers a traditional correspondence school program with an optional video version. Their textbooks and materials are also available for purchase.

Advanced Training Institute of America, Box One, Oak Brook IL 60522-3001. James A. Sammons, President, 1984, (312) 323-9800, F'G'HI'P'QS'UVX'cdefghk. ATIA is affiliated with the Institute in Basic Youth Conflicts. Applicants must have attended or plan to attend an IBYC Advanced Seminar. "The goal of ATIA is to train entire families how to be mighty in Spirit" by becoming wise, mature, knowledgeable and successful. Required core, expanded by topics chosen by the student.

Alpha Omega Publications, P.O. Box 3153, Tempe AZ 85281. J. Richard Fugate, 1978, (800) 821-4443, E'FGHIKNPVWZ-efghk.

Alta Vista Home School Curriculum, P.O. Box 222, Medina WA 98039. Tim Krell, Project Director, 1965, (206) 454-7691, DG'Vfghk. The Alta Vista curriculum presents studies of God's world in the light of His written Word, the Bible, in order that families may learn to know God and to respond to Him in loving service. Sample materials, $3.00.

American Home Academy, 2770 S. 1000 W. Perry UT 84302. Joyce Kinmont, 1975, (801) 723-5355, ABFH'IKLMTVWej. See Appendix H (bibliography) for a description of Joyce Kinmont's book.

Associated Christian Schools Curriculum, P.O. Box 27115, Indianapolis IN 46227. Don Boys, Ph.D., President, 1980, (317) 881-7132, GHILNPUWXYZacdfij. A sample packet of materials used in the home school division is available for $25 ($63 value). Includes scope and sequence.

Basic Education, P.O. Box 610589, D/FW Airport TX 75261-0589. Dr. Frank H. Owens, Director, 1970, (800) 852-2742 or (214) 462-1909, BFGIKLMNPQRSTUVW-XYZabcdefghk. Curriculum built around "self-pacs" and "self-texts" widely and successfully used. Bible based, self taught, diagnostically assigned, continuous progress, Kindergarten to 2nd year college. For home and private schools.

Basic Learning Network, 9669 E. 123rd, Hastings MN 550333. (612) 437-3049. Sharon Hillestad. Evolved from the Minnesota Homeschool Network.

Cair Paravel - Latin Satellite School, 1108 Bank IV Tower, Topeka KS 66603. 1983, (913) 233-4122 or (913) 357-0558, BGHLNOPQRSTUXcdefghk. CP-LSS assists families in providing the best home training program possible with a structure of accountability. Emphasis is on involvement of both parents.

Calvert School, 105 Tuscany Rd., Baltimore MD 21210. Susan Weiss, Principal, (301) 243-6030, NPQRTUVYZacdefgh. Courses include full lesson plans, all material, and textbooks. The integrated curriculum for kindergarten through grade eight includes all basic subjects and enrichment areas. Optional advisory teaching service (guidance and grading through the mail).

Christian Liberty Academy Satellite Schools, 502 Euclid Ave., Arlington Heights IL 60004. Paul Lindstrom, Supt., 1968, (312) 259-8736, GHILM'PQSTU-VWXYZabcdefhk. CLASS also offers Christian textbooks on typical school subjects and an independent achievement testing service for any family.

Christian Light Education (Division of Christian Light Publications), P.O. Box 1126, Harrisonburg VA 22801. Paul E. Reed, (703) 434-0750, BDHILNPQWXZ-cdfhik. CLE's student options: (1) basic information kit plus student materials, (2) complete training program plus materials, (3) training, support services and materials. CLE's worktexts are used. Also vocational training and workshops.

Classic Plan, 20969 Ventura Blvd., #213, Woodland Hills CA 91364. Sally Jordan, 1985, (818) 883-4093, C'FHIKLNPVWX-bfghk.

Clonlara School Home Based Education Program, 1289 Jewett St., Ann Arbor MI 48104. Pat Montgomery, Director, 1979, (313) 769-4515, ABNOPQRSTUVXZabc-defghjk. Open-type educational program. Families form their own programs with the administrative guidance of the school. "Guidebooks" suggest objectives for basic skills. Real life experiences including community service are stressed.

Country Garden School, P.O. Box 6, College Place WA 99324. Gwen Hawkins, Director, 1975, (509) 525-0125, 1-12, FGILNQTWabcefgh. Please send $5 for catalog.

Creative Christian Education, P.O. Box K, Angwin CA 94508. (707) 695-3004 or (707) 695-3411. BFHILNPQSVWXZab-cdefghjk. Joyce George, an experienced Christian teacher, has been providing quality, individualized home school support since 1976. Contact teachers associated with the school are available in some areas. Elementary and secondary diplomas are granted to students meeting the organization's requirements.

Daystar Educational Exchange, 733 S. Main #43, Willits CA 95490. Sol E. Day, Ph.D., 1985, ABDFIJKNPQRUVWZ'bcdfghk. "Students are placed in materials at their level. Except for beginning reading and math, materials are generally self-directed and need little parent teaching time."

Hewitt Research Foundation, P.O. Box 9, Washougal WA 98671. 1964, (206) 835-8708, BFGHIKLNPQSTUVWXY-bcdefghj2k. Hewitt tailors the curriculum to individual interests and abilities. They are prepared to work with families of children with special needs.

Home Study International, 6940 Carroll Ave., Takoma Park MD 20912. George P. Babcock, President, 1909, (202) 722-6570, DEHJKLNPQRUVXYacdefghk. I am familiar with the operation of HSI and can recommend their program. You get professional supervision, thorough and

frequently updated courses, carefully selected textbooks, and optional Bible courses.

International Institute, P.O. Box 99, Park Ridge IL 60068. 1965. Planned courses for K-8 which include textbooks, instructions and assignments. "Advisory service" optional. Christian emphasis.

Lindenwood Academy, P.O. Box 3405, Fort Smith AR 72913-3405. Nicholas D. Graham, 1980, (501) 782-6277, FGHILN-PUWX2abcdefghk. Diagnostic testing helps individualize the curriculum. Materials from Accelerated Christian Education and Basic Education. Monthly billing.

Living Heritage Academy. Home study division of Basic Education.

Magic Meadow School, P.O. Box 662, North San Juan CA 95960. Jayanthi Malley, 1985, (916) 292-3209, ABDFPVWbcdefghj.

McGuffey Academy, Box 656, Milford MI 48042. Gary Elfner, Ph.D., (313) 685-8773, BHIL'NPQRSTUVWXYZ-abcdefhk. "We specialize in the educational philosophy and texts of the 19th century. The academics are brought up to date through the use of workbooks that are currently being developed."

Mountain School Summer Camp, The, P.O. Box 246, Boonville CA 95415. J. David Colfax, Ph.D. 1987, (707) 895-3241, ABFNPTUefghk. Programs planned for a few youth who want to discover the adventures of learning in a "camp" program.

National Home Education Guild, 515 N.E. Eighth St., Grants Pass OR 97526. Elizabeth Brown, 1985, (503) 474-1501, ABFHINPQTUVbefijk. K-6. Send $5 for a catalog, $1 for a sample of the newsletter.

Oak Meadow School, P.O. Box 712, Blacksburg VA 24060. Lawrence Williams, 1975, (703) 552-3263, ABNPQRUVWYabcdefghjk. Creative expression emphasized. Parent sensitivity training and teacher training offered. Based on the Waldorf philosophy.

Our Christian Heritage, 7923 W. 62nd Way, Arvada CO 80004. Samuel R. Noel, 1972, (303) 421-0444, CFGHILNPQRST-UVWXZfgh. OCH publishes books for grades 1-5 with a scriptural, principle approach to the teaching of geography, history, and government. Lessons planned to build Christian character and teach about responsibility, self-government, authority and freedom. Send $23.50 for all 5 books and postage. Add tax if Colorado.

Our Lady of Victory School, P.O. Box 5181, Mission Hills CA 91345. William L. Bowman, 1973, (818) 899-1966, CILM'P-UXYZabcdefhk. A program for Catholics.

Pinewood School, Rt. 2, Box 409, Pine CO 80470. Olivia Loria, 1981, (303) 838-4418, ABDFJKNPTUVXacdfghjk. Alternative school. Member of the National Coalition of Alternative Community Schools (NCACS). Individual study programs planned.

Santa Fe Community School, P.O. Box 2241, Santa Fe NM 87504. Ed Nagel, 1968, (505) 471-6928, ABDFJKNPQRST-Uabcdefghjk. Send $2 for a sample periodical issue.

School of Home Learning, P.O. Box 92, Escondido CA 92025. John Boston, 1970, (916) 749-1522, ABG'JKNPQRSTUVWX-YZabcdefghj. Enrollment in this state-attested, accredited, diploma-awarding, K-12, private school qualifies the home-centered learning family as a satellite classroom and the parents as volunteer, invited, private school teachers. For sample issue of their periodical send $1.

Seton Home Study School, One Kidd Lane, Front Royal VA 22630. Mary Kay Clark, 1981, (703) 636-9990, CFHILNOPQUVX-YZabcdefghjk. A Catholic program offering all subjects, grades K-12. Associated with a resident school. The staff includes a lawyer and a learning disability consultant. Counseling by phone or mail.

Summit Christian Academy, P.O. Box 802041, Dallas TX 75380. Doree Tate, Executive Director, 1984, (214) 991-2096, HINPVWXYZcdfgh. Diagnostic testing and phone consultation (by toll-free line) also available.

Sycamore Tree, The, 2179 Meyer Place, Costa Mesa CA 92627. William & Sandra

Gogel, 1982, (714) 650-4466, BFGHILN-PQRUWXabcdefghk. You'll appreciate their large descriptive catalog. $3 (discounted from your first order). They also provide a quality guidance service helping you plan and operate your school according to the individual needs of your child.

Teaching Effective Academics and Character at Home (TEACH), 4350 Lakeland Ave. No., Robbinsdale MN 55422. (612) 535-5514. Robert Newhouse, Director, 1983. AG'HI'NPQ-STUVWXabcdgj. "We feel motivation and maintaining curiosity in children and giving them the skill to find information . . . are crucial." Three levels of service. Certified teacher supervision and training programs are available. You may apply for state-recognized accreditation from TEACH. The organization appears serious about quality. Ask for free information brochures and/or a copy of their newsletter.

Universal Academy: Parent-Mentors' Association, etc. 602 N. Main-Monroe Middletown OH 45044. Alyce Ehrmann Bowling, Coord., 1975, (513) 539-7547, NPQRUYZabcdefhij. Curriculum recommendations. Registration and communication in political coalition or lobby for learning alternative freedom. Organization offers individualized academics with family life values, etc.

Weaver Curriculum Series, 2752 Scarborough, Riverside CA 92503. Becky Avery, 1985, (714) 688-3126, A'B'C'F'-G'HL'M'Wbefghk. A K-6 home study program weaving academics and Scripture into lives through direct Bible study. Coordinated for teaching children in different grades. Supplements available for grades 7-9. What I see looks interesting. You might want to adapt it. For $5 they will send you a sample.

Windsong Lifeschool, 535 W. Center St., Pomona CA 91768. Barbara Lawson, Director, 1985, (714) 622-6461, ABFGHIKMNPTUV-Wcdej. Assistance (but not legal counsel or legal advice) based upon experience as an attorney *in*

propria persona (a legal term meaning an attorney "in one's own proper person").

Part 2, Secondary correspondence schools

Again in this section I have used an alphabet code to describe characteristics of secondary correspondence schools. I have not intended to imply that any school is unsatisfactory. The most important factors—course quality and course availability—can't be shown in a listing as we have here. Course fees, as well as other items in the list are subject to change.

Many of the organizations shown in the previous section also offer guidance for high school youth.

Below is the key to the code letters:

l   90% of the lessons are graded and back in the mail within 1 or 2 working days of the time they are received.
m   They are back in the mail within 3 or 4 days.
n   It usually takes longer than 4 days.
o   The base fee for 1/2 unit is more than half of the fee for 1 unit.
p   The fee per unit is less when several courses are taken at once.
q   An additional fee is charged for the syllabus or study guide.
r   An additional fee is charged for admission or registration.
s   Textbook costs are *included* in the tuition fees.
t   Science course(s) with lab kit(s) are available.
u   Audio cassettes are used in some courses.
v   Video cassettes are used in some courses.
w   Less than 1 year is granted for completion of a course (unless special arrangements are made).
x   An extension of six months or more is available (possibly for a fee).
y   All failed exams (not lesson submissions) may be repeated. at least once (possibly for a fee).
z   A student may drop a course and apply at least part of the fee to another course.
!   Enrolled students may call the school toll free.
@   Teachers are either available for phone consultation during most business hours or their direct phone numbers are usually available.
#   A computer is used to help in grading some lessons or tests.
$ Fire-resistant record storage.
%   National Home Study Council accreditation.
&   National University Continuing Education Association membership.
+   A diploma is offered by the correspondence school.

American School, 850 E. 58th St., Chicago IL 60637. (312) 947-3344. Tuition $45.00 - $82.00 per half unit. The cost depends on how many courses are taken and for how many years the student is enrolled. mopstuxyz@$%+.

Arizona, University of, Correspondence/Independent Study, Room 1201, 1717 E. Speedway, Tucson AZ 85719. (602) 621-3201. Tuition $60.00 per half unit. muw$&.

Arkansas, University of, Department of Independent Study, #2 University Center, Fayetteville AR 72701. (501) 575-3647. Tuition $40.00 in-state, $45.00 out-of-state, per half unit. nqwxz!$&+.

Citizens' High School, 5575 Peachtree Rd., Atlanta GA 30341. (404) 455-8358. Tuition $90.00 - $125.00 per unit. The basic foundation cost ranges from $395 for 4 courses to $725 for 16 needed for a diploma. Monthly payment plan. mpsuxyz@$%+.

Colorado at Boulder, University of, Division of Continuing Education, Box 178, Boulder CO 80309. (303) 492-8756. Tuition $55.00 per half unit. mqtuvwxz!@&.

Florida, University of, Independent Study by Correspondence, 1223 N.W. 22nd Ave., Gainesville FL 32609. (904) 392-1711, (800) 327-4218 (national), (800) 255-5927 (Florida). $55.00 / half unit. nqxyz!&.

Granton Institute of Technology, 263 Adelaide St. W., Toronto Ontario M5H 1Y3. (416) 977-3929. The school offers a variety of job training courses as well as high school courses by correspondence. Serves both the U.S. and Canada. For the high school program, you take 3 courses: English, Math, and Canadian Studies which are prerequisite to three "specialist" subjects. Current cost: $2350 at registration or $2970 on a payment plan.

Hadley School for the Blind, 700 Elm St., Winnetka IL 60093. (312) 446-8111. No charge for courses. Prerequisite: legal blindness. nuxy!@$%&+.

Home Study International, 6940 Carroll Ave., Takoma Park MD 20912. (202) 722-6570. Tuition $97.50 per half unit. mqrtuxyz#$%&+. See note for this same school in the first section of this appendix.

ICS Newport/Pacific High School, Oak St. & Pawnee Ave., Scranton PA 18509. (717) 342-7701. Priced by program. lsxy!@#%+.

Idaho, University of, Correspondence Study in Idaho, University of Idaho CEB-116, Moscow ID 83843. (208) 885-6641. Tuition $80.00 per half unit. mnxz@$&.

Indiana University, Independent Study Program, School of Continuing Studies, Indiana University, Owen Hall, Bloomington IN 47405 Attn: Enrollments Section (See if you can get all that on the front of the envelope.) (800) 457-4434 except IN, AK and HI. (800) 822-4762 IN except local. Otherwise, (812) 335-3693. They have a respectable program even if they did leave me to fill out my own questionnaire. $43 for a half unit plus $7 or $5 for a learning guide plus textbooks, etc.

Kansas University of, Lawrence KS 66045. (913) 864-4440. Tuition $45.00 per half unit. oqwz!@#$&.

Kentucky, University, Eastern, Division of Extended Programs, Coates 27 A, Richmond KY 40475-0931. (606) 622-2003. Tuition $22.00 / half unit. ny@&.

Learning and Evaluation Center, 479 Drinker St., P.O. Box 616, Bloomsburg PA 17815. (717) 784-5220. Tuition $50.00 per unit. lswy@#$%. "We work only with failed junior or senior high school students for credit make up. Courses are 30 hours with a six-week limit for completion. . . . service to school districts."

Massachusetts Dept. of Education Correspondence Instruction, 1385 Hancock St., Quincy MA 02169. (617) 770-7582. Tuition approx. $30 for a half unit or $57 for a full unit. nruxyz&.

Minnesota, University of, Department of Independent Study, 45 Westbrook Hall, 77 Pleasant St. S.E. Minneapolis MN 55455. (612) 624-0000. Tuition $80.00 per half unit. ntxyz$%&.

Mississippi State University, Continuing Education, P.O. Drawer 5247, Mississippi State MS 39762. (601) 325-2649. Tuition $53.00 per half unit. nxyz!@&.

Missouri, University of, Center for Independent Study, 136 Clark Hall, Columbia MO 65211. (314) 882-6431. Tuition $46.00 per half unit. lmuwyz#$&.

Nebraska, University of, Independent Study, 269 Nebraska Center, Lincoln NE 68583-0900. (402) 472-1926. Tuition $51.00 resident, $59.50 nonresident per half unit. mqtux@$&+.

North Dakota Division of Independent Study, State University, State University Station, Box 5036, Fargo, ND 58105-5036. (701) 237-7182. Tuition $20.00 / half unit resident, $40.00 nonresident. lquvx@$&+.

Oklahoma, University of, Independent Study Department, 1700 Asp, Rm B-1, Norman OK 73037. (405) 325-1921. Tuition $55.00 per half unit. Call toll free from within Oklahoma. nuvxzl'@'&.

Oregon State System of Higher Education, Independent Study, P. O. Box 1633,

Portland OR 97207. (503) 464-4865. Tuition $55.00 per half unit. mxyz!&.

Pennsylvania State University, Independent Learning, P.O. Box 3207, 128 Mitchell Bldg., University Park PA 16802. (814) 865-5403. $40.00 / half unit. mqxz!@$&.

South Dakota, University of, Independent Study Division, 414 E. Clark, Vermillion SD 57069. (605) 677-6108. Tuition $35 per half unit. nqtuxyz!&.

Tennessee, University of, Center for Extended Learning, 420 Communications Bldg., Knoxville TN 37996-0300. (615) 974-5134. $42.00 / half unit. mvuxz@$&.

Texas Tech University, Division of Continuing Education, Independent Study by Correspondence, P.O. Box 4110 TTU, Lubbock TX 79409. (806) 828-6392. Tuition $67.00 per half unit. muw!@&.

Texas, University of, at Austin, EIMC-Independent Learning, P.O. Box 7700, Austin TX 78713-7700. (512) 471-0220. Tuition $45.00 per half unit. nqtuwyz!#&.

Utah State University, Independent Study, UMC 5000, Logan UT 84322. (801) 750-2132. Tuition $40 / half unit. novx&.

Washington State University, Independent Study Program, 202 Van Doren Hall, Pullman WA 99164-5220. (509) 335-3557. Tuition $60 / half unit. nuvxz@$&.

Wisconsin, University of, Extension, Independent Study, 432 North Lake St., Madison WI 53706. General information, (608) 263-2055. Tuition $50.00 varying with subjects per half unit. nuxz&.

Wyoming, University of, Correspondence Study Department, 3294 University Station, Laramie WY 82071. (307) 766-5632. Tuition $30.00 per half unit.

Part 3. Suppliers of books and other materials

Abbott Loop Christian Ctr., 2626 Abbott Rd., Anchorage AK 99507. (907) 349-9641, BGHILWfghk. Curriculum materials are offered by this Anchorage area support group (currently for K-2).

Blue Bird Publishing, 1713 E. Broadway #306, Tempe AZ 85282. Cheryl Gorder, 1985, (602) 968-4088, AUeghk. Publishes Home Schools: An Alternative, Revised 1987, and Home Education Resource Guide. Plus an assortment of other books. See Appendix H.

Bob Jones University Press. See App. B.

Brook Farm Books, P.O. Box 277, Lyndon VT 05849. ABF'IWej. *The First Home-school Catalog,* U.S. $8.00 postpaid, and other materials. Free brochure.

Builder Books, P.O. Box 7000-748, Redondo Beach CA 90277. (213) 373-7657. A reliable source for home school supplies. Some discounted.

Children's Book & Music Center, P.O. Box 1130, Santa Monica CA 90406-1130. (800) 443-1856 or for Calif., (213) 829-0215. Big, well-organized catalog of books and recordings.

Children's Books. See Mile-Hi Publishers, (This section).

Conservative Book Club, 15 Oakland Ave., Harrrison NY 10528. "We offer a very broad variety of books of interest to political, religious and economic conservatives." Every bulletin announces one or more books for parents with young children. Check their ads or just write for info.

Creation's Child, P.O. Box 3004 #44, Corvallis OR 97339. Paula Carlson. Time line charts for teaching history, history book reprints, phonics based on Bible words and many more interesting items. SASE appreciated.

Eagle Star Network, 19655 Campbell Rd., Black Forest CO 80908. Barbara Keeler, 1986, ABIJKTUWg. "We have a huge selection of children's literature as well as select learning materials for alternatively schooled children. Eagle Star Foundation is an educational foundation teaching people about alternative right living." Catalog $1 (refundable).

Family Educator, The, P.O. Box 309, Templeton CA 93465. Eric M. Luthi, 1987, (805) 434-0249, FHILWefghk. Carefully selected books and educational materials listed by grade: history, arithmetic, art, music, nature, science, phonics, grammar, domestic arts, etc.

Gazelle Publications, 5580 Stanley Dr., Auburn CA 95603. Ted Wade, 1976, (916) 878-1223, BEFHUWefghj. We currently have 5 titles in print including this book. Also, *Science Activities for Christian Children,* $5.50 and *Bubbles, Poetry for fun and meaning,* an enjoyable book with activities and notes, $9.00.

Great Christian Books, 1319 Newport Gap Pike, Wilmington DE 19804. (302) 999-0595. A discount book source carrying a wide selection of titles on home educ.

Home Run Enterprises, 12531 Aristocrat Ave., Garden Grove CA 92641. Cathy & Mike Duffy, 1986, (714) 638-7956, E'H-TUWehj. *Christian Home Educators' Curriculum Manual* (1988 ed., $14.95 + $1.50 mail and tax if Calif.) Math Mouse Games. Seminars and lectures cover topics such as: choosing curriculum, learning styles, methodology, unit studies, etc.

Home School Supplies, 3446 N. Avenida de la Colina, Tucson AZ 85749. Pat Gentala, 1984, (602) 749-2685, EHILWefhi. Send $3.50 for a catalog. Add 13 cents tax for Arizona addresses.

Home School Supply House, 3254 E. Mitchell, Petoskey MI 49770. Kim Overton, 1987, (616) 347-8158, Wefghk. A wide variety of books and materials. Fastest service available.

Intrepid Books, P.O. Box 179, Rough and Ready CA 95975. Jean Ryland, 1987, (916) 432-3197, FGHILMWefhij. Intrepid publishes *America's Christian History* workbooks for grades 1-8 using the principle approach.

John Holt's Book and Music Store, 729 Boylston St., Boston MA 02116. Many items for those interested in natural (and general) learning. M / V charge cards accepted. Call between 10 and 4 M-F, (617) 437-1583.

KONOS Curriculum, P.O. Box 1534, Richardson TX 75083. Jessica Hulcy, 1985, (214) 669-8337, BF'HI'KWefghk. The Konos Character Curriculum is coordinated around character themes. K-6. Seminars and cassettes explain how

to use the program. For the two-hour cassette presentation, *Building a Good Writer,* send $9.00.

Learning at Home, P.O. Box 270, Honaunau HI 96726, (808) 328-9669, Judith Wilson and Ann Pervinkler, 1984, ABI'NUVWefghk. Teaching guides for grades 1-5, testing service (1-12), supplies for art and science. M / V charges.

LibertyTree Network, 6600 Silacci Way, Gilroy CA 95020. 1986, (415) 981-1326, CG'IKM'UWefhik. Books, audio and video tapes, etc. relating to America's heritage of liberty, free markets, etc.

Library & Educational Services, P.O. Box 146, Berrien Springs MI 49103. Dick Proctor, 1976, (616) 471-1400. This supplier really means business about good prices. Catalog available without charge.

Life For Little Learners, P.O. Box 701616, Tulsa OK 74170. David Film, 1979, (918) 827-3367, ABFGHIQWej. Interesting products. Check them out.

Manna Computing Concepts, P.O. Box 527, Woodstock GA 30188. Steve & Cindi Combs, 1984, (404) 479-7178, GHIKLM'-UWhi. A wide range of interesting software in most popular formats. Categories: (1) Bible-related educational and recreational, (2) Bible study, (3) ministry, (4) practical and (5) educational. The $1 catalog fee is refundable.

Mile-Hi Publishers, P.O. Box 19340, Denver CO 80219. (303) 922-5876. Timothy E. Nelson. 1978. HIWfghk. Selected books. Some special prices.

National Book Company, P.O. Box 8795, Portland OR 97207-8795. 1965. (503) 228-6345. IWZj2. I didn't learn much about this company, but for two stamps you can find out about them.

Pratte Religious and Educational Supplies, 7021 Omaha Ct., Fort Wayne IN 46804. David Pratte. 1980. (219) 432-4434, ILMUWehj.

Riverside Schoolhouse Resource Center, HCR Box 181A, Bemidji MN 56601. Daniel and Kathryn Duerst, 1984. (218) 751-8227, BFHINWe. In addition to their mail-order bookstore, the Duersts offer workshops on the curriculum, the unit method, etc. Catalog $1 (refundable).

Rod and Staff Publishers, Highway 172, Crockett KY 41413. Duane E. Miller and James Boll, 1960, (606) 522-4348, CFGH-ILMQRWk. Rod and Staff publications have been used by many home schools over the years. Request a free catalog and/or sample periodical issue.

Shekinah Curriculum Cellar, 967 Junipero Dr., Costa Mesa CA 92626. Michele Robinson, 1984, (714) 751-7767, BE'GILNUW. Their large catalog describes many interesting items to help

your home school—some at discount prices. Send $1 (refundable).

Sycamore Tree. A large materials provider. See Part 1 of this section and Chapter 10.

Textbooks for Parents, P.O. Box 209, Kendrick ID 83537. (208) 883-0991, A'B'CDEINPWZefhj. A large selection of standard school textbooks including teachers' editions. You can call and explain your situation, and Clara Emery will suggest which books are best. You can get a single book or a basic group for a certain grade. Used books sometimes available. Also, you can sell back.

Part 4, Various organizations serving home education

Alberg, Patty, Curriculum consultant, seminar speaker and teacher, 23247 Robert Rd., Torrance CA 90505.

Association for Children & Adults with Learning Disabilities, 4156 Library Rd., Pittsburg PA 15234. Mrs. Jean Petersen, Exec. Dir. 1963, (412) 341-1515, UVWhk. Information and referrals.

Brackin & Sons Publishing Co. P.O. Box 359, Burtonsville MD 20866. Ron Brackin, 1987, (301) 421-1473, BFGHLM-NPORTUVWefhj. Full-day writing workshops for home school parents. Also See *Home School Gazette* in Appendix H, Part 2.

Christian Life Workshops, 180 S.E. Kane Rd., Gresham OR 97080. Gregg Harris, 1981, (503) 667-3942, BFGHILQSTUW-eij. Gregg Harris is speaker for the Home Schooling Workshops.

Education Services, 6410 Raleigh, Arvada CO 80003. Ruth Beechick, 1981, (303) 429-6941, HU. Dr. Beechick's books help parents make better use of preplaned curriculum materials or put together their own program. Common sense approach. See the bibliography (Appendix H). Consulting service for authors of home schooling teaching materials.

Educational Spectrums, P.O. Box 1014, Placerville CA 95667-1014. Jane Williams, (916) 677-1445, BKNUWefghj.

Guidance for home schooling and for supplementing a regular school program.

Golden Shell, The, 2211 E. James St., West Covina CA 91790. Rachelle Schreiber, 1987, (818) 967-6649, AFJKQRUWb.

Holt Associates, 729 Boylston St., Boston MA 02116. Patrick Farenga, President, 1977, (617) 437-1550, N'QRTUWj2. Publishes *Growing Without Schooling*. See Appendix H, Part 2. "Holt Associates is a national clearinghouse for information about home education, John Holt's work, and how people of all ages can learn outside of school. We believe children are good at learning and that learning is not separate from the rest of life. We are interested in how teaching and learning can best be supported outside of schools, and how adults can best respond to and nurture children's growth."

Home Education Press, P.O. Box 1083, Tonasket WA 98855. Publishers of *Home Education Magazine.* Also *Alternatives in Education,* 120 pp. $10.75. *Home School Primer,* valuable advice for getting started and finding resources, $6.50, *Networking Directory.* Remember tax for WA. For information on the magazine, see Appendix H, Part 2.

Home Free, CBN Center, Virginia Beach VA 23465-9989. See Appendix H, Part 2.

Home School Legal Defense Association, P.O. Box 950 (731 Walker Rd. E2), Great

Falls VA 22066. 1983, (703) 759-7577, Code letter: O. Membership with HSLDA is $100 yearly. A quarterly newsletter on legal issues sent to members. Legal counsel and defense is available only to members.

Home-Educator Computer Users Group, 26824 Howard Chapel Dr., Damascus MD 20872-1247. Jim Mayor, (301) 253-5467, QRUk. Computer electronic bulletin board system for home schoolers.

Homeschoolers for Peace, P.O. Box 74, Midpines CA 95345. Pam Gingold, 1984, (209) 742-6802, ABIJKNReij. A nationwide support group for families interested in working for a peaceful world. Children write on assigned topics. Peace projects include pen pals, sending school supplies to world areas in need. Newsletter $10 for 12 issues; sample 75¢.

Learning at Home. See Part 3 of this appendix. They also offer testing and counsel.

National Assn. for the Legal Support of Alternative Schools, P.O. Box 2823, Santa Fe NM 87504. Ed Nagel, 1975, (505) 471-6928, NOQTUVWjk. Legal insurance which provides attorneys for counsel and defense as needed. Newsletter, $1.

National Coalition of Alternative Community Schools, 417 Roslyn Rd., Roslyn Heights NY 11577. Jerry Mintz, Nat'l Coordinator, 1976, (516) 621-2195, AF'NPSTUjk. Send $12.50 for the NCACS Directory, $6.00 for a sample issue of their journal, Skole.

National Home Study Council, 1601 18th St. N.W. Washington DC 20009. William A. Fowler, Exec. Dir. 1926, (202) 234-5100, Uk. Accrediting agency for home study schools.

National Institute for Christian Home Education, Rt 3, Box 543, Rustburg VA 24588. Rick Boyer, Director, 1983, (804) 845-8345, BD'EFGHILMNQTUWej. "Our ministry is basically parent education. Manuals, tapes and lectures on a variety of interesting topics.

National University Continuing Education Association, One Dupont Circle N.W.

#420, Washington DC 20036. 1915, (202) 659-3130, U. A professional organization including university-based correspondence schools. Peterson Guides publishes The *NUCEA Guide to Independent Study Through Correspondence.*

Parent Scene, P.O. Box 2222, Redlands CA 92373. Kay Kuzma, 1982, (714) 792-2412, FGHIJKLQUk. Dr. Kuzma is an author, seminar speaker, mother and founder of the family ministry and radio program, Parent Scene. You will appreciate her common sense approach from a Christian background.

Reading Reform Foundation, 949 Market St., Suite 436, Tacoma WA 98402. Marian Hinds, President, 1961, (206) 572-9966, INQSUWFGH. RRF is dedicated to restoring literacy through intensive phonics to our nation's schools. A clearinghouse for phonics materials. $2 donation for information.

Riggs Institute, 4185 S.W. 102nd Ave., Beaverton OR 97005. Myrna McCulloch, 1979, (503) 649-9459, CIKLTUVWZefgh. A college-level training program for teachers or parent-teachers in intensive phonics and a total language arts. $1 for catalog.

Rutherford Institute, P.O. Box 510, Manassas VA 22110. John W. Whitehead, 1982, (703) 369-0100, OUh. A nonprofit legal and educational organization. Also mentioned in the introduction to Appendix C.

Taunta Danque's Home Schooling Data Bases, P.O. Box 832, Bellville TX 77418. (409) 865-9467. Taunta Danque is a home schooling mother and a Montessori Directress who edits *Home Schooling, The Neurological Frontier of Giftedness,* a quarterly collection of comments and reprints from here and there. The data bases are to provide a diversity of Home-schooling information. Ask for information.

Teaching Home, The, See Appendix H.

WE CAN, Incorporated, 601 Brandywine Dr., Goshen IN 46526.

B

Publishers

Classification of home schooling organizations is difficult because many that publish also teach and many that support also publish, and so on. This list includes publishers that, as a rule, are not operating home education teaching programs.

The chapter, "Teaching in the home school," suggests how to select textbooks and other learning materials. This appendix lists sources which are not included in Appendix Sections A and H and it cross references some that are.

Many major home school support organizations sponsor curriculum fairs where you can see materials on display. Major textbook publishers (a few of which are included below) however, are less apt to be represented before home schooling groups.

Major subject areas in which each publisher specializes are generally listed.

Remember to *add tax* if you are ordering from a publisher in your own state.

If you know what books you want from major publishers—title, publisher, date, etc., you may be able to get used copies through Wilcox & Follett Book Company, 1000 West Washington Blvd., Chicago, IL 60607; (800) 621-4272. Have your charge card ready. Books are priced according to their condition. Workbooks are new.

Ampersand Press, 691 26th St., Oakland CA 94612. From the descriptions, these look like excellent learning games. Emphasis on science.

A Beka Book Publications, Box 18000, Pensacola, FL 32523. (904) 478-8933. An evangelical Christian publisher providing a full line of textbooks.

Accelerated Christian Education, Inc., P. O. Box 1438, Lewisville, TX 75067. (214) 462-1776. Individualized Christian curriculum for church schools, K-college. Academic core subjects, electives, learning to read and word building. See their Basic Education subsidiary for home schooling.

Addison-Wesley Publishing Co., 2725 Sand Hill Rd., Menlo Park, CA 94025. (415) 854-0300. Subject areas: English/language arts, math, music, art, reading, science, and social studies, for both elementary and secondary grades.

Allyn and Bacon, Inc., Rockleigh NJ 07647. (800) 526-4799; in NJ (800) 932-0117.

Alpha-Omega Publications, See Appendix A.

American Bible Society, 1865 Broadway, New York, NY 10023. (212) 581-7400. Although no response was received to my request for information, I thought you should have this address.

Amsco School Publications, 315 Hudson St., New York NY 10013. (212) 675-7000. Textbooks covering basic subjects plus some standard literary works. The catalog is mostly a list of titles and prices. Teacher's editions and keys are available only through licensed teachers.

Aristoplay, Ltd., P.O. Box 7028, Ann Arbor MI 48107. (800) 634-7738. Interesting educational games. For example, In *Made* *for Trade* players earn shillings in an early American setting minimizing taxes and escaping indentured service. 4 levels of play. $20 + $3 shpg. + tax if MI. Also a game about world geography, one about running for president, one about dinosaurs, one about musical instruments, etc.

Association of Christian Schools International, P.O. Box 4097, Whittier, CA 90607-4097. (800) 367-0798, (213) 694-4791. Curriculum and administration guides, ethics materials. The catalog description of their *Character Foundation Curriculum* looks interesting. You can get the pupil book for any grade K-8 for $5.00 + 1.50 shpg. + tax if CA. Teacher editions and supplementary materials are available to go with the program.

Audio Memory Publishing, 1433 E. 9th St., Long Beach CA 90813. *Grammar Songs,* and *Multiplication Songs.* See Appendix H, Part 4.

Blue Bird Publishing. See Appendix A.

Bob Jones University Press, Greenville, SC 29614. (800) 845-5731 or (803) 242-5100, Ext. 4300. Quality curriculum materials for conventional Christian schools and home educators. Textbooks and teacher's editions in all subjects and grade levels. Also material available for special areas such as computer science, speech and elementary music. Wholesale prices available to home schools. Complete catalog available.

Bookstuff, 4B SW Monroe, Box 200, Lake Oswego OR 97034, Suite 139. Operated by Nancy Cross Aldrich and Patricia Reinold. (503) 288-3805. "Our materials provide a 'family-experience' approach to language development, logical thinking and reading." Parents and children use the workbooks together. You can get *My First Bookstuff,* an invitation to reading, for $5.95 + 1.50 shpg. + tax if OR. Or just send them an SASE (Self-addressed stamped envelope) for a catalog.

Bradshaw Publishers, P.O. Box 277, Bryn Mawr CA 92318. (714) 796-6766. Bible story beginning readers suitable through the second grade. Phonics based, progressive. Large print with flowing,

rhythmic style and structure. Full color pictures. Children love them.

Brook Farm Books. See Appendix A.

CBN Publishing, CBN Center, WOSC 336, Virginia Beach VA 23462. Peter Bradley, (804) 424-7777, HIQTVWefghk. CBN Publishing offers the Homefree membership plus the following products: (1) *Sing, Spell, Read & Write,* (2) *Exploring Creation* (life science program with video), (3) *Songs of America's Freedoms* (Constitution learning program by music), (4) *Winning* (Adult literacy program), (5) *Home Free* newsletter (sample issue without charge), (6) Super Book / Flying House Videos, (7) G.T. Scripture Memorization tapes, etc.

Chaselle, Inc., 9645 Gerwig Ln., Columbia, MD 21046. (301) 381-9611. Arts, crafts, educational aids, toys, school and office products, computer software. Specify your interest when requesting catalogs.

Christian Education Music Publishers, 2285 185th Place, Lansing, IL 60438. (312) 895-3322. Books, cassettes and other materials for K-4. Teaches concepts of praise to God. *Your Musical Friends* series. Catalog available.

Christian Schools International, P. O. Box 8709 Grand Rapids, MI 49508. Curriculum materials for Christian schools.

Crossway Books, 9825 W. Roosevelt Rd., Westchester IL 60153. Crossway is a division of Good News Publishers and has published several books of interest to home educators.

David S. Lake Publishers, 19 Davis Dr., Belmont, CA 94002. (415) 592-7810. Special ed. and material for reading, math, vocational ed., social studies.

DIDAX Educational Resources, Inc., 5 Fourth Street, Peabody, MA 01960. (508) 532-9060 or (800) 458-0024. Teaching aids and learning resource materials for mathematics, science, readiness skills, reading, language development and social studies at preschool and elementary school levels. Originators of the Unifix Structural Mathematical materials.

DLM Teaching Resources, P.O. Box 4000, Allen TX 75002. (800) 527-4747, or (800)

442-4711 for Texas. Supplementary learning materials: books, workbooks, games, videotapes, computer programs, etc. Costs could be shared by a lending program through your support group.

Eagle's Wings Educational Materials, P.O. Box 502, Duncan OK 73534. *Letterland Phonics 1.* Also a math packet.

Educators Publishing Service, Inc., 75 Moulton St., Cambridge, MA 02238-9101. (800) 225-5750, (617) 547-6706. Two catalogs are available. One in language arts; the other, for students with learning difficulties. Popular titles include: *Explode the Code,* and *Primary Phonics.* A periodical and special screening tests are also available. For grades K-12.

EduSoft. See Key Curriculum Press.

Elijah Company, P.O. Box 12483, Knoxville TN 37912-0483. (615) 691-1310. *Keyboard Capers.* A music reading and theory book with activities. From beginning to advanced. Based on the Suzuki method. Money back guarantee. $16.70 postpaid. Add tax only for TN.

ESP Publishers, Inc., P.O. Box 5037, Jonesboro AR 72403. (800) 643-0280. The "Super Workbooks" published by ESP contain from 544 to 832 pages each and cover the major subjects taught in each grade. Teaching instructions included. $18 (+ tax if AR) for each grade you want, K-6. And they guarantee satisfaction so you can order to see for yourself if you're not sure.

Every Day Is Special, 1602 Naco Place, Hacienda Heights CA 91745. An activity calendar for home schooled kids. Includes art ideas, puzzles, games and recipes as well as activities keyed to holidays, famous birthdays and historical notes.

Family Life Institute, The Bible in Living Sound, P.O. Box 234, Nordland WA 98358-0234. (206) 385-0234. See Appendix H.

Family Pastimes, RR 4, Perth, Ontario K7H 3C6. (613) 267-4819. Games designed for cooperation rather than competition. Both the U.S. and Canada are served. Send $1 for a catalog.

Flaherty, H.E., and Co., 7313 Simsbury Cir., Las Vegas NV 89129. See Appendix H, Part 4.

Gazelle Publications, 5580 Stanley Dr., Auburn, CA 95603. (916) 878-1223. Thank you for buying (or borrowing) this book. We would love to help you get a chance to find out about our other titles. Ask your favorite home school supplier, or you can contact us directly. See Appendix sections A and H.

Harvest House Publishers, 1705 Arrowsmith, Eugene OR 97402. (800) 547-1979 or (503) 343-0123. Two of the titles from Harvest House that may be of interest to a number of home school families are: *Man in Demand* for teenage boys and *Christian Charm Course* for girls. They explain spiritual growth as part of personal development. $4.95 each. Teacher manuals are $7.95 each. Call for shipping charge information if you order direct.

Home Education Press. See Appendix A, Part 4, and Appendix H, Part 2.

Home School Headquarters. Now under the direction of Blue Bird Publishing.

Imperial International Learning Corporation, 162 East Court St., Kankakee IL 60901. (815) 933-7735. A Bible oriented publisher of supplemental learning materials for grades K-12, using audio cassette, filmstrip, microcomputer and videotape media.

Key Curriculum Press, P.O. Box 2304, Berkeley, CA 94702. (800) 338-7638; (415) 548-2304. K-12 math workbooks with simple explanations and diagrams. Priced from $1.40 each. Apple II software $35 and up per program from their EduSoft section.

Knickerbocker Publishing, P.O. Box 113, Fiskdale MA 01518. (508) 3477-2039. Michael Glaser has been producing Discovery Crew science kits. Now he has published several small science books. Ex: *Does Anyone Know Where a Hermit Crab Goes?* a poem book about Purmitt Drab the hermit crab. $3.95 + $1 shpg.

Laidlaw. See Scribner-Laidlaw.

Leonardo Press, Box 403, Yorktown Heights NY 10598, (914) 962-7856. Learning materials for spelling (with attention to word structure and phonics) and for basic math computation. Skills are broken down by author Raymond E. Laurita into narrow categories and taught one by one. I'm a little afraid that this emphasis would reinforce the natural tendency to try to get the "answer" by following a rule rather than by understanding the principle. I'm in favor of teaching one concept at a time, but a little mixing of past concepts would encourage learning principles and help develop more intuitive rather than rote understandings. And it wouldn't be so boring. The quality of appearance and manufacture also leaves room for improvement. If you like Laurita's ideas, your kids will probably learn from the materials. I have not examined the design of all of the other learning programs as closely. Similar comments might be made about some of them.

Manna Computing Concepts. See Appendix A, Part 4.

Midwest Publications, P.O. Box 448, Pacific Grove CA 93950. (408) 375-2455. Critical thinking and reasoning skills for math and reading. K-12. A wide range of challenges in booklets mostly at $5.95. Also some software. Caution: You may get hooked by the samples shown in their free catalog.

Modern Curriculum Press, 13900 Prospect Rd., Cleveland, OH 44136. (800) 321-3106; (216) 238-2222. Spelling, phonics, reading, language arts, math, science, social studies, computer software, and testing and assessment.

Moody Press, 2100 W. Howard, Chicago, IL 60645. (312) 508-6850.

Mott Media, 1000 E. Huron, Milford, MI 48042. (800) 521-4350, (313) 685-8773. This firm specializes in "classic" textbooks—revised reprints of the ones used in the good old days: Harvey's Grammars, Spencer's Penmanship, McGuffey's Readers and Spellers, and Ray's Arithmetic. They also publish biographies and a few other titles.

Open Court Publishing Company, La Salle, IL 61301. (800) 435-6580. Major textbook publisher.

Pacific Press Publishing Assn., P. O. Box 7000, Boise, ID 83707, (208) 465-2512. *Listen* magazine, Bible Story series, and Bible related materials.

Paradigm Co., The, P.O. Box 45161, Boise ID 83711. (208) 322-4440. Peter F. Watt, President, 1984. GILMQSTUVWk. Publisher for books by Samuel L. Blumenfeld. See listings under his name in Appendix H.

Parent Scene. See Appendix A.

Play 'n Talk, "Phonics in Action," P.O. Box 98, Oceanside CA 92054. (619) 438-4330. Marie A. LeDoux, Ph.D. C'GHIKL. The $210 package includes 3 books that go with 12 records plus games and other materials. A language arts program based on detailed phonics instruction. Send $1 (plus your child's age and grade, and your phone number) for the basic information packet or $5 for a big packet including a cassette, sample lessons and teaching information you will find useful even if you don't buy their program.

Positive Approach, 4378 Eldamain Rd., Plano IL 60545. (312) 552-8910. *The Mortensen Math System,* "Easy-to-learn, step-by-step curriculum.

Praise Hymn, Inc., P.O. Box 1080, Taylors SC 29687. "God Made Music" workbook series, "We Sing Music" song books and cassettes, etc.

Professor Phonics System, **S.U.A. Phonics Department,** 1339 East McMillan St., Cincinnati OH 45206. (513) 961-3410. Students begin reading real words from the first page. The 42 regular sounds of the 26 letters are taught first. Book, instruction manual, word list and word cards, $13.20 + 1.80 shpg. The advanced book with instructions is priced at $4.80. Use it especially for middle grades, or for older students with reading/spelling problems, or for foreign students. You get everything for $19.80. Add tax if in Ohio. By the way in case you are curious like I was, S.U.A. stands for St. Ursula Academy.

Rainbow Specialty Products, P.O. Box 870, Columbia MD 21044. Marilyn Rockett has "invented" the *Time Minder,* a convenient system for organizing your home school. It gives you space to define your goals, to organize your school year, your weekly lesson plans, field trips, school projects, and student evaluation and grade records. It even has pages for working in your nonschool activities. New edition has forms for assignments and health records. If you are already organized you can adapt this to your needs adding sheets to the loose-leaf binder. If you are new to managing a school at home, this tool will help you keep it all under control. $24.95 plus $3 shipping and tax if MD.

Rod and Staff Publishers. See Appendix A.

Scholastic, 902 Sylvan Ave., Englewood Cliffs NJ 07632. Books, software and classroom magazines. See Appendix H.

Scribner-Laidlaw, P.O. Box 500, Riverside NJ 08075. Major textbook publisher. If you request a catalog, specify K-8 or 7-12.

Silver Burdett & Ginn, Customer Service Center, P.O. Box 2649, Columbus OH 43216. Major textbook publisher.

School Zone Publishing Co., P.O. Box 777, Grand Haven, MI 49417. Supplementary workbooks, flash cards, puzzles, beginning reading books and audio and video cassettes. (800) 253-0564. Reading books tend to have 16 pages and cost $1.95. The workbooks: $1.95 for 32 pages. The samples I have are attractive.

Sound Principles., 304 East D, Hillsboro KS 67063. (316) 947-2505. Publisher of and interesting math and money-handling game. See appendix H, Part 4.

Timberdoodle, The. See Appendix A.

Tin Man Press, P.O. Box 219, Stanwood WA 98292. (206) 387-0459. Tin Man Press develops and markets innovative, effective materials designed to foster thinking skills. The "discover!" series uses everyday objects as the focus for thinking challenges.

Victory Drill Book, Reading with phonics. See Enderlin, August, in Appendix H.

White Lion Media, P.O. Box 120190, San Antonio TX 78212. (800) 777-LION. A producer and distributor of Christian films and videos including *The Good Time Growing Show* for children, as set of six episodes with activity guides. You may purchase or rent them.

Worthy Publishing, 3934 Sandshell, Fort Worth TX 76137, (817) 232-3166. *The Everyday Bible, International Children's Bible,* and other Christian books.

Xerox Educational Publications, 245 Long Hill Rd., Middletown CT 06457.

Your Story Hour, P.O. Box 15, Berrien Springs MI 49103. (616) 471-3701. The "largest and finest library of Bible and character-building stories ever assembled on cassette." In addition to Bible stories, they have biographies of people like Mueller, Nightengale, Pasteur and Moody. There are lots of other stories like "Pa and the Violin" on overcoming difficulties and "Ellen's Cross-road" on resisting cheating. Also, books with cassettes.

Zaner-Bloser, P.O. Box 16764, Columbus OH 43216. (614) 486-0221. K-8 language and other areas. Their new series, *Spelling Connections,* looks very good. It builds a whole language arts program of spelling, word recognition (by phonics and other means), vocabulary, grammar and writing from weekly sets of words. These are regular, quality, school textbooks. Softcover texts: $7.38 per grade, list; or $5.55, school price. We have appreciated Zaner-Bloser permitting us to use their handwriting letter models for our cover.

Zephyr Press, 430 S. Essex Ln., Tucson AZ 85711. (602) 745-9199. Books to supplement the standard curriculum by developing creativity, self-esteem, dance, etc. Other topics include futuristics and ancient cultures. Prices tend (in my opinion) to push the upper limit just a bit. I do like the book they sent for review: *Search: A Research Guide for Science Fairs and Independent Study.* If your child wants to submit a project for a fair at a local school, or just to do some research on his own, this book could be valuable. It discusses selecting a topic, acquiring information, analyzing data and making the display. It gives examples and specific ideas for where to look for information. 94 pp. paper, $14.95 + $2.50 shpg. + tax if AZ.

Zondervan Bible Publishers, 1415 Lake Dr. S.E., Grand Rapids, MI.

C

Information by region for the United States

The purpose of this appendix section is to provide starting points for finding information specific to particular states.

The law information is not intended to be complete. And by the time this book is in your hands, some of it may have changed. Even with a few changes in time, it can provide worthwhile clues about what you might expect. *Nothing in this book constitutes legal advice.* Chapter 4 discusses facing legal problems in the establishment of home schools. You will find suggestions there about obtaining more complete and up-to-date information.

Several organizations provide legal advice and counsel for home schools and better information than we show here: For $11.50 (packet and handling) The Rutherford Institute will send current information for a specific state. A quarterly magazine on the work of the Institute is available without charge.

The Home School Legal Defense Association is a similar organization and provides legal insurance for home schools. Their stated purpose is "to establish the fact that responsible home schooling is legally permissible in every state." They believe "that God imposes a responsibility on all parents to train their children in a manner

pleasing to Him. . . ." You may send them $20 for an *Analysis of the Home School Laws and Regulations in the 50 States*. Both this and the information from the Rutherford Institute are updated periodically.

A third organization, the National Association for the Legal Support of Alternative Schools also provides legal insurance. Their focus includes home education that is not religiously oriented. These three organizations are also listed in Appendix A, Part 4.

In this appendix section, we also provide information about home schooling support organizations. We are aware of other groups but have, as a rule, not listed ones that did not return our questionnaire. Support organizations change frequently. They are usually administered by volunteers. Although some of the people whose addresses are listed may no longer be home education leaders by the time you want to contact them, they will probably be willing to direct you to those who can help you.

Dates indicate when the organization was founded.

For an explanation of the code letters at the ends of the entries, see the introduction to Appendix Section A.

ALABAMA

Legal requirements highlights: Home schools must either (1) operate as private schools meeting certain requirements including certification for their teachers, or (2) qualify as a "church school" under the control of a local church, in which case teacher certification is not required, or (3) use a private certified tutor. Approval is handled by the local board or superintendent. The beginning attendance age is 7. *This information is not necessarily sufficient for arranging to teach children at home. Also, it may not be currently accurate. See the beginning of this appendix section and Chapter 4 for general explanations.*

State government information: Charles L. Saunders, Educational Consultant, Private Schools Unit, Room, 348, State Office Building, Montgomery AL 36103. (205) 261-2910.

Supporting organizations:

Alabama Home Educators, 819 Joryne Dr., Montgomery AL 36109. James Hart, President. 1984. (205) 277-1614. AHE is a nonsectarian organization with a network of local support groups. You may subscribe to the newsletter for $6.00 or send $1.50 for a sample issue by writing to *The Voice*, Rt. 3, Box 37-B, Tallassee AL 36078. NQSTUjk (See the beginning of Appendix A to translate the code letters).

Alabama Home Educators - Tuscaloosa Area, Rt. 3 Box 633, Cottondale AL 35453. Barbara & David Brasfield, Area Representative. 1984. (205) 556-1464. Home schoolers in the Tuscaloosa area can expect a lot from this group! They'll tell you what church schools provide a "covering" and they give start-up guidance. Monthly meetings and field trips are planned. The public is educated through news contacts. And "an occasional shoulder to cry on" may even be available. BNSUj.

ALASKA

Legal requirements highlights: A student in Alaska may study at home if he or she "is equally well-served by an educational experience approved by the school board." The request for approval must be made in writing. Alternatively, the student may enroll in "a full-time program of correspondence study approved by the department" or be tutored by a certified teacher. Attendance is required beginning at age 7. *This information is not necessarily sufficient for arranging to teach children at home. Also, it may not be currently accurate. See the beginning of this appendix section and Chapter 4 for general explanations.*

State government information: Darlene M. Wicks, Education Administrator, Centralized Correspondence Study, Department of Education, P.O. Box GA, Juneau AK 99811-0544. (907) 789-350 350 2835.

Supporting Organizations:

Abbott Loop Christian Center, 2626 Abbott Rd., Anchorage AK 99507. Lloyd Bellamy, Home School Consultant. (907) 349-9641. Services available to enrolled families. Enrichment classes in art, music and physical education in addition to home materials for (currently) grades K-2. BGHILPSWXYabcdfghk.

Valley Homeschoolers Network, HC 30 Box 5370-A, Wasilla AK 99687. Nancy Stich, Coordinator. 1985. (907) 373-0740. Statewide newsletter, *Alaska Home Learners Gazette*, $6.50/yr. SASE for current issue. BQRj.

ARIZONA

Legal requirements highlights: To teach their own children, Arizona parents must pass a proficiency test and file an affidavit. The child must take standardized tests. Compulsory attendance begins at age 8. *This information is not necessarily sufficient for arranging to teach children at home. Also, it may not be currently accurate. See the beginning of this appendix section and Chapter 4 for general explanations.*

State government information: Dr. Gary Emanuel, Deputy Associate Superintendent,

Department of Education, 1535 W. Jefferson St., Phoenix AZ 85007. (602) 255-5387.

Supporting organizations:

Arizona Families for Home Education, 639 E. Kino Dr., Mesa AZ 85203. Shirley Gardner (with the assistance of her husband). 1982. (602) 964-7435. Information packet with state requirements, $2. Sample of newsletter, $1. ABEFGHIKLQS.

Home School Supplies, 3446 N. Avenida de la Colina, Tucson AZ 85749. Pat Gentala, Owner. 1984. K-8. (602) 749-2685. Supply center open by appointment. Catalog $3.63 including tax. EHILWefhi.

ARKANSAS

Legal requirements highlights: Parents who wish to teach their children at home must notify the local public school superintendent in writing by August 15. Certain information is to be included in the notification. All children of school attendance ages (beginning at 7) must take an annual standardized test according to several options. *This information is not necessarily sufficient for arranging to teach children at home. Also, it may not be currently accurate. See the beginning of this appendix section and Chapter 4 for general explanations.*

State government information: Jim P. Franks, Administrative Advisor, Department of Education, Room 404-B, #4 State Capitol Mall, Little Rock AR 72201. (501) 682-4252.

Organization: Arkansas Christian Home Education Association, P.O. Box 501, Little Rock AR 72203. Tom Holiman, Board Member. 1982. (501) 753-7790. Send $4 for information. BCEGHIKLNQRSTUj.

CALIFORNIA

Legal information highlights: Teaching certificates are not required for private schools and, currently, most parents who teach their own children in California are filling out an affidavit (form furnished by the school district office) to open a private

school. Dr. L. P. Hartzler points out that "home schooling, as such, is not a legal option in California." and that although it is possible to establish a private school in the home, "the Department of Education strongly urges parents . . . to exercise their legal option for independent study—an educational alternative which generally enables home-based schooling and the student's enjoyment of the services and materials which are allocated to all public school students. "Under independent study, instruction must be consistent with the school district's course of study." I understand that many public school supervising teachers are flexible, and that some private schools also offer independent study. Not all public school districts in the state provide services under this option. Dr. Hartzler's suggests that if independent study is not available for your area, you may wish to consider an inter-district transfer to a district that offers it. *This information is not necessarily sufficient for arranging to teach children at home. Also, it may not be currently accurate. See the beginning of this appendix section and Chapter 4 for general explanations.*

State government information: Dr. L. P. Hartzler, Consultant. Alternative Education Unit State Department of Education, P.O. Box 944272, Sacramento CA 94244-2720. (916) 322-1048.

Supporting Organizations: *We have used bold face type to help you select by city although some, like Christian Home Educators Association of California, are statewide organizations.*

American Heritage Christian Academy, 9027 Calvine Rd., **Sacramento** CA 95829. Franklin F. Stover, Headmaster. 1974. (916) 682-2382. "We well recognize that children are 'an heritage from the Lord' and desire to assist you in fulfilling your responsibility. . . ." Individualized curriculum, meetings, counsel. DEFHILMNPSTUVXabcdefghjk.

Baldwin Park Christian School, 13940 E. Merced Ave., **Baldwin Park** CA 91706. Rev. Erling W. Hofseth, Administrator/Principal. 1957. (818) 337-8828. CEFHILNPSTVXacdj.

California Coalition of People for Alternative Learning Situations, P.O. Box 92, **Escondido** CA 92025. John A. Boston, State Director. 1982. (619) 749-1522. ABG'JKNPQRSTWj. Ideas exchange, networking. The organization's newsletter, *Communications Network,* deals with issues affecting home-centered learning in California, $4/year; sample issue, $1.

Center For Educational Guidance, P.O. Box 445, **North San Juan** CA 95960. Josette Luvmour, Director. 1984. (916) 292-3623. Fertility awareness advice. A Holt-style learning club. Computer link ups. ABFIJKNPQRSTUVefghjk.

Christian Home Educators of the County of Kern (CHECK), 2808 Hollins St., **Bakersfield** CA 93305. Pam Geib, President. 1982, reorganized 1988. (805) 398-8363. Field trips, parties, meetings. No charge for brochure or newsletter sample. BHILPQRSTUXj.

Christian Family Educators of Orange County, 2462 Norse Ave., **Costa Mesa** CA 92627. Bethany Bennett, County Coordinator. 1982. (714) 642-6405. NQSTej

Christian Family Schools, P.O. Box 2066, **El Cajon** CA 92021. Randi Flynn, Coordinator. 1982. Primarily a support group. Newsletter $6/yr. sample free. A'BDEFGHIKLQSTefik.

Christian Home Educators Association of California, P.O. Box 28644, **Santa Ana** CA 92799-8644. Philip Troutt, Executive Director. 1982. (714) 537-5121, 15-min. recorded message (no incoming calls). Contact this group for information on local affiliated groups throughout the state (more than are shown here). Conventions sponsored. $25 membership fee includes *The Teaching Home* and other benefits. NQSTUk.

Corona Heights Christian School, 930 E. Ontario Ave., **Corona** CA 91719, (714) 734-5578. Branches at 8291 Arcadia Ave., **Hesperia** CA 92345, (619) 244-2355 and at 1245 South "A" St., **Perris** CA 92370, (714) 943-6290. Sherry Hartman, Administrator. 1985. CHCS is a structured support system to help parents in areas surrounding the 3 school locations, to provide quality home education. Some 150 families are currently enrolled. Activities beyond academic guidance include field trips, drama and assemblies. B'F'GHILMNPQRSTUXabcdefghj.

Discovery Christian Schools, 5547 Alabama Dr., **Concord** CA 94521. Patrick Clifford, Superintendent. 1983. (415) 672-2736. Workshops and curriculum recommendations are also offered. BHILNPSUXcdefghk.

Educational Services, 175 Gladys Ave., #7 **Mountain View** CA 94043. Kathryn S. Means, Consultant. 1983. (415) 965-2594. DEFGKNQRSTUVWefghj.

Holy Home, The, P.O. Box 262, **Tehachapi** CA 93561. 1988. BGHINQ'RTUefghj.

Home Learning Exchange, 295 Karel Ave., **Red Bluff** CA 96080. Celia Surman, Coordinator. 1987. (916) 527-6553. NPQRS'Tefgh.

Learning Tree Inc. / Academy, P.O. Box 4855, **Auburn** CA 95604. Rick Pryor, Principle. 1985. (916) 823-2349. The Learning Tree is a guidance center offering a variety of programs and counsel for choosing the right combination for each child. A 4-year high school diploma program is also offered. BDFH'ILPSVWXYZabcdefgh.

Monterey County Office of Education Independent Study, P.O. Box 80851 **Salinas** CA 93901. Bill LaPlante, Director of Alternative Programs. 1986. (408) 755-6457. "We provide a professional support system to families who have chosen to educate their children at home." DFPSTUVXZabcdgk.

Northern California Homeschool Association, 3345 Santa Paula Dr., **Concord** CA 94518. Connie Pfeil, Chairman & Editor. 1987. (415) 674-1294. This group meets the interests of those who are not comfortable in the existing religious groups. This group meets the interests of those who are not comfortable in the existing religious groups. NQSUj.

North Santa Clara Valley Homeschoolers, 795 Sheraton Dr., **Sunnyvale** CA 94087. Jane Becktel. 1985. (408) 735-7525. Open to any home schoolers regardless of philosophical or religious beliefs. Social meetings weekly. Lessons 3 times/wk. ABNSj.

Pilgrims School, P.O. Box 1776, **Porterville** CA 93258. Jonathan Lindvall, Superintendent. 1981. (209) 782-0402. BFGHILMNPQSTUXabcdefghj. Offerings are appreciated from those wishing information or a sample of the newsletter. I quoted from Johnathan Lindvall in the chapter on social development.

Peninsula Homeschoolers, 2427 Grandby Dr., **San Jose** CA 95130. Jill Boone. (408) 379-6835.

Sacramento Council of Parent Educators (SCOPE) P.O. Box 163720, **Sacramento** CA 95816. Laurie A. Johnson, Chairman. 1985. Pre (916) 366-7393. Group lessons and field trips. A'DEFGHILMNPQSTUVWefghj.

South Valley Homeschoolers Association, P.O. Box 961, **San Martin** CA 95046. 1985. Ann Bodine, Coordinator, (408) 683-4802. Sample newsletter available for $1 and long SASE. NQRSTU.

COLORADO

Legal information highlights: Although certification is not required for home teaching parents, they are required to fill out an "annual notification" form and to file a complete instructional plan. Annual achievement tests are required, but students may place as low as the 13th percentile. The beginning compulsory attendance age is 7. *This information is not necessarily sufficient for arranging to teach children at home. Also, it may not be currently accurate. See the beginning of this appendix section and Chapter 4 for general explanations.*

State government information: Roma Duffy, Staff Assistant II, State Office of Education, 201 E. Colfax Ave., Denver CO 80203. (303) 866-6678.

Supporting Organizations: *We have used bold face type to help you select by city although some are statewide organizations.*

Alternative Education Resources, 4344 Bryant St., **Denver** CO 80211. David W. Snow. (303) 477-8482. ABKNUefghj.

Colorado Home Educators Association, 1616 17th St., Suite 372, **Denver** CO 80202. Mike Dwyer, Chairman. 1986. Sent $1 for a sample periodical issue. CHEA is an association of Colorado support groups. Any 3 or more families may form a group. NQSTUj.

Colorado Homeschooling Network, 7490 W. Apache, **Sedalia** CO 80135. Judy Gelner. 1981. (303) 688-4136. No specific philosophy is endorsed although participants tend to be those interested in the ideas of John Holt. Send 50c for a sample newsletter or $6.50 for the "Guide to Hmeschooling in Colorado" which gives current laws and legal climate. ABDKNQSUj.

Colorado Springs Home School Support Group, P.O. Box 26117, **Colorado Springs** CO 80936-6117. Mr. & Mrs. Dean Goossen. 1982. (719) 598-2636. Many, but not all, participants are Christian. Recorded message line. Legislative involvement and updates. NOQRSTUVXjk.

Concerned Parents of Colorado, P.O. Box 62062, **Colorado Springs** CO 80920-2062. (719) 598-8444 or (719) 687-6722. Mr. & Mrs. Dean Goossen and Mr. & Mrs. Peter Schneeberger. 1987. Parenting classes in addition to services indicated by the code letters. Homeschooling handbook, $3.00. NQRSTUefghjk.

Front Range Eclectic Educators, 6505 Hillside Way, **Parker** CO 80134. David & Marie Reeves, 1985. (303) 841-5267. The group is predominantly but not exclusively composed of Christians. A sample of their newsletter is available without charge. They plan frequent activities for children. NQSe.

North Suburban Home Schoolers, 11529 Ogden, **Northglen** CO 80233. Carrie Farmer, Contact Person. 1985. (303) 450-0305. The group is mostly fundamentalist Christians, but any homeschooler is welcome to join. Field trips, crafts, parties, etc. NPQSTj.

Northern Colorado Home School Association. 4721 Harbor View Ln., **Fort Collins** CO 80526. Ms. Tighe Yovanoff,

Facilitator. 1984. (303) 223-6026. A support group for John Holt style home schoolers, but cooperation with other groups. Active members include people qualified to administer standardized tests in Colorado. Newsletter sample for 45¢ postage. ABNQSUX.

Rainbow Ranch Christian Family School. **Woodland Park** CO 80863-9110. Mr. & Mrs. Peter Schneeberger, Headmaster and Principal. 1983. 1-12. (719) 687-6722. Certified teachers. Phone or direct counseling for enrolled families. BDEGHIKL'NOPSTUXZcefghjk

South Jefferson County Homeschoolers, 7331 So. Upham St., **Littleton** CO 80123. Benita Howell. 1984. (303) 978-0707. This group believes in "Encouragement," for beginners as well as others. ABDEHIKLNPTj.

Teller County Home Educators. Association. c/o Box 155, **Divide** CO 80814-0155. Mr. & Mrs. Ken Kish, Treasurers. 1983. (719) 687-2012. Membership, newsletter, $3.00 per year. NQRSTUVWXefghk.

CONNECTICUT

Legal information highlights: Parents can educate a child at home by showing that he or she is "elsewhere receiving equivalent instruction in the studies taught in public schools." Attendance records are also required. According to the State Board of Education policy, "when a parent wishes to educate a child at home, the board of education . . . will determine whether the instruction is equivalent. . . ." Certification is not required. Compulsory attendance begins at the age of 7. The Department of Education uses terms like "educating a child at home" rather than "home schooling." *This information is not necessarily sufficient for arranging to teach children at home. Also, it may not be currently accurate. See the beginning of this appendix section and Chapter 4 for general explanations.*

State government information: Maria Della Bella, PhD., School Approval Consultant,

State Department of Education, P.O. Box 2219, Hartford CT 06145. (203) 566-5234.

Support group: Connecticut Homeschooler's Association. 98 Bahr Rd., Deep River CT 06417, (203) 526-0962. JoAnne Malcarne, Coordinator. 1980. Nk. The $12 yearly membership fee includes the bimonthly state newsletter. No specific philosophy has been adopted. About 80% of the group is Christian.

DELAWARE

Legal information highlights: Regular and thorough instruction as required for public schools may substitute for school attendance if the local superintendent and an official designated by the state board of education agree that it qualifies, and a written examination substantiates it. A certificate from the teacher or principal in charge of a private school may substitute for the examination as evidence of proper instruction. Annual reporting is required. *This information is not necessarily sufficient for arranging to teach children at home. Also, it may not be currently accurate. See the beginning of this appendix section and Chapter 4 for general explanations.*

State government information: Department of Public Instruction, P.O. Box 1402, Dover DE 19903. (302) 736-4629.

FLORIDA

Legal information highlights: A parent may qualify to provide "sequentially progressive instruction" at home by having a teaching certificate. Or the home instruction may be offered by (a) notifying the county superintendent, (b) giving the names of the students, (c) maintaining a teaching log, and (d) having the child "evaluated." School attendance is required in Florida beginning at age 6. *This information is not necessarily sufficient for arranging to teach children at home. Also, it may not be currently accurate. See the beginning of this appendix section and Chapter 4 for general explanations.*

State government information: Don Darling, Administrator of Student Services, Department of Education, Tallahassee FL 32301. (904) 488-8974.

Supporting Organizations:
Circle Christian School, 3300 Edgewater Dr., Orlando FL 32804. (407) 422-5357. Jim Werner, Administrator. NPQSTVWXacdehij3.

Florida Association for Schools at Home, 1000 Devil's Dip, Tallahassee FL 32308. Karen Jackson, President. 1978. ABIKNThj.

Florida at Home, 7615 Club House Estates Dr., Orlando FL 32819, Linda Werner.

Florida Parent-Educators Association, Inc. 9245 Woodrun Rd., Pensacola FL 32514-5519. Dr. Larry Walker, Registered agent. 1984. (904) 477-9642. The group keeps in contact with the department of education and is active in lobbying. For a sample newsletter send postage for two ounces (45c). NQSTU.

GEORGIA

Legal information highlights: A parent in Georgia who is a high school or holds a G.E.D. diploma may operate a home school without being certified as a teacher. The parent need not seek approval of the authorities, but a declaration of intent to home study must be filed. Certain regulations apply. School-attendance laws apply to a student beginning at his seventh birthday. *This information is not necessarily sufficient for arranging to teach children at home. Also, it may not be currently accurate. See the beginning of this appendix section and Chapter 4 for general explanations.*

State government information: Norris Long, Division Director, Regional Education Services, Georgia State Department of Education, 1662 Twin Towers E., Atlanta GA 30334. (404) 656-2446.

Supporting Organizations:
Mountain Homeschoolers, Linda Rigell, Rt. 1 Box 1426, Clayton GA 30525. 1987. (404) 782-3920. ABFJKNSefghj.

Still Waters, Rt. 3, Box 1180, LaFayette GA 30728. Lewis & Trisha Gibson, Leaders. 1983. (404) 397-2941. CFGILMNQTeij.

HAWAII

Legal information highlights: The parent or employed tutor must have a bachelor's degree. The "superintendent" must approve the program according to certain information provided. Compulsory attendance begins at 6. *This information is not necessarily sufficient for arranging to teach children at home. Also, it may not be currently accurate. See the beginning of this appendix section and Chapter 4 for general explanations.*

State government information: Department of Education, P.O. Box 2360, Honolulu HI 96804. (808) 548-6405.

Supporting Organization: Hawaii Home Based Educators, Arleen and John Alejado, 91-824 Oama St., Ewa Beach HI 96824, (808) 689-6398. Milton and Kathy Yamada, 45-681 Kuahulu Pl., Kuahohe HI 96744, (808) 235-0220. 1984. Na Makua Ho' Olako, (means "parent enriched.") A contact group for other support groups. Works for favorable legislation. For newsletter subscription, send $5 to Arleen Alejado. DE'F'GHILMNQRSTUWXj.

Also see Appendix A for Learning at Home.

IDAHO

Legal information highlights: Teacher certification may be required if the local board of trustees considers it necessary for meeting the legal stipulation of being "comparably instructed." The beginning compulsory attendance age is 7. *This information is not necessarily sufficient for arranging to teach children at home. Also, it may not be currently accurate. See the* *beginning of this appendix section and Chapter 4 for general explanations.*

State government information: Department of Education, Len B. Jordan Office Building, Boise ID 83720. (208) 334-2165.

Supporting organizations:
Family Learning Organization. See listing under Washington.

Idaho Family Education Association, 2835 Balboa Dr., Idaho Falls ID 83401. Nancy Trued, Support Group Leader, 1985, (208) 529-4123. BDEFHIKLNQSk.

Idaho Home Educators / The Family Act, P.O. Box 4022, Boise ID 83711-4022. Bennett & Molly Brown, Chair Parents. 1982. BC'F'G'HIKNOQRSTUVWXej.

Information Network for Christian Homes. See listing under Michigan.

ILLINOIS

Legal information highlights: Parents have not generally had difficulty teaching their children at home in Illinois. They are not required to be certified teachers, but must teach their children "the branches of education taught to children of corresponding age and grade in the public schools." The beginning attendance age is 7. *This information is not necessarily sufficient for arranging to teach children at home. Also, it may not be currently accurate. See the beginning of this appendix section and Chapter 4 for general explanations.*

State government information: State Board of Education, Research and Evaluation, W-279, 100 N. First St., Springfield IL 62777. (217) 782-3950.

Supporting organizations:
Illinois Christian Home Educators, P.O. Box 261, Zion IL 60099. 1984. Ask them how to contact a support group near you. Send $3.75 for a sample issue of *The Teaching Home.* QSTUWefghijk.

Information Network for Christian Homes. See listing under Michigan.

INDIANA

Legal information highlights: To satisfy attendance requirements (beginning at age 7) a child may be taught in "some other school" and provided with "equivalent" instruction. The courts have viewed home schools as private schools and have not held for certification. *This information is not necessarily sufficient for arranging to teach children at home. Also, it may not be currently accurate. See the beginning of this appendix section and Chapter 4 for general explanations.*

State government information: Joseph E. Blankenbeker, Ed.D, Indiana Department of Education, Room 229, State House, Indianapolis IN 46204-2798. (317) 232-6614.

Supporting organizations:
Fort Wayne Area Home Schools, 4321 Mirada Dr., Fort Wayne IN 46816. Mike and Janice Sasser, Leaders. 1983. (219) 447-0425. Although operating from a Christian base, the group welcomes participation from anyone. Excellence is encouraged. Orientation meetings, book fair, etc. QRSTUeh.

Greater Lafayette Home Educators, 926 N. 19th St., Lafayette IN 47904. Eric and Margie Haley, Contact persons. 1983. (317) 448-4988. The group is diverse although mostly Christian. It is loosely organized and offers field trips and special classes. BHINj.

Indiana Association of Home Educators, P.O. Box 50524, Indianapolis IN 46250. 1983. (317) 849-3780. NQSTUk.

Information Network for Christian Homes. See listing under MIchigan.

Jackson County Home Educators, 715 W. Spring St., Brownstown IN 47220. Salvilla Huffman, Secretary-treasurer. 1986. (812) 358-2487. We provide monthly field trips, testing service and get-togethers. BEFKLNPQSVegj.

IOWA

Legal information highlights: Teacher certification has been required. The home schooling requirements are being studied as this books goes to press and parents who file their intent to home teach along with lesson plans by September 1, 1988 are exempt from prosecution for the 1988-1989 school year. By the next year, new legislation should be in place. Compulsory attendance begins at age 7. *This information is not necessarily sufficient for arranging to teach children at home. Also, it may not be currently accurate. See the beginning of this appendix section and Chapter 4 for general explanations.*

State government information: Kathy L. Collins, Legal Consultant, Department of Education Consultant, Iowa Department of Education, Grimes State Office Building, Des Moines IA 50319-0146. (515) 281-5295.

KANSAS

Legal information highlights: Parents who want to teach their children at home should register with the State Board of Education as operating a private school. Teacher certification is not required. The school year is to be "substantially equivalent"—180 days. Compulsory attendance begins at age 7. *This information is not necessarily sufficient for arranging to teach children at home. Also, it may not be currently accurate. See the beginning of this appendix section and Chapter 4 for general explanations.*

State government information: Topeka KS. (913) 296-4961.

Supporting organizations:
Alpha Christian School, Rt. 1, Perry KS. Stuart Merrill, Principle. 1983. (913) 597-5822. CFGILMNPVWXcdhij.

Teaching Parents Association, P.O. Box 3968, Wichita KS 67201. Jim Farthing, President. 1982. (316) 945-0810. An organization composed primarily of fundamentalist Christians. But home schoolers from all backgrounds are welcomed and assisted. BFHIMQSTXefghjk.

KENTUCKY

Legal information highlights: Parents who teach their children are to hold school for 185 days a year, keep attendance records, and teach certain subjects. Standardized testing is required. Attendance ages: between 6 and 16. *This information is not necessarily sufficient for arranging to teach children at home. Also, it may not be currently accurate. See the beginning of this appendix section and Chapter 4 for general explanations.*

State government information: William K. Evans, Advisor of non-public schools, Kentucky Department of Education, Capital Plaza Tower, Frankfort KY 40601. (502) 564-2116.

Supporting organizations:
Kentucky Christian Home School Association, 1301 Bridget Dr., Fairdale KY 40118. Victoria Kays, President. 1985. (502) 363-5104. Send $5 for a sample periodical issue. ABDEHIJLMNPQRSTUVXacek.

Kentucky Homeschoolers, 3310 Illinois Ave., Louisville KY 40213. Ruth McCutchen, Contact Person. 1983. (502) 636-3804. For communication and fellowship. NQRSTUej.

LOUISIANA

Legal information highlights: Home schools must be "approved by the Board of Education." The law specifies conditions expected for approval, thus limiting the freedom of the board to arbitrarily turn down the application. The home-school teacher need not be certified, but a "sustained" curriculum "at least equal" in quality to that of the public schools is required. The beginning compulsory attendance age in Louisiana is 7. *This information is not necessarily sufficient for arranging to teach children at home. Also, it may not be currently accurate. See the beginning of this appendix section and Chapter 4 for general explanations.*

State government information: Sue Starling, Assistant Director, Department of Education,

P.O. Box 94064, Baton Rouge LA 70804. (504) 342-3473.

Supporting Organization: Louisiana Citizens for Home Education, 3404 VanBuren, Baker LA 70714. Terri and Cathi Edward, State Leaders, 1981. (504) 775-5472. NSTUXZefgj. Send $2 for their information catalog.

MAINE

Legal information highlights: Home-school teachers in Maine are not required to be certified, but they are required to file for approval 30 days before starting school. The home school must be approved by the local school board and by the commissioner of education according to extensive criteria. The beginning compulsory attendance age is 7. *This information is not necessarily sufficient for arranging to teach children at home. Also, it may not be currently accurate. See the beginning of this appendix section and Chapter 4 for general explanations.*

State government information: Willian Doughty, Consultant, Department of Educational and Cultural Services, Augusta ME 04333. (207) 289-5923.

Supporting Organization: Maine Homeschool Association, Incorporated, P.O. Box 3283. Auburn ME 04210. (207) 784-2094. Steve Moitozo, President. 1985. BFLNQSTUefhk.

MARYLAND

Legal information highlights: Parents may qualify to provide "home instruction" (the term "school" means something different) by the local superintendent's approval of their application using a provided form. The program is to be periodically reviewed to retain approval. A teaching certificate is not required. Alternatively, an approved correspondence program may be supervised by a school or church. Compulsory attendance begins at age 6. *This information*

is not necessarily sufficient for arranging to teach children at home. Also, it may not be currently accurate. See the beginning of this appendix section and Chapter 4 for general explanations.

State government information: Mary Kalbrittain, Chief Pupil Services Branch, State Department of Education, 200 W. Baltimore St., Baltimore MD 21201-2595. (301) 333-2433.

Supporting Organizations:
Family Centered Learning Association, 6415 Dolphin Ct., Glen Burnie MD 21061. Susan Whetzel, contact person. 1984. (301) 850-4496, Call between 3 and 5 pm or between 6:30 and 8. ABHKLNSUei.

Maryland Association of Christian Home Education Organizations, 3529 Hepburn Ct., Burtonsville MD 20866. Ron Brackin, Acting President. 1987. (301) 421-1473. Currently loosely formed. Contact with support group and satellite school leaders. NPQ'Sefhj.

Maryland Home Education Association (MEHA), 9085 Flamepool Way, Columbia MD 21045. Manfred W. Smith Coordinator. 1980. (301) 730-0073. ABNOQRS'TUefghjk.

Montgomery County Support Group, 26824 Howard Chapel Dr., Damascus MD 20872-1247. Terry and Jim Mayor. (301) 253-5467 or (301) 428-0217. QSUk.

MASSACHUSETTS

Legal information highlights: Home education must be approved by the local superintendent or school committee. They may consider (1) teacher qualifications (but certification or a college degree are not required); (2) the school program (180 days, specified subjects and suitable textbooks and lesson plans); (3) the use of progress reports or standardized tests. Attendance ages are 6 to 16. *This information is not necessarily sufficient for arranging to teach children at home. Also, it may not be currently accurate. See the beginning of this appendix section and Chapter 4 for general explanations.*

State government information: Department of Education, 1385 Hancock St., Quincy MA 02169.

Supporting Organizations:

Massachusetts Home Learning Association, P.O. Box 248, Harvard MA 01451. Susan Ostberg, Coordinator. 1987. Occasional regional events. Membership open to all. Not church affiliated. NQRSU'j.

North Shore Home School Support Group, 211 Forest St., So. Hamilton MA 01982. Marcia Anthony, Coordinator. 1986. (617) 468-4663. Activities planned for families. CFHk.

South Shore Home Schoolers, 163 Hingham St., Rockland MA 02370. Karen C. Kimball. 1982. (617) 878-8093. Monthly discussions meetings. AIJKNT.

MICHIGAN

Legal information highlights: All instruction (900 hours required) is to be given by a certified teacher! Check the "Nonpublic School and Home School Compliance Procedures." The state has no procedure for approving home schools, but they can disapprove. *This information is not necessarily sufficient for arranging to teach children at home. Also, it may not be currently accurate. See the beginning of this appendix section and Chapter 4 for general explanations.*

State government information: Department of Education, P.O. Box 30008, Lansing MI 48909. (517) 373-3324. Unconfirmed address and phone information. I received no response to my questionnaire.

Supporting Organizations:

Information Network for Christian Homes (INCH), 4150 Ambrose N.E., Grand Rapids MI 49505. Dennis Smith. 1984. (616) 364-4438. NQSTUk.

Michigan Alliance of Families, 30327 Pembroke, Warren MI 48092. Elaine Andreski, Home School Chairman. 1978. (313) 751-4497. Traditional approach to education. Contacts may be arranged with nearby home school families. Curriculum

manual, $7.50 postpaid. CE'ILNPQTUXZcefij.

Sunnyridge, A branch of Clonlara School, HCO 1, Box 134, Pelkie MI 49958. Ray Krumm, Director. 1987. (906) 334-2788. "Sunnyridge's basic philosophy is to trust children as natural learners." Serves Michigan's Upper Peninsula. ABFIJKNPQRSTUVWXabc'defghj.

MINNESOTA

Legal information highlights: Attendance is required beginning at age 7. Parents without a state teaching license may teach their own children. Reports must be filed by October 1 each year and quarterly during the year. The children must be tested annually. *This information is not necessarily sufficient for arranging to teach children at home. Also, it may not be currently accurate. See the beginning of this appendix section and Chapter 4 for general explanations.*

State government information: Barry Sullivan, Government Relations, Minnesota Department of Education, Room 710, Capitol Square Building, 550 Cedar St., St. Paul MN 55101. (612) 296-6595.

Supporting Organizations:

Basic Learning Network. See Appendix A, Part 1.

Minnesota Association of Christian Home Educators, P.O. Box 188, Anoka MN 55303. (612) 434-9004. Roger K. Schurke, Executive Director. 1984. NOQRSTUXefghk.

Teaching Effective Academics and Character at Home (TEACH), 44350 Lakeland Ave. No., Robbinsdale MN 55422. (612) 535-5514. Described in Appendix A, Part 1.

MISSISSIPPI

Legal information highlights: The law in Mississippi specifically provides for home schooling and does not require either that the school be approved by the authorities or that its teachers be certified. The school may not be for the "purpose of avoiding or circumventing the compulsory attendance law." A "certificate of enrollment " must be filed by September 15. School attendance is required of a child who is "6 years old by September 1 and has not attained age 14." *This information is not necessarily sufficient for arranging to teach children at home. Also, it may not be currently accurate. See the beginning of this appendix section and Chapter 4 for general explanations.*

State government information: Nan Tarlton, Coordinator of Dropout Prevention, State Department of Education, P.O. Box 771 Suite 601, Jackson MS 39205. (601) 359-3598.

Supporting Organization: Mississippi Home Schoolers' Support Group, #1 Tally Ho Dr., Starkville MS 39759. Gerald & Babs Nelson, State Coordinators. 1984. (601) 324-2666. You may request information about the support group nearest to you. Sample of the state edition of The Teaching Home, $3.50. QSWjk.

MISSOURI

Legal information highlights: The statutes specifically allow for home schooling and do not require the teacher to be certified. The home school is required to maintain certain records and samples of the student's work. School attendance in Missouri is required from age 7. *This information is not necessarily sufficient for arranging to teach children at home. Also, it may not be currently accurate. See the beginning of this appendix section and Chapter 4 for general explanations.*

State government information: Russell McCampbell, Administrative Assistant, Department of Elementary and Secondary Education, P.O. Box 480, Jefferson City MO 65102. (314) 751-7602.

Supporting Organizations:
    Christian Home Educators Fellowship, 601 Madison Dr., Arnold MO 63010. Philip Lancaster, President. 1988. (314) 296-0120. The organization promotes formation and growth of support groups. BCFGHILNST.
    Families for Home Education, Rt. 1, Box 234, Independence MO 64050. Steve

Fortney, Executive Director, Donna Fortney, Secretary. 1983. (816) 796-0978. All home schoolers are welcomed. For a sample newsletter a $2 donation is appreciated but not required. Send a long envelope with your address on it for information. NQSTUVWk.

MONTANA

Legal information highlights: Montana parents wanting to teach their children at home must notify the county superintendent and provide an organized course of study as specified by the Board of Public Education. Also required are immunization and attendance records, compliance with health and safety regulations and the provision of the equivalent of 180 days of instruction. Attendance at school is required beginning at age 7. *This information is not necessarily sufficient for arranging to teach children at home. Also, it may not be currently. accurate. See the beginning of this appendix section and Chapter 4 for general explanations.*

State government information: Rick Bartos, Assistant State Superintendent, Office of Public Instruction, Room 106, Capitol Station, Helena MT 59620. (406) 444-4402.

Supporting Organizations:
    Flathead Homeschool Association, 360 One Way, Columbia Falls MT 59912. Janice Shamp. 1982. (406) 892-4052. BFILNQSTUWefghj.
    Homeschoolers of Montana, P.O. Box 40, Billings, MT 59103. Keith Babcock, Executive Board Member. 1983. (406) 248-6762. Karen Yost and Lu Olson, Newsletter editors, P.O. Box 40, Billings, MT 59103. (406) 656-3971 or (406) 248-3051. Sample periodical issue (with the Teaching Home), $3.00. FHIKL'MQSUefghj.
    Cascade County Home School Support Group, 417 5th Ave. N., Great Falls MT 59401. Sue Johnson & Lynn Baber (current leaders). 1987. (406) 454-2958. BDEFG'HK'NQRSTeik.

NEBRASKA

Legal information highlights: Home schools operate as private schools which are not required to meet accreditation standards. They must offer instruction in certain subjects. Teachers must be "qualified." Taking a minimum competency test may substitute for submitting qualifications. Parents must state that accreditation requirements and state approval violate their sincerely-held religious belief. An annual notice must be sent to the local superintendent by August 1 or 30 days before school is opened. Regular achievement testing is required. Compulsory attendance applies for ages 7 through 15. *This information is not necessarily sufficient for arranging to teach children at home. Also, it may not be currently accurate. See the beginning of this appendix section and Chapter 4 for general explanations.*

State government information: Bob Peterson, Program Director, State Department of Education, 301 Centennial Mall, South, Lincoln NE 68509. (402) 471-2783.

Supporting Organization: Lincoln Area Mother's Home School Support Group, 2441 Bretigne Dr., Lincoln NE 68512. Linda Stroh, Coordinator. 1983. (402) 423-1196. BEFGHI.

NEVADA

Legal information highlights: Parents have several quite restrictive options for their first year of home schooling. They may (1) hire someone with a teaching certificate, (2) qualify for one themselves, (3) be supervised by a certified teacher, or (4) enroll the child in an "approved correspondence program." After the first year, if the child shows "reasonable educational progress," parents may teach without supervision. Application for home school is made to the county school board. New regulations require testing and identification of the children taught. Ask for details. *This information is not necessarily sufficient for arranging to teach children at home. Also, it may not be currently accurate. See the beginning of this appendix section and Chapter 4 for general explanations.*

State government information: Dr. Doris Walker, Private Schools Consultant, Nevada State Department of Education, Basic Education Branch, 400 West King St., Carson City NV 89710. (702) 885-3136.

NEW HAMPSHIRE

Legal information highlights: School attendance is required beginning at age 6. Children taught at home may be excused from compulsory attendance by either (1) claiming religious exemption and explaining why the regulations are a threat, or (2) submitting a letter of intent to the local superintendent 90 days before beginning school. For details, request the publication, *Regulations and Procedures for Home Education Programs in New Hampshire* from the State Department of Education. *These legal highlights are not a precise or complete reflection of the law and are not offered as sufficient for arranging to teach children at home. Also, they may not be currently accurate. See the beginning of this appendix section and Chapter 4 for general explanations.*

State government information: Dr. Judith D. Fillion, Director, Division of Standards and Certification, 101 Pleasant St., Concord NH 03301. (603) 271-3453.

Supporting Organization: New Hampshire Home Educators Association, 9 Mizoras Dr., Nashua NH 03062. Elaine D. Rapp, Chairman. 1983. New Hampshire Home Schools Newsletter, c/o Abbey Lawrence, P.O. Box 97, Ctr. Tuftonboro NH 03816. Send $3.00 to get six bimonthly issues. QSUehj.

NEW JERSEY

Legal information highlights: Parents in this state are required to cause their children between the ages of 6 and 16 to attend a public school, or . . . a day school . . . or "to receive equivalent instruction elsewhere than at school." Parents have the responsibility to provide evidence of "equivalent instruction" to the local superintendent. *This information is not necessarily sufficient for arranging to teach children at home. Also, it may not be currently accurate. See the beginning of this appendix section and Chapter 4 for general explanations.*

State government information: Saul Rossien, Coordinator, non-public school services, New Jersey Department of Education, 225 West State St., CN 550, Trenton NJ 08625. (609) 292-5161.

Supporting Organization:

New Jersey Family Schools Association, RD 2 Box 236, Califon NJ 07830. Jenny Nepon, Coordinator. 1979. (201) 832-7217. "Support group for families who are home schooling on an informal basis. Sometimes we meet as a group especially when one family has a good idea for an outing. Then we all go together." ABJ'KNTj.

Unschoolers Network, 2 Smith St., Farmingdale NJ 07727. Nancy Plent. 1978. (201) 938-2473. An important purpose of this group is to establish people connections. ABF'JKNQSTUVWefghj. $1 for a newsletter sample.

NEW MEXICO

Legal information highlights: The state of New Mexico does not require either that a home school win the approval of the authorities or that the parents be certified to teach. The parents must, however, notify the superintendent of what they are doing and, unless the superintendent waives the requirements, the parent must hold a baccalaureate degree. School attendance is required from the age of 5 to 18. Annual standardized testing is required. *This information is not necessarily sufficient for arranging to teach children at home. Also, it may not be currently accurate. See the beginning of this appendix section and Chapter 4 for general explanations.*

State government information: Mary H. Beavis, Assistant Superintendent / Instructional Support, Department of Education, Education Building, Santa Fe NM 87501-2786. (505) 827-6515.

Supporting Organization:

New Mexico Christian Home Educators, Inc., 7417 Santa Fe Trail N.W., Albuquerque NM 87120. Phil Schultz, President. 1985. (505) 265-7016. Legal liaison, networking. Sample periodical, $3.00. New handbook expected to cost $5.00. Discounts on materials. FGHNQSTUWefhik.

New Mexico Family Educators, 678 Lisbon Ave., S.E., Rio Rancho NM 87124. Elvira Guillen and Katy Fuchs, Chairmen. 1982. (505) 892-5783. Join some 50 active families and participate in science fair, talent show, picnic, etc., and receive a valuable newsletter. Sample issue $1. ABE'HILNQRSTUX'ehij.

NEW YORK

Legal information highlights: The law permits attendance "elsewhere" than at public school with instruction "at least substantially equivalent." Local boards determine this equivalence. Parents must be "competent" but are not required to be certified. New regulations have been passed by the Board of Regents which clarify the responsibilities of parents and of superintendents in dealing with home instruction: An annual "intent to home instruct plan" is to be filed by a certain date; attendance reports, testing and quarterly progress reports are required. Attendance ages are from 6 to 16. *This information is not necessarily sufficient for arranging to teach children at home. Also, it may not be currently accurate. See the beginning of this appendix section and Chapter 4 for general explanations.*

State government information: Carl Friedman, State Education Department, Bureau of Pupil Support services, Room 362, Education Bldg. Annex, Albany NY 12234. (518) 474-6943.

Supporting Organizations:

Home Education Workshops, Christian Homesteading Movement, RD #2-SM, Oxford New York 13830. Richard Fahey, Director. 1961. For a newsletter sample send stamps for 2 ounces. ABDEFHIKLNQRTefhj.

Home Schoolers' Exchange, R.D. 1, Box 172 E, East Chatham NY 12060. Katharine Houk. (518) 392-4277. 1983. All are welcome. NQRSTUefhij.

Long Island Family Educators (LIFE), P.O. Box 283, Sayville NY 11782-0283. Vivian Martin. 1986. (516) 589-7844. A Christian-based group open to all. Monthly meetings focus on specific topics. NSUej.

Loving Education At Home (LEAH), P.O. Box 332, Syracuse NY 13205-0332. (315) 469-0564. Sharon Grimes, State Coordinator. 1983. Sample periodical issue, $3.50. F'HILNQSTUefhij.

NORTH CAROLINA

Legal information highlights: Home teachers are required to submit written documentation showing high school graduation or the equivalent. Standardized testing is required each year. The fire and teacher health clearance requirements have been dropped. Compulsory attendance is required beginning at age 7. *This information is not necessarily sufficient for arranging to teach children at home. Also, it may not be currently accurate. See the beginning of this appendix section and Chapter 4 for general explanations.*

State government information: Division of Non-Public Education, 532 N. Wilmington St., Raleigh NC 27604. (919) 733-4276.

Supporting Organization: North Carolinians for Home Education, P.O. Box 5182 Emerywood Station, High Point NC 27262-9998. Walt Goforth, President. 1983. (704) 553-1369. NQSUj.

NORTH DAKOTA

Legal information highlights: North Dakota law allows excuse from public school

attendance if the child "is in attendance for the same length of time at a parochial or private school approved by the county superintendent." No such school shall be approved unless the teachers therein are legally certificated . . ." Certain requirements also pertain to the course of study. Several court cases are currently challenging these requirements. Compulsory attendance begins at age 7. *This information is not necessarily sufficient for arranging to teach children at home. Also, it may not be currently accurate. See the beginning of this appendix section and Chapter 4 for general explanations.*

State government information: Patricia Herbel, Dir. of Elem. Educ., Education, Department of Public Instruction, State Capitol, Bismark ND 58505. (701) 224-2295.

Supporting Organization: North Dakota Home School Association, P.O. Box 539, Turtle Lake ND 58575. Clinton Birst, Executive Director. 1984. (701) 448-9193 or res. (701) 448-2646. A resource center is being considered. NQSTUX.

OHIO

Legal information highlights: The law currently holds the superintendent of schools responsible to determine whether the home schooling program (including the teacher) is "qualified." A recent court case has ruled in favor of the parents on the basis that the State Board lacks minimum standards. Attendance is to begin at age 6. 182 days and certain subjects are required. *This information is not necessarily sufficient for arranging to teach children at home. Also, it may not be currently accurate. A task force is working on more specific regulations. Get current information. See the beginning of this appendix section and the chapter on legal requirements for general information.*

State government information: Department of Education, Columbus OH 43215. (614) 466-2761.

Supporting organization: Christian Home Educators of Ohio, P.O. Box 1224, (1100

Summit Rd.), Kent OH 44240. William Ihde, Board Chairman, 1983. (216) 673-7272. NQSTUefghk.

OKLAHOMA

Legal information highlights: A child of school age (7 to 18) must be compelled to attend "unless other means of education are provided for the full term. . . ." (180 days). Apparently home schools are considered as legitimate private schools and are not regulated. Attendance records and certain subjects are specified by law. *This information is not necessarily sufficient for arranging to teach children at home. Also, it may not be currently accurate. See the beginning of this appendix section and Chapter 4 for general information.*

State government information: State Department of Education, Oklahoma City OK 73105. (405) 521-3308.

Supporting Organizations:
The Family Learning Connection, P.O. Box 1938, Durant OK 74702. Joyce Spurgin. 1986. (405) 924-1436. ehj.

Alpha Christian School. See listing under Kansas.

OREGON

Legal information highlights: Parents who wish to teach at home are required to notify the local superintendent in writing before the beginning of each school year. Standardized tests are required. Certain courses must be taught. School attendance is compulsory from age 7. *This information is not necessarily sufficient for arranging to teach children at home. Also, it may not be currently accurate. See the beginning of this appendix section and Chapter 4 for general explanations.*

State government information: Terry Kramer, Specialist, State Department of Education, 700 Pringle Parkway S.E., Salem OR 97310. (503) 378-3702.

Supporting Organizations:
Family Learning Organization, P.O. Box 7256, Spokane WA 99207-0256. Kathleen McCurdy, Director. 1984 (as Wash. Assoc. of H. Educ.). (509) 467-2552. "The real purpose of education is survival. A good character may be helpful thereto. The whole concept of 'school' for children is false as well as unbiblical." Courses on homeschooling. *Homeschool Resource Guide*, $7.50. List of homeschool groups and people. Sample periodical issue, $2. A'BNPQRSTUVXZejk.

Jackson County Home Educators, 790 Cherry St., Medford OR 97501. Don & Zana Walker, Board member. 1984. K-12. NQSUXefghj.

Mustard Seed Educational Services, 1911 N.E. Thompson, Portland OR 97212. (503) 287-4812. Molly Moreland, Educational Consultant. 1988. Tutoring in math through calculus, parent counseling and testing for the deaf, job placement and career counseling, student body cards. BHINTUWXcdefghj.

Parents Education Association, P.O. Box 1482, Beaverton OR 97075. Dennis R. Tuuri, Executive Director. 1984. (503) 241-4585. Lobbies for home schools and private schools. "The chief end of man is to glorify God and enjoy Him." CHILMOQSTUj.

Portland Area Tri-County Homeschoolers (PATCH), P.O. Box 5345, Oregon City OR 97045. Laura Pritchard, Coordinator. 1985. (503) 657-6671. A group of families with different lifestyles. Field trips, networking. ABJKNSUej.

PENNSYLVANIA

Legal information highlights: "Regular daily instruction in the English language, for the time herein required by a properly qualified private tutor" satisfies the school attendance requirement. District superintendents across the state, however, apply quite different standards to determine satisfactory qualifications. Some expect teacher certification. Alternatively, a home school might be acceptable if operated by a "bona fide* religious institution. Children must be in school "not later that at the age of 8." *This information is not necessarily sufficient for arranging to teach children at home. Also, it may not be currently accurate. See the beginning of this appendix section and Chapter 4 for general explanations.*

State government information: Division of Advisory Services, Pennsylvania Department of Education, 333 Market St., Harrisburg PA 17126. (717) 783-3750.

Supporting Organizations:
Pocono Homeschoolers, 1743 Pokono Ave., Stroudsburg PA 18360. Ann Cameron-Schick, Director. 1983. K-12. (717) 421-5022. Information available by phone. Time does not allow written correspondence. Calls returned collect. A'BFI'KNPe.

Pennsylvania Homeschoolers, R.D. 2, Box 117, Kittanning PA 16201. Susan and Howard Richman, Editors. 1982. (412) 783-6512. QRSTUefghj. From what I understand about their newsletter, you may want to subscribe. It has long articles and a kids "Backpack" section. No dues for the organization beyond the newsletter fee. For $2.25 they'll send a sample issue.

RHODE ISLAND

Legal information highlights: Parents may provide a "course of at-home instruction" approved by the local school committee. Or they may present a certificate declaring that their child is enrolled as a local school's satellite program. School attendance is required between the ages of 7 and 16. *This information is not necessarily sufficient for arranging to teach children at home. Also, it may not be currently accurate. See the beginning of this appendix section and Chapter 4 for general explanations.*

State government information: J. Troy Earhart, Commissioner of Education, Department of Education, 22 Hayes St., Providence RI 02908. (401) 277-2031.

Supporting Organization: Parent Educators of Rhode Island, P.O. Box 546, Coventry RI 02816.

SOUTH CAROLINA

Legal requirements highlights: Parents who teach their own children are required to have a high school diploma and are evidently also required to pass the qualifying test given to college education students. School attendance is required from the age of 5.

State offices: Department of Education, Columbia SC 29201. Public information (803) 734-8500, legal services (803) 734-8783.

SOUTH DAKOTA

Legal information highlights: A child in South Dakota may be "otherwise provided with competent alternative instruction for an equivalent period of time . . . in the basic skills." Parents teaching their children must submit an application to the local superintendent and be "competent" (but certification is not required). An annual standardized achievement test is required. Compulsory attendance begins at age 6. *This information is not necessarily sufficient for arranging to teach children at home. Also, it may not be currently accurate. See the beginning of this appendix section and Chapter 4 for general explanations.*

State government information: Leonard Powell, Consultant A. E., State Division of Education, Kneip Office Building - 700 Governors Dr., Pierre SD 57501-2293. (605) 773-4662.

Supporting Organization: Western Dakota Christian Home Schools, 8016 Katrina Court, Rapid City SD 57702. Carol Schoen, Secretary. 1983. (605) 343-6523. BHINSUj.

TENNESSEE

Legal information highlights: Parents or legal guardians conducting home schools must have a high school diploma or G.E.D. to teach grades K-8, and a baccalaureate degree to teach grades 9-12. Also, a home school may operate as a "satellite" of a church-related school (as defined by TN law) if the church-related school supervises the home school and gives the home school students standardized achievement tests. Attendance at school is required from age 7. *This information is not necessarily sufficient for arranging to teach children at home. Also, it may not be currently accurate. See the beginning of this appendix section and Chapter 4 for general explanations.*

State government information: Office of the Commissioner, Department of Education, 102 Cordell Hull Building, Nashville TN 37219. (615) 741-2963.

Supporting Organization: Home Education Association of Tennessee, 3677 Richbriar Ct., Nashville TN 37211. (615) 834-3529.

TEXAS

Legal information highlights: Home schools may operate as private or church schools if they offer certain courses. The State may make "reasonable inquiry" to assure attendance (compulsory from age 7). Certification is not required. *This information is not necessarily sufficient for arranging to teach children at home. Also, it may not be currently accurate. See the beginning of this appendix section and Chapter 4 for general explanations.*

State government information: Joe L. Price, Director, Texas Education Agency, 1701 N. Congress, Austin TX 78701. (512) 463-9734.

Supporting Organizations:
El Paso Home School Association, Star Rt. Box 87, Anthony TX 79821. Becky Powers, Coordinator. 1985. (915) 877-2417.

Home Oriented Private Education for Texas (HOPE), P.O. Box 402263, Austin TX 78704. Debi Short, Secretary-treasurer. 1986. (512) 477-4673. Home schooling information: *Handbook for Texas Home Schoolers,* $5.00 postpaid. Sample of Texas edition of *The Teaching Home Magazine,* $3.50, or just subscribe for only $15. B'C'FGHIKLMNQSTUefghjk.

UTAH

Legal information highlights: Home school parents in Utah are not required to be certified, but they must win the approval of the local school board. School attendance is required beginning at the age of 6. *This information is not necessarily sufficient for arranging to teach children at home. Also, it may not be currently accurate. See the beginning of this appendix section and Chapter 4 for general explanations.*

State government information: Joyce Hansen Educational Specialist, State Office of Education, 250 E. 500 S., Salt Lake City UT 84111. (801) 533-6040.

VERMONT

Legal information highlights: To qualify as an alternative public school attendance, a home study program must include certain subjects and not enroll more than two children outside the home unless all they are all from the same family. An initial enrollment notice must be submitted. To continue, a new notice must be submitted each year after March 1. The commissioner will respond by acknowledgement, by asking for more information or by calling for a hearing. Home study programs are required to annually assess the progress of each student by one of several options. Mandatory attendance in Vermont begins at age 7. *This information is not necessarily sufficient for arranging to teach children at home. Also, it may not be currently accurate. See the beginning of this appendix section and Chapter 4 for general explanations.*

State government information: Kevin Colling, Home Study consultant, State Office Building, 120 State St., Montpelier VT 05602. (802) 828-3412.

VIRGINIA

Legal information highlights: Four options allow instruction by parents: (1) a baccalaureate degree, (2) teacher certification, (3) enrollment in an approved correspondence course, (4) a curriculum meeting the division superintendents' approval. Annual evaluation (which may be the SRA test) is required. The curriculum must be approved (which may also satisfy option (4) above.) Attendance is required from age 5 unless the parent requests a delay until age 6. *This information is not necessarily sufficient for arranging to teach children at home. Also, it may not be currently accurate. See the beginning of this appendix section and Chapter 4 for general explanations.*

State government information: Department of Education, P.O. Box 6Q, Richmond VA 23216.

Supporting Organizations:

Home Educators Association of Virginia, P.O. Box 1810, Front Royal VA 22630. Michael Ferris. 1984. (703) 635-9322. NOQSTUXefghk.

Home Instruction Support Group (HIS group), 217 Willow Terrace, Sterling VA 22170. Mark and Mary Ellen Tedrow, Founders/Directors. 1986. (703) 430-9544. HILNQSTUXj.

WASHINGTON

Legal information highlights: Washington parents have a variety of options for meeting legal requirements: (1) instruction supervised weekly by a certificated individual: (2) instruction by a parent with 45 College credits, (3) by a parent having completed a course in home instruction, or (4) by a person deemed qualified by the local superintendent. "An approved private school may operate an extension program for parents . . . to teach children in their custody. Public schools may provide courses and/or ancillary services for home-based students. A standardized test is to be administered annually by a qualified person. The program must include certain courses and be conducted for a minimum number of hours. An annual "intent" must be filed by September 15. A certificated parent may request to operate a private school. Compulsory attendance begins at age 8. *This*

information is not necessarily sufficient for arranging to teach children at home. Also, it may not be currently accurate. See the beginning of this appendix section and Chapter 4 for general explanations.

State government information: Barbara L. Mertens, Director, Office of Private Education, Superintendent of Public Instruction, Old Capitol Building FG-11, Olympia WA 98504. (206) 753-2562.

Supporting Organizations:

Christian Home Educators Co-operative (CHEC), 182 N. Columbia Hts. Rd., Longview WA 98632. Barb Shelton, Community Resources Chariman, 1985. (206) 577-1245. BDEFHILNQSUj. A local area group focusing on ages 4-12.

Family Learning Organization of Washington (FLO), P.O. Box 7256, Spokane WA 99207-0256. Kathleen McCurdy, Director. 1984. (509) 467-2552. "The real purpose of education is survival. A good character may be helpful thereto. The whole concept of 'school' for children is false as well as unbiblical." Courses on homeschooling. Information on Washington laws. *Homeschool Resource Guide* $7.50. List of homeschool groups and people. Sample periodical issue, $2.00. A'BNPQRSTUVXZejk.

Homeschoolers' Support Association, 23923 S.E. 202nd, Maple Valley WA 98038. Dianne Leber, President. Janice Hedin, Public Relations Coordinator. 1985. (206) 432-9805. HSA is a large and growing group which welcomes families of all philosophical backgrounds. Affiliated groups have been established in Issaquah and Pierce County. NQSTUX.

Information Network for Christian Homes (INCH), 4150 Ambrose NE, Grand Rapids MI 49505. Dennis Smith. 1984. (616) 364-4438. Sample periodical issue available without charge. NQSTUk.

Responsible Education Achieved in the Christian Home (REACH), 20800 Hubbard Rd., Lynnwood WA 98036. Stephanie Martindale, Co-Coordinator. 1983. (206) 672-7416. Resource guide for the Snohomish and King county areas, $5.00.

Weekly activities for children: skating, swimming lessons, choir, etc. ABDEFGHILMNPQSTUWXek.

River Valley Learning Center, P.O. Box 1488, Okanogan WA 98840. Sherrie Farrell, Director. (509) 422-5309. An affiliate of Family Centered Learning Alternatives, a state-approved private school offering regular high school credit for work done under supervision at home. ABD'IKNPSTVWXYZabcdefghk.

Snohomish County Christian School, 17931 64th Ave. W., Lynnwood WA 98037. Mrs. Debbie Schindler, Principal. 1981. Pre-school-12. (206) 742-9518. BFHILNPUVXacdghj.

Teaching Parents Association, 16109 N.E. 169th Place, Woodinville WA 98072. Julie Diamont, Chairman. 1984. (206) 483-2376. ABFKNQSTXek.

Washington Baptist Teachers College, 2402 S. 66th St., Tacoma WA 98409. James M. Bramblet, Chairman Division of Education. 1976. (206) 472-9675. GHI'Lfghk.

Washington Homeschool Organization (WHO), 23335 264th Ave. S.E., Maple Valley WA 98038. Sandi Hall, Chairman. 1986. (206) 432-3935. WHO supports all home schoolers regardless of their philosophy. I'm very impressed by the scope of topics and the level of organization represented by a convention announcement I just looked at. NQSTUj. WHO's journal is *Washington Homeschool Report*, 10029 48th Ave. W., Everett WA 98204. Craig and Carolyn Kunard, Editors. (206) 745-8478.

WEST VIRGINIA

Legal information highlights: Exemption from public school attendance may be obtained for home schools in either of two ways: (A) the instructor must be considered "qualified" in the judgment of the county superintendent and board; and school must be conducted as long as the county schools in the county are; and attendance, instruction and progress records must be furnished. Or under (B) the second option, (1) the home instructor must file a notice of intent. (2)

He/she must show evidence of qualification by either having completed formal education of four years more than any pupil, but at least have received a high school diploma, or by a satisfactory score on the National Teachers Examination. (3) He/she must submit an instructional plan (4) The child must pass standardized tests. Compulsory attendance begins at age 6. *This information is not necessarily sufficient for arranging to teach children at home. Also, it may not be currently accurate. See the beginning of this appendix section and Chapter 4 for general explanations.*

State government information: Office of classification and accreditation, Complex, B-346, (304) 348-3788; or Dr. Tom McNeel, Superintendent, West Virginia Department of Education, Capitol Complex, Building 6, Room B-358, Charleston WV 25305. (304) 348-2681.

Supporting Organizations:

Homeschool Education Association, Rt. 1, Box 353, Alderson WV 24910. Richard Dulee, President. 1981. (304) 445-7667. Family counseling is also available. ABFJKNTefghj.

West Virginia Home Educators Association, P.O. Box 266, Glenville WV 26351. Donald D. Fox, President. 1986. (304) 462-8296. BFHIKLNQRSTUVWXefghj.

WISCONSIN

Legal information highlights: Parents who wish to teach their children at home in the state of Wisconsin are not required to be certified as teachers or to receive prior approval from the school authorities. The home school must, however, comply with certain regulations covering such things as the number of hours of instruction to be provided during the school year, and the nature of the curriculum. School attendance is required from the age of 6. *This information is not necessarily sufficient for arranging to teach children at home. Also, it may not be currently accurate. See the beginning of this appendix section and Chapter 4 for general explanations.*

State government information: Marvin Berg, Consultant, Private School Education, State of Wisconsin Department of Public Instruction, 125 S. Webster St., P.O. Box 7841, Madison WI 53707. (606) 266-5761.

Supporting Organization:
Home Offered Meaningful Education (Wisconsin HOME), 1428 Woodland Ave., Eau Claire WI 54701. Mary Peterson, Editor. 1983. (715) 835-2869. A secular support group. Sample periodical issue $2. KQj2.

Wisconsin Parents Association, P.O. Box 2502, Madison WI 53701. 1983. Ask about their Handbook on home education in Wisconsin. NQWTUjk

WYOMING

Legal information highlights: School attendance is required for children who are 7 by September 15. Parents conducting home schools are to submit their curriculum (materials and plans for using them) for the approval of the local superintendent. If the home school is operated under the auspices of a local religious congregation it may be exempted from all attendance requirements. *This information is not necessarily sufficient for arranging to teach children at home. Also, it may not be currently accurate. See the beginning of this appendix section and Chapter 4 for general explanations.*

State government information: Audrey M. Cotherman, Deputy Superintendent, State Department of Education, Hathaway Building, Cheyenne WY 82002. (307) 777-6202.

Supporting Organization:
Homeschoolers of Wyoming, Box 2197, Mills WY 82644. (307) 235-4928. Denise Nobs. NPQSUVej. Referrals to other homeschoolers. Materials loaned.

Wyoming Home Educators Network, (WHEN), 1084 Sybille Creek Rd. Wheatland WY 82201. Jay R. and Shelly Ann Halle, Directors. 1982. (307) 322-4976. HNk.

D

Information by region for Canada

The purpose of this appendix section is to provide starting points for finding information specific to particular provinces and territories in Canada.

Although the legal information is not intended to be complete and some of it may have changed by the time you read this book, we offer it as clues about what you might expect. *Nothing in this book constitutes legal advice.* Chapter 4 discusses facing legal problems in the establishment of home schools and includes suggestions about finding more complete and up-to-date information.

In this appendix section, we also provide information about organizations of specific interest to home schooling families in each province. Support group leadership changes frequently. Although some of the people whose addresses are listed may have other responsibilities by the time you want to contact them, they will probably be willing to direct you to those who can help

you. Plan to send a self-addressed stamped envelope when requesting information.

Also there are no doubt many groups we are unaware of. We invite you to keep us informed for future editions of this book.

NATIONAL ORGANIZATIONS

In addition to many of the U.S. based organizations which also serve Canadian families (See Appendix A), we have confirmation for listing several others in Canada which operate on a national level:

Canadian Alliance of Home Schoolers. Look under Ontario.

Granton Institute of Technology, a correspondence school based in Toronto. See Appendix A, Part 2.

Hewitt-Moore Canada. In British Colombia.

King's Education Advisory. Also in B.C., Tunya Audain. (According to old information.)

ALBERTA

Legal information highlights: "A school board may excuse a pupil 6 years of age and up to 16 years . . . from attendance . . . if the Superintendent certifies in writing that the pupil is under efficient instruction at home." School boards are to monitor and evaluate the educational progress. Provincially administered achievement tests for grades 3, 6 and 9 are usually required. Request the

Foundation Programs information brochure on home schooling.

Provincial office information: For information relating to home schooling education programs contact a regional office: <1> Grand Prairie Regional Office, 5th Floor Nordic Court, 10014 99th St. T8V 3N4. (403) 538-5130. <2 & 3> Edmonton Regional Office, 3rd Floor Edwards Building, 10053 111 St., T5K 2H8. (403) 427-2952. <4> Red Deer Regional Office, 3rd Floor

West, Provincial Building, 4920 51 St., T4N 6K8. (403) 340-5262. <5> Calgary Regional Office, Room 1200, Rocky Mountain Plaza, 615 Macleod Trail S.E., T2G 4T8. (403) 297-6353. <6> Lethbridge Regional Office, Provincial Building, 200 5th Ave. S., Bag Service 3014, T1J 4C7. (403) 381-5243. For general information call (403) 427-7219. Correspondence school: (403) 674-5333.

Supporting Organizations:

Alberta Federation of Homeschool Associations, 16 Fonda Close S.E., Calgary T2A 6G3. (403) 255 0080. See the beginning of this appendix for nationwide organizations.

Homeschoolers' Association of Northern Alberta, 10239A- 150 St., Edmonton Alberta T5T 1T4. Ruth Plumb, President. 1985. (403) 486-3417. NQSUj. Although not a Christian- based group, many Christians are members. Membership $15/yr. Newsletter sample, $1.

BRITISH COLUMBIA

Legal information highlights: Laws are subject to change and often depend on particular circumstances. See the chapter "Keeping peace with school authorities" for suggestions for finding current information and interpretations. The following summary is not intended as legal advice. The law requires attendance of all children "over the age of 7 years" but shows as an "exemption": "that a child is being educated by another means satisfactory to the justice or tribunal before whom the prosecution takes place." "The local board of each school district shall enforce the provisions of this Act. . . ."

Provincial government information: Field Liason Branch, Ministry of Education, Parliament Buildings, Victoria BC V8V 2M4. (504) 356-2575. For the Ministry of Education: (604) 387-4311.

Supporting organizations:

Home Learning Resource Centre (HLRC), Box 61 Quathiaski Cove, B.C. V0P 1N0, or Box 438, Fort Langley, B.C. V0X 1J0. Mary Turner, President, 1986. (604) 285-3926.

Hewitt-Moore Canada, Box 500, Lillooet, B.C. V0K 1V0, Rhona Kwiram, 1983. (604) 256-7487. BFGINPQTUVWXbefghjk. See the beginning of Appendix A for the key for the alphabet codes.

Victoria Homeschoolers, 4 Ethos Place, Victoria, B.C. V9A 7A3. Jan Hunt. 1987. (604) 386-0508. Or contact Cindy Barker at (604) 383-7618. ABJKNSeghj.

See the beginning of this appendix for nationwide organizations.

MANITOBA

Legal information highlights: Home Schools need official approval from the provincial office of education. Approved correspondence courses meet school-attendance requirements for any family wishing to use them. Home instruction must be "equivalent to the standard in public school." Children whose ages are 7 to 16 are required to attend school. This information may soon change since an advisory committee has reviewed home schooling and is reporting to the Minister of Education.

Provincial office information: E. A. Woods, Education Administrative Consultant, Room 116, 1200 Portage Ave., Winnipeg, Manitoba R3G 0T3. (204) 945-8321.

Correspondence School at 528 St. James St., Winnipeg, Manitoba R3G 3J4. (204) 945-7612.

Supporting organization:

Manitoba Association for Schooling at Home (MASH), 89 Edkar Cr., Winnipeg, Man., R2G 3N8. Henrietta Hielema, President. 1982. (204) 334-4763. BDF'KNPQRSTUefghj (Code interpreted at the beginning of Appendix A). Also, "Family values are of paramount importance in developing self- assured, competent, contributors to society." Children's activities organized. Send $1 for a sample periodical issue. See the beginning of this appendix for nationwide organizations.

NEWFOUNDLAND and **LABRADOR**

Legal highlights information: Mandatory attendance ages 6 to 15.

Department of Education: P.O. Box 4750, St. John's, Newfoundland A1C 5T1. (709) 576-3020.

Supporting organizations: See the beginning of this appendix section for nationwide organizations.

NEW BRUNSWICK

Legal highlights information: Attendance at school for children between 7 and 15 is not required where "in the opinion of the Minister a child is under efficient instruction elsewhere." Thus home programs are evaluated by a Department of Education consultant.

Department of Education, P.O. Box 6000, Fredericton, N.B. E3B 5H1. (506) 453-3678.

NORTHWEST TERRITORIES

Department of Education, Media and Information Services, 1st Floor, Lahm Ridge Tower, Yellowknife, N.W.T. X1A 2L9. (403) 873-7529.

Supporting organizations: See the beginning of this appendix for nationwide organizations.

NOVA SCOTIA

Higdon, P. O. Box 1650, Halifax, N.S. B3J 2Z2. (902) 424-5445. The Department of Education office address is P.O. Box 578, Halifax B3J 2S9.

Supporting organizations: See the beginning of this appendix for nationwide organizations.

ONTARIO

Legal highlights information: School attendance is required for children who are six years of age on or before September 1 of the given school year. Certification is not required for home teachers. Correspondence courses are offered by the Independent Learning Center (same address). These courses do not generally satisfy the attendance requirement.

Department of Education: John W. Rogers, Provincial School Attendance Counselor, 900 Bay St., Mowat Block, Queen's Park, Toronto, Ontario M7A 1L2. (416) 963-2456.

Supporting organizations:
Canadian Alliance of Home Schoolers, 195 Marksville Rd., Unionville, Ont., L3R 4V8. Wendy Priesnitz, Coordinator. 1979. (416) 477-3641. ABJKQSTUefgk. See the bibliography (Appendix H) for information on Wendy Priesnitz's book.
Ontario Homeschoolers, P.O. Box 60, (260 Adelaide St., East,) Toronto, Ont., M5A 1NO. 1983. (705) 456-3186 (Gail). Extensive resource list available. Includes information, materials, people, places, etc. ABF'HKNOPQRSTUefghik.

PRINCE EDWARD ISLAND

Sketch of the legal situation: From correspondence received in 1983 and confirmed in 1985, the school act excuses a child from public school attendance if, in the opinion of the Minister, he/she is under efficient instruction elsewhere. Private schools are permitted under this section of the law. Presumably home schools would be, too. Attendance is mandatory beginning with age 7.

Department of Education: P.O. Box 2000, Charlottetown, P.E.I. C1A 7N8.

Support: See the beginning of this appendix for nationwide organizations.

QUEBEC

Legal highlights information: Jocelyn Maskerman of the Quebec Homeschooling Advisory writes: "Parents teaching their own children at home do not need any particular 'permission' but if called to task will have to prove that the child receives 'effective instruction' (Pgh 273) which may involve testing. They also have to satisfy the child's 'right to an education' clause under the Youth Protection Act.

"This whole area of homeschooling/ correspondence/ private schools, etc. is due to come under closer scrutiny in the future as more and more parents inquire at the Ministère de l'Education du Québec."

You might get a different response from the Ministry of Education or the local school commission. The person in the office I wrote to before contacting Jocelyn Maskerman evidently responded to my inquiry as if I were asking about establishing a private school. In this case, teachers need to be certified.

Mandatory attendance begins at age 6.

Ministère de l'Education, Direction générale de l'enseignement privé, 1035 rue de la Chevrotière, 9è Etage, Québec, QC G1R 5A5. (418) 643-8156. Yvon Charbonneau, Directeur Générale.

Support:
Quebec Home Schooling Advisory, 4650 Acadia, Lachine, Quebec H8T 1N5. Jocelyn

Maskerman. 1983. NQSTUefghj (See the beginning of Appendix A). Information fee $5. Newsletter subscription $5. Service by correspondence (not phone) in English or French.

See the beginning of this appendix for nationwide organizations.

SASKATCHEWAN

Legal notes: Parents may educate their children using . . . any means which meets the approval of the local director or superintendent of education. See The Education Act, Section 156(a). Parents may arrange to establish private schools. "The issue of private schooling is currently under review and . . . some changes may be made in legislation or policies."—personal correspondence 5/88. Attendance required from the 7th to the 16th birthdays.

Correspondence school, Saskatchewan Education, London Life Place, 3rd Floor, 1855 Victoria Ave., Regina, Sask. S4P 3V5 (800) 667-7166 or (306) 787-6024.

Support: See the beginning of this appendix for nationwide organizations.

YUKON TERRITORY

Legal information: No laws now address the subject of home schooling. Legislation is expected to appear in 1989. The beginning mandatory attendance age is 6.

Department of Education, Box 2703, Whitehorse, Yukon Territory Y1A 2C6. (403) 667-5607.

Support: See the beginning of this appendix for nationwide organizations.

E

Information for countries outside North America

In this appendix section, we provide information about organizations of specific interest to home schooling families in several countries. Our listing here does not imply endorsement. We do not know the people or the histories of these groups. Also there are no doubt many other organizations we are unaware of. We invite you to keep us informed for future editions of this book.

In addition to the organizations shown here, some U.S. based correspondence schools have overseas branches or affiliates. Others offer overseas service from their U.S. offices.

The alphabet code letters indicate characteristics of the various groups and are interpreted at the beginning of Appendix A. Plan to send a self-addressed envelope with appropriate stamps when requesting information.

AUSTRALIA

Accelerated Christian Education Parent Home Education Program, P.O. Box 10, Strathpine, QLD. 4500. Suzanne Priest, Coordinator. 1982. (07) 205-7503. BCFGHILNOPSTUVXZcdefghk.

Alternative Education Resource Group, Inc., Vic., 39 William St., Hawthorn, Victoria, 3122. Sue Simpson, Co-ordinator. 1980. (03) 819-2629, (03) 297-044. ABJKQRSTUeijk. Send A$4.00 for a sample issue of their periodical.

Brisbane Home Schooling Group, 148 Henson Rd., Salisbury, Brisbane 4107. Lyn Cargill, Contact Person. 1981. (07) 277-7945. ABKNQSUj.

Homeschoolers Aust. Pty. Rtd, P.O. Box 346, Seven Hills, NSW 2147. Mrs. Jo-Anne Beirne, President. 1985. (02) 629-3727. BDFNPQRSTUVWXZeik. A catalog and a sample newsletter are available for $4 each.

GREAT BRITAIN

Education Otherwise, 25 Common Lane, Hemingford Abbots, Cambs. PE18 9AN. Membership is open to anyone. A network of some 70 local co-ordinators are usually willing to give personal help and are backed by people with specialised experience in various aspects of education "otherwise."

NEW ZEALAND

Christian Home Schoolers of New Zealand, 4 Tawa St., Palmerston North. (063) 74-399. Craig S. Smith Director.

New Zealand Home Schooling Advice Network, 120 Eskdale Rd., Auckland 10. Anne Denny and Jean Harris, Editors of the network magazine, PRUNES. 1981. 480-5570. BDNQRSTUefghj. "Most people in New Zealand send their children to school at age 5, but it is not compulsory until 6. Exemption from enrollment is relatively straightforward."

F

Typical course of study

The pages which follow show topics commonly studied at each grade level, kindergarten through high school. A particular subject in a given school system may not cover all the topics listed; and classes are often added or subtracted especially at the high school level. Subjects which are not included in the main academic areas of the list, but which should be considered in a full curriculum come under categories such as music, art, physical education, vocational education, home economics and foreign languages. A school with a religious orientation would add Bible or religion.

I have not included this listing to show you specifically what to teach but as a reference for comparison. Home teaching is naturally in danger of achieving a very narrow range of objectives even with some of the packaged programs. Standardized tests measure only the bare essentials—the common elements all children need. Compare this list with what you plan to teach, and consider expanding in selected areas you feel are important.

This outline of courses and topics was developed from three major research studies plus curriculum guides from a professional organization and from many state and local offices of education across the United States.

As time passes, other revisions will be made. For information about obtaining a current copy, write to: Educational Services Department, World Book, Inc., Merchandise Mart Plaza, Chicago, IL 60654.

The curriculum outline which follows is from *Typical Course of Study* by William H. Nault, A.B., M.A., Ed.D. © 1986 Field Enterprises Educational Corporation. Revised printing 1987.

By permission of World Book, Inc.

___ Kindergarten ___

SOCIAL STUDIES _____
Meaning of holidays. ►Role of home and family. ►Characteristics of home and family. ►Location of home and school. ►Diagram of home and school. ►Relationship between home and school. ►Relationship of individuals to the group. ►Children in other lands. ►Why things change. ►Where things come from. ►How things change. ►What people do (jobs).

SCIENCE _____
►Weather and seasons (observations). ►Interrelationships of plants and animals. ►The sun—our principal source of energy. ►Classification of living things. ►Simple measurements. ►How plants are alike and

different. ►Farm animals. ►Care of pets. ►Observing animals. ►Indoor plants. ►Earth, moon and stars.

LANGUAGE ARTS
►Listening to music, poetry, choral reading. ►Social listening. ►Listening for correct speech habits and word usage. ►Constructing visual images while listening. ►Organizing ideas. ►Relating events and experiences using complete sentences. ►Reading readiness activities.

HEALTH AND SAFETY
►Personal hygiene. ►Good eating habits. ►Good clothing habits. ►Care of teeth. ►Safety to and from school.

ARITHMETIC
►Simple counting. ►One-to-one relationship. ►Correspondence of quantities. ►Ordinal-cardinal relationship. ►Number-numeral relationship. ►Recognition of basic sets. ►Elementary geometry (shapes). ►Calendar and clock. ►Denominations of money.

____ Grade 1 ____

SOCIAL STUDIES
►Citizenship. ►Neighborhood helpers. ►What people do (jobs). ►Our American heritage. ►National heroes. ►School-community. ►Homes in other lands. ►Make and read a simple neighborhood map. ►Holidays: Christmas, Mother's Day, Lincoln's Birthday, St. Valentine's Day, Halloween, Thanksgiving, Father's Day Washington's Birthday, Hanukkah.

SCIENCE
►Animals and pets: Farm animals, Zoo and circus animals, Woodland animals, Common birds. ►Where plants live. ►Where animals live. ►Grouping and classification. ►Air and water. ►Seeds, bulbs, plants and flowers. ►Day and night. ►Sun, moon, stars. ►Seasons and weather. ►Fire and temperature. ►Simple machines.

LANGUAGE ARTS
►Reading: Phonetic analysis; Structural analysis; Establishing sight vocabulary; Reading informally—names, labels, signs, etc. ►Enunciation and pronunciation. ►Simple capitalization and punctuation. ►Write name and simple words in manuscript.
►Create stories and poems. ►Tell favorite stories. ►Simple pantomimes and dramatic play. ►Use table of contents. ►Learn to handle books. ►Organize ideas and impressions. ►Take part in group discussion. ►Present information orally, in sequence and with clarity.

HEALTH AND SAFETY
►Safety rules to and from school. ►Good eating habits. ►How to dress for weather and activity. ►Exercise and rest. ►Personal hygiene. ►Common cold.

ARITHMETIC
►Number line use. ►Place value and numeration. ►Count and write through 99. ►Simple properties of sets. ►Count by 2's to 40. ►Simple properties of zero. ►Simple number patterns. ►Use of 10 as basic unit. ►Concepts of quantity and size. ►Geometric configurations. ►Concepts of ordinal and cardinal numbers. ►Value of penny, nickel, dime. ►Meaning of inch, foot, yard. ►Recognize time: clock and calendar. ►Handle ½ and ¼ in appropriate situations. ►Solve simple word problems. ►Estimation.

____ Grade 2 ____

SOCIAL STUDIES _____

►Community services and helpers.
►Holidays and festivals: Easter, Passover, Christmas, Hanukkah. ►Patriotic celebrations. Our food: Dairy and bakery, Garden and greenhouse, Markets and stores.
►Shelter. ►What people do (jobs).
►Families around the world.
►Communities in other lands. ►World heroes. ►Interdependence of people.

SCIENCE _____

►Animals of our neighborhood. ►Useful and harmful animals. ►Birds and insects in winter. ►Animal babies. ►How plants and animals get their food. ►Plant reproduction. ►How animals protect themselves and their young. ►Effects of seasons on lives of people, animals, and plants. ►Weather and how it affects our earth. ►Heat and temperature. ►The sun. ► The moon. ►The earth and sky. ►Simple constellations. ►Gravity. ►Air and atmosphere. ►Magnets and forces. ►Exploring space.

LANGUAGE ARTS _____

►Write independently in manuscript form.
►Develop methods of word attack.
►Simple capitalization and punctuation.
►Refine manuscript writing. ►How to study spelling. ►Listening skills. ►Give simple book reviews. ►Compose brief and simple letters. ►Use table of contents and index of book. ►Alphabetize through second letter. ►Use guide words in dictionary. ►Read silently for specific purposes. ►Use and meaning of quotation marks in reading. ►Develop increased skill in handling books. ►Organize ideas and impressions. ►Dramatizations and interpretive or oral reading.

HEALTH AND SAFETY _____

►Know basic food groups. ►Dental hygiene. ►Personal cleanliness. ►Safety in the neighborhood. ►Communicable diseases. ►Preventive measures against disease.

ARITHMETIC _____

►Decimal numeration system. ►Addition and subtraction facts through 18. ►Counting by 1's to 999. ►Reading and writing numbers through 999. ►Common measures of time, weight, length, liquid, and shape. ►Place value through 100's. ►Introduction to multiplication and division. ►Multiplication properties of zero and one. ►Telling time and using the calendar. ►Count by 10's to 990. ►Handling of money (coins). ►One-step problem solving. ►Using ordinal numbers through 10. ►Using sets and number facts.

____ Grade 3 ____

SOCIAL STUDIES _____

►Community helpers. ►Kinds of careers. ►History and development of local community. ►American Indians and pioneers. ►Shelters of animals and people. ►Transportation today and yesterday. ►Communication today and yesterday. ►Sources of our food. ►Sources of our clothing. ►Shelter. ►Some great Americans. ►Holidays and folk customs. ►Flat maps and the globe.

SCIENCE _____

►How the face of the earth is changed.
►The atmosphere. ►Motions of the earth.
►Earth satellites. ►Stars and moon.
►Energy and its sources. ►Sound.
►Weather and climate. ►Rocks and soil.
►How animals serve people. ►Plants and animals of the desert. ►Plants and animals of the sea. ►Life cycle of animals.
►Common birds, trees, and flowers.
►Forest plants. Conservation of plants and

animals. ►Ocean life. ►Magnets and electricity. ►Great names in science.

LANGUAGE ARTS
►Silent reading in increasing amounts and difficulty. ►Reading prose and poetry aloud. ►Report experiences orally with accuracy. ►Write short original stories and poems. ►Develop methods of word attack. ►Use period, comma, question mark, apostrophe, and quotation marks. ►Use common contractions, such as "can't," "aren't," and "doesn't." ►Develop dictionary skills. ►Beginning index skills. ►Alphabetize through third letter. ►Begin cursive writing. ►Spelling. ►Concept of paragraph. ►Homonyms.

HEALTH AND SAFETY
►Correct names for various parts of the body. ►Simple first aid. ►Proper balance of activities. ►Prevention and control of diseases. ►Care of eyes and ears. ►Health with relation to food, shelter, and clothing. ►Safety in the community.

ARITHMETIC
►Numeration systems. ►Properties of one. ►100 subtraction facts. ►Problem-solving analysis. ►Units of measurement. ►Graphs and charts. ►Two-step problems. ►55 addition facts and their reverse facts. ►Basic multiplication facts through the 6's. ►Division facts corresponding with multiplication facts. ►Distributive property of multiplication. ►Roman numerals through XII. ►Reading and writing numbers to five places. ►Simple fractions and equivalents. ►Count by 2's, 3's, and 4's through 100. ►Introduction to metric measurement.

____ Grade 4 ____

SOCIAL STUDIES
►History and development of the local state. ►Relationship of the state to its region, the nation, and the world. ►Geographic or climatic regions of the world: Regions of four seasons, Hot, dry desert regions, Cold regions, Hot regions, Mild regions, Mountainous regions. ► Types of community life. ► Why we have laws. ►Uses of the globe.

SCIENCE
►Environment of local state. ►Measurement systems (including metric). ►Plants and animals of the past. ►Earth and its history. ►Balance of nature. ►Classification systems. ►Structure of plants. ►Influence of weather. ►Causes of seasons. ►Solar system and the universe. ►Oceans and the hydrosphere. ►Climate. ►Rocks and minerals. ►Plants and seeds. ►The insect world. ►Biological organization. ►Living in space. ►Air and water pollution. ►Great names in science.

LANGUAGE ARTS
►Spelling. ►Silent and oral reading. ►Choral reading. ►Listening skills. ►Simple outlining. ►Write letters and informal notes. ►Creative writing. ►Use of the telephone. ►Make and accept simple introductions. ►Develop dictionary skills. ►Develop skills in locating information. ►Summarize simple information.

HEALTH AND SAFETY
►The body and its functions. ►Care and proper use of the body. ►Personal and mental hygiene. ►Principles of digestion. ►Basic good groups. ►Good nutrition habits.

ARITHMETIC
►Numeration systems. ►Subsets. ►Reading and writing numbers. ►Roman numerals through L. ►Addition—4 numbers of 3 digits each. ►Multiplication facts through the 10's. ►Division facts of through 9's. ►Multiplication by one-, two-, or three-digit numbers. ►Division with one-digit

divisor. ►Algorithms. ►Measurement. ►Meaning of mixed numbers. ►Find simple averages. ►Problem-solving methods.

►Simple geometric concepts. ►Develop ability to compute. ►Metric measurement. ►Use of calculator.

____ Grade 5 ____

SOCIAL STUDIES _____
►Exploration and discovery. ►Establishment of settlements in the New World. ►Colonial life in America. ►Pioneer life in America. ►Westward movement. ►Industrial and cultural growth. ►Life in the United States and its possessions today. ►Presidents and other famous people. ►Natural resources of the United States. ►Environmental issues. ►Geography of the United States. ►Relationship of the United States with Canada. ►Fundamental map skills.

SCIENCE _____
►How living things adapt. ►Plants and their food. ►Properties of air. ►Properties of water. ►Chemical systems. ►Time and seasons. ►Molds. ►Bacteria. ►Trees. ►Sun. ►Milky Way. ►Great names in science. ►Use and control of electricity. ►Magnetic fields. ►Latitude and longitude. ►Space and space explorations. ►Conservation. ►Biotic communities. ►Biological adaptations.

LANGUAGE ARTS _____
►Spelling. ►Silent and oral reading. ►Present original plays. ►Listening skills. ►Parts of sentences. ►Kinds of sentences. ►Plurals and possessives. ►Commonly used homonyms. ►Synonyms and antonyms. ►Homophones. ►Write letters, stories, reports, poems, plays. ►Dictionary use for word meaning, analysis, and spelling. ►Use of study materials: keys, tables, graphs, charts, legends, library file cards, index, table of contents, reference materials, maps. ►Make two kinds of outlines. ►Types of literature. ►Prepare simple bibliography. ►Use a thesaurus.

HEALTH AND SAFETY _____
►Elementary first aid. ►Community health resources. ►Our water supply. ►Sewage disposal. ►Bicycle and water safety. ►Care of the eyes. ►Dental hygiene. ►Nutrition and diet. ►Facts about coffee, tea, soft drinks, candy, etc. ►Germ-bearing insects and pests.

ARITHMETIC _____
►Fundamental processes involving whole numbers and common fractions. ►Set of the integers. ►Associative and distributive properties. ►Read and write numbers through millions. ►Common and decimal fractions. ►Numeration systems. ►Nonneg-ative rational numbers. ►Roman numerals to C. ►Long division concepts. ►Algorithms. ►Simple decimals through hundredths. ►Metric measurement. ►Extension of geometric concepts. ►Tables, graphs, scale drawings. ►Per cent. ►Multiple-step verbal problems. ►Use of calculator.

____ Grade 6 ____

SOCIAL STUDIES _____
►Countries and cultures of the Western Hemisphere. ►Canada and Mexico. ►Our neighbors in Central America and the West Indies. ►Our neighbors in South America. ►Australasia. ►Relationships among nations. ►United Nations. ►Transportation and communication. ►World trade.

►Eurasia and Africa. ►Map-reading skills. ►Reading charts and graphs. ►School camping (optional).

SCIENCE _____

►Helpful and harmful insects. ►Improvement of plants and animals. ►Classification of living things. ►Food for growth and energy. ►Microbes. ►Algae and fungi. ►Energy and simple machines. ►Climate and weather. ►Motors and engines. ►Electricity and its uses. ►Simple astronomy. ►Elemen-tary geology. ►Elements of sound. ►Light and heat. ►Heat engines. ►Equilibrium systems. ►Atom and nuclear energy. ►Inventions and discoveries. ►Great names in science. ►Space and space travel. ►Ecology and environment. ►Recycling of resources. ►Energy futures. ►Conservation.

LANGUAGE ARTS _____

►Nonlanguage communication. Write: letters, outlines, factual matter (newspaper article, reports), verse (limerick or ballad), creative prose (diary, stories). ►Extend dictionary skills. ►Use reference materials and indexes. ►Types of literature. ►Sentence structure. ►Simple note taking. ►Concepts of noun, pronoun, verb, adjective, and adverb. ►Work on speech errors and punctuation. ►Vocabulary building. ►Spelling. ►Listening skills. ►Reading silently and skimming. ►Use roots, prefixes, and suffixes. ►Bibliography building. ►Organization of a book.

HEALTH AND SAFETY _____

►Cure and prevention of common diseases. ►Facts on tobacco, alcohol, and narcotics. ►Great names in the field of health. ►Our food supply. ►The heart. ►Safety and first aid. ►Personal appearance. ►Health maintenance.

ARITHMETIC _____

►Ancient numeration systems. ►Fundamental operations with decimals. ►Fundamental operations with compound denominate numbers. ►Relationship between common and decimal fractions. ►Roman numerals to M. ►Multiply and divide common fractions and mixed numbers. ►Measures of areas and perimeters. ►Metric system. ►Operation of powers. ►Exponents. ►Factoring. ►Volume of rectangular solids. ►Simple problems in per cent. ►Interpret and make bar, line, and picture graphs. ►Set of the integers. ►Problem analysis. ►Introduction to symbolic logic (Boolean algebra). ►Use of calculator.

_____ Grade 7 _____

SOCIAL STUDIES _____

►Lands and peoples of the Eastern Hemisphere. ►Prehistoric people. ►Greek and Roman civilizations. ►The Middle Ages. ►Age of Discovery. ►Industrial Age. ►Yesterday and today in the Middle East. ►Yesterday and today in the Far East. ►Yesterday and today in continental Europe. ►Yesterday and today in Scandinavia. ►Yesterday and today in the British Isles. ►Yesterday and today in Russia. ►Yesterday and today in the Mediterranean. ►Yesterday and today in Africa. ►World trade and resources. ►Social institutions. ►The study of human beings. ►The family. ►Reading charts and graphs. ►Advanced map-reading skills. ►Exploring careers.

SCIENCE _____

►Scientific method. ►Scientific classification. ►Bacterial mutations. ►The cell. ►Life cycle of insects. ►Anatomy and physiology. ►Genetics. ►Rocks and soil. ►Minerals. ►Air pressure. ►Atmosphere. ►Energy crisis. ►Alternative energy sources. ►Conservation. ►Properties and uses of water. ►Effects of weather and climate. ►Changes and uses of materials. ►Ecology and environment. ►Famous scientists and their contributions.

LANGUAGE ARTS _____
►Spelling. ►Work on reading skills.
►Clauses and phrases. ►Parts of speech.
►Person, number, and gender of nouns and
pronouns. ►Compound sentences.
►Punctuation of conversation. ►Plan and
produce dramatizations. ►Writing descriptions, reports, and letters. ►Note taking and
outlining. ►Organization of the library.
►Extend reference skills—atlases,
encyclopedias, magazines, directories.
►Refine dictionary skills. ►Speech
activities. ►Listening skills. ►Literary
terms. ►Myths and legends. ►Types of
poetry. ►Autobiography. ►Biography.
►Ballads. ►One-act plays.

HEALTH AND SAFETY _____
►Practice of good health habits. ►Good
grooming and posture. ►Personality of
development. ►Effects of stimulants and
narcotics. ►Personal and public safety.
►Accident prevention. ►Circulation and
respiration. ►Functions of the body.
►Germ theory. ►Chemotherapy.
►Antibiotics. ►Toxins and antitoxins.
►Immunization.

MATHEMATICS _____
►Numeration. ►Properties of nonnegative
integers. ►Rational numbers and fractions.
►Three cases of per cent with applications.
►Finite, infinite, and empty sets. ►Contin-
ued growth in developing number skills.
►Measurement. ►Areas and volumes of
geometric forms. ►Basic geometric
concepts. ►Ratio and proportion.
►Elementary business practices. ►Reading
and constructing graphs. ►Development
and use of formulas. ►Metric system.
►Computer literacy.

_____ Grade 8 _____

SOCIAL STUDIES _____
►Our Old World backgrounds.
►Exploration and discovery. ►Colonial life.
►Struggle for independence. ►United
States Constitution and Bill of Rights.
►Westward movement. ►Civil War and
Reconstruction. ►Growth and development
of the United States. ►The U.S. as a world
power. ►Our American culture. ►Our
economic system. ►Energy and society.
►The U.S. political system. ►Meaning of
democracy. ►Advanced map-reading skills.
►Exploring careers.

SCIENCE _____
►Scientific method. ►Science nomen-
clature. ►Scientific measurement. ►Water
and its uses. ►Magnetism and electricity.
►Composition of the earth. ►The earth's
movement. ►Weathering and erosion.
►The ocean. ►The atmosphere.
►Weather. ►The universe. ►The Milky
Way. ►Space and space travel.
►Conservation. ►Contributions of scientists.
►Astronomy. ►Heat. ►Light. ►Machines.
►The atom. ►Chemical changes. ►Wave
energy. ►Mechanical energy. ►Nuclear
energy. ►Ecology and environment.
►Recycling of resources.

LANGUAGE ARTS _____
►Spelling. ►Independent reading.
►Figures of speech. ►Advanced dictionary
work. ►Speech activities. ►Listening
activities. ►Creative dramatics. ►Extended
vocabulary. ►Biographies of great
Americans. ►American poets and
storytellers. ►Short story. ►Narrative
poetry. ►Nonfiction. ►Improving skills in
the use of basic reference materials. ►Kinds
of sentences and their essential parts.
►Functions of sentence elements. ►Writing
simple business letters. ►Report-writing
skills. ►Study of infinitive, participle,
gerund, predicate nominative, predicate
adjective, direct and indirect object.

HEALTH AND SAFETY _____
►Safety. ►Sanitation. ►Mental hygiene.
►First aid. ►Grooming. ►Types and

functions of foods. ►The body's utilization of food. ►Functions of the body. ►Community sanitation and health.

MATHEMATICS _____

►Maintaining skills in fundamental operations. ►Application of percent. ►Use of fractions and decimals. ►Simple formulas and equations. ►Study of insurance, banking, and taxes. ►Scale drawing. ►Metric and nonmetric geometry. ►Polynomials. ►Powers and roots. ►Equalities and inequalities. ►Graph of an equation. ►Factoring and products. ►Sets and simple sentences. ►Numeration systems. ►Probability statistics. ►Metric system. ►Computer literacy.

____ *Grade 9* ____

SOCIAL STUDIES _____

►Basic human communities. ►Community government. ►State government. ►National government. ►Political parties and elections. ►Conservation (including human conservation). ►Resource management. ►Elementary economics. ►Labor and management. ►Taxation. ►The Constitution. ►Rights and responsibilities of good citizenship. ►The United Nations. ►Foundations of American democracy. ►Contributions of ethnic groups. ►City planning. ►Cities—then and now. ►Exploring careers.

SCIENCE _____

►Air and air pressure. ►Heat and fuels. ►Weather and climate. ►Air masses and fronts. ►Erosion. ►Nature and uses of light. ►Water and its uses. ►Air and water pollution. Electricity and electronics. ►Solar energy. ►Nuclear energy. ►Molecular theory. ►Earth science. ►Ecology and environment. ►Space and astronomy. ►Space travel. ►Metals and plastics. ►Sound and music. ►Nature and causes of disease. ►Health and safety. ►Nature and uses of chemicals. ►Simple and complex machines. ►Transportation and communication. ►Effects of alcohol and narcotics on the human body. ►Careers in science.

LANGUAGE ARTS _____

►Spelling. ►Fundamentals of composition. ►Analyzing poetry. ►Dramatic poetry. ►Using poetry anthologies. ►Language systems. ►Vocabulary. ►Grammar. ►Folklore and myths. ►Parable and allegory. ►The novel. ►Reading the newspaper. ►Advertising. ►Structure of a play. ►Extend reference skills. ►Report-writing skills. ►Listening skills. ►Preparing a speech. ►Analyzing propaganda. ►Evaluate material for accuracy. ►The unabridged dictionary. ►Foreign words used in English. ►Review of the card catalog. ►Special indexes.

MATHEMATICS _____

►General mathematics: Mathematical vocabulary, Direct measurement, Banks and banking, Investment, Budgeting, Insurance, Taxation, Graphs and tables, Informal geometry, Elementary algebra, Indirect measurement, Metric system. ►Algebra: Sets and their relationships, Properties of polynomial forms, Equations, Signed numbers, Fundamental operations, Equations of the first degree, Ratio, proportion, and variation, Relations and functions, Special products and factoring, Fractions and fractional equations, Square roots, Radicals, Quadratic equations, Elements of probability.

_____ Grade 10_____

SOCIAL STUDIES _____
►Prehistoric people. ►The earliest civilizations. ►The early Greeks. ►The Romans. ►The Middle Ages. ►The Renaissance. ►The rise and fall of monarchies. ►Birth of modern democracy. ►The French Revolution. ►The Industrial Revolution. ►Nationalism. ►Imperialism. ►Science and industry. ►World War I. ►Between the World Wars. ►World War II. ►The Cold War. ►The Vietnam War. ►The search for peace. ►Role of women in today's society.

SCIENCE _____
►Characteristics of life. ►Vertebrate life. ►Mammals and birds. ►Conservation of human resources. ►Plant life. ►Behavior. ►The scientific method. ►Disease and disease control. ►Genetics. ►Heredity. ►Human biology. ►The human being—a changing organism. ►Microscopic life. ►Classification. ►DNA-RNA. ►Nutrition and digestion. ►History of plants and animals. ►Reproduction and growth. ►Biology and space travel. ►Environmental issues. ►Energy in ecosystems. ►Careers in biology.

LANGUAGE ARTS _____
►Techniques of writing. ►History of writing. ►History of the alphabet. ►The short story. ►The novel. ►Writing short stories. ►Spelling. ►Listening skills. ►Vocabulary. ►Grammar. ►Lyric poetry. ►Sonnet. ►The essay. ►American literary heritage. ►Folklore and ballads. ►Regional customs, traditions, folkways, and language. ►Geographical dialects. ►Persuasion and argumentation. ►Understanding and writing poetry. ►Writing plays. ►Extend dictionary skills. ►Construction of footnotes. ►Distinguish between fact and opinion.

MATHEMATICS _____
►Plane geometry: Sets, Origin and uses of geometry, Simple constructions, Parallel lines, Circles, Polygons, Converse theorems, Inductive reasoning, Nature of proof, Inequalities, Locus, Ratio and proportion, Measurement of geometric figures. ►Intermediate algebra: Relations and functions, Square roots, surds, radicals, Quadratic equations, Binomial theorem, Imaginary numbers, Exponents and radicals, Logarithms, Progressions, Higher degree equations, Vectors, Determinants.

_____ Grade 11 _____

SOCIAL STUDIES _____
►Age of exploration and discovery. ►Colonization of America. ►The new nation is born. ►The Constitution of the United States. ►Development of the new nation. ►Period of nationalism. ►Sectionalism. ►Civil War and Reconstruction. ►The United States as a world power. ►Struggle for women's rights. ►Between the World Wars. ►World War II. ►The Cold War. ►The atomic era. ►Delinquency and crime. ►Problems of mental health. ►Urbanization. ►Public education. ►Role of women in today's society.

SCIENCE _____
►Chemistry: Matter and its behavior, Carbon and its compounds, Formulas and chemical equations, Acids, bases, and salts, Atomic theory, Periodic law, Water and solutions, Oxidation-reduction, The nonmetals, Ionization and ionic solutions, The metals and alloys, Colloids, suspensoids, and emulsoids, Electrochemistry, Equilibrium and kinetics, Nuclear reactions, Radioactivity, Careers in chemistry.

LANGUAGE ARTS _____
►American literature. ►Analysis of plays. ►Vocabulary development. ►Grammar.

►Architecture and sculpture. ►Mass communication. ►Music and painting. ►Propaganda techniques. ►Spelling. ►Listening skills. ►Advertising. ►Story writing. ►Editorial writing. ►Journalistic writing. ►Proofreading symbols. ►Use of *Reader's Guide*, etc. ►Miscellaneous reference aids. ►Vocabulary of poetry. ►Critical and evaluative reading.

MATHEMATICS
►Solid geometry: Lines and planes in space, Dihedral and polyhedral angles, Locus Polyhedrons, Cylinders and cones, Spheres, Photogrammetry, Slide rule. ►Trigonometry: Solution of right triangles, Use of tables and interpolation, Measurement of angles, Properties of trigonometric functions, Complex numbers and vectors, Graphs of functions, Solutions of oblique triangles, Logarithms, Identities and equations, General triangle solutions, Slide rule. ►Computer programming.

____ Grade 12 ____

SOCIAL STUDIES
►The democratic ideal. ►Agriculture in the United States. ►Urbanization. ►Conservation. ►Business and industry in the United States. ►American party system. ►Propaganda and public opinion. ►Democracy vs. Communism. ►Crime and delinquency. ►Labor-management relations. ►Taxation and finance. ►International relations. ►International organizations. ►Distribution and exchange. ►Public education. ►Principles of U.S. government. ►Free enterprise system. Consumer education. Role of women in today's society. ►Family economics and management.

SCIENCE
►Physics: Mechanics, Heat, Electricity and magnetism, Sound and acoustics, Light and optics, Wave motion, Nuclear physics, Electronics, Force, Work, energy, and power, Space, time, and motion, Relativity, Solid-state physics, Careers in physics.

LANGUAGE ARTS
►Spelling. ►Listening skills. ►Shakespeare. ►Current periodical literature. ►Problems of communication. ►Mass communication. ►Comparative study of mass media. ►Radio and television. ►Literary, social, and political heritage of England. ►The theater. ►Techniques of acting. ►Nature of tragedy and comedy. ►Social and business letters. ►Writing book reviews, precis, essays. ►Identify verbals. ►Parliamentary procedures. Bibliography development. ►World literature. ►Report writing. ►Film as an art form. ►Critical and evaluative reading.

MATHEMATICS
►Analytic geometry: Coordinates of a point, Slopes of lines, Equations of straight lines and circles, Plotting equations, The conics, Parametric equations, Polar coordinates. ►Elementary calculus: Derivative of a function, Computation of derivatives, Rate of change of a quantity, Maxima and minima, Integrals, Length of curves, Volume and surface areas. ►Elementary statistics: Tabular data, Graphs, Measures of central tendency, Quartiles and percentiles, Measures of dispersion, Simple correlation, Statistical inference. ►Advanced algebra: Sets of numbers, Binomial theorem, Progressions, Complex numbers, Theory of equations, Permutations, Functions and their graphs, Combinations, Probability, Determinants, Inequalities, Matrix algebra Mathematical induction, The derivative (optional). ►Computer science.

G

Ideas that work

In the area of human behavior, research results are usually elusive. Human circumstances are much more complex than those of fish or wheat or stars. What worked in a classroom in New York may not work at all in your home school. The collection of research evidence in this appendix, however, is some of the most certain and most practical. These ideas have been sifted and checked and clarified. They represent the heart of an 86-page book published in 1978 by the U.S. Department of Education under the title *What Works, Research About Teaching and Learning.**

I believe you will find the majority of this material very valuable if you consider it in relation to your goals. If you feel that an idea that promotes intellectual achievement, for example, might interfere with character development, you may not want to apply it as suggested.

The book, *What Works,* contains 59 findings along with explanations. We list all the findings but quote selectively from the explanations, choosing portions that would seem to be the most important for home school parents. Ellipsis points indicate only material cut from within the sentences we have included.

To find specific principles in this section, refer to the general index.

Parents are their children's first and most influential teachers. What parents do to help their children learn is more important to academic success than how well-off the family is.

Parents can do many things at home to help their children succeed in school. . . .

They can create a "curriculum of the home" that teaches their children what matters. They do this through their daily conversations, household routines, attention to school matters, and affectionate concern for their children's progress.

Conversation is important. Children learn to read, reason, and understand things better when their parents: ● read, talk, and listen to them, ● tell them stories, play games, share hobbies, and ● discuss news, TV programs, and special events.

In order to enrich the "curriculum of the home," some parents: ● provide books, supplies, and a special place for studying, ● observe routine for meals, bedtime, and homework, and ● monitor the amount of time spent watching TV and doing after-school jobs.

The best way for parents to help their children become better readers is to read to them—even when they are very young. Children benefit most from reading aloud when they discuss stories, learn to identify letters and words, and talk about the meaning of words.

. . . children whose parents simply read to them perform as well as those whose parents use workbooks or have had training in teaching.

The conversation that goes with reading aloud to children is as important as the reading itself. When parents ask children only superficial questions about stories, or don't discuss the stories at all, their children do not achieve as well in reading as the children of parents who ask questions that require thinking and who relate the stories to everyday events. Kindergarten children who know a lot about written language usually have parents who believe that reading is important and who seize every opportunity to act on that conviction by reading to their children.

Children improve their reading ability by reading a lot. Reading achievement is directly related to the amount of reading children do in school and outside.

Independent reading increases both vocabulary and reading fluency. Unlike using workbooks and performing computer drills, reading books gives children practice in the "whole act" of reading, that is, both in discovering the meanings of individual words and in grasping the meaning of an entire story. But American children do not spend much time reading independently at school or at home. In the average elementary school, for example, children spend just 7 to 8 minutes a day reading silently. At home, half of all fifth graders spend only 4 minutes a day reading. These same children spend an average of 130 minutes a day watching television.

Research shows that the amount of leisure time spent reading is directly related to children's reading comprehension, the size of their vocabularies, and gains in their reading ability. Clearly, reading at home can be a powerful supplement to classwork. Parents can encourage leisure reading by making books an important part of the home, by giving books or magazines as presents, and by encouraging visits to the local library.

Children who are encouraged to draw and scribble "stories" at an early age will later learn to compose more easily, more effectively, and with greater confidence than children who do not have this encouragement.

Studies of very young children show that their carefully formed scrawls have meaning to them, and that this writing actually helps them develop language skills. Research suggests that the best way to help children at this stage of their development as writers is to respond to the ideas they are trying to express.

Very young children take the first steps toward writing by drawing and scribbling or, if they cannot use a pencil, they may use plastic or metal letters on a felt or magnetic board. Some preschoolers may write on toy typewriters; others may dictate stories into a tape recorder or to an adult, who writes them down and reads them back. For this reason, it is best to focus on the intended meaning of what very young children write, rather than on the appearance of the writing.

Children become more effective writers when parents and teachers encourage them to choose the topics they write about, then leave them alone to exercise their own creativity.

A good way to teach children simple arithmetic is to build on their informal knowledge. This is why learning to count everyday objects is an effective basis for early arithmetic lessons.

A good foundation in speaking and listening helps children become better readers.

When children learn to read, they are making a transition from spoken to written language. Reading instruction builds on conversational skills: the better children are at using spoken language, the more successfully they will learn to read written language. To succeed at reading, children need a basic vocabulary, some knowledge of the world around them, and the ability to talk about what they know. These skills enable children to understand written material more readily.

Research shows a strong connection between reading and listening. A child who is listening well shows it by being able to retell stories and repeat instructions. . . .

Parents and teachers need to engage children in thoughtful discussions on all subjects. . . .

Excessive television viewing is associated with low academic achievement. Moderate viewing, especially when supervised by parents, can help children learn.

Watching television more than 2-3 hours a day often hurts children's achievement in reading, writing, and mathematics, especially if it disrupts homework and leisure reading. . . .

Moderate TV viewing can, however, actually help students from backgrounds in which books, magazines, and other mind-enriching resources are in short supply.

Many highly successful individuals have above-average but not extraordinary intelligence. Accomplishment in a particular activity is often more dependent upon hard work and self-discipline than on innate ability.

High academic achievers are not necessarily born "smarter" than others, nor do people born with extraordinary abilities necessarily become highly accomplished individuals. Parents, teachers, coaches, and the individuals themselves can influence how much a mind or talent develops by fostering self-discipline and encouraging hard work. . . .

Studies of accomplished musicians, athletes, and historical figures show that when they were children, they were competent, had good social and

communication skills, and showed versatility as well as perseverance in practicing their skills over long periods.

Belief in the value of hard work, the importance of personal responsibility, and the importance of education itself contributes to greater success in school.

Parental involvement helps children learn more effectively. Teachers who are successful at involving parents in their children's schoolwork are successful because they work at it.

Children get a better start in reading if they are taught phonics. Learning phonics helps them to understand the relationship between letters and sounds and to "break the code" that links the words they hear with the words they see in print.

Because phonics is a reading tool, it is best taught in the context of reading instruction, not as a separate subject to be mastered. Good phonics strategies include teaching children the sounds of letters in isolation and in words (s/i/t), and how to blend the sounds together (s-s-i-i- t). . . .

If phonics instruction extends for too many years, it can defeat the spirit and excitement of learning to read.

Children get more out of a reading assignment when the teacher precedes the lesson with background information and follows it with discussion.

Good teachers begin the day's reading lesson by preparing children for the story to be read—introducing the new words and concepts they will encounter. Many teachers develop their own introductions or adapt those offered in teachers' manuals. . . .

In the discussion after the reading lesson, good teachers ask questions that probe the major elements of the story's plot, characters, theme, or moral. . . . When children take part in a thought-provoking discussion of a story, they understand more clearly that the purpose of reading is to get information and insight, not just to decode the words on a page.

Students in cooperative learning teams learn to work toward a common goal, help one another learn, gain self-esteem, take more responsibility for their own learning, and come to respect and like their classmates.

Telling young children stories can motivate them to read. Storytelling also introduces them to cultural values and literary traditions before they can read, write, and talk about stories by themselves.

Children learn science best when they are able to do experiments, so they can witness "science in action."

Although students need to learn how to find exact answers to arithmetic problems, good math students also learn the helpful skill of estimating answers. This skill can be taught.

Research has identified three key steps used by good estimators; these can be taught to all students: ● Good estimators begin by altering numbers to more manageable forms—by rounding, for example. ● They change parts of a problem into forms they can handle more easily. In a problem with several steps, they may rearrange the steps to make estimation easier. ● They also adjust two numbers at a time when making their estimates. Rounding one number higher and one number lower is an example of this technique.

Before students can become good at estimating, they need to have quick, accurate recall of basic facts. They also need a good grasp of the place value system (ones, tens, hundreds, etc.).

Children in early grades learn mathematics more effectively when they use physical objects in their lessons.

The type or design of the objects used is not particularly important; they can be blocks, marbles, poker chips, cardboard cutouts—almost anything.

Students will become more adept at solving math problems if teachers encourage them to think through a problem before they begin working on it, guide them through the thinking process, and give them regular and frequent practice in solving problems.

Good mathematical problem solvers usually analyze the challenges they face and explore alternative strategies before starting work. Unsuccessful problem solvers often act impulsively when given a problem and follow the first idea that occurs to them. Too often, school instruction emphasizes and rewards the rapid solving of problems and fails to recognize and reinforce thoughtful behavior. . . .

After different strategies are identified, students can begin to solve the problem. If a plan does not work, the teacher can ask additional questions or provide hints to help students formulate other approaches. After the problem is solved, the teacher can have students analyze their strategies and consider alternatives.

Frequent practice in solving problems is most effective when teachers ask students questions about their thinking, give them hints when they are stumped, and help them see how some problems are related. These practices help students learn how to think problems through for themselves. They can also be taught other techniques to help them correctly solve problems, such as adding a diagram, removing extraneous information, and reorganizing data.

The most effective way to teach writing is to teach it as a process of brainstorming, composing, revising, and editing.

Students learn to write well through frequent practice. Good writing assignments are often an extension of class reading, discussion, and activities, not isolated exercises.

An effective writing lesson contains these elements:

● Brainstorming: Students think and talk about their topics. They collect information and ideas, frequently much more than they will finally use. They sort through their ideas to organize and clarify what they want to say.

● Composing: Students compose a first draft. This part is typically time-consuming and hard, even for very good writers.

● Revising: Students re-read what they have written, sometimes soliciting reactions from teachers, classmates, parents, and others. The most useful teacher response to an early draft focuses on what students are trying to say, not the mechanics of writing. Teachers can help most by asking for clarification, commenting on vivid expressions or fresh ideas, and suggesting ways to support the main thrust of the writing. Students can then consider the feedback and decide how to use it to improve. On the next draft, teachers may want to focus on chosen aspects of good writing such as combining sentences to improve structure and add variety. Through such exercises, teachers can help students realize that varying sentence length and structure within a paragraph yields more interesting prose. Discussing these alternatives while working on a draft emphasizes to students the importance of writing clear, interesting, and concise sentences that are appropriate for the writer's audience and goals.

● Editing: Students then need to check their final version for spelling, grammar, punctuation and other writing mechanics, and legibility.

Prompt feedback from teachers on written assignments is important. Students are most likely to write competently when schools routinely require writing in all subject areas, not just in English class.

Children learn vocabulary better when the words they study are related to familiar experiences and to knowledge they already possess.

Teachers can use students' personal experiences and prior knowledge to build vocabulary. Instruction in which children establish relationships among words is more effective than instruction that focuses only on word definitions. . . .

Teachers can foster connections between words by having students group them into categories such that relationships among the words become clear. Children can use their own experiences to create a cluster of synonyms, such as neat, tidy, clean, and spotless. They can consider similarities and differences in related words, such as examine and scrutinize. They can also group words according to certain features, such as suffixes or prefixes. Encouraging students to talk about personal experiences associated with particular words helps them grasp meanings and relationships among new words and ideas.

Using analogies is another way to help children see the relationship between old and new words. For example, when children are learning the word "province," the analogy "state is to the United States what province is to Canada" relates prior knowledge to a new concept.

Well-chosen diagrams, graphs, photos and illustrations can enhance students' learning.

Teachers who set and communicate high expectations to all their students obtain greater academic performance from those students than teachers who set low expectations.

Hearing good readers read and encouraging students repeatedly to read a passage aloud helps them become good readers.

Helping students learn to read aloud smoothly and easily is an important—but often overlooked—goal of reading instruction. Some authorities have called it the "missing ingredient" in early reading instruction. Teachers can help students become fluent readers by including supported and repeated readings as part of individualized, small group, or classroom instruction.

In supported reading, a child listens to—and reads along with—a good reader. The model can be an adult reader, another student able to read the passage fluently, or a rendition that has been tape recorded. Initially, the student follows along silently or in a soft voice. In subsequent readings of the same passage, the student becomes more fluent and the model gradually fades into the background. In repeated readings, students read a passage over and over until they can read it with ease.

Students may balk at having to read a passage more than once. Teachers can overcome this by providing instructional activities in which repeated readings are a natural component. For example, teachers can have students practice and perform dramatic readings, emphasizing the meaning and emotion of the passage. Teachers can also have students practice reading short stories and poems in unison, and practice singing popular songs together. These types of activities require repeated readings for proficient performance.

Children's understanding of the relationship between being smart and hard work changes as they grow.
When children start school, they think that ability and effort are the same thing; in other words, they believe that if they work hard they will become smart. Thus, younger children who fail believe this is because they didn't try hard enough, not because they have less ability.

Because teachers tend to reward effort in earlier grades, children frequently concentrate on working hard rather than on the quality of their work. As a result, they

may not learn how to judge how well they are performing.

In later elementary grades, students slowly learn that ability and effort are not the same. They come to believe that lower ability requires harder work to keep up and that students with higher ability need not work so hard. At this stage, speed at completing tasks replaces effort as the sign of ability; high levels of effort may even carry the stigma of low ability.

Consequently, many secondary school students, despite their ability, will not expend the effort needed to achieve their potential. Underachievement can become a way of life.

Once students begin believing they have failed because they lack ability, they tend to lose hope for future success. They develop a pattern of academic hopelessness and stop trying. They see academic obstacles as insurmountable and devote less effort to learning.

Teachers who are alert to these beliefs in youngsters will keep their students motivated and on task. They will also slowly nudge their students toward the realism of judging themselves by performance. For example, teachers will set high expectations and insist that students put forth the effort required to meet the school's academic standards. They will make sure slower learners are rewarded for their progress and abler students are challenged according to their abilities.

As students acquire knowledge and skill, their thinking and reasoning take on distinct characteristics. Teachers who are alert to these changes can determine how well their students are progressing toward becoming competent thinkers and problem solvers.
Students ordinarily go through four changes as they master skills and acquire knowledge.

● The isolated ideas and initial explanations with which students begin to learn a new topic become integrated and more widely applicable. For example, children just beginning to learn about dinosaurs tend to classify them in terms of visible characteristics, such as size and skin texture. Children who are more familiar with dinosaurs make more elaborate classifications in which sensory features become less important than more abstract features such as dietary habits.

● When confronting problems, competent learners identify fundamental principles that allow them to reach solutions smoothly, instead of wrestling with details. Where beginning physics students tend to classify problems in terms of surface features, more accomplished learners classify the same problems in terms of underlying physical principles. For example, beginning students view problems in mechanics as involving inclined planes and pulleys; more competent learners see the same problems as involving mechanical principles such as conservation of energy.

● Besides grasping rules and principles, competent learners are aware of the range of conditions under which these principles apply. In the example mentioned above, accomplished learners not only understand the principle of conservation of energy, but are also aware of problems that can be solved using such principles.

● Tasks that beginning students carry out with concentration are performed automatically by students with more expertise. This frees them to direct their attention to analysis, critical thinking, and other demanding aspects of performance. For example, when children first learn to read, they must devote much attention to the process of translating printed letters into pronounceable words. As their expertise increases, children more quickly and accurately recognize printed words. This frees them to devote more attention to grasping the meanings conveyed by the text.

By monitoring these changes, students and teachers can assess progress toward competence.

How much time students are actively engaged in learning contributes strongly to their achievement. The amount of time available for learning is determined by the instructional and management skills of the
teacher and the priorities set by the school administration.

Teachers must not only know the subjects they teach, they must also be effective classroom managers. . . .

Effective time managers in the classroom do not waste valuable minutes on unimportant activities; they keep their students continuously and actively engaged. Good managers perform the following time-conserving functions:

● *Planning Class Work:* choosing the content to be studied, scheduling time for presentation and study, and choosing those instructional activities (such as grouping, seatwork, or recitation) best suited to learning the material at hand;

● *Communicating Goals:* setting and conveying expectations so students know what they are to do, what it will take to get a passing grade, and what the consequences of failure will be;

● *Regulating Learning Activities:* sequencing course content so knowledge builds on itself, pacing instruction so students are prepared for the next step, monitoring success rates so all students stay productively engaged regardless of how quickly they learn, and running an orderly, academically focused classroom that keeps wasted time and misbehavior to a minimum.

Good classroom management is essential for teachers to deal with students who chronically misbehave, but such students also benefit from specific suggestions from teachers on how to cope with their conflicts and frustrations. This also helps them gain insights about their behavior.

When teachers explain exactly what students are expected to learn, and demonstrate the steps needed to accomplish a particular academic task, students learn more.

The procedure stated above is called "direct instruction." It is based on the assumption that knowing how to learn may not come naturally to all students, especially to beginning and low-ability learners. Direct instruction takes children through learning steps systematically, helping them see both the purpose and the result of each step. In this way, children learn not only a lesson's content but also a method for learning that content.

The basic components of direct instruction are: ● setting clear goals for students and making sure they understand those goals, ● presenting a sequence of well- organized assignments, ● giving students clear, concise explanations and illustrations of the subject matter, ● asking frequent questions to see if children understand the work, and ● giving students frequent opportunities to practice what they have learned.

Direct instruction does not mean repetition. It does mean leading students through a process and teaching them to use that process as a skill to master other academic tasks. Direct instruction has been particularly effective in teaching basic skills to young and disadvantaged children, as well as in helping older and higher ability students to master more complex materials and to develop independent study skills.

Students become more interested in writing and the quality of their writing improves when there are significant learning goals for writing assignments and a clear sense of purpose for writing.

Teachers often assign writing tasks to encourage specific types of learning. For example, a teacher may assign a summary if she wants students to identify all the important concepts of a particular topic. Another teacher may assign an analytic essay if he wants students to narrow their focus and examine one aspect in greater depth.

What students learn by writing depends on what they do when they write. Those who simply paraphrase when the assignment calls for analysis may learn facts, but may not be able to draw connections or make inferences about the content. Good teachers identify what they want their writing

assignments to accomplish and tell students what those goals are.

Also, students feel the keenest sense of purpose when the audience for their writing extends beyond the teacher. Publishing student writing in school literary magazines and newspapers is one effective way to do this. Students can also write books for the elementary school library, guides to high school life for entering junior high school students, letters, or scripts for school-produced audio and video programs.

Teachers can encourage their students to write for audiences outside of school by having them enter writing contests, write letters to the editors of local newspapers, and correspond with students in other states and countries.

Teachers of all subjects can use writing to help students analyze and understand content. Science teachers, for example, can have students record and organize their ideas about complex concepts in learning logs. History teachers can have students study the life of a turn-of-the-century American immigrant and then interview a present-day immigrant; an article comparing the two experiences can be written for the school or local newspaper. A health teacher can have students write about the causes and effects of morphine addiction during the Civil War and relate that information to present-day drug problems. Such exercises help students and teachers see more clearly what the student understands—or doesn't yet understand.

Good teachers help students understand that the choices they make in writing affect the quality of their learning in ways that go well beyond the writing itself.

Constructive feedback from teachers, including deserved praise and specific suggestions, helps students learn, as well as develop positive self-esteem.

Teachers should not underestimate the impact of constructive feedback on their students. Providing positive and timely comments is a practice that teachers at all levels can use. These comments help students correct errors and give them recognition when deserved. Helpful feedback praises successful aspects of a student's work and points out those areas that need improvement.

Useful feedback, whether positive or negative, is prompt, germane, and includes specific observations and recommendations. It tells students what they are doing, how they are doing it, and how they can improve. Whether written or spoken, effective feedback is initiated by the teacher and is given privately rather than in front of the class. An example of effective feedback: "Your book report is well written, Paul. The content is clear because the ideas are presented in a logical order and the details support your main idea. Your use of some clever examples makes your book report enjoyable to read. Next time, let's work harder to organize your time so that you will meet the assigned deadline." An example of ineffective feedback is: "Your book report is well written, Paul. But it is late and I'm upset about that."

Students who are accustomed to failure and who have difficulty mastering skills react more positively to encouragement and praise from teachers than to criticism. Effective teachers successfully use praise to motivate their low-achieving students. On the other hand, higher-achieving students respond more to specific comments and suggestions about their work.

Through constructive, timely feedback, teachers can reinforce and help develop positive self-esteem in their students. Students who believe they can succeed are usually more successful than those with low self-esteem when it comes to participating in activities, working independently, getting along with others, and achieving academically.

Students tutoring other students can lead to improved academic achievement for both student and tutor, and to positive attitudes toward coursework.

Tutoring programs consistently raise the achievement of both the students receiving instruction and those providing it. Peer tutoring, when used as a supplement to regular classroom teaching, helps slow and underachieving students master their lessons and succeed in school. Preparing and giving the lessons also benefits the tutors themselves because they learn more about the material they are teaching.

Of the tutoring programs that have been studied, the most effective include the following elements: ● highly structured and well-planned curricula and instructional methods, ● instruction in basic content and skills (grades 1-3), especially in arithmetic, and ● a relatively short duration of instruction (a few weeks or months).

Memorizing can help students absorb and retain the factual information on which understanding and critical thought are based.

Most children at some time memorize multiplication tables, the correct spelling of words, historical dates, and passages of literature such as the poetry of Robert Frost or the sonnets of Shakespeare. Memorizing simplifies the process of recalling information and allows its use to become automatic. Understanding and critical thought can then build on this base of knowledge and fact. Indeed, the more sophisticated mental operations of analysis, synthesis, and evaluation are impossible without rapid and accurate recall of bodies of specific knowledge.

Teachers can encourage students to develop memory skills by teaching highly structured and carefully sequenced lessons, with frequent reinforcement for correct answers. Young students, slow students, and students who lack background knowledge can benefit from such instruction.

In addition, teachers can teach "mnemonics," that is, devices and techniques for improving memory. For example, the mnemonic "Every Good Boy Does Fine" has reminded generations of music students that E, G, B, D, and F are the notes to which the lines on a treble staff correspond. Mnemonics helps students remember more information faster and retain it longer.

Comprehension and retention are even greater when teachers and students connect the new information being memorized with previous knowledge.

Student achievement rises when teachers ask questions that require students to apply, analyze, synthesize, and evaluate information in addition to simply recalling facts.

Even before Socrates, questioning was one of teaching's most common and most effective techniques. Some teachers ask hundreds of questions, especially when teaching science, geography, history, or literature.

But questions take different forms and place different demands on students. Some questions require only factual recall and do not provoke analysis. For example, of more than 61,000 questions found in the teacher guides, student workbooks, and tests for 9 history textbooks, more than 95 percent were devoted to factual recall. This is not to say that questions meant to elicit facts are unimportant. Students need basic information to engage higher level thinking processes and discussions. Such questions also promote class participation and provide a high success rate in answering questions correctly.

The difference between factual and thought-provoking questions is the difference between asking: "When did Lincoln deliver the Gettysburg Address?" and asking: "Why was Lincoln's Gettysburg Address an important speech?" Each kind of question has its place, but the second one intends that the student analyze the speech in terms of the issues of the Civil War.

Although both kinds of questions are important, students achieve more when teachers ask thought-provoking questions and insist on thoughtful answers. Students' answers may also improve if teachers wait longer for a response, giving students more time to think.

The ways in which children study influence strongly how much they learn. Teachers can often help children develop better study skills.

Research has identified several study skills used by good students that can be taught to other students. Average students can learn how to use these skills. Low-ability students may need to be taught when, as well as how, to use them.

Here are some examples of sound study practices:

● Good students adjust the way they study according to several factors: (1) the demand of the material, (2) the time available for studying, (3) what they already know about the topic, (4) the purpose and importance of the assignment, and (5) the standards they must meet.

● Good students space learning sessions on a topic over time and do not cram or study the same topic continuously.

● Good students identify the main idea in new information, connect new material to what they already know, and draw inferences about its significance.

● Good students make sure their study methods are working properly by frequently appraising their own progress.

Student achievement rises significantly when teachers regularly assign homework and students conscientiously do it.

Extra studying helps children at all levels of ability. One research study reveals that when low-ability students do just 1 to 3 hours of homework a week, their grades are usually as high as those of average-ability students who do not do homework. Similarly, when average-ability students do 3 to 5 hours of homework a week, their grades usually equal those of high-ability students who do no homework.

Homework boosts achievement because the total time spent studying influences how much is learned. Low-achieving high school students study less than high achievers and do less homework. Time is not the only ingredient of learning, but without it little can be achieved.

Teachers, parents, and students determine how much, how useful, and how good the homework is. On average, American teachers say they assign about 10 hours of homework each week—about 2 hours per school day. But high school seniors report they spend only 4 to 5 hours a week doing homework, and 10 percent say they do none at all or have none assigned.

Well-designed homework assignments relate directly to classwork and extend students' learning beyond the classroom. Homework is most useful when teachers carefully prepare the assignment, thoroughly explain it, and give prompt comments and criticism when the work is completed.

To make the most of what students learn from doing homework, teachers need to give the same care to preparing homework assignments as they give to classroom instruction. When teachers prepare written instruction and discuss homework assignments with students, they find their students take the homework more seriously than if the assignments are simply announced. Students are more willing to do homework when they believe it is useful, when teachers treat it as an integral part of instruction, when it is evaluated by teacher, and when it counts as a part of the grade.

Assignments that require students to think, and are therefore more interesting, foster their desire to learn both in and out of school. Such activities include explaining what is seen or read in class; comparing, relating, and experimenting with ideas; and analyzing principles.

Effective homework assignments do not just supplement the classroom lesson; they also teach students to be independent learners. Homework gives students experience in following directions, making judgments and comparisons, raising additional questions for study, and developing responsibility and self-discipline.

Frequent and systematic monitoring of students' progress helps students, parents, teachers, administrators, and policymakers identify strengths and weaknesses in learning and instruction.

Teachers find out what students already know and what they still need to learn by assessing student work. They use various means, including essays, quizzes and tests, homework, classroom questions, standardized tests, and parents' comments. Teachers can use student errors on tests and in class as early warning signals to point out and correct learning problems before they worsen. Student motivation and achievement improve when teachers provide prompt feedback on assignments.

Students generally take two kinds of tests; classroom tests and standardized tests. Classroom tests help teachers find out if what they are teaching is being learned; thus, these tests serve to evaluate both student and teacher. Standardized tests apply similar gauges to everyone in a specific grade level. By giving standardized tests, school districts can see how achievement progresses over time. Such tests also help schools find out how much of the curriculum is actually being learned. Standardized tests can also reveal problems in the curriculum itself.

When teachers introduce new subject matter, they need to help students grasp its relationship to facts and concepts they have previously learned.

The more students already know about a particular subject, the easier it is for them to acquire new information about it. Teachers can help students learn new information by organizing courses and units of study so that topics build on one another and by helping students focus on relevant background knowledge. Teachers can also help students grasp relationships between new information and old. Not all students spontaneously relate prior knowledge to new information. . . .

By identifying central and recurrent patterns in content areas, teachers can help students focus on important information and not get overwhelmed by minor details.

The most important characteristics of effective schools are strong instructional leadership, a safe and orderly climate, school-wide emphasis on basic skills, high teacher expectations for student achievement, and continuous assessment of pupil progress.

Schools that encourage academic achievement focus on the importance of scholastic success and on maintaining order and discipline.

Good character is encouraged by surrounding students with good adult examples and by building upon natural occasions for learning and practicing good character. Skillful educators know how to organize their schools, classrooms, and lessons to foster such examples.

Educators become good role models through their professionalism, courtesy, cooperation, and by demanding top performance from their students. They maintain fair and consistent discipline policies, including matters of attendance, punctuality, and meeting assignment deadlines.

The use of libraries enhances reading skills and encourages independent learning.

Research has shown that participating in library programs reinforces children's skills and interest in reading. Summer reading programs offered by public libraries, for example, reinforce reading skills learned during the school year. Library programs for preschool children encourage children's interest in learning to read. Both types of programs provide many opportunities for reading, listening and viewing materials.

Public and school libraries can enhance reading instruction by offering literature-based activities that stress the enjoyment of reading as well as reading skills. Hearing stories and participating in such activities help young children want to learn to read.
. . .

Use of both public and school libraries encourages students to go beyond their textbooks to locate, explore, evaluate and use ideas and information that enhance classroom instruction.

Schools contribute to their student's academic achievement by establishing, communicating, and enforcing fair and consistent discipline policies.

For 16 of the last 17 years, the public has identified discipline as the most serious problem facing its schools. Effective discipline policies contribute to the academic atmosphere by emphasizing the importance of regular attendance, promptness, respect for teachers and academic work, and good conduct.

A school staff that provides encouragement and personalized attention, and monitors daily attendance can reduce unexcused absences and class-cutting.

Successful principals establish policies that create an orderly environment and support effective instruction.

When schools provide comprehensive orientation programs for students transferring from one school to another, they ease the special stresses and adjustment difficulties those students face. The result is apt to be improved student performance.

Underachieving or mildly handicapped students can benefit most from remedial education when the lessons in those classes are closely coordinated with those in their regular classes.

Students benefit academically when their teachers share ideas, cooperate in activities, and assist one another's intellectual growth.

Teachers welcome professional suggestions about improving their work, but they rarely receive them.

Many children who are physically handicapped or have emotional or learning problems can be given an appropriate education in well-supported regular classes and schools.

Students read more fluently and with greater understanding if they have knowledge of the world and their culture, past and present. Such knowledge and understanding is called cultural literacy.

In addition to their knowledge of the physical world, students' knowledge of their culture determines how they will grasp the meaning of what they read. Students read and understand passages better when the passages refer to events, people and places—real or fictional—with which the students are familiar.

Students' understanding of the subtleties and complexities of written information depends on how well they understand cultural traditions, attitudes, values, conventions, and connotations. The more literate students are in these ways, the better prepared they will be to read and understand serious books, magazines, and other challenging material.

Most school teachers, college professors, journalists, and social commentators agree that the general knowledge of American students is too low, and getting lower. . . .

In the United States, the national community comprises diverse groups and traditions; together they have created a rich cultural heritage. Cultural literacy not only enables students to read better and gain new knowledge; it enables them to understand the shared heritage, institutions, and values that draw Americans together.

The best way to learn a foreign language in school is to start early and to study it intensively over many years.

Most students who take a foreign language study it for 2 years or less in high school and do not learn to communicate with it effectively.

The stronger the emphasis on academic courses, the more advanced the subject matter, and the more rigorous the textbooks, the more high school students learn. Subjects that are learned mainly in school rather than at home, such as science and math, are most influenced by the number and kind of courses taken.

Students often handicap their intellectual growth by avoiding difficult courses.

Handicapped high school students who seek them are more likely to find jobs after graduation when schools prepare them for careers and private sector businesses provide on- the-job training.

Skimpy requirements and declining enrollments in history classes are contributing to a decline in students' knowledge of the past.

The decline in the study of history may hinder students from gaining an historical perspective on contemporary life.

Advancing gifted students at a faster pace results in their achieving more than similarly gifted students who are taught at a normal rate.

High school students who complement their academic studies with extracurricular activities gain experience that contributes to their success in college.

When students work more than 15 to 20 hours per week, their grades may suffer. They can benefit, however, from limited out-of-school work.

Students can benefit from jobs, however, if work hours are limited, the experience is well-selected, and the job does not interfere with their school work. Such jobs help improve knowledge about the workplace, foster positive attitudes and habits, and open up possibilities for careers.

Business leaders report that students with solid basic skills and positive work attitudes are more likely to find and keep jobs than students with vocational skills alone.

As new technologies make old job skills obsolete, the best vocational education will be solid preparation in reading, writing, mathematics, and reasoning. In the future, American workers will acquire many of their job skills in the workplace, not in school.

They will need to be able to master new technologies and upgrade their skills to meet specialized job demands. Men and women who have weak basic skills, or who cannot readily master new skills, to keep pace with change, may be only marginally employed over their lifetimes.

Business leaders recommend that schools raise academic standards. They point to the need for remedial programs to help low-achieving students and to reduce dropping out.

Business leaders stress that the school curriculum should emphasize literacy, mathematics, and problem-solving skills. They believe schools should emphasize such personal qualities as self-discipline, reliability, perseverance, teamwork, accepting responsibility, and respect for the rights of others. These characteristics will serve all secondary students well, whether they go on to college or directly into the world of work.

H

Books, periodicals and other media

These are samples of the many good books of interest to the home schooling community. Ordering information is subject to change.

The line which begins some entries indicates that the author is the same as for the preceding entry.

Part 5 in this appendix is a cross reference showing books, magazines, programs, etc. by title.

Part 1, Books

Baker, Virginia Birt, *Teaching Your Children at Home,* 1984 (with update inserts), 54+ pp. Write to Mrs. Baker at Route 1, Box 297, Van TX 75783. (214) 963-5133. Ginny Baker tells you how she did it. She shows you the materials she likes for each grade (although other materials are on the market now). She adds some notes on how to use them. She tells you how to set up a fairly precise weekly schedule. You will also find legal information, lists of other books and periodicals, and a chapter on discipline. $8.75 postpaid.

Ballmann, Ray E., *The How and Why of Home Schooling,* Crossway Books (See Appendix B). Pastor Ballmann makes a good case for Christian home schooling. The book seems to be stronger on "why" than on "how."

Barbe, Walter B., *Growing Up Learning,* Acropolis Books, 1985. 205 pp. Available from Sycamore Tree, 2179 Meyer Pl., Costa Mesa CA 92627, for $8.95 + $2.75 shipping + tax if Calif.

Beatty, Susan, *An Introduction to Home Education,* 3rd ed., 1987. Christian Home Educators Assoc. of Calif., P.O. Box 28644, Santa Ana CA 92799-8644. $8 plus $1 shpg. + tax. Covers most of the basic questions for Calif. families: filling out an affidavit, report cards, getting started, etc. Approx. 90 pages.

Beechick, Ruth, *A Biblical Psychology of Learning: How Your Mind Works,* 158 pp., 1982. $10 postpaid from Education Services, 6410 Raleigh St., Arvada CO 80003 (Add tax if Colo.). Dr. Beechick has the ability to develop theory and make it interesting (and practical) for ordinary people. Although I would come to some different conclusions on a few points relating to Bible terms, I heartily agree with her idea that the Scriptures need to be the basis of our study of human thinking.

_____ *You CAN Teach Your Child Successfully.* As I expected, Ruth Beechick's preparation of this book is professional, practical, and understandable. It discusses teaching methods for all the major subjects including Bible, art and music for grades 4 to 8. It also covers grammar, achievement test scores, spelling, new history teaching ideas, how to use textbooks, and so on. Order from Educational Services, 6410 Raleigh St., Arvada CO 80003. 1988, 388 pp. $13.70 postpaid for the paperback edition or $18.95, hardcover. (Add tax if Colo.)

Blumenfeld, Samuel L., *Alpha-phonics, A Primer for Beginning Readers,* Described as "an effective, step-by-step intensive phonics program. . . ." The Paradigm Co. (See Appendix B.) Paperback, $21.95 + $1.50 shpg. + tax if ID.

____, *How to Tutor,* The Paradigm Co. (See Appendix B.), 1986, 298 pages, $11.95 + $1.50 + tax if ID. From its description, the book seems good. The idea was to help parents help their children achieve in school. 117 lessons on reading, 73 on writing and 67 on arithmetic.

Brackin, Ron, *The Writing Christian,* Brackin & Sons Publishing Co., P.O. Box 359, Burtonsville MD 20866. According to this book, writing is relevant "to God and to the world. . . ." It shows "how anyone who can learn to read can learn to write." $6.95 postpaid. (Add tax if MD).

Christian Home Education Association of California, *To the parents of Children with Learning Disabilities,* and *Learning Disabilities follow-up Packet.* $2 + $5 + $1 shpg. + tax if CA.

Christian Liberty Academy Satellite Schools, *Legal Manual.* Explains how home school parents can learn for themselves how to avoid legal pitfalls. Cassette tape commentary introduces the manual. The cassette and the manual are both sent to those who ask and make a $10 donation. Or you can send $5 for one or the other. Write to CLASS, 502 W. Euclid Avenue, Arlington Heights, IL 60004.

Clinard, Linda M., *The Reading Triangle,* David S. Lake Publishers. 133 pp. 1985. Explains parents' responsibility in preparing children to communicate and read.

Colfax, David and Micki, *Homeschooling for Excellence,* Warner Books, 666 5th Ave., New York NY 10103. Although this book's thrust is outside the arena of Christian philosophical viewpoints, it has some good thoughts about general principles of education. I describe a few of the concepts from it in the chapter, "Educating for Superior Achievement." The edition from Warner books will be out shortly after this book is so I don't have the price information. It is fairly brief.

Degering, Etta B., *My Bible Friends,* Review and Herald, 55 W. Oak Ridge Dr., Hagerstown MD 21740. 1964. The nicest children's Bible story books I have seen; for preschool and primary grades.

Duffy, Cathy, *Christian Home Educators' Curriculum Manual,* Home Run Enterprises (See Appendix A). The 1988 edition has been extensively revised. Cathy Duffy explained to me: "I have incorporated information on learning styles throughout the book. I have increased the amount of commentary so that people can better see the differences between similar materials. I have also indicated in some instances which materials are more appropriate for different learning styles." The book tells you how to choose materials and methods and where to find resources. Specific suggestions by subject for elementary and high school. 165 pp. including planning forms to copy. $14.95 plus $1.50 book rate or $2.50 UPS. (and tax if you live in Calif.).

Enderlin, August C., *Victory Drill Book, A phonetic approach to reading with an emphasis on speed,* 1987, tough hardcover, 78 pp., Victory Drill Book, 501 Pecan Way, LaHabara CA 90631. (213) 697-2128. This appears to me as a straight-forward and effective approach that would not overdo the phonics training. Typography is clean and clear (not done with a typewriter). The Drill Book is to supplement reading books. Cost is currently $9.50 + $5 handling for up to $30 orders + tax if CA. The $5.50 cassette demonstrates high-speed pronunciation and is a teaching guide keyed to the book. I think I would order the book and tape, then decide whether or not to also get the teachers' manual or the worksheets. Consider the *Victory Pre-drill Book* ($3.00) if your child needs it for mastering the alphabet. It also has phonetic letter combinations. For more information, request their brochure.

Flotzer, Monica, *Professor Phonics Gives Sound Advice.* See Professor Phonics in Appendix B.

Fugate, Richard, *What the Bible Says About Child Training.* Sold through *The Teaching Home* magazine.

Gorder, Cheryl, *Home Schools: An Alternative,* Revised, 1987. Blue Bird Publishing (See Appendix B). 203 pp. The book's title is an appropriate reflection of its contents. Cheryl Gorder clearly sets forth the advantages and issues involved in home education and shows the opinions of professional educators. Chap. 12 gives a helpful discussion of learning materials and tells you where to get them. $12.95 postpaid. + tax if AZ.

_____, editor, *Home Education Resource Guide,* Blue Bird Publishing (See Appendix B). Although the 1988 edition is to appear after this book is already in print, I expect it to be a helpful resource judging by its earlier editions and the abilities of its new editor. $11 postpaid + tax.

Granger, Bill, *The Magic Feather,* E.P. Dutton, 1986, 259 pp. A book denouncing special education programs with the idea that most children don't need them and can be helped at home.

Harris, Gregg, *The Christian Home School,* Wolgemuth & Hyatt, 1988, hardcover, 168 pp. Available from Christian Life Workshops, 180 SE Kane Rd., Gresham OR 97080, for $13.95 + tax if OR. Harris explains advantages of home education emphasizing those aspects he sees as important from a his Christian viewpoint. He also offers a few suggestions on how to get started. One chapter deals with three of his special topics: the ministry of hospitality, a home business and storytelling.

Hegener, Mark and Helen, *Home School Primer.* A get-started booklet for "anyone seriously interested in home schooling." Mark and Helen edit *Home Education Magazine* and keep this book up to date. $6.50 postpaid. P.O. Box 1083, Tonasket WA 98855.

_____, *Home School Reader,* to be ready fall or winter 1988. A collection of articles.

_____, *Homeschoolers Networking and Travel Directory,* $3.75 postpaid, from *Home Education Magazine.* Updated twice a year. The directory currently has 20 pages and lists nearly 200 families who would like to meet other home schooling families. Special interests and accommodations, if any, for travelers are shown. You may even want to be listed.

Hoffman, Jane, *Backyard Scientist,* (The "original"), P.O. Box 16966, Irvine CA 92713. This booklet of "experiments that kids can perform using things found around the house" is designed to help children 6 to 12 make science a mystery-solving adventure. The 10 experiments are simple and well-explained. Jane Hoffman refined her program in presenting it to schools. A relatively small book of 57 pages. $8.50 + $1 shpg. + tax if CA.

_____, *Backyard Scientist, Series One,* 52 pp. 25 experiments similar to those in the book listed above. Same price.

Holt, John, *Teach Your Own, a Hopeful Path for Education*, Dell. 1981. A secular approach to home schooling described by experiences. Available from John Holt's Music and Book Store, which is associated with the periodical, *Growing Without Schooling*, 729 Boylston St., Boston MA 02116. $11.95 + $4 UPS shipping. + tax for MA.

Hunt, Dave, and T. A. McMahon, *The Seduction of Christianity*, Harvest House Publishers (See Appendix B) 1985. Although this book isn't really about home schooling, it touches an area close to most of us—occult influences that are changing the Christian churches. It's a well documented and clearly explained exposition. $7.95.

Keller, Clifton, and Jeanette Appel, *Science Activities for Christian Children*, Revised edition, Gazelle Publications. 1986. 119 pp. A hundred activities using common materials and organized by process skills such as observing, measuring, and predicting. A spiritual lesson is suggested for each activity. Early to middle grades. Worth its price even if you are using a structured science program. $5.50 plus $1.00 shpg. + tax if CA. If you order direct and would like a list of extra Bible references, add 25¢. For only the extra references, send 75¢.

Kendall, Ingeborg U. V., *School at Home*, ICER Press, P.O. Box 877, Claremont CA 91711. 1982. $6.95 + $1 shpg. + tax if CA. Ingeborg Kendall discusses reasons why home schooling meets educational needs of various families. The second half of the book explains how to devise a strategy for meeting academic, social, religious and physical needs. She discusses advantages offered in correspondence school programs and also how to plan the whole program yourself.

Kilpatrick, William Kirk, *Psychological Seduction, The Failure of Modern Psychology*, Thomas Nelson Publishers, 1983. 236 pp. A look at "the disturbing results of a society seduced by the claims of psychiatry." Kilpatrick feels that "many Americans equate self-esteem and personal growth with personal salvation" and that "positive thinking often takes the place of God." He sees the thrust of modern psychology as a type of religion.

Kinmont, Joyce, *Home School Decisions*, 2770 South 1000 West, Perry UT 84302. $5.95 + $1 for postage. Add tax if in Utah. The book deals with 22 educational issues including socialization, impatient parents, and how much time should be spent at desk work. The Kinmonts also distribute Brite Music books and cassettes. *Standin' Tall*, for example, is a series on 12 character traits like courage, gratitude and honesty. The booklet and cassette for each trait cost $8.95 (for both).

Maxwell, Arthur S., *The Bible Story*, Review and Herald, 55 W. Oak Ridge Dr., Hagerstown MD 21740. 1957. A ten-volume set, well written and well illustrated, with attention to accuracy.

Moore, Raymond and Dorothy, *Better Late than Early*, McGraw- Hill and Reader's Digest. 1975. This initial book sets the basis of the reasons for delaying formal education and explains what to do for various age levels. $6.00 +. The Moore's books are available from Hewitt Research, P.O. Box 9, Washougal WA 98671. Add 8% for shipping with a minimum of $2.50 for mail or $5.00 for UPS. Remember tax if in WA.

____ *Home-Spun Schools*, Word Books. 1982. Success stories of people who have done it. $6.00 plus shipping and tax. (The line in front of the book title means that the author is the same as for the preceding book.)

____ *Home-Grown Kids*, 1981. Chapter titles include: The hand that rocks the cradle; Parents in charge; Setting the stage for birth; Getting a good start . . . ; The winsome ones and twos; The exploring threes and fours; the . . . fives and sixes; The . . . sevens, eights and nines; Sources of . . . materials, etc. $7.00 plus shipping and tax.

____ *Home-Style Teaching*, 1984. Topics include: Confidence as a teacher, Starting home schooling, Organizing time, Students as teachers, Making reading instruction easy, Teaching creative thinking and writing, Tests, Studying, Remotivating a burned-out child, Curriculum, Consistent reasoning, Readiness and "super baby," Grandparents, Transition to regular school, Submission to state control, etc. $10.00 plus shipping and tax.

____ *School Can Wait*, 1979. A defense of delayed formal education backed by reference to research studies. $8.00 shpg. and tax.

National University Continuing Education Assn., *NUCEA Guide to Independent Study Through Correspondence Instruction*, Peterson's Guides. P.O. Box 2123, Princeton NJ 08540. A listing of member schools and courses in various topics (mostly secondary, college and adult noncredit).

National Wildlife Federation, *Nature Scope*, 1412 Sixteenth St. N.W., Washington DC 20036-2266. A collection of issues (books) published in conjunction with *Ranger Rick's* magazine. Designed for teaching specific nature topics.

Pagnoni, Mario, *The Complete Home Educator*, Larson Publications, 4936 Route 414, Burdett NY 14818. 1984. The experience and ideas of a classroom teacher who taught his boys at home for a year. Most readers would not consider it to be very "complete," but it does offer some good thoughts on social influences, etc., from a secular viewpoint. About half of the 229 pages are about computers.

Pride, Mary, *The New Big Book of Home Learning*, 347 pp. 1988. Crossway Books, 9825 West Roosevelt Rd., Westchester IL 60153. Mary Pride's lucid evaluation of most of the learning materials that are catching the interest of home educators. She also covers home school providers and organizations. Each section begins with advice on aspects of home schooling that relate to it. Informative and helpful. $17.50. Available from most home schooling suppliers.

____ *The Next Book of Home Learning*, Crossway Books, 1987. This is an extension of *The Big Book* . . . . It tends more to cover supplementary materials.

Priesnitz, Wendy, *School Free*, Village Books, 109 pages, 1979. Described as a "definitive profile of deschooling in Canada . . . from the experience of . . . Canadian deschooling families." Simple information for getting started and discussion of issues such as socialization and the variety of philosophies. Available for $15.95 (Can.) postpaid from Canadian Alliance of Home Schoolers, 195 Markville Rd., Unionville ONT L3R 4V8.

Reed, Donn, and others, *The First Home School Catalogue*, 1986 edition, 135+ pages. $8.00 postpaid. Brook Farm Books (See Appendix A). Mostly a listing of learning materials and resources.

Rice, Mary F., and Charles H. Flatter, *Help Me Learn, A Handbook for Teaching Children from birth to Third Grade*, Prentice-Hall, 1979. Full of practical ideas.

Scott, D. H., *The Parent as Teacher, A Guide for Parents of Children with Learning Difficulties*, David S. Lake Pub., 6 Davis Dr., Belmont CA 94002.

Samson, Richard W., *Thinking Skills, A Guide to Logic and Comprehension*, Innovative Sciences, Inc., 300 Broad St., Stamford CT 06901. 1965.

Texas Home School Coalition, *Home Education, Is it Working?* A 12-page booklet designed to convince skeptical relatives, state legislators, school board officials and others. Suitable for all 50 states. Fully documented. Available on a donation basis of $5 or more for 5 copies. P.O. Box 835105, Richardson TX 75083. (214) 231-9838.

Wade, Theodore E. Jr., editor, *Bubbles, Poetry for Fun and Meaning,* Gazelle Publications, 5580 Stanley Dr., Auburn CA 95603. (916) 878-1223. 1987. A hundred poems and verses selected to help young minds enjoy thinking. The extensive notes section tells about the 54 main authors, what inspired the poems, how they help us understand poetry, and it suggests activities that spring from them. Well illustrated, hardcover, 159 pages. Currently underpriced at $9.00. Add $1.35 for shpg + 6% if CA.

_____, editor, *With Joy, Poems for Children,* Gazelle Publications (See Appendix A). 1988 revision in the works. 48 pp. $2.00 plus $1 shpg + tax if CA. A delightful collection of verses. Find out who the "funny, string bean face" belongs to. Listen while "roundabout, the rain patters on the pane." Or think of pets like the cat "who doesn't care if I am here or I am there."

_____ *School at Home.* 1980. Out of print. The material has been mostly revised and included in this book. See the listing under Kendall for a book with the same title.

Wallace, Nancy, *Better Than School,* Larson Publications, 1983. A story of natural learning at home. Intro. by John Holt. Check with the John Holt Music & Book Store. (See App.A.)

Ward, Mary Lou, *Writing Step by Step, Developing Paragraphs by Asking Questions,* instruction manual and cassette for teaching writing in primary and intermediate grades. Appears to be an approach that really works and would be simple to teach. Available from Builder Books (App. A, Part 3).

Whimbey, Arthur, with Linda Shaw Whimbey, *Intelligence Can Be Taught, Why and How You Can Become Extra-intelligent,* Innovative Sciences, Inc., Bantam Books. 1975.

Whitehead, John W. and Wendell R. Bird, *Home Education and Constitutional Liberties,* 1986. From The Rutherford Institute. 147 pp. Published by Crossway Books. $5.95 + $1 shpg. + tax if IL. The authors discuss home education from both historical and constitutional perspectives.

Part 2, Home schooling periodicals

Most support groups have newsletters which are not shown here.

Catholic Home School Newsletter, 688 11th Ave., N.W., New Brighton MN 55112. (612) 636-5761. Approximately 3 issues per year. Send a long SASE to get a sample copy.

Christian Educator, The, Published by Christian Liberty Academy Satellite Schools, 203 E. McDonald Rd., Prospect Heights IL 60070. (312) 259-8736.

Creative Learning Magazine, P.O. Box 37568, San Antonio TX 78237. Shelley A. Ashcroft, Editor. Dozens of learning activities around a monthly theme. ABFIJKihjk (Code defined in beginning of App. A). Sample issue $1.

Family Learning Exchange, See Appendix A for Family Learning Organization of Washington.

Family Resources, The Christian Family Magazine, SMS Publications, Inc., 1418 Lake St., Evanston IL 60201. (312) 328-3386. Practical articles; curriculum helps; ideas for family ministry; reviews of books, videos and music; and advertisements of particular interest to home educators. Subscription price, $7.95, 4 issues/yr. $3 for sample issue. Article manuscripts considered. (Include SASE when submitting work to any publisher.)

Growing Without Schooling, 729 Boylston St., Boston MA 02116. Articles, letters from home schoolers, learning ideas, reader directory. From Holt Associates (See App, A, Part 4). Bimonthly. $20 for 6 issues or $36 for 12.

Home Education Magazine, P.O. Box 1083, Tonasket WA 98855. Mark and Helen Hegener, 1983, (509) 684-9855, ABQRUj. A leading home school periodical. Articles and "kids' pages" for home schoolers with a wide variety of interests. $24 for 6 48-page issues. Sample issue $4.50.

Home Free, A bimonthly publication for Christian home educators, from CBN Publishing, CBN Center, Virginia Beach VA 23463. (804) 424-7777. The first issue was for January/February, 1988. It is professionally prepared and will no doubt turn out to be an excellent journal. *Home Free* is sent to those who join the Home Free Club. The $29.95 yearly membership fee also entitles you to special discounts on other home schooling materials. Call or write for more details.

Home School Digest, Wisdom Publications, P.O. Box 3154, LaVale MD 21502. (301) 759-3218.

Home School Gazette, P.O. Box 359, Burtonsville MD 20866. Ron Brackin, Publisher, 1987, (301) 421-1473, BFGHLMNPQRTUVWefhj. The Home School Gazette is discussed in the chapter on teaching writing. Sample issue, $1.

Also, look under "Brackin" in Appendix A, Part 4.

Home School Researcher, Science Education Department, Oregon State University, Corvallis OR 97331. Byron Ray. A report on research studies.

Hostex News, P.O. Box 2241, Santa Fe NM 87504-2241. Stories, poems, drawings, pen pals, for and by home study students. The paper's appearance leaves room for improvement, but it provides a nice opportunity for kids to get into print. Contributions solicited. $10 for 8 issues. Sample, $2.00.

KidsArt News, P.O. Box 274, Mt. Shasta CA 96067. Kim Solga, 1985, (916) 926-5076, ADFIJKQRWefghj. A sixteen-page quarterly magazine with art activities for children. An art print is included and discussed with each issue. $8.00 per year. Sample issue, $2.50. Also ask for a copy of the free "All Time Greatest Art Products" catalog.

Learning Edge, The, See Clonlara School in Appendix A.

Parent Educator and Family Report, Hewitt Research Foundation, Box 9, Washougal WA 98671. Bimonthly newsletter giving homeschool advice, legal updates, materials for sale, etc. Subscription by donation to Hewitt Research Foundation.

Parent Scene, A brief but interesting and professionally prepared newsletter sent without charge. Dr. Kuzma's ministry is described in Appendix A, Part 4.

Teaching Home, The, P.O. Box 20219, Portland OR 97220-0219. (503) 253-9633. Magazine for Christian home school families. A quality publication. Affiliated support organizations in 22 states plus Australia currently consider TTH their official journal and furnish material to include in center inserts for copies for their territories. Subscribe through a cooperating state organization or through the office in Wash. $15 per year. Also, I highly recommend the TTH *Home School Information Booklet* (Q&A, resources, "socialization," organizations). $5 postpaid.

Part 3, Magazines of more general interest

Gifted Children Monthly, P.O. Box 115, Sewell NJ 08080. "For parents who want to help their children reach their full potential." Articles, consumer information, pullout section for children and a catalog.

Good Apple Newspaper, Box 299, Carthage IL 62321. (217) 357- 3981. 16 giant size pages on good quality paper with activities teachers can use. The sample I saw has an activity of naming states by shape and pasting on a little paper with the name of a science point of interest in the state; a "literature unit" about the Easter bunny with discussion prompts; an astronomy page with blanks to fill in; 2 pages about seeds with a song; patterns; etc. 5 issues/yr., for grades 2-8 (although I would say 2-6) $13.95. Single copy, $3.50.

Highlights for Children, 803 Church St., Honesdale PA 18431. (717) 253-1080. A nice periodical which you have probably already seen. 1 year's subscription (11 issues), $19.95.

Instructor, P.O. Box 6099, Duluth MN 55806. (218) 723-9215. Teaching and learning strategies, arts and crafts, stories, poems, plays and poster inserts. For K-8 classroom teachers. 9 issues/yr. $20 U.S. or $27 foreign.

Lollipops, for preschoolers and early grades. Activities, things to make, discussion, etc. 64-pages 5 issues per year, $15. Sample, $4.00. From Good Apple (In this list).

National Geographic World, P.O. Box 1269, Washington DC 20013. $10.95. For U.S. addresses only. Of special interest to children in grades 3 through 8.

Nature Friend Magazine, P.O. Box 73, Goshen IN, (219) 534- 2245. BHIRefj3.

". . . a colorful, cheery magazine that *involves* young readers through puzzles, projects, high- quality stories, illustrations, etc. It is the *only* full- scale nature/science magazine that is Bible-based and nonsectarian." $10.75 for 12 monthly, 36-page issues. ($13.25 for Canada or $18.00 elsewhere, U.S. funds) $2 for two sample issues.

Educational Oasis, by Good Apple (In this list). For grades 4-9. The sample issue I saw features England, Vietnam and tutoring. It has quizzes with blanks to fill in on literature, etc. and a 2-sided poster. 64 pages, 5 issues/yr. $20, or single copy $4.50.

Popular Science Monthly, Editorial offices at 380 Madison Ave., New York NY 10017. Official subscription price is $13.94, but special prices are generally available. Buy a newsstand copy and see if a card drops out.

Ranger Rick's Nature Magazine, An excellent magazine for youngsters 6-12. 12 monthly issues, $14.00. 1412 16th St., N.W. Washington DC 20036.

Scholastic Magazines, Inc. 902 Sylvan Ave., Englewood Cliffs NJ 07632. This company publishes a number of good periodicals for students. Reasonably priced per student, but you must order for 10 students.

Xerox Educational Publications. Classroom magazines. 245 Long Hill Rd., Middletown CT 06457.

Your Big Backyard, Companion to *Ranger Rick's* for youngsters 3-5. 12 issues, $10. 1412 16th St., N.W., Washington DC 20036-2266.

Part 4, Nonprint media: Recordings, games and computer software

A number of the publishers listed in Appendix B offer computer software in addition to print media.

Ampersand Press. Science game publisher. See Appendix B.

Aristoplay. Game publisher. App. B.

Bible in Living Sound, The, Family Life Institute, Nordland WA 98358-0234. Bible stories on records or cassette tapes. The institute offers the whole Bible narrative in professionally prepared, dramatized stories. The 450 episodes, true to the Bible account, come on 75 cassettes or 75 records! I really enjoyed the six stories on the cassette they sent me. For only $1 to cover some of the postage and handling, they will send you a sample cassette along with information on how to get more.

Christian Home Education Association of California, *Cassette Tape Catalog.* Price to be determined. P.O. Box 28644, Santa Ana, CA 92799-8644.

Generosity, Sound Principles, 304 East D, Hillsboro KS 67063. (316) 947-2505. Advertised as "a quality fun-filled board game that promotes Judeo-Christian values." Ages 9-Adult. Deals with math and biblical attitudes about money. $19.95 + $2.50 shpg. + tax if KS.

Grammar Songs, Audio Memory Publishing, 1433 E. 9th St., Long Beach CA 90813. Cassette, song book / workbook, teacher's guide, $16.95. *Multiplication Songs,* Cassette covers the multiplication facts. $5.00. I haven't seen these, but they appear to be worthwhile.

Manna Computing Concepts. See Appendix A, Part 3.

Math-it. A unique and effective approach to learning math computation. $31.50 postpaid from Hewitt Research Foundation, P.O. Box 9, Washougal WA 98671.

Safari through Multiplication Jungle, A packet including: cassette, teacher's guide, learning cards and board game. Money back guarantee. $19.95 with postage if prepaid. (Add tax if in NV.) H.E. Flaherty and Co., 7313 Simsbury Cir., Las Vegas NV 89129. (800) 828-0090.

Your Story Hour. Sound recordings. See Appendix B.

Part 5, Title cross reference

For publications mentioned in this book. Letters after the title indicate the appendix in which it may be found.

TITLES FOR CHILDREN'S USE.

TITLES DEALING WITH HOME SCHOOLING OR EDUCATION IN GENERAL

OTHER TITLES

I

Notes and references

Chapter 1: The home school alternative
* Washington Homeschool Research Project, "Report from the 1987 Washington Homeschool Testing," Jon Wartes, March, 1988. Available for $7 from Washington Homeschool Research Project, 16109 NE 169 Pl., Woodinville WA 98072.

Chapter 3: When not to try home schooling
* Information Center, Council for Exceptional Children, 1920 Association Drive, Reston, VA 20091 (703) 620-3660. Or The National Information for Handicapped Children and Youth (Closer Look), P. O. Box 1492, Washington, DC 20013.

Chapter 4: Keeping peace with school authorities
1. *Pierce* v. *The Society of Sisters,* 268 U.S. 510 (1925); *Wisconsin* v. *Yoder,* 406, U.S. 205 (1972).
2. *Welch* v. *United States,* 398 U.S. 333 (1970).
3. *State of Ohio* v. *Whisner,* 47 Ohio St. 2d 181 (1976). See also, "Ohio" in Appendix Section C.
4. *Kentucky St. Bd. of Elem. & Sec. Educ.* v. *Rudasill,* 589 S.W. 2d 877 (Ky 1979).
5. *State of Michigan* v. *Peter and Ruth Nobel,* S 791- 0114-A (1979).
6. *Perchemlides* v. *Frizzle,* Civil No. 16641 (Hampshire Superior Court, 11/13/78).

Chapter 5: Battle for the right to teach
* From recommendations relating to home study issued by the National Education Association's Standing Committee on Instruction and Development, October 11, 12, 1984.

Chapter 6: Helping children learn
1. Testimony of Professor Donald Erickson in the trial of *Michigan* v. *Peter and Ruth Nobel,* 57 Michigan State, S 79- 0114-1 (1979).
2. James L. Hymes, Jr., *A Child Development Point of View,* Copyright 1955, p. 26. Reprinted by permission of Prentice-Hall, Inc., Englewood Cliffs, New Jersey.
3. *Ibid,* pp. 43, 44.
4. *Ibid,* p. 100.

Chapter 8: Developing an educational framework
1. Prepared by the 1955 White House Conference on Education.
2. Patricia M. Lines, "An Overview of Home Instruction," *Phi Delta Kappan,* March 1987, pp. 510-517.
3. See John Holt in *The Radcliffe Quarterly,* March 1978, *The Underachieving School,* Dell, 1969. pp. 202, 203, and other books he has written.

Chapter 9: Teaching in the home school
* For example, see John Holt, *What Shall I Do Monday?,* Chapter 27, 1970, or Betty H. Yarborough and Roger A. Johnson, "Research That Questions the Elementary School Marking System," *Phi Delta Kappan,* April 1980, pp. 527,528, or Howard Kirschenbaum, et al, *Wad-ja-get? The Grading Game in American Education.* 1971.

Chapter 10: Structure for learning
1. Kathleen McCurdy, Washington Association of Home Educators, personal correspondence, October 1, 1985.

2. See *The Teaching Home* June/July, August/September and October/November, 1985 for a discussion of the "lost tools of learning."

3. Wilford M. Aikin, *The Story of the Eight-year Study*, Harper & Brothers, 1942. And James Hemming, *Teach Them to Live*, Longmans, Green, 1948, 1957.

Chapter 13: Support groups
  * From *The Teaching Home,* "Support Groups," Apr./May, 1988, Used by permission.

Chapter 14: Early education
  1. Census bureau information by telephone 3/30/88.

2. For a well-documented report of the Moores' analysis of research, see their book, *School Can Wait.* It and other of their books are listed in the bibliography (Appendix H).

3. Copyright 1983, *USA TODAY.* Reprinted with permission.

4. See L. J. Schweinhart and D. P. Weikart, *Young Children Grow Up: The Effects of the Perry Preschool Program on Youths Through Age 15.* High/Scope Educational Research Foundation, 600 N. River St., Ypsilanti, MI 48197. 1980.

5. For reports on the Brookline Early Education Project, see Donald E. Pierson, et al, *School-based Programs for Parents and Young Children,* prepared for publication in the *Personnel and Guidance Journal.* 1983. Also, Pierson, et al, "The Impact of Early Education: Measured by Classroom Observations and Teacher Ratings of Children in Kindergarten," from *Evaluation Review,* April, 1983.

6. Neal W. Finkelstein ("Aggression: Is It Stimulated by Day Care?" *Young Children,* September 1982) refers to studies finding undesirable social behavior in children who have had day care. Then he describes how one experimental center overcame aggression problems they found. See also three articles in a special section of the September 1982 issue of *Parents Magazine* entitled "Day-Care Days."

7. "A Few Clear Words About the Montessori 'Method,'" *Montessori News,* May 1984, p. 2. International Montessori

Society, 912 Thayer Ave., Silver Spring, MD 20910.

8. "Creativity," *Montessori News,* May 1984, p.4.

9. *Trade Announcement,* Anthroposophic Press, Winter/Spring, 1988, p. 8. Bell's Pond, Star Route, Hudson, NY 12534.

10. *Ibid,* p. 9.

11. "What Makes a Good Preschool Program?" and "Child- Initiated Learning—What About the Teachers?" *High/Scope ReSource,* Fall 1986. If you are serious about preschool education, see *Young Children in Action, A Manual for Preschool Educators* ($25 postpaid from High/Scope Press, 600 N. River St., Ypsilanti, MI).

Chapter 15: Teaching values
  1. See Benjamin Bloom, et al, eds., *Taxonomy of Educational Objectives, Handbook I: Cognitive Domain.* 1956. McKay. Objectives for the affective domain were worked out by David R. Krathwohl and others. See *Taxonomy of Educational Objectives, Handbook II: Affective Domain.* 1964. McKay.

2. Copyright 1988, by *The Teaching Home.* Used by permission.

3. *Ibid.*

Chapter 16: Teaching reading
  1. Rudolph Flesch. *Why Johnny Can't Read.* Harper & Row, Publishers, NY, 1956.

2. Rudolph Flesch. *Why Johnny Still Can't Read.* Harper & Row, Publishers, NY, 1981.

3. "Reading and Pre-first-grade: A Joint Statement of Concerns about Present Practices in Pre-first-grade Reading Instruction and Recommendations for Improvement." *Young Children,* September 1977, pp. 25, 26.

4. Jim Trelease, *The Read-Aloud Handbook.* Penguin Books, Middlesex, England and New York, 1982.

5. Summarized by Jim Trelease (reference above). See Dolores Durkin, *Children Who Read Early,* Teachers College, 1966.

6. Harry F. Walters. Article in *Newsweek.* February 21, 1977, p. 63.

7. Less than half of the students leaving high school in 1984 had advanced beyond

what the NAEP defines as the "intermediate" level in "proficiency and reading complexity." This is the 3rd level out of 5. National Assessment of Educational Progress, *The Reading Report Card.* Published by Educational Testing Service.

8. Jeanne S. Chall, *Learning to Read: the Great Debate.* McGraw-Hill, New York, 1967, p. 307.

9. Roma Gans, *Fact and Fiction About Phonics.* © 1964 by Bobbs-Merrill Co., Inc. Indianapolis. Quotation from page 87 used by permission.

10. Nancy Larrick, "De-trivializing our methods of reading instruction," *Phi Delta Kappan,* November 1987, pp. 184-189. By late spring, 1987, all 350 first graders in the Open Sesame project were reading in English, and all but three (who had been in this country less than six months) passed a comprehension test given by a school district evaluator. The project is based on an earlier research study comparing ten second-grade classes learning from this approach with ten more using conventional readers.

11. Pam Palewicz and Linda Madaras. *The Alphabet Connection.* Socken Books, NY, 1979.

Chapter 17: Teaching literature
    * Alexander Pope, *Essay on Man,* Epis. ii, 1.217.

Chapter 18: Teaching writing
    1. National Council of Teachers of English, *How to Help Your Child Become a Better Writer,* NCTE, 1111 Kenyon Rd., Urbana IL 61801. Single copies are available for sending a Self-addressed stamped envelope.
    2. Jessica Hulcy, "Write! Write! Write!" *The Teaching Home,* Oct./Nov., 1987, pp. 14, 15.
    3. Two good books to help you build writing skills are: Peter Elbow, *Writing With Power, Techniques for mastering the writing process,* Oxford University Press, 1981. 384 pp. And Harry Shaw, *Errors in English and Ways to Correct Them, The practical approach to correct word usage, sentence structure, spelling, punctuation and grammar,* Harper & Row, Publishers, 10 E. 53rd St., New York, NY 10022, 1986, 288 pp.

Chapter 19: Teaching math
    1. Washington Homeschool Research Project, "Report from the 1987 Washington Homeschool Testing." Referenced under Chapter 1 in this appendix.
    2. National Council of Teachers of Mathematics. *An Agenda for Action: Recommendations for School Mathematics in the 1980s.* Reston, VA, NCTM, 1980.

Chapter 21: Teaching social studies
    * Lawrence Kohlberg, "The Cognitive-Developmental Approach to Moral Education," *Phi Delta Kappan,* 56 (June 1975), 672.

Chapter 24: Social development
    * J. W. Taylor, V., *Self-concept in Home-schooling Children,* (doctoral dissertation) Ann Arbor, MI; University of Michigan, 1986.

Chapter 31: Educating for superior achievement
    1. David and Micki Colfax, *Homeschooling for Excellence,* Mountain House Press, p. 88. See Appendix H.
    2. *Ibid,* pp. 32-45.
    3. Jules Archer, "Educating Children, a Personal Perspective," *Home Education Magazine,* February, 1987, pp. 6, 7; and *The National Forum,* Fall, 1986, pp. 38-43.

Appendix G: Ideas that work
    * United States Department of Education, *What Works, Research About Teaching and Learning.,* 1987. 86 pp., paper. For ordering information, write to What Works, Pueblo CO 81009 or phone (202) 783-3238.

General
    Letter models on the cover are reproduced with permission from Zaner Bloser, Inc. from the series *Handwriting Basic Skills and Application,* Copyright 1984.

Index